BLACK POWER
AND THE
AMERICAN
PEOPLE

BLACK POWER AND THE AMERICAN PEOPLE

The Cultural Legacy of Black Radicalism

RAFAEL TORRUBIA

BLOOMSBURY ACADEMIC
LONDON • NEW YORK • OXFORD • NEW DELHI • SYDNEY

BLOOMSBURY ACADEMIC
Bloomsbury Publishing Plc
50 Bedford Square, London, WC1B 3DP, UK
1385 Broadway, New York, NY 10018, USA
29 Earlsfort Terrace, Dublin 2, Ireland

BLOOMSBURY, BLOOMSBURY ACADEMIC and the Diana logo
are trademarks of Bloomsbury Publishing Plc

First published in Great Britain 2016
Paperback edition published 2022

Copyright © Rafael Torrubia, 2016, 2022

Rafael Torrubia has asserted his right under the Copyright,
Designs and Patents Act, 1988, to be identified as Author of this work.

Cover design by Holly Bell

All rights reserved. No part of this publication may be reproduced or
transmitted in any form or by any means, electronic or mechanical,
including photocopying, recording, or any information storage or retrieval
system, without prior permission in writing from the publishers.

Bloomsbury Publishing Plc does not have any control over, or responsibility for,
any third-party websites referred to or in this book. All internet addresses given
in this book were correct at the time of going to press. The author and publisher
regret any inconvenience caused if addresses have changed or sites have
ceased to exist, but can accept no responsibility for any such changes.

A catalogue record for this book is available from the British Library.

A catalog record for this book is available from the Library of Congress.

ISBN: PB: 978-0-7556-3810-9
ePDF: 978-1-7867-3088-6
eBook: 978-1-7867-2088-7

To find out more about our authors and books visit
www.bloomsbury.com and sign up for our newsletters.

CONTENTS

Preface vii

Introduction 1

1. Hotheads and Demagogues: What is Black Power? 28
2. Why Black Power? 45
3. A Nation of Militants? 97
4. 'Dramas-of-Aggression': Black Power in Sports 133
5. Behind Bars and Under Fire 162
6. Chariots to the Stars 184
7. Culture from the Midnight Hour 226

Conclusion   The Long History of Black Power 265

Notes 270
Bibliography 326
Index 347

This book would not exist without the help of many people, but very particularly my wonderful PhD supervisor and mentor, Professor Gerard DeGroot, and my unfailingly supportive parents, who remain inexplicably proud to have raised an historian.

PREFACE TO THE NEW EDITION

Writing a preface to a new edition of this book, which seeks to touch on the connections between Black Lives Matter and the long history of Black Power and the American people, is something of a Sisyphean endeavour. The America that I wrote about just a few short years ago, which already seemed on a knife-edge of conflict, has had its racial divisions sharpened and broadcasted by four years of a white supremacist presidency which has treated the lives and liberties of black Americans as inconsequential. Much like their Black Power predecessors, protestors in this environment have found themselves reckoning with 'an American empire that demands black death for its functionality'.[1]

As Angela Davis warned, freedom remains a constant struggle.[2] Within this struggle, the American police, the active power of the state, have provided a litany of torture, cruelty and state-sanctioned murder almost daily to newsrooms and social media around the world, which has inevitably coloured the act of composition. As I attempt to pull this preface together, the roll of disappeared names shifts like the tide, threatening to erase the individuality of each life lost. In this high-speed age, the preservation of loss is an ongoing contest, with each news cycle threatening to cast aside the bodies of the previous days' dead. Walter Scott, Botham Jean, Atatiana Jefferson, Breonna Taylor and Elijah McClain have all been casualties of the American policing system since I began to write. I have started and restarted this opening dozens of times, and each time, I've returned to the outset, as the American political landscape has convulsed, first with the election of Donald Trump, then under his four years of truly spectacular racial brutality, and yet again with the victory of Joe Biden in the 2020 election, followed by a predictable, and dispiriting, wave of desperate Republican litigation, culminating in the storming of the US Capitol by a group of neo-fascist insurrectionists, conspiracy theorists and Nazis, encouraged by the departing incumbent himself.[3]

I have had to start telling this story over and over, because the story America tells itself about race is constantly reiterated, and the 'truths' it holds sit uneasily against the historical record. Part of that story is familiar now, depressingly so. Black Lives Matter (BLM), like much of the preceding Black Power movement, was catalysed by a communal response to state violence – specifically the July 13, 2013, acquittal of George Zimmerman for the murder of seventeen-year-old Trayvon Martin.

Eight impossibly long years ago, Mark O'Mara, Zimmerman's attorney, fretted over the presence of a 'fringe element' of protestors, bent on seeking revenge against his client.[4] The founders of BLM, however, were less concerned with revenge than with justice and, like Black Power advocates before them, with access to the basic dignities of survival under the American regime. One of those founders, Alicia Garza, then a community organiser with the National Alliance of Domestic Workers, now principal of the policy organization Black Futures Lab, watched the Zimmerman verdict live, before writing a Facebook post which concluded: 'Black people. I love you. I love us. Our lives matter.'[5] Her friend, the prison reform activist Patrisse Cullors, commented '#blacklivesmatter' on Garza's post, and from that, a new addition to the American protest lexicon was born.

Now, as Confederate monuments tumble and with the death of George Floyd, BLM protests have erupted around the world and the slogan itself has been daubed in massive yellow letters on the approach to the White House.[6] Steered by Garza, Cullors and immigration activist Opal Tometi, BLM has grown from a hashtag into an international protest movement. With more than forty chapters worldwide, it's important to note that BLM is one of around fifty organizations in the Movement for Black Lives (M4BL). Even here in the UK, campaigns such as BLM in the Stix seek to build on the June and July protests over George Floyd's death in over 260 UK towns and cities stretching from South Wales to Shetland.[7]

Somewhat feverishly positioned by commentators as an uprising which 'spans from Ferguson to Baltimore ... Minneapolis to Salt Lake City ... London to Tokyo',[8] the success of the M4BL is founded, like Black Power, on direct, grassroots action and community solidarity. As with their forebears, integrating with local networks, 'being able to show up and work alongside the activists leading the way' was key.[9] Following the 2013 Martin case, BLM found itself on the ground protesting the murder of Mike Brown in August 2014, bringing over six hundred activists to coordinate actions in Ferguson and St Louis.[10] Participating in a series of October protests dubbed the Ferguson 'Freedom Rides' by Tometi, using tactics that consciously moved in the shadow of the 1960s civil rights movements, BLM's work in Brown's name catapulted it to national prominence.[11] By July 2015, the first ever National Convening of the Movement for Black Lives took place in Cleveland, Ohio, attended by more than two thousand activists and organisers.[12]

Despite its structured approach, much of the early reportage around BLM treated it as a movement which emerged from nowhere. For anyone conscious of the long history of Black Power in America and the parallel history of white oppression, it was apparent that this was not the case. However, acknowledging connections and inheritances does not come without complications. Since its inception, there has been a rush to position BLM as the vanguard of a new civil rights movement, styling it as the successful inheritor of the partially unfulfilled legacies of twentieth-century struggles.[13]

There are elements of truth to this. Tactically, BLM sits somewhere between the Panthers and Martin Luther King's Southern Christian Leadership Conference (SCLC), working immediately at the grassroots via community chapters, but with a functioning, well-funded network at the national level to lend organisational assistance to local direct action. These strategies are evident in everything from BLM's protest of the Cleveland Republican convention and presidential debates, through transit shutdowns and police defunding protests, to their operations in solidarity with Native protests contesting the Standing Rock pipeline on the Sioux reservation.[14]

BLM is primarily differentiated, both from its opponents and its Black Power predecessors, by its intersectionality. Key BLM figures like Tometi exemplify this shift, advocating for action against police violence and for black empowerment but also for the political mobilisation of women and expanded labour rights.[15] Tometi is only one of many BLM members who are veteran community organisers with long experience bridging the interlinked battles over immigration, accommodation, incarceration, gender, class and medicine which exemplify the experience of being black in America.

Another major point of difference between earlier Black Power movements and BLM lies in the latter's reception. On the one hand, achingly familiar narratives have been mobilised – right-wing pundits have labelled BLM a terrorist organization as recently as May 2021.[16] This comes despite the production of statistics showing that BLM protests are overwhelmingly peaceful, with the main source of violence coming from conservative counterprotestors and the police.[17] However, others have taken issue with its queer-friendly focus – an issue which has been extant since the 1960s Black Power era organisations, which often had a complex and contested relationship with gender and sexuality, seeking allies in other oppressed minorities, and reliant on women, but mixing this with a culture of machismo, and the internalised homophobia and misogyny which accompanied it.[18]

Some superficial similarities are similarly complicated – the Panthers, a party consistently reliant on the leadership of women, whose membership was 60 percent female,[19] and which had a stated policy of gender equality from the outset, struggled to centre those same women. The group wrestled with a hypermasculine image, elevating prominent sexual offenders and misogynists like Eldridge Cleaver to influential positions within the party. Conversely, BLM owes its existence not just to the three women behind its foundation but also to the countless others who have sustained it in local chapters and affiliated organisations in the years since.[20]

BLM, in its diversity, inherits a more authentic and, until recently, more often obscured legacy of protest in America – protest guided and catalysed by Bayard Rustin and Ella Baker, by Marsha P. Johnson, Silvia

Rivera and Storm De Larverie, by Ernestine Eckstein, by Barbara Jordan and James Baldwin, and all those other queer activists who are rarely mentioned in the same breath as Dr King and Malcolm X.

What has emerged is a profoundly inclusive twenty-first-century organisation – BLM has been outspoken about violence against the black queer community and has consistently centred LGTBQ members, whether in the Black Trans Lives Matter rally of June 2020, one of the largest transgender-focused protests in history, or the Juneteenth celebrations of last year organised by The Blacksmiths art collective, which culminated in a reading of Linda LaBeija's 'Vogue, bitch', an incendiary call to action against transphobic violence.[21] This focus places the M4BL squarely as an intersectional, modern iteration of the civil rights and Black Power movements.[22] In response, BLM's critics have included both expected sources like Fox News and Breitbart hacks, and the unexpected: National Association for the Advancement of Colored People (NAACP) leaders struggling to reconcile with the movement's direct action tactics[23] and even former Black Panther chairperson Elaine Brown, who accused BLM of having a 'plantation mentality' as a consequence of their reduced focus on self-defence and decentralised structure.[24]

Accordingly, much of BLM's energy, as befits an organisation birthed in the disinformation age, is devoted to providing credible counter-narratives to the dominant hegemony, from both white and black America. Unsurprisingly, their efforts in this direction mirror those of Newton, Carmichael and other Panthers who tried to advocate for their organisation, as well as cultural commentators such as Muhammad Ali and Larry Neal who placed their careers on a collision course with American assumptions.

While it's overly glib to place the Black Panthers and the BLM movement as points on one single historical continuum, there are numerous points of connection between the two organisations that situate them as part of the long history of Black Power. Both these movements emerged from the experience of American racism – from its political and economic frameworks and its cultural milieu. It's no coincidence that both the Panthers and BLM originated in Oakland, which experienced some of the sharpest points of contact with the racism of the American state, or that the Panthers' Ten-Point Program advocated for self-determination, education and the cessation of police brutality, while the M4BL issued an analogous agenda, demanding 'an end to the criminalization, incarceration, and killing of our people' and calling for the 'accountability of entire police departments'.[25] The demands are the same, because the problems remain the same – they began with the American slave system, and they have remained unaddressed since.

Connection is sharpened by retrospect. From the outset, both the Black Panthers and BLM placed themselves in confrontation with the foundational structures of American racism. Both groups sought intersectional alliances in order to resist these structures and were international in their outlook. The key here is context – while both the Black Panthers and BLM are part of the long history of Black Power, their contexts are profoundly different. The Panthers came to prominence following decades of decolonisation struggles in the Global South, capped by the advent of Cuban independence, while BLM has been shaped by decades of neoliberal scouring of black communities, coupled with a contingent expansion of the for-profit prison system and a concomitant evisceration of support for public education.[26] Thus, while it's tempting to see linear continuities between historic Black Power struggles and BLM, often the river we follow is more like a delta, a shifting net of overlapping influences and confluences demarcating ongoing efforts for liberation, streams of resistance that have moved over American soil since the first slave revolt.

For some activists, BLM is not just an inheritor of the Black Power era but a clear evolution, part of a chain of connected cultural and political expression through time.[27] In this respect, earlier iterations of the Black Power movement are both inspiration and cautionary tale, providing lessons in direct action but also warning against allowing the fractures and divisions that undercut earlier manifestations of Black Power protests to splinter these more modern movements.

The internal and external stressors on the late-1960s Black Power movement are well documented, from its patriarchal, misogynist culture to its internecine strife, exacerbated by FBI surveillance and COINTELPRO sabotage.[28] For today's protestors, technological evolution has meant increasingly sophisticated repression. The firehoses of Selma have been replaced by a panoply of near science-fiction interventions, from sonic disruptors[29] to signal harvesters, with DC police requesting the use of a heat ray against BLM protestors, months before some in their own ranks opened the gates to allow armed white rioters into the Capitol.[30]

This technological brutalisation has been met with technological innovation – the real-life manifestation of the sonic warfare which Underground Resistance dreamed up in the Detroit music scene. In this new protest parallel, audio engineers like Dave Rife and Gabe Liberti, designers of an audio shield against sonic cannons, are as valuable and essential as medics, mouthpieces and mantras.[31] Science fiction is real, and it's on our streets. This should come as no surprise. BLM exists at the nexus of direct action gone digital – the interface of street-level protest, grassroots organisation and technological resistance.

Protest via direct action has been an intrinsic component of resistance since the colonial origins of the United States, but the flavour of the direct action served by BLM has proven unpalatable to centrist commentators, when placed in comparison to disingenuous recollections of the classic 'non-violent' civil rights movement. Photogenic artefacts of the Freedom Rides, the sit-ins or the Montgomery boycott become anaesthetised into a false dichotomy between the acceptable, justified protest of the past and the supposedly unwelcome, disruptive protest of the present.[32] One need only take note of the varying degrees of treatment afforded the recent Capitol rioters, alongside shooters like Kyle Rittenhouse, in comparison to activists like Tiana Arata, to see that America treats its disruptions very differently and gives white terrorism a far longer leash than black protest.[33]

If BLM protest is held in a different reality to that of the civil rights and Black Power era, the essentials of the struggle are the same. BLM has had to revisit historic strategies for survival, what the Panthers called their 'survival programs', in order to persist in our fraught modern context. Consequently, part of BLM's work is advancing policies and social strategies that ameliorate the oppression of life in America, perhaps most recently seen in the launch of the BLM Survival Fund, a program which often moved more swiftly than federal aid when reaching affected communities during the pandemic.[34]

We cannot deny the deep challenges of modern protest. We exist in a world which burns every summer, wildfires scouring California.[35] We exist in a world wracked by viral plague.[36] We exist in a world of rising rents and eviction notices. We exist in a world of water poverty, and historic red line delineation and defunding.[37] For protest to succeed in this world, life must be sustainable. As the Panthers put it, the possibility of struggle predicates the need for survival.[38] That struggle for survival is constantly scrutinised. The praxis and politics of black empowerment, as this book discusses, are often conducted under the lenses of the American media, and for a variety of audiences.

We have moved beyond Gil Scott-Heron's admonishment that the revolution will not be televised. Not only is the televisation of the M4BL an inevitable factor in our daily lives, the broadcast of these protests, both consensually and non-consensually, by media at all levels places protestors' identities and lives into profound jeopardy. In both Trump's and Biden's America, protest exists in a virulently confrontational information battleground. Companies and agencies attempt to recruit journalists to record, document and disclose the identities of BLM activists, and to disclose or fabricate links with anti-fascist protest.[39]

Where most historic Black Power adherents had to contend only with television, radio and print media, the M4BL is a product of the internet era, mycorrhizal in its reach, and also correspondingly diverse and open to manipulation. Historically, groups like the Panthers courted and positioned themselves within the relatively limited media frames available to them, and were able to base their protests on enshrined constitutional rights.[40] One need only contrast this with the recent attempts by state governors and legislatures to restrict camping on state property and dial up the cost of bail funds to realise that even the right to protest is a debated possibility in what remains of American democracy.[41]

In order to defend this right to protest, BLM activists, like the Panthers, have chosen to place themselves in front of a varyingly sympathetic American audience in an era which erodes anonymity and promotes retribution against legitimate protest.[42] To survive this gaze, BLM protestors have been obliged to inherit and adapt a range of protest tactics, ethics and aesthetics from their Black Power predecessors, and by extension from the long history of Black Power and the American people.

Much of this book charts the centrality of the cultural inheritances of the Black Power movement to its late-1960s tactics. This long history of resistance conditioned the relationship between the politics, poetics, ethics and aesthetics of groups like the Panthers, and their successors in BLM. Black Power, perhaps even more so than the 'mainstream' civil rights movement from which it emerged, thrived on dramatic, highly stylised conversations, declarations and protest actions, grounded in an extended heritage of black resistance to oppression. This set of tactics constrained the Black Power movement at the time but presents a much wider set of communication possibilities, for those elements of the M4BL bequeathed similar strategies. Symbol, song, art and poetry place BLM squarely in front of its audience and define its shape as much as its concrete protest actions.

This engagement heightens as many Americans become increasingly cognisant of the tightening grip of Republican hegemony over the past four years, aided by the fact that, despite being a country with marked and dramatic historical farragoes, the United States until recently was helmed by a president so mercurial and venal that he prompted comparison with the Third Reich, the Reagan era and the original civil rights struggle simultaneously.[43]

Having a thinly veiled white supremacist in office has perhaps had the concomitant effect of a partial reckoning with the white supremacy stitched into American history. Visible protest actions around sites of history, memory and oppression in the current moment create the impression of an apparently seismic shift in how individuals, corporations and institutions are engaging with that history, suggesting a mass effort to reckon with America's endemic racism.

Progress towards this reckoning is halting. High-profile cultural repositories like the British Museum and the Met – both with substantial historic ties to colonialism – comfortably adopt the BLM slogan while moving in fits and starts to address their own roles in the euphemistically phrased 'race problem'.[44] While some institutions such as the Walker Art Center in George Floyd's Minneapolis have stopped contracting local police for events, the move to divest America's cultural institutions from the grip of the police has a long way to go, as demonstrated by the recent Whitney Museum controversy.[45]

Control over culture remains central to the attainment of equality. The following chapters demonstrate that the persistent presence of Black Power's cultural legacy in American history inflected art, music, dance, painting, poetry and theatre. It informed the secular religion of sports, and more conventional theologies. It occupied the diners of America via soul food, and the clothes and hairstyles worn on nights out. It changed the language of its adherents, from Black Is Beautiful to rap, and some of its gestures have become eternally enduring, none more so than the raised Black Power fist, which has found itself emblazoned on citizen shield walls in the later round of protests, and misappropriated immediately thereafter.[46]

Writing now, decades into the twenty-first century, there is a base parallel to be drawn between the inheritances and targets of the Black Power movement, and its successors in the M4BL. Both sustained their immediate survival by deploying a multitude of cultural forms, often with profound historical connections. Both groups also demanded substantial shifts in the forms and exercise of American power in order to ensure the continuance of that survival within the American state. This is most clearly seen in the growing efforts amongst BLM advocates to defund or abolish the police, channelling the egregious amount of money currently allocated to most state police budgets into community support and security funds.[47] While many of the more ossified elements of the American political spectrum have dismissed these attempts as a pipe dream, the popularity of politicians like Alexandra Ocasio-Cortez, Stacey Abrams and Ilhan Omar, along with the ire they draw, speaks to the groundswell in support of some fundamental change.[48] Several city budgets have already adjusted in the wake of recent protests, and it seems that more may follow.[49] As Damon Williams of the #LetUsBreathe collective puts it, 'Redistributing resources away from carceral institutions and militarism now feels achievable in ways I did not expect to see in my lifetime.'[50]

Such optimism can be hard to sustain. As I write, we are just over a year out from the paralysis of Jacob Blake, shot seven times in the back while opening a car door – an act described by Wisconsin police as 'within policy'.[51] Daily news shows convoys of American police rolling through the communities they ostensibly protect, macing protestors from behind riot shields and out of the windows of military-style vehicles designed to evoke the machismo and fascist strength-signifiers of a failing regime. Were these scenes happening in a country which more readily fits Occidental notions of instability and collapse, we would be quick in recognising the protest sweeping America as a profound new phase of direct action against an abusive political regime. Regardless of whether observers are sympathetic or not, the conflict itself is undeniable. A change is being sought, and the brutality of the American policing system has advanced to a point where it is impossible to ignore. The police, as the Panthers recognised since their inception, are both 'a reflection of antiquated systems that have for too long been in place' and the most immediate point of contact and control utilised by the state.[52] Accordingly, confrontations with the police are the most immediate staging ground for the ethics and aesthetics of the Black Power movement to be exhibited within the M4BL.

As will be seen, the drama and flair of Black Power's leaders and demagogues, coupled with a groundswell of community support, propelled the movement front and centre by 1967, on the back of a series of summer riots in Los Angeles, Chicago, Detroit and Newark. The Kerner Commission assigned to investigate the riots concluded that they marked the emergence of 'two Americas, one Black, one white'.[53] The protest divisions exhibited in today's BLM movement are perhaps more complex. On one side are ordinary Americans who have been brutalised on multiple fronts, first through the economic impacts of the last century, from the legacy of redlining through to the subprime crash, later via the vampiric tendencies of the American medical system, such that the sight of a GoFundMe to save a desperately ill person is now par for the course. These same Americans daily witness acts of horrendous brutality in their communities as black bodies are asphyxiated, beaten, hung and shot by a police force which often appears to have entirely abandoned its purpose as a tool of community security, and enshrined itself as a paramilitary complex for authoritarian, majority white interests. On the other side of the divide, we have an American plutocracy which appears to be positioning itself to bleed America dry even as it burns.

Much as the Black Power movement attempted to give shape to the rage and fury which had fuelled the riots of the late 1960s, the M4BL has striven to turn anger, heartbreak and desolation into powerful political action. These efforts are partially similar to early Black Power drives because so little has changed. In the early 1960s, Black Power figureheads spoke out against systematic degradation across the American system, a death of a thousand cuts that played out through racism, substandard provision in education, accommodation and healthcare, and persistent, unrelenting police brutality. Little has changed, save that the mass-mediated age we've moved into has brought the edges of this system into even sharper relief.

The following pages are not comprehensive, but they hopefully provide a sense of the evolution of the struggle for empowerment in America by examining a series of connected cultural expressions across time – aggregate streams in the wider delta of the struggle for black empowerment. The M4BL stands as an inevitable modern iteration of these struggles, and an inheritor of the historic legacies of American racial violence. It is in many ways perhaps uniquely placed to effect fundamental change in American society – it has at points held a more sympathetic audience, and it has a greater range of digital and conventional tools at its disposal than its predecessors. BLM arguably holds the presence in popular culture that groups like the Panthers strove for, combined with significant political influence and grassroots, street-level power. The directions it takes now will be influenced by both its inheritances from the long history of Black Power and its ability to navigate the particular alchemies of the modern moment. It's evident that BLM strives for a liberated, inclusive, intersectional future – whether Americans choose to embrace this or whether American society is held back by an atavistic attachment to the divisive power structures and systems established over the last few centuries remains to be seen.

INTRODUCTION

'QUESTION: What is Black Power, Daddy? ANSWER: ?' So began the Pulitzer Prize winning playwright Charles H. Fuller's eponymous piece, published in 1979 as the Black Power movement faded from America's political consciousness.[1] Yet while Fuller put pen to paper almost forty years ago, it's a question we still have trouble answering even today. In part, this book hopes to address that issue. Post-Ferguson, in an increasingly racialised America where the lines between black and white Americans seem once more to be thrown into stark relief the legacy of the Black Power movement is on the rise. While the mainstream media remain mostly content with the occasional dewy-eyed retrospective on philosophers and demagogues softened by the passage of the time, and while the more thoughtful outlets might remark upon the political and economic legacies left by the Black Power movement's political heyday, the quiet legacy of Black Power; its long history in American culture and its profound influence on the American racial imagination remains something of a whisper, barely heard beneath the microphone static and ghost-gun rattle of a political and social revolt too quickly dismissed in our collective recollection, or too easily blended with the broader sweep of the civil rights struggle.

Black Power was both part of, and distinct from, the more familiar civil rights milieu. Its adherents drank from many of the same wells, but also ranged widely, voraciously and creatively in their search for new identities of resistance. This book hopes to take you down some of the paths they trod, and to give you a sense of the diversity and complexity present in the evolution of Black Power's relationship with the American people.

There is, perhaps, no better time to do so. The long history of the Black Power movement, evidenced in a series of connected cultural expressions across time, has been and continues to be instrumental in defining America's relationship with its citizens of colour. Its images of community, beauty, strength, empowerment and resistance inform today's dialogues. Its emphasis on controlling the means of culture creation to control your identity remains ever more relevant. When protestors today chant 'Hands Up, Don't Shoot', when they walk the streets bearing signs asking 'Am I next?', there remains the sense of a society in opposition with itself. When those same chants change into 'Hands Up, Shoot Back', they echo present and past frustrations alike. We also see in the mass protests that have swept the country the interaction between local and national solidarity which lay at the heart of Black Power, and the wider civil rights movement. Black Power, at its root, was an ideology of self-defense. Adherents sought to protect their community, their loved ones, at base, their life and identity from an inimical dominant society. It was an ideology which emphasised the creativity, beauty and potential of America's people of colour and their ability to drive society forward in a multitude of unexpected and essential ways. Yet it was also an ideology which divided and terrified much of late-1960s America.

Writing now, it seems ever more pressing to understand where these fears came from and to develop a more coherent picture of Black Power's place in American history. Not to teleologically shape our actions in the present, but so we can act and react with an understanding of past struggle which includes the long history of the Black Power movement as an essential component of the changing dynamics of the American people and American society.

While we cannot and should not draw easy parallels with a complicated past, the relationship between Black Power and the American people is a strong strand in a tapestry of racial oppression, resistance and reconciliation which still affects us all today. Understanding the ways in which Black Power has manifested through American history gives us a clearer sense of its enduring appeal, and a more lucid lens with which to examine the events in America today.

Constructing that lens requires some delicate work. The evolution of Black Power is an historical puzzle that has created confusion from its first 'official' utterance on the Meredith March in 1966 to the present day. This book seeks to explore Black Power's long history; to trace its evolution through American culture and society by reconsidering the growth of Black Power sentiment as a series of connected cultural expressions across time. In this endeavour, I am not alone. There have been innumerable attempts to encapsulate these two incendiary words and understand their meaning for the American nation. So, how should we think about this mercurial historical phenomenon? When he strove to answer his unsettling question, Fuller himself reinforced the most accepted interpretation of the political movement. He wrote, 'The concept of Black Power embodies a clearly thought out, step by step process, which if initiated by the national Black community, will put control of those areas of government, which directly relate to us, into our hands.'[2] However, painting Black Power by its politics has only ever provided part of the picture.

Defining Black Power at its political zenith was comparatively simple – defining it over the course of its long relationship with the American people is substantially more complicated. Historical assessment has reached the point where Black Power as a political term is comparatively well-defined, but Black Power outside the political sphere, and its attendant black militancy, remains amorphous. In January 1967, Black Panther Party member Stokely Carmichael remarked that, 'the first need of a free people is to define their own terms', and if any reassessment of the long cultural history of Black Power in America is to be undertaken, we first need to ask ourselves what exactly we mean when we say those iconic words. Black Power.[3]

Black Power is not a static term. Nothing ever entirely is. The associations we ascribe to a phrase change with the decades, with deaths, with triumphs, with historical reflection. Yet even in its earliest years, some of Black Power's pertinent qualities were clearly and lucidly enunciated. Perhaps the simplest definition was retrospectively provided by Solomon P. Gethers, executive director of United Neighbors for Progress, a community organisation based in Wilmington, North Carolina. Writing in the December 1969 issue of *Negro Digest*, Gethers reasoned 'Black Power is a call to Black people to rediscover the richness of their own possibilities; to open themselves spiritually, morally, and psychologically to the true meaning of their lives as expressed in the Black man's own unique historically evolving culture.'[4] For activists, this personal development was a logical parallel to the political thrust of the movement, which was equally pithily defined by the National Coalition of Negro Churchmen (NCNC) as 'the power to participate.'[5] Yet to many observers, there appeared to be a clear contradiction between the practicality of political Black Power and the apparently ephemeral nature of cultural Black Power's demands for psychological and spiritual reinvention. As the social critic Harold Cruse wrote, there was an apparent gulf between the connotative and denotative meanings of Black Power, a 'conceptual gap between shadow and substance'.[6] As one of the pivotal figures in the growth of the African-American studies movement, Cruse was better placed than most to view the tensions at its heart, but even he conceded, 'Whatever Black Power is supposed to mean to its adherents and its foes, its implications cannot be clearly understood unless one examines the slogan's aims and origin.'[7] In part, that is what this book aims to do.

This is no easy task, primarily because America itself was unsure of Black Power's aims, nowhere more profoundly than in the heart of the civil rights establishment. At the 1966 convention of the National Association for the Advancement of Coloured People (NAACP) in Los Angeles, the group's Vice President Hubert Humphrey declared, 'we must reject calls for racism, whether they come from a throat that is white, or one that is black'.[8] Echoing Humphrey, Executive Director Roy Wilkins excoriated the Black Panther Party as, 'a reverse Mississippi, a reverse Hitler, a reverse Ku Klux Klan ... the father of hatred and the mother of violence'.[9] Panic amongst the luminaries of the civil rights establishment was mirrored in the breathless response of the white mainstream media, but while the horror and indignation present in the press may have varied in its conviction, it undoubtedly made good copy.[10]

This makes the historian's task particularly daunting. To observers at the time the Black Power aesthetic was often magnetically alluring, but it was also overwhelming, a sensory assault from 'an alien world'.[11] To be young, black and militant at this point in time was to be 'all of white America's nightmare of the black revenge come chillingly to life'.[12] The heralds of the new creed, *Newsweek* wrote, were foreign, strange and hostile 'bitter young men who lounge at every corner ... the dynamite in the ghetto – the likeliest to be ignited'.[13] The politicisation of young black America, then as now, was an unsettling prospect. As Elaine Brown recalled on the formation of the LA Black Panther chapter, 'those ... gritty young Brothers ... sent chills through everybody.'[14]

White America needed to beware – according to *Life* magazine, the main concern of young African-Americans was 'How to Get Whitey'.[15] In the fevered world of early Black Power journalism, it seemed somehow plausible that 'Red-Hot Young Negroes Plan a Ghetto War'[16] or that 'Young apostles of violence' nurtured in 'hate-filled ghettoes' could give rise to 'a strutting band of hyper militants.'[17] In the absence of palatable information, the white media filled in the blanks with fear.

This confusion was compounded by the fact that the same media outlets delineated acceptable forms and frames of protest. By the time the Black Power movement emerged, articles were less about reprobation and more salivation. A new language of crisis and conflict characterised the 1960s commentary.[18] A growing dichotomy was created between the 'Responsible Negro Leaders' and the emergent, allegedly novel, Black Power delinquents. Surrounded by vociferous media judges, and suffering dissension within its own ranks, the established civil rights movement suffered an uncertainty over how to respond, summarised by Bayard Rustin who declared, 'we are in the valleys of confusion'.[19] It is into this polarised swamp of memory and interpretation that any historian of Black Power must plunge, confronting a nation afraid of itself, afraid of the consequences of its own history, and a civil rights movement unable to fully grasp the speed and extent of its own evolution. Somewhere in these murky waters, we need to fish for a definition of Black Power. Good luck down there. It is strange, deep and weird.

How to proceed then? Well, despite the title of the book, and while Black Power is logically often presented as an American phenomenon, emerging from American circumstances, the view from across the pond was often clearer. In the closing years of the decade, a multipart series by *The Times* described the Black Power movement as 'efforts by the Negro to discover his own cultural and historical origins, long buried beneath white civilization'.[20] Yet even as the estimable journalists of *The Times* were wrapping their heads around Black Power, it seemed all too familiar to ordinary black Britons who saw the televised clash between Black Power activists and the American state unfold with such drama that they got to know the names and faces of American militants 'better than the next door neighbours.'[21] Media familiarity and ready iconography had created a new transatlantic protest connection. So, our definition has to recognise that by virtue of its long history, Black Power was eminently transmissible. Again *The Times* skirted close to the truth in its predictions for the movement's future, when it speculated that, '[Black Power activists] may well have the effect of creating folk heroes ... particularly among the young, who are ardently in search of manhood and self-respect.'[22]

This search paid little heed to conventional geographical boundaries. On both sides of the Atlantic, the sensation generated by the movement's emergence guaranteed activists an attentive national audience, and the ear, if not yet the heart, of the man in the street. The stark nature of the movement's soundbites matched the blunt impact of their alien style. Carried on waves of iconoclastic language, Black Power hit the evening news, bringing black militancy into the living rooms of America. On the screens of a stunned nation, Stokely Carmichael warned that America stood 'on the brink of becoming a nation of murderers' while the Congress of Racial Equality's (CORE) National Director Floyd McKissick spat that, 'The greatest hypocrisy we have is the Statue of Liberty. We ought to break the young lady's legs and point her to the Mississippi.'[23]

Here lies the next problem for the historian of Black Power – the theatrics and hyperbole initially favoured by many of the movement's speakers were not easy for contemporary observers to distinguish from any tangible threat. The potential of Black Power was feared more than the reality of its existence. Here was Cruse's gulf between shadow and substance – as former Black Panther press secretary Kathleen Cleaver explained: 'frequent television exposure subtly legitimised the image of the Black Panthers but its sensationalising made the Panthers loom far more glamorous and ferocious than they actually were.'[24] As the most voluble and iconic of the early Black Power groups, the problems faced by the Panthers mirrored those of the movement as a whole.

However, we also have to realise that despite the predominantly negative nature of the media coverage, young African-Americans appeared to be profoundly influenced by the images of Black Power dissent presented by the media. Looking back on his life before the Party, former Black Panther Minister of Culture Emory Douglas reminisced it was 'like being in a movement you'd seen on TV and now you could participate and share in that movement; when you'd seen Malcolm on TV, when you heard talk about Stokely Carmichael, Rap Brown ... to become part of that brought a sense of pride'.[25] To view the movement on print or on screen was simply another way to feel part of the movement, a foretaste of things to come.

We need to find the meaning and origins of a movement which was terrifying, yet alluring to white observers. Confusing yet familiar to black observers. Empowering yet already reaching beyond its physical scope. Black Power, virtually from the outset, became an umbrella term, but one which often obscured. It was the blanket draped over the budgie's cage. Who needed to worry about the frantic cries from beneath, when the general shape of the thing could be seen at a glance?

Black Power advocates rapidly issued bitter complaints about the media's inattention to the root causes of the movement. This was perhaps unsurprising. The white gaze of the media inevitably narrowed the range of commentary. As McKissick remarked to newspaper editors in 1967, 'all you can hear are two words: "Black Power." You would like us to stand in the streets and chant "Black Power" for your amusement ... You'd rather know us by Black Power than by our programme.'[26] According to McKissick, any attempt to analyse the militant African-American struggle in detail was punished by news blackouts.[27] Here lies a key reason for our current incomplete understanding of the movement. Black Power was only fit for print when it sold papers, and it only sold papers when it was loud, alien, frightening and violent.[28] To the militants, it seemed the media invariably twisted any statement made by a Black Power spokesperson to suit this purpose. As Malcolm X ruefully noted, 'If I had said "Mary had a little lamb", what probably would have appeared was "Malcolm X Lampoons Mary".'[29] Similarly, *US News and World Report* happily recorded Carmichael's strident declaration that "We're Going to Shoot the Cops' but less diligently omitted was Carmichael's qualifier '(who are shooting our black brothers in the back).'[30] So, we need to define a movement which relied on a media outwith its control. We need to find the ethos of a protest form which was being edited even as it was being born. Can we then look to its great figures?

Hardly. The icons of the movement drew attention, but narrowed focus. Stories structured around leaders such as H. Rap Brown, James

Forman, Floyd McKissick and Stokely Carmichael, offered little exploration of context and often painted them as little more than, as Forman ruefully noted, 'monsters thirsting for the blood of whites.'[31] During the 1967 Sacramento State Capitol protest, Bobby Seale recalled stupefied white observers muttering 'Niggers with guns, niggers with guns'.[32] This maudlin mantra typified a larger problem.

New media framing strategies which placed the emphasis on individual personalities offered no context for Black Power's origins, nor any attempt to situate them in the long history of Black Power. Reporters were too focused on trigger fingers to see where they were pointing, and they generally had no intention of looking back past a gun-wielding man to divine his inspirations. This was compounded by the fact that almost all of these gun-wielding men came from that most iconic of Black Power organisations, the Black Panther Party for Self-Defense. Founded in Oakland, California on 15 October 1966, the Black Panthers have become virtually consanguineous with the Black Power movement. Tough, macho and articulate, the Panthers, led by Huey Newton, Bobby Seale, Eldridge Cleaver and David Hilliard have stormed our hearts, minds and historiography.

While there's been a lot of great work done to add detail to this picture – examining the role of women within the party, its grass roots diversity and its community origins, the fact remains that when we talk about Black Power, we talk about the Panthers. This is partly, a legacy of their '60s emergence. For all the complaints levelled at the movement, the mainstream media rapidly enshrined Black Power and the Black Panthers as 'subjects worthy of popular attention'.[33] As this cult of celebrity developed, the Black Panthers increasingly functioned as a signifier for black militancy. This is problematic for historians as it obscures the growth of Black Power sentiments not directly linked to the Panthers. Nonetheless, America's media loved the voyeuristic thrill provided by Black Power's violent image and when it was not readily available it was manufactured, as noted in the 1968 *Report of the National Advisory Commission on Civil Disorders* (informally, the Kerner Report), which exposed the propensity of reporters to encourage black youths to act up for the cameras.[34]

This desire for drama is partially explained by the fact that aspects of Black Power culture inevitably resonated with the splits in white America. A generation in the throes, or in fear, of rebellion inevitably found great fascination with the photogenic images and tropes which spattered the nightly news. As this coverage expanded, definitions evolved and changed with startling rapidity, shifting to fit immediate imperatives or contorting themselves around pre-defined frames of interpretation and understanding. As George Krowter, a reporter for Selma's WBWC confessed, the facts of Black Power events could be bent, hammered and beaten to fit whichever agenda would draw the most listeners.[35]

The stakes were high. African-American identity was part of a malleable set of representations which were fought over by the media like jackals. Simplified organisational frameworks allowed commentators not only to reinforce perceived stereotypes of blackness, but also to distil and refine threatening ideologies into more easily dismissed ciphers. Challenging these existing frameworks, and constructing new, more empowering bases for identity construction was a continuing theme throughout the long history of Black Power, with its participants empowered and inspired by a series of connected cultural expressions throughout time.[36]

During this period, the media not only controlled what Americans saw, but how they saw it. The emergent Black Power movement, in part, seemed so startlingly violent only because the media's construction and presentation of the preceding comparatively non-violent movement had carefully elided any more militant response which did not fit the myth being constructed. The extent of this revision has only recently become clear. Studies, such as Simon Wendt's *The Spirit and the Shotgun* have examined the presence of violence in the non-violent movement, while commentators such as Jenny Walker have argued that 'the press underrepresented the relatively high incidence of black violence ... that occurred around the edges, and occasionally in the midst, of the putatively non-violent movement.'[37] A nationally constructed illusion of calm and moderation made the Black Power movement seem, frenzied, aberrant and removed from historical connection.

In the drive to alternately glamourise and demonise the demonstrations convulsing America, little attention was given to the concerns behind this dramatic upsurge in militant action or to analysing the results.[38] Accordingly the initial explosion of Black Power sentiment received shallow, disjointed and manipulated media coverage, which warped mainstream America's subsequent perceptions of the movement. Within a span of months, political Black Power was trivialised, marginalised and pigeon-holed. Cultural Black Power however, was an altogether trickier beast to cage. Pushing beyond Du Bois's 'veil' – that great conceptual divide which distorted views of race in America – required cultural expressions of unusual potency and permanence, appropriated by average African-Americans trying to define their identity outwith the perceptions of the white media and white society, and also by political groups who sought to construct the separate realm of 'blue sky and great wandering shadows' from which Du Bois looked down on white America in despair.[39]

Their success in doing so is highlighted by the way in which Black Power persists vibrantly in our collective memory. However, this memorialisation tends to settle at a surface level. Commentators have mourned the passing of the Black Panthers, alongside their apparently ephemeral political rhetoric and symbolism and ignored the deeper roots which helped give rise to these expressions. The long history of Black Power was a formative part of the attempts by innumerable black activists to give the techniques and tools of representation to people previously denied them.

Scholars like Jane Rhodes have noted that political groups like 'The [Black] Panthers ... invented themselves and delivered the goods' but the *tools* with which these groups invented themselves and the *frameworks* within which they did so stemmed from the long history of Black Power.[40] The political Black Power movement existed within a complex cultural matrix that was intimately connected to a series of cultural expressions across the American and African-American past: the long history of Black Power.

Thus when the political arm of the movement gained prominence, it was inevitable that, as Rhodes noted, it would exist in 'a hyperreal state in which it was unclear whether the meaning ... [the Panthers] embodied was ... replaced by the signs, symbols, and rhetoric that swirled around them.'[41] The Panthers argued that it was the reality of their politics which defined them, rather than their immediate cultural context, but they were shaped by a pre-existing cultural and historical inheritance which lent their politics a rootedness and relevance which it otherwise might have lacked. The Panthers' emergence was not the culmination of Black Power's long history, but their political existence was a significant shaping period which would colour and constrain the forms and frames it took thereafter.

By examining the long heritage of the political Black Power movement this book will explore how historically developed forms of cultural expression served to broaden the appeal and facilitate the acceptance of Black Power tenets in everyday life. Cultural forms of advocacy contributed significantly to making the Black Power movement a lasting influence in American society – one whose presence could be discerned long after its exclusively political agenda had disintegrated and which was instrumental in shaping changing notions of 'American' identity. Considering these connected cultural expressions across time and acknowledging the existence of Black Power's long history elevates the 1960s movement to a position where it can be effectively compared to other areas of the civil rights struggle and provides a novel perspective for discourse on culture, identity and group definition.

Recent works have situated the roots of the late twentieth century black aesthetic in the political movement of the same time, but it is increasingly useful to consider the politics of the 1960s as a phase of black cultural development, rather than its genesis.[42] Political Black Power was the ideological articulation and attempted implementation of certain persistent cultural tropes and images of African-American freedom via a structural programme. Cultural Black Power was the evolution, expression and adaptation of these persistent tropes across time which created a framework for political articulations. This cultural framework was in turn modified by the twentieth century political movement during the period where the two intersected.

A delineation needs to be made between the late 1960s manifestations of cultural nationalism and the long history of Black Power which this book seeks to examine. While cultural nationalism sought to provide an immediate, systematic and politically constructed antidote to the alleged omnipresence of African-American self-hate and self-destruction, examining the long history of Black Power offers an alternative perspective in which independent and evolving African-American identities have persisted across time in a series of connected cultural expressions. These expressions produced a legacy of resistance which informed the political Black Power movement, in both its cultural, nationalist and less overtly Africanist aspects. Black cultural nationalism, with its new approaches to and images of blackness, was an *aspect* of the complex network which comprised the cultural inheritance of the Black Power movement, but was not its sole component.

However, cultural nationalism not only predicated the reshaping of that inheritance into an African-centred world view, but the repudiation of, and separation from, American mainstream culture. Conversely, the book, by examining the long history of Black Power, does not limit itself to instances of repudiation, but seeks to explore the far more complex process of infiltration, adaptation, dissemination and intermingling of African-American cultural life with white cultural forms. Viewing the evolution of Black Power as a series of connected cultural expressions across time not only presents it as a contiguously present aspect of American culture, but demonstrates the manner in which the forms and iterations of cultural Black Power provided a framework for the political movement.

However, this is itself deceptive – these cultural forms both *shaped* and *were shaped by* their political contexts. Examining cultural Black Power requires a consciousness of the persistence of cultural tropes, but also of their remarkable evolution, adaptability and appropriation. The long history of Black Power consists of a series of connected cultural events across the time that both condition and are conditioned by the political forms arising alongside them. These connected cultural events share a set of tropes, symbols, ideas and icons which provide a common well of empowering identity construction tools.

As a consequence, cultural Black Power falls somewhere between the more familiar poles of cultural nationalism and political nationalism, but wholly cleaves to neither. However, it does provide an overlapping form which can bridge these two often virulently opposed ideological standpoints. The heterogeneous process of transmission and infiltration of cultural tropes was often an immersive phenomenon for its participants and is accordingly hard to trace. Cultural Black Power did not travel simply via lines of political discourse but rode these chains of rhetoric and surrounded (or appeared to surround) its adherents. Transmitted via tropes and symbols, history seemed to be repeated via not just aspirational figures, but ascriptional avatars onto which and from which ordinary black Americans could place and draw a new sense of identity. These more personal identities were not only constructive, but protective structures against the dangers of modern mass society.

As Toni Morrison explained, they functioned as 'strategies for survival' fashioned in 'response to predatory western phenomena'.[43]

As cultural expressions of Black Power were more malleable, they were therefore more capable of adaptation and utilisation by different facets of the Black Power struggle and, importantly by black Americans lacking a sense of identity and agency. Cultural Black Power was an individualised, personalised revolution, a revolution of the mind which could be experienced differently by each person and which could also be partially tailored by that person's choice of reference points. These reference points were in turn tailored by their emergence from a series of connected cultural expressions expressed across Black Power's long history. Thus, gaining an interest in the long history and cultural aspects of Black Power did not always occur in the same manner for every black American, nor did it produce the same results, beliefs or affiliations. What it did provide was a vast and potent reservoir which individuals could draw upon to create a new identity which they found to be empowering, liberating and uplifting, with their blackness situated as a central aspect of that identity, alongside their gender, belief, ideologies and ethnicities. Analysing the use of that reservoir and its interactions with the political dynamics of race in America requires some caution.

Often these days, historians speak of the civil rights and Black Power movements in the same breath, but conflating civil rights and Black Power damages the history we write by obscuring its complexity; conflating the political and cultural aspects of the Black Power movement injures it still further. To avoid this reductionism we need to pay more attention to the cultural and intellectual dimensions of the black liberation movement. Civil rights activists could shoot guns, and Black Power adherents could run candidates for political office. Yet superficially similar protest practices served different goals and long-term plans and the people involved thought about them differently. Whereas civil rights activists saw culture as a sustaining force to aid resistance to oppression in the freedom struggle, most notably expressed in the freedom songs of the movement, Black Power activists saw culture as a means to craft a separate identity both on an individual and a group basis.[44] For Black Power adherents and their militant predecessors culture was a weapon rather than a sustaining force for passive endurance, a tool for shaping a new identity in opposition to an existing system, rather than for reinforcing an established identity within that system. While many advocates of Black Power saw cultural forms as a necessary aspect of resistance, they were always, to paraphrase the Black Panther maxim, a means of 'survival pending revolution', in this case, a revolution of the mind.[45]

When historians favour 'Civil Rights' as an umbrella term, Black Power is cast as simply a militant episode in civil rights history. This reduces it to a set of tactics at best, and virtually erases it at worst, removing its leaders, followers, symbols and cultural legacy from our narrative. This book seeks to argue that the Black Power movement drew upon a particular set of cultural forms seen in a series of connected expressions across time and that the long history of Black Power, although intertwined with, *is distinct from* the history of civil rights in general.

To maintain this distinction, I have tried to respect Adam Fairclough's injunction that to avoid descending into 'homogenized mush' the civil rights and Black Power movements need to be presented as distinct waves within a wider struggle.[46] While the Black Power and civil rights movements both sought a clearer identity for African-Americans, the ways in which they did so and their conceptions of freedom were fundamentally different. This difference can be acknowledged even as the chronology under assessment is extended backward to consider the precedents, antecedents and heritage present in the long history of Black Power. This history was not simply a structural underpinning for the political movement of the 1960s, but an evolving series of cultural expressions that both shaped and was shaped by the political Black Power movement during the historical space when the two existed concurrently.

To explore these expressions, our interpretation of culture needs to be open to a much wider range of chronological and conceptual influences from the plantation forward. Future work requires an analytical framework which considers not simply the Africanist leanings of cultural nationalism, but the unconscious as well as the conscious selection of elements from the African-American past. Groups like the Panthers may have dreamt Africa, but they lived America and it was from their shared American experience that the bulk of their tropes, imagery and charismatic power stemmed. Moreover, it bears repeating that while scholars have a natural tendency to position the Black Panther Party as the zenith of Black Power expression, in reality they were simply one of a selection of expressions in the long history of the Black Power movement. Potent, charismatic and powerful, yes, but neither an end point nor a lacuna.

Even after setting aside the differences in contemporary interpretations, 'culture' is itself a problematic term. Like many others before me, I find that the anthropologist Clifford Geertz provided a solid foundation from which to begin approaching the concept and in many respects, a significant portion of this discussion will treat culture 'as the "webs of meaning" within which people live'.[47] However applying Geertz's relatively static conception of culture (penned as it is within a particular locale, period or social group), to the turbulent milieu of the 1960s and the decades that followed is difficult, if not impossible. The 1960s saw the rise of mass media and mass mediated culture, and exploring Black Power's relationship to the American people within that chronological framework requires flexibility.[48] Gently put, Geertz's concept 'needs some creative stretching to fit mass-mediated lives.'[49] On one level, this book attempts, albeit roughly and imprecisely, to translate Geertz's static story sources into the long history of Black Power by presenting them as a series of expressions linked throughout time, which became particularly pronounced in the 1960s due to the critical catalytic combination of the mass media upsurge, the stress of domestic politics and the growing national and transnational pressures of the anti-colonial, anti-imperialist and third world movements. Looking at the long cultural history of Black Power helps us partially understand why late twentieth century African-Americans felt as they did and what role cultural forms played in the formulation and reformation of militant identities in response to these events.

Culture, most of us are likely to agree these days, at least provides us with a shared system of meanings, and in the process 'dictates what we pay attention to, the way we act, and our value presumptions.'[50] The world we are immersed in, along with its past, shapes the way we respond to it, the way we think about it and the way we think about ourselves. At the most basic level 'culture sustains us'.[51] Many Black Power activists would have gone one step further and declared that culture could be used both as a sustaining force and as a weapon. So, where is this 'culture' to be found? In his recent work, communications theorist Fons Trompenaars sensibly stresses the relationship between an 'observable reality' which he takes to include 'language, food, buildings, markets, fashion, and artefacts', and a deeper level of culture of which these things are symbolic.[52] If we allow ourselves to think in this manner, the explicit realities of African-American culture can be tied to their chronological place, be that in the 1960s or earlier, but may also hold a deeper layer of symbolic meaning which is applicable in a more mediated, anachronistic form. The long history of Black Power provided a set of tools to solve the political problems of the 1960s but it also shaped the way in which those problems would be solved. The ensuing interaction created a new framework and a new set of tools, as did each point of cultural expression across time.

To show these interactions, any consideration of the long history of Black Power has to combine the visible realm of artefacts, rituals, practices and myth with the invisible, internal realm of values, beliefs and perceptions. This is a balancing act. Culture remains a complex phenomenon, especially in today's transnational environment.[53] While Geertz's webs of meaning likely still exist, they are expansive and complex beyond easy reckoning. Accordingly, rather than enumerating static instances of resistance and difference, this book seeks to trace the development of cultural Black Power through the long history of black militant expression, evidenced in a series of connected, reciprocally evolving and influential cultural expressions throughout time.

When examining this expression, it is important to realise that the theoretical and ideological lenses through which people viewed their actions matter as much as what they actually did. During the late 1960s, African-Americans' perceptions of themselves and their place in the world changed fundamentally. To periodise the black liberation movement, to write its history, we must take these mental changes into account. The civil rights movement tempts us toward easy generalisations, which we need to add complexity to by looking at the personal, cultural, intellectual and social motivations behind activism. Working with the cultural legacy of the movement is particularly challenging, as cultural creators can express events with a passion, vehemence and often imprecision which is outwith the traditional purview of historical analysis.

Matters become clearer if we accept that between 1965 and 1975 there was not a geographical shift in the movement, or a sea change in its protest activities, but that ordinary Americans understanding of the goals, ideology, discourse and symbols surrounding those activities changed fundamentally. The fervid climate of the 1960s and early 1970s partially explains why the long history of Black Power emerged with such force and potency at the time. The impact of federal anti-poverty programmes and spreading urban riots combined with a society in which segregation was legally outlawed, but racial oppression was practically implemented. Working in an environment where there was a backlash not only against the movement, but against the perceived dominance of federal intervention, some protestors inevitably gravitated to radical nationalist ideologies. With the war in Southeast Asia, American foreign policy was far more overtly hardline when dealing with revolutionaries and nationalists abroad, enabling Black Power activists to see themselves as part of a wider anti-imperialist movement. Facing increasingly draconian conditions, young militants found themselves seeking alternative responses to oppression, many of which could be found within the cultural history of Black Power, a wellspring of available and accessible tropes. Importantly, the long history of Black Power not only provided the means for that expression and resistance but conditioned the forms it would take.

When examining Black Power's long history it rapidly becomes apparent that none of the political actors of the 1960s functioned separately from their historical and cultural context – the images, stereotypes, tropes and myths produced across the long history of Black Power were firmly etched into the American nation's conception of race and identity. The relationship between Black Power and the American people which received such dramatic expression in the late 1960s, was only one iteration in a much longer process of racial confrontation, which merits further analysis. This is what the book hopes to achieve; to steer our conception of Black Power towards a longer history which both acknowledges the distinctiveness of the 1960s political phase and more sensitively places the roots of that political phase in the long history of African-American cultural militancy – the relationship between Black Power and the American people.

With this goal in mind, the book provides a broad-based reappraisal of the Black Power movement's relationship with the American people which operates on several levels. In the process of writing, I found that any such reappraisal must be an aesthetic as well as a utilitarian history. Accordingly, the book takes a wide-angle view of American history, emphasising the continuity of militant sentiment from its earliest expressions, exploring the impact of this political and cultural heritage on the formation of Black Power concepts during the traditional 1965–75 period and reconsidering why a Black Power movement developed during the latter half of the twentieth century.

To do so, I have sought to reorient our historical emphasis towards the long evolution of Black Power and to explore the way militant and iconoclastic sentiments manifested in a series of linked cultural expressions across time. In reconsidering the evolution and formation of differing beliefs, the book shows that the self-definition at the heart of all Black Power ideology was culturally driven – shaped, bounded, promulgated and formulated by cultural expression and production. In the process, I have tried to trace the emergence of a plurality of Black Power perspectives in the streets and on the campuses, in schools and town halls, far-flung barracks and simmering Southern towns.

By redefining militancy in a cultural context it becomes possible to consider iterations of Black Power on campus, in labour, in sports, film and the performing arts, in speech and thought, in music and science-fiction as well as in the 'Total Institutions' – the military and the prisons. Expanding the historical definition of Black Power and building on our existing concepts of militancy, enables a far more significant demonstration of how these individuals and their ideologies interacted with the broad-based cultural infrastructure of the movement.

Black Power and American mainstream culture experienced a mercurial historical relationship and this book seeks to document and explore these shifting perceptions. Changes in political and personal perspectives often manifested in everyday life and accordingly this book offers a series of connected vignettes which demonstrate the revolution of the mind occurring for ordinary Americans as Black Power infiltrated their consciousness. This book charts a course through the growth of the literary and the performing arts, the evolution and adoption of novel cultural definitions, the gradual surge of militancy in Hollywood, its explosive arrival in the sporting arena and most crucially the redefinition and cultural reappropriation of history by the Black Power movement, culminating in the creation of a new mythology of empowerment, the strategic use of history as a tool for liberation and the acquisition of African-American culture as a potential road map to a more empowered future.

Although any analysis of the Black Power movement must acknowledge its political decline in the 1970s, reading the movement's story from a new, integrated cultural perspective demonstrates a convincing cultural legacy bequeathed by the Black Power movement to American society and one whose repercussions radiate outward through American history. In order to challenge the crippling notion that Black Power was nothing but a short-lived flurry of noise without substance, the book strives to present future historians with a long-term evolution in the American cultural sphere that holds more resonance for history and society than isolated considerations of the political aspects of Black Power and compliments the current fashion for focused, single-issue studies by placing them within a wider framework. From this perspective, culture can be seen not as the offshoot of politics, but as carrying political ideology, birthing it and altering it, as a fundamental factor in the construction of African-American identity and crucially, as a central force in not just Black Power, but American and world history.

This fundamental consideration explains the primary rationale for the topics selected in the following pages. The book focuses on those cultural expressions which offered the most pronounced and significant challenge to white American cultural dominance and which significantly shaped the interaction between the Black Power ethos and the American people. Accordingly, one of our most immediate cultural touchstones – music – is addressed primarily as a catalyst for the transformation of the mind occurring amongst its African-American audience and in its transatlantic and futuristic manifestations. Despite its widespread popularity across the race divide, much African-American music offered little significant challenge to the citadel of white cultural hegemony. Its very popularity and acceptance meant that it seldom provoked a profound collision with established perceptions, and, when it was controversial, a flicked switch or a turned dial could remove its presence easily and rapidly. The exceptions which prove this rule merit attention as the most profound moments of mental iconoclasm, and I leave a broader consideration of the cultural presence of African-American music to other scholars with greater scope in which to address its fundamental integration with American life.

The same logic has been applied to the presence and potency of religion within the African-American community. Although I have touched upon the subject of spiritual empowerment, as befits such a profoundly personal protest movement, I have endeavoured to limit myself to the points where the spiritual profoundly influenced the secular, and where the strands of religion most clearly shaped the reality of African-American life. To fully study the interplay between African-American identity and spirituality in America is a life's endeavour in itself and would require another monograph to do it justice.

Similarly, while several scholars have recently reintroduced gender as a shaping dynamic within the civil rights and Black Power movements, I have attempted to address black women as the sources tended to write about themselves: as individuals experiencing the twin pressures of life as black Americans, and black women.[54] The revolution of the mind explored throughout the book entailed a fundamental redefinition of what it meant to be African-American and it appears that many women engaged with emergent versions of the Black Power ethos were concerned with formulating a concrete African-American identity while also exploring their existence as women within that matrix. When the two desires conflicted, I have endeavoured to explore the ramifications for identity construction.

In keeping with the book's focus on presenting the most fundamental challenges to white American hegemony, it makes sense to consider women within the Black Power movement primarily as one would any other activists reassessing their self-perceptions. Put simply, feminism and the role of women in the struggle appear to have been more prominent issues in the political Black Power movement, where gender was a primary shaping factor. Within the cultural movement, being black and celebrating that fact tended to initially take precedence over one's gender. However, the endemic and intertwined nature of American racism and American misogyny ensured that these facets of protest could never be entirely separated.

In the process of writing, two key areas for further research have become apparent. Firstly, while I have begun to explore the influence of cultural Black Power on suburban African-Americans, there remains scope for a much broader study of suburban responses to the classic tropes of black cultural empowerment. Again, within the limited space of the book, I chose to focus on the rapid acceptance of the 'Blaxploitation' genre by many ordinary Americans as being the exemplar which offered the most direct and pronounced challenge to cultural and personal assumptions among both black and white viewers.

The scope of this analysis limits the ability to push beyond the 1970s demise of the political movement in any comprehensive form, but this undoubtedly remains the most fertile ground for future research, identifying not only the legacies and ramifications of the 1960s movement, but the persistence of identifiable cultural tropes across the long history of Black Power. Scholars would do well to turn their attention to structuring and dissecting the contribution of the Afrofuturist movement in creating new hybrid identities and there may well be room to move toward new concepts of identity using the matrix of Paul Gilroy's Black Atlantic. I have attempted to provide some points of embarkation from which new voyages into this fertile sea might be made.

Ultimately, to understand the evolution and emergence of Black Power, historians must view the movement in a broad, expansive cultural context across the movement's long history. Despite the media-prescribed distortion of events, the importance of Black Power to modern American history cannot be dismissed as the actions of young demagogues and 'negro hotheads' fuelled by vitriol and craving anarchy. Neither was Black Power a fringe movement endorsed only by a small but vocal minority of African-Americans with an aberrant passion for racism and violence. Rather, Black Power should be considered a movement focused on gaining equality of influence, respect and power. The power it sought began with the power to influence the affairs and address the concerns of the average African-American.

The long history of black cultural militancy became the building blocks of the political Black Power movement, a solid foundation which would endure when later structures toppled and which guided African-America through one of its most challenging, surprising and difficult eras. However, the cultural forms which reinforced the structure of the political movement were not bounded by it, diversifying and proliferating to endure long after the political aspects of the movement had faded.

In the chapters that follow, the Black Power movement will be analysed in several contexts. In the first chapter, I have attempted to answer the question 'What is Black Power?' by considering the definitions formulated during the 1965–75 period, beginning with the political statement itself and expanding outwards to cover the initial scholarly, media and cultural flurry to comprehend the movement's political emergence and subsequent cultural expressions of the concept. The chapter discusses the use of sensationalism as initial publicity and what took its place. An analysis is made of militant responses to popular stigmatisation and activists' reactions to the allegations that Black Power was incapable of making a permanent contribution to American life. I argue that Black Power was almost always more popular in its cultural aspects than as a political expression. In doing so, I have attempted to explore the role of Black Power's long history in the creation of a new African-American cultural consciousness and a catalyst for processes of group and individual redefinition within the wider American society.

The chapter concludes that Black Power was a revolutionary cultural concept which demanded important changes in extant patterns of American cultural hegemony, but that to grasp the essence of the term, historians must view Black Power in an inclusive, chronologically extended, cultural context. By defining African-Americans as culturally distinct from white Americans, black militants constructed a power base in territory they knew best – the area of black life with which outsiders were most unfamiliar. The long history of black culture was the seedbed of the political Black Power movement but existed in parallel, having an independent vitality of its own.

Chapter 2 examines why a Black Power movement developed during the latter half of the twentieth century. Black Power was not a concept which sprang fully formed from Stokely Carmichael's lips in 1965, but one which exhibited a long history and clear cultural evolution seldom discussed by historians. Accordingly, the chapter traces the emergence of Black Power concepts from the earliest days of the plantation, through the bohemian foment of the awkwardly named 'Harlem Renaissance' to its later distillation in the work of the Black Arts Movement, and other, less frequently lauded grassroots and community groups such as the Free Southern Theater (FST). African-American cultural history was an ongoing quest for clarity and self-definition amidst the wider American milieu and this evolution gave birth to a new mythology of empowerment which featured clear, recognisable tropes that could be identified in the political as well as the cultural arena.

Chapter 3 considers some of the individuals who carried Black Power ideology forth into American life. It attempts to redefine the concept of a 'militant' in a cultural context, by considering the diverse iterations of Black Power on campus and the manner in which the movement was framed by the mainstream media. The process of identity construction interacted with the complex university environment, across not only lines of race but also generation and ultimately transferred into the wider community via the lenses of white America. The chapter explores the predisposition of the media to framing student protest in terms which reinforced existing cultural stereotypes, in order to demonstrate that student protest was part of the wider American cultural milieu and that America was not as homogenous in its reaction to the protests as the media, or some current historiography, might suggest. In the process, it contends that for student protesters of the late 1960s education and empowerment were intrinsically linked.

Investigating the incarnation of this linkage in the Institute of the Black World (IBW), the chapter explores how the drive toward Black Studies promoted the study of African-American history and culture, in the process introducing new value concepts, identity images and cultural standards to African-American youth. Responsive to the needs of its audience, the IBW's existence was proof that institutionalised Black Power conformed to no single pattern of development, adapting existing institutional forms to the needs of the black liberation movement.

The chapter closes by discussing the concept and implications of the potential emergence of a 'communiversity' where the campus itself was the sidewalk of the black community, arguing for the cultural importance of an aspirational educational facility dependent upon ordinary African-Americans for standards and values and, accordingly, more responsive to local needs than traditional institutions. The section concludes that the programmatic measures adopted by advocates of Black Power in higher education were important steps toward black self-definition and empowerment and essential in maintaining connections with the movement's long history. A student vanguard took the revolution home, striving to transmit their values across the generation gap, encouraging relatives to join in politicising their local communities and spreading the Black Power message beyond the academy.

Chapter 4 attempts further to revise our conceptions of militancy, by considering iterations of Black Power in sports. Black Power archetypes of militancy were more visible in the cultural arena and, crucially, their messages of self-definition were more easily interpreted when conveyed through the lens of familiar cultural forms. Exploring the interaction between the Negro and Major Leagues in American baseball illuminates a complex net of cultural relations and inter-racial interactions seldom discussed and at variance with much common perception. In the process, the long historical legacy of some of America's most lauded players is exposed as part of an intricate cultural network.

Conversely, the cultural legacy of African-American boxing is revealed as a form of cultural catharsis. Boxers themselves became archetypes of the ways in which both white and black Americans wished to perceive their country. The chapter demonstrates the reciprocal relationship between culture and politics; the manner in which sports could be used as a frame of reference for the interpretation of political ideologies and its dual function as an arena for archetypes of empowerment and a mirror to contemporary concerns.

This perspective challenges the persistent public memory of the 1968 Olympic boycott as a single iconic moment. In the process, the cultural and historical impetus for the boycott is analysed, alongside organiser Harry Edwards's progression from aspirational cultural archetype to modern-day establishment figure. The chapter concludes that the heterogeneous responses to the boycott epitomised the ability of sporting protest to alter American cultural assumptions and its power as a carrier for militant rhetoric and imagery.

Similarly, Chapter 5 explores the durability of the militant ethos within America's 'Total Institutions', commencing with an examination of the transmission of militant culture within the armed forces which considers the cultural impetus for rebellion once inducted and the way in which army militants crafted separate identities in defiance of a decaying system. The reasons behind radicalisation are explored, to demonstrate that the African-American GIs defined their place in the struggle for freedom by their cultural heritage and culture heroes, as much as by their political beliefs.

In comparable manner, the chapter examines the militant assertion that prison was a transformative experience and the cultural avenues of resistance available in this most disempowering of environments. The importance of belief and self-image in survival and parole are examined, alongside the flourishing of revolutionary thought and the creation of modes of internal communication which integrated political Black Power with a cultural iteration far more aptly tuned to penitentiary survival. In the process, I have attempted to move our focus from the transmission of militant ideology amongst inmates, to its practical implementation, in order to show that cultural forms of Black Power provided essential tools that enabled incarcerated African-Americans to retain their own identity behind bars. The flourishing of militant culture in the penitentiary was testament to the strength of the cultural forms which carried it.

The continuing strength of these cultural forms is further explored in Chapter 6, which examines the potent and persistent series of cultural tropes and artefacts that the long history of Black Power has bequeathed to modern American thinkers. Studying the long ignored interaction of black music and black speculative fiction presents new perspectives on the construction of a modern black identity. From the iconic myth of blues man Robert Johnson's diabolic trade for the secret of the blues to the aluminium glamour of Labelle and the neon strut of Parliament Funkadelic, the chapter analyses the interaction between African-America's musical heritage and its futurist thought.

As contemporary culture creators sifted the long history of Black Power, they integrated aspects of their African-American heritage and diasporic artefacts to inform musical genres from funk to hip-hop and techno. This composite, transatlantic culture was also evident in the pages of African-American science fiction. These visions of a black future challenged prevailing notions of race and gender, the assumed binaries of American culture and ultimately, accepted social reality.

In closing, the chapter contends that the musicians and writers of the late twentieth century worked from a shared set of historically produced cultural forms and tropes which allowed their audience to briefly transcend the limits of their skin colour and which acted as a catalyst for the revolution of the mind. These writers articulated themes of alienation, transportation, abduction and colonisation which were appropriated by the Afrofuturist movement to construct a modern, hybrid transatlantic identity. In effect, a second revolution of the mind, but one with its roots in the acceptance and integration of the long history of Black Power into everyday American life.

Chapter 7 elaborates on this conclusion by exploring manifestations of this empowering African-American culture in everyday life, in order to demonstrate the profound change occurring in many African-Americans' self-perception and to explore the degree to which the African-American community accepted these new cultural manifestations.

Elaborating upon the importance of black culture to the long militant history of African-America explored in Chapter 2, the chapter examines the relationship between African-American art and the black public and the resulting implications for an evolving African-American identity. Moving from the counterculture subversion of the early twentieth century Harlem Renaissance to the brazen boldness of the 1970s Black Arts Movement the chapter concludes that there was a basic commonality in these works – the presence of a rich and vibrant cultural tradition repeatedly refuted by black and white alike.

This commonality emphasises the importance of little analysed practical manifestations of Black Arts ideology in street culture, from smoky dancehalls to the glossy pages of *Ebony* and highlights the tangible change occurring in African-American cultural perspectives. Accordingly, the chapter concludes that the politics of the street and the cultural legacy of the Black Power movement were not distinct, but interrelated parts of a greater whole, each informing and driving the other. As fast as militant culture evolved white capitalism attempted to co-opt it, resulting in an American *milieu* increasingly infiltrated by the militant aesthetic.

The diversity of this aesthetic is supported by an examination of the ways in which African-American theatre brought history to the community, serving as both a stimulus to commemoration and a catalyst for political action. Focusing on the grass roots approach of the Free Southern Theater, the section argues that although theatre seldom led to direct change, it was an opportunity for critical assessment, of self and society, a catalyst to wider action and a means of reshaping established modes of thought.

In counterpoint, the chapter also explores African-America's response to the white cultural *milieu*. It argues that even the most ostensibly 'passive' individuals reacted to the changing culture around them and demonstrates that the revolution of the mind was also occurring behind the white picket fence and in front of the silver screen, as African-America's cultural landscape was changed forever by the lurid arrival of Blaxploitation cinema. The diverse reactions to the militant images contained therein provide a basis from which to explore the growing integration of the Black Power aesthetic with American mainstream culture. The chapter asserts that African-America was becoming increasingly engaged with its evolving culture, debating its merits and casting it against the expectations of mainstream society.

The book closes with an analysis of the movement's lasting historical and cultural presence in order to challenge the prevailing view of the Black Power movement as the 'poor cousin' of the civil rights movement which failed to achieve lasting gains for the black American populace. It contends that the 1960s and 1970s Black Power movement was the product of a long history of militant empowerment, which enabled it to be far more resonant and permanent in its cultural aspects than its political manifestations. Ultimately, it is my hope readers will begin to acknowledge that the cultural Black Power movement existed long prior to and long after the political movement, and that it should be viewed as a phenomenon in its own right. Our historiography needs to change accordingly and take account of the poets, sportsmen, artists and film stars as much as of the protesters and the pickets.

CHAPTER 1

HOTHEADS AND DEMAGOGUES: WHAT IS BLACK POWER?

Understanding Black Power first entails grappling with the images that accompanied its emergence into American popular culture. From the outset, Black Power was presented in a two-dimensional manner due to white America's aversion to investigating beneath the surface of a photogenic and alluring image. From this perspective, the movement's diversity and constant evolution was manifested as chaos and disorganisation, with ideological and practical distinctions obscured in the media avalanche of berets, shotguns and snarling beasts.

    The media and the militants were occasionally complicit in the creation of Black Power's iconic imagery, most obviously demonstrated in the regalia of the Black Panther Party for Self-Defense. A carefully crafted enterprise from the start, everything about the Panthers' iconography, from their snarling symbol, 'a bold beautiful animal, representing the strength and dignity of black demands today', to the classic garb of beret, dark glasses, shotgun and the oft-forgotten law book; was designed to project an image of resilience, confidence and a willingness to push back if pushed.[1] This often proved a double-edged sword. As David Hilliard, Panther Chief of Staff, commented, there was a fine line between the use of violent imagery and its appropriation toward a negative stereotype.[2] Even Malcolm X admitted, '[The press was] looking for sensationalism, for something that would sell papers and I gave it to them'.[3] News coverage may have brought the image of

Black Power to the forefront, but popular discussions of the concept remained clouded by misperception, assumption and fear.

This has persisted to the present day. As recently as 2003, *San Francisco Chronicle* journalist Kate Coleman rather archaically castigated the Panthers as a 'bunch of thugs' who continue to 'capture the imagination of American intellectuals' while fringe academic David Horowitz unsurprisingly sees any faith in the positivity of the Panther legacy as the preserve of 'acolytes, idolaters and the credulous.'[4]

In order to conceive of how Black Power could have left a consistent cultural legacy the term needs clarification. The drive to 'understand' this new and frightening phenomenon often compromised the initial street-level surveys. Rather than explore the psychological and social factors behind militancy, surveys focused on the followers and support received by the movement. The qualifiers used to define militancy were often so vague as to be almost useless; small scale, marginal samples were used to give the aura of a clear public sentiment without being genuinely representative.[5]

The overriding insinuation of such surveys was that Black Power was nothing more than a fringe element which seldom matched the approval rate of the civil rights establishment.[6] When black Chicagoans were asked who best represented their position, almost twenty times as many respondents favoured Martin Luther King as did Stokely Carmichael.[7] The pattern seemed endlessly repeated, and yet when one 1967 study of Watts found 58 per cent of respondents favoured Black Power and only 24 per cent opposed it, the conclusion was that Black Power would fail as 'most urban Negroes simply reject the Black Power ideology'.[8] The initial flurry of media interest apparently seduced analysts into conflating wishful thinking and social science gospel. The conception of black militancy as some ephemeral, marginal force was so pervasive that in Harlem, a street gang known as the 'Five Percenters' named themselves after the oft-touted assumption that only 5 per cent of African-Americans were sufficiently militant to achieve change.[9] There was a real problem here; as the 'Five-Percent Nation' demonstrated, even inaccurate interpretations of Black Power had a distinct influence on the society of the block and ghetto.

Overall, studies which show minimal support for militancy obscure the fact that Black Power was consistently more significant in its cultural aspects than as a political expression. In a 1966 national survey on contributions to the fight for African-American rights, the first African-American Major League Baseball player of the modern era, Jackie Robinson, received ten times the endorsement given to the 'Black Muslims', a term which incorporated the Nation of Islam, a political group fundamentally involved in practical community support projects.[10] Despite his conservative politics, perceptions of Robinson's cultural contribution were so prevalent that the *Umbra* co-founder Calvin C. Hernton, on applying for a prestigious job, was informed he had the potential to become the 'Jackie Robinson' of the company, not for his skills, but for what he represented.[11]

Outside of class, Black Power rode the statistics into African-American cultural consciousness.[12] Distinctive new trends in clothing, cuisine, hairstyles and music found purchase with a surprisingly wide range of age groups within African-America.[13] Seventy-six per cent of young northern black Americans, tellingly dubbed the 'Stokely Generation' by pollsters, liked the new natural hairstyles, but more significantly 45 per cent of all African-American respondents in 1969 saw the appeal.[14] A 1968 survey found approximately 40 per cent of African-Americans in Detroit endorsed the wearing of dashikis while eight out of ten enjoyed soul food and music.[15] With greater wealth appeared to come greater approbation of the new aesthetic, as 'middle-income' African-Americans both North and South took to the dashiki and buba quicker than their impoverished counterpoints.[16]

Surveys which assessed abstract cultural concepts like 'soul', 'black is beautiful', and collective identity suggested the cultural aspects of the Black Power movement possessed a profound and distinct appeal.[17] Regrettably, the implications of these surveys were seldom explored.[18] There was a more immediate concern with creating a scale of militancy, a barometer of African-American discontent, so that America could predict where and among whom the next outbreak of militant fever would strike.[19] Hampered by overly subjective topics and poorly constructed samples, such surveys are unwieldy tools for investigating the foundations of the movement.

More relevance can be gleaned from individual interpretations of the meaning of Black Power. Responses of white people differed greatly from those of black people. In a Harris opinion poll towards the end of the decade, 60 per cent of white respondents expressed concern about the Black Panthers, compared to only 20 per cent of the black Americans surveyed.[20] Earlier, and more explicitly, a 1967 University of Michigan survey of community perspectives found almost 60 per cent of white people equated Black Power with African-American supremacy, civil disorder and racism.[21] As interviewers were matched with respondents based on race, the perspectives which emerged spoke to potentially genuine fears. Like the media, many of these ordinary men and women (a significant proportion of whom lived in the less urban lakeside areas of Grosse Pointe and Harper Woods) were intimidated and confused by the rapid and strident emergence of Black Power onto the national scene.[22] At the far end of the spectrum, some white commentators warned of a complete 'Black takeover' effected by fervent Black Panthers arming for 'a last-stand guerrilla fight in what ... members believe will be a white war of extermination against Negroes.'[23] These fears were primarily a white construction; according to the same surveys, fewer than 9 per cent of black people interviewed held similar views.[24]

Yet perception mattered. When Russell Sackett warned that 'in secret recesses of any ghetto in the US there are dozens and hundreds of black men working resolutely toward an Armageddon in which whitey ... is forced to his knees', his claims were not isolated vitriol.[25] Police officers believed the Panthers would 'invade their homes ... killing wives and children', as late as January 1970.[26] Consistently, the nascent Black Power movement was pitched against the earlier nonviolent struggle, with the contrast established repeatedly and carefully, word by loaded word. Whereas civil rights protests had been framed as marches and assemblies, the Panthers roamed, stalked and forced their way into events.[27] In a country wracked by conflict and unrest, fragmented whispers of terror slithered in from every state. Look out, the news wires hummed, look out. The blacks are coming to kill you, and they are going to do it in style.[28]

Panic over African-American militancy was not confined to the late twentieth century, for all contemporary newspapers might have created the impression of a new and terrifying phenomenon. As early as 6 October 1919 the *New York Times* cautioned its readers to beware a 'Planned Massacre of Whites', while in the closing months of the war the same organ warned weary Manhattanites that they risked becoming the victims of a '200 pound Negro armed with a Shark Knife' who had been seen wading through rioting streets thronged with excited negroes, armed with revolvers, knives, stones and bottles.'[29]

The *Times'* provocations were indicative of how many newspapers of the era 'uncritically mediated and disseminated prevailing ideologies of race'.[30] As a consequence, African-American militancy existed within a narrow spectra from the outset. If the black rioters of the early twentieth century were seen as an impulsive and politically naïve threat to the social order, the militants of the late 1960s fared little better. An article in the *San Francisco Sunday Chronicle* again attempted a pithy definition, asserting that 'Black Panthers; Wear Guns, Talk Revolution.'[31] Here the dependable allure of the Black Panthers was highlighted, with members cast as 'stars of a movie melodrama of revolution', placing the Panther party as magnetic centres of a poorly defined whole.[32]

Lack of definition became the *bete noire* of media coverage of Black Power. Part of the problem lay in the fact that, for many media observers, extremists were extremists, whether they wore white hoods or black berets. Simplistic analysis cast the Panthers as the black analogue of white terror, and assumed they would threaten American life in the same way.[33] The Panther's taint of lawlessness, readers were informed, 'pervades the American scene.'[34] Too often, the media preferred moral judgements before simple observation. It was no wonder that when surveyors and pundits took white America's pulse that it ran feverish and hot.

Media commentary and popular survey may have revealed differences in white and black perceptions of the new militant phenomenon but did little to clarify any analytical definition of Black Power. Nonetheless, there are sufficient enthusiastic refutations of the many apparently misguided conceptions articulated by predominantly white observers throughout the political Black Power period that historians can begin to construct an explanation. According to one of its highest, most militant exponents, Black Power was emphatically neither a negative term nor intrinsically violent; it was a clear plan for community control. Revolutionary rhetoric, it was argued, was designed to engage the average African-American, not to breed riots.

In perhaps the clearest definition of the political movement, the Student Nonviolent Coordinating Committee's (SNCC) Stokely Carmichael spoke of Black Power as 'the coming together of black people to elect representatives to speak to their needs'.[35] The people, it was argued, could never come together if they remained insulated and stifled by American mainstream culture. As Carmichael remarked in 1970, 'The first stage is waking up our people ... to the impending danger. So we yell, Gun! Shoot! Burn! Kill! Destroy! They're committing genocide! until the masses of our people are awake.'[36] According to doctrine, violence was only justified in self-defence. Black Power advocates believed the will and ability to retaliate was an essential survival skill for an abusive political and cultural environment.

The lack of actual violence proved mystifying for some white observers. As *US News and World Report* almost wistfully remarked on the Sacramento State Capitol Penal Code protests of 2 May 1967: 'No shots were fired. There was no violence beyond a few scuffles. What was it all about?'[37] The answer to this question, it often seemed, depended on who was asked.

For some Black Power adherents, it was about exposing the consequences of American racial violence. As Carmichael explained in *The Politics of Liberation*, one of the most lucid manifestos for Black Power, 'Nothing more quickly repels someone bent on destroying you than the unequivocal message: "O.K. fool, make your move, and run the same risk I run – of dying".'[38] The Black Power appeal tapped into cultural conventions which reasoned that individuals were justified in using force to preserve their safety, property or identity. Carmichael phrased this concept more prosaically, and with greater resonance for the average African-American: 'what man would not defend his family and home from attack?'[39] Activists felt that American culture was itself an assault on African-American freedom, and to escape its stifling, vampiric influence, a new cultural militancy needed to evolve.[40] As H. Rap Brown commented, 'We put america on notice; IF WHITE FOLKS WANT TO PLAY NAZIS, BLACK FOLKS AIN'T GOING TO PLAY JEWS.'[41] Brown's rhetoric had been prefaced by Stokely Carmichael in his earliest speeches. American fascism, Carmichael alleged, was a relic of an older time, with rules that no longer applied. As he told a UC Berkeley audience, 'this is not 1942 and if you play like Nazis, we playing back with you this time around.'[42] This oppressive conceptualisation of their contemporary situation shaped Black Power policy. Carmichael and other Black Power advocates believed that the American system had profoundly failed them, and to expect acquiescence to the same system was idiocy, since 'there can be no social order without social justice.'[43]

Within this schema, the *potential* for black violence was intended to deter white Americans from responding physically to interracial confrontation.

At its most basic root, Black Power was seen by its advocates as a primarily positive pacifying force. African-American militancy, it was argued, would dissuade inter-racial confrontations by making white belligerents consider the full repercussions of violence.[44] As John Oliver Killens wrote in 1966, 'It keeps everybody nonviolent. It stays the hands of the practitioners of violence ... We must teach the brutalizers how it feels to be brutalized.'[45]

Clarifying the role of violence in militancy required refuting charges that Black Power gave *carte blanche* to black racism, giving rise to Roy Wilkins's 'reverse Ku Klux Klan'.[46] Movement participants countered that vituperative reactions to Black Power were another attempt to obfuscate white American racial prejudices with accusations of reverse discrimination. Militants argued that some white people – especially those with vested interests in the failing American system – sought to bolster their support by branding militants as racial supremacists, thereby turning undecided Americans against the movement.[47]

Beneath these accusations lay a more sinister contention: that distaste for violence in reality masked a distaste for blackness and black America. Waxing lyrical at Berkeley, Carmichael argued that an overarching fear of blackness permeated white culture. In this context white advocacy of non-violence was a tool to control unsettling elements of the African-American population. Any attention to the violence so endemic in American culture was conspicuous by its absence. Carmichael's litany was scathing: 'Black people cut themselves every night in the ghetto ... Lyndon Baines Johnson is busy bombing the hell of out Vietnam ... White people beat up black people every day – don't nobody talk about nonviolence'.[48] It was only when black people began to assert themselves, Carmichael complained, that 'the double standard' began to emerge.[49]

Conversely, white liberals and black moderates were accused of lambasting Black Power supporters to reinvigorate an increasingly stagnant civil rights campaign. In this context, accusations of black racism were designed to ostracise fractious militants and reinforce the decaying façade of mid-1960s civil rights reform.[50] Established campaigners feared the new militancy would drive an insurmountable wedge through the coalition. Thus to an extent cries of black racism were a panicked response to a dissolving status quo.

In rebuttal, activists argued that charges of black racism were profoundly ahistorical. Contending that the entirety of African-America's history had been a bitter struggle against discrimination, militants argued it was impossible to end racism by perpetuating racism. Bobby Seale encapsulated the issue in a 1968 speech:

> When the Man walks up and says that we were anti-white, I scratch my head ... I say, 'Wait a minute man, let's back up a little bit. That's *your* game, that's the Ku Klux Klan's game ... to hate *me* and murder *me* because of the colour of my skin' ... If you got enough energy to sit down and hate a white person *just* because of the colour of his skin, you're wasting a lot of energy. You better take some of that same energy ... and start dealing with those oppressive conditions.[51]

To the emergent Black Power militant, white prejudice had no tangible black equivalent. Intrinsically, racism involved discrimination designed to institute and maintain a system of societal subjugation. In the American context, this had historically been a white endeavour. For black campaigners to embrace white racism would be a suicidal enterprise.[52] As Eldridge Cleaver wrote, racism 'will only get us killed, and it will destroy the world'.[53] From the militant perspective, what white America perceived as racism was simply a necessary cultural construction to survive and advance in an antagonistic environment; it was, as the Panthers repeatedly claimed, a means of 'survival pending revolution'.[54] As Julius Lester wearily explained in *Sing Out!* magazine, 'There is too much to do to waste time and energy hating white people.'[55]

In effecting survival, Black Power aspired to become a preservationary force for African-American values. Racism was fought through community solidarity and the creation of a new African-American cultural consciousness that uplifted the militants' own social group. Recognising the problems of representation, militants laid the blame for the perversion of this ethos squarely at the feet of a racist national media, alternately raging against the temerity of unlicensed white commentary and succumbing resignedly to the perils of external definition. Stokely Carmichael reflected morosely after an awkward appearance on the Dick Cavett show in 1970: 'They're not going to let us ... really break down the truth to our people.'[56] Carmichael was perhaps right to be concerned that the Panthers might be reduced to a curiousity on the evening news, but it was also an essential conduit for the movement. The media at the time spread familiar images via a confusing mix of tropes, but it also, for the first time introduced a vast audience to the Panther's symbolic universe. Stuart Hall has argued that the media actually presented a space within which white perspectives of black America could be 'articulated worked on, transformed and elaborated.'[57] There was a transformative potential here for both black and white Americans; the very alien nature of these images presented a world 'so extraordinary that belief in the feasibility of revolution grew.'[58]

The majority of Black Power activists argued that white perceptions of black violence were indicative of deep-rooted lesions in the white American psyche, culminating in a pathological fear of power placed in African-American hands, at the root of which lay a twisted cultural concept of what it meant to be black – a libidinous, primal, lascivious image constructed without reference to reality. As Toni Morrison noted, African-America was always a dissident, provocative presence in the American imagination, capable of absorbing national fears and anxieties.[59] Accordingly, much cultural analysis of Black Power emerged from 'a fabricated brew of darkness, otherness, alarm and desire that is uniquely American'.[60] In particular, there is some value to John Fiske's claim that 'the figure of the Black male out of control is a cultural nightmare for whites' – many press accounts tapped into racially coded frames of understanding which reinforced traditional stereotypes of African-America.[61] Underneath the rhetoric of law and order, more exotic and terrifying understandings lay in shallow graves.

According to militant rhetoric, for white people, the very concept of blackness conjured terrifying images. As Julius Lester wrote with quiet fury in *Look Out Whitey!* 'Black! That word. BLACK! And the visions came of alligator-infested swamps arched by primordial trees ... and out of the depths of the swamp, the mire oozing from his skin, came the black monster ... raping everything white that wore a dress, burning, stealing, killing. BLACK POWER!'[62] Certainly, increased 'attention to ... Black Power inflamed long buried white American anxieties' or, as Eldridge Cleaver explained with typical delicacy, 'The black man's penis was the monkey wrench in the white man's perfect machine.'[63]

While Cleaver and Lester's remarks may have struck a certain guilty chord among white observers, African-Americans were in the process of constructing a more complex series of associations for Black Power. As Fuller noted, 'The concept ... is a valid one, but the term, connected to the concept by virtue of language, does not always translate, or ... come close to the meaning of the concept.'[64] What then was the meaning of Black Power for black people? Here lies the problem of negative definition: militants generally found it simpler to refute white misconceptions than formulate succinct explanations. African-Americans found themselves in possession of a nascent identity which was 'at once self-evident and needed definition.'[65] As one student acerbically put it, 'You're black, no matter what you do to yourself.'[66] However, the assumption by some adherents that the meaning of Black Power was too obvious to merit articulation is of less use to historians.

It seems important to note that the cultural exploration that proliferated during the civil rights struggle developed into a more deliberate rethinking of the meanings of blackness in the course of the Black Power movement. The Black Power movement did not create an identity *sui generis*. Rather, it embraced and redefined elements of pre-existing identities, collated and conflated from a series of connected cultural expressions across time. The result was a consistently malleable, composite, complicated identity matrix.

Despite this emergent and persistent complexity, militants often made the daunting assertion that any African-American who claimed not to understand Black Power's basic implications was deluded or mad. Yet at the time, 'Within different organizations, black was variously defined as African, revolutionary and communal, urban and poor, or Muslim.'[67] Navigating this sea of referents, assertions and dire warnings was profoundly challenging, yet any confessions as to confusion over the meaning of Black Power flagged the confessor as part of the conspiracy to discredit the movement.[68] Despite such militant bravado there was a reluctance actually to define the term, something which led commentators to find the Black Power concept complex and ambiguous, remaining unsure of its practical repercussions. As one anonymous 'Observer' mused:

> Does 'Black Power' mean *more* or does it mean *less* new model automobiles lining up in the Harlem streets? More Hi-Fi phonographs and television sets and tape recorders and transistor radios? More high rise middle-income apartments and young black nationalists with pointed shoes and sharp continental cut

suits? Does it mean more or less fancy togs and cocktails to go along with the African hair do's? Or does it mean austerity and sacrifice? And who will be elected to do the sacrificing?[69]

In an attempt to answer these questions, an incredibly varied selection of definitions was advanced. At one end of the spectrum, a profoundly contributionist perspective cast Black Power as a variant of the traditional African-American freedom struggle. It was 'People getting together to accomplish things for the group'; obtaining employment, self-esteem and respect, thereby compelling white society to realize their worth.[70] At this end of the spectrum, and perhaps surprisingly, African-American newspapers were often more able to distil 'the multifarious elements of Black Power'.[71] An *Oakland Tribune* reporter came near to the truth when he noted that for many people it was as simple as: 'bread on the table, money in the pockets and Negro officeholders in towns and counties.[72] Often disapproving or unsure of the methods being employed, these commentators nonetheless acknowledged that the movement was worth watching, offering 'an awareness of social responsibility which differs sharply from the negative image ... which the daily press has created in the minds of thousands of readers.'[73] One teenager explained things on a more personal level: 'It means mostly equality ... to have the power to go up to a person ... no matter what his skin colour is and be accepted on the same level ... it doesn't necessarily have to mean that you gotta take over everything and be a revolutionary ... just as long as people are going to respect you.'[74] Such rhetoric was powerful at both the local and the national level. As Bayard Rustin reflected, somewhat ruefully, 'while we're talking about a poverty programme, the extremists are telling him [black youths] how he can be black and still feel like a *man* ... there are a lot of brothers-too many who think it sounds pretty good.'[75]

The Reverend Franklin Florence, President of Rochester-based militants F.I.G.H.T. (Freedom, Independence, God, Honor, Today) presented this alluring formula in a convenient acronym.[76]

POWER. The 'P' stands for *Persistence*: You got to wear them down ... The 'O' stands for *Organization*: In Rochester, that's spelled F-I-G-H-T ... The 'W' stands for *Whitey* – He's got all the power ... You have to get your share ... it won't be given – you just have to take it. The 'E' is for *Effort*: That's the sweat and heart aches you have to invest ... The 'R' is for ... Results. The name of the game is to win.[77]

Although Florence had obtained his theological degree in what he referred to as 'the school of hard knocks', his prescription for revolution was triumphant against Kodak hiring policies in Rochester.[78] Such local success perhaps stemmed from the fact that this interpretation of Black Power was profoundly pragmatic. It acknowledged, perhaps more clearly than the moderate civil rights movement, that American society was motivated not by morality but by power. Living at the sharp end of American *realpolitik*, militants recognised that power was often seized, seldom shared. Accordingly, any attempt to better the African-American position needed to occur from a position of strength. Power was needed to escape the welfare state and to shape political proposals affecting the African-American community. As Black Panther co-founder Huey P. Newton explained, such militant goals were entrenched within the American socio-political tradition. To Newton, power was, 'the ability to first of all define phenomena, and secondly the ability to make these phenomena act in a desired manner'.[79] And so, in the iconic expression 'all power to the people' the Panthers articulated African-America's desire to control its own destiny, politically and culturally.

This statement of purpose was echoed and amplified by many other Black Power activists. Spreading far beyond the media, this desire for self-definition often resonated more with the challenges faced by ordinary African-Americans than the enraged cry of 'Get Whitey!' and self-definition was nowhere more developed than within the cultural sphere. Far removed from most white perceptions of Black Power, African-America was building a new cultural Black Power on the film screen, in juke joints, universities, libraries and on the stoops of America. The voices of the militants themselves suggest the African-American view of Black Power was a far more complex construction, vastly different in content and focus from that perceived by white America and reported via its mainstream media.

In some respects, the growth of black militancy was a logical product of the civil rights movement's efforts to achieve equality, dignity and freedom. This was not always immediately apparent, as a heavy layer of attitude, style and rhetoric cloaked the most salient similarities. Nevertheless the ultimate concerns of the two movements were consanguineous. There would have been no Black Power without civil rights and the 1960s movement was an incomplete precursor to the 1970s evolution of African-American consciousness.

However, Black Power sought more than guarantees of legal equality and renewed governmental attention to constitutional rights. Militants wanted control of the defining force of American society – power, both actual and psychological, by 'any means necessary'.[80] In retrospect, these means came to encompass a bewildering array of cultural forms.

Historians and the wider public still have problems grasping the scope and form of Black Power. Our collective historical memory is inevitably shaped by mass culture, and as Marita Sturken noted, the processes of representation which we choose, or are chosen for us, block out difficult to represent memories, replacing them with simpler ciphers, a commemorative shorthand.[81] Our current difficulties in anatomising the complexity of the Black Power movement lie in its mid-1960s origins. Despite the fact that as James Forman noted 'by 1966 the problems of black people across the United States had become similar in all their fundamentals', mainstream coverage suffered from confused and inconsistent framing, amid a quest for definable leaders and symbols amidst polarising rhetoric.[82]

During the period, comprehensive enquiries which might have illuminated the movement's cultural richness and diversity of thought were seldom attempted. Aspirational ideology and street-smart swagger were given roughly equal page space. The press rushed to cover race issues with little self-critique; neither routines nor approaches changed – the same sources were used and the same stories proliferated, using 'values of conflict, proximity, prominence and the unusual occurrence'.[83] Any attempt by contemporary social scientists to delineate the ideological variants of Black Power and locate common denominators would have been of immeasurable value, as would a more informed understanding of the diverse manner in which militants aspired to acquire power. This gap in source material is understandable. At the popular level the strategies and goals of 1960s campaigners were often entangled. Often methodologies were interpreted as goals, and vice versa. The international climate lent itself to fears of spontaneous anarchy. Most importantly, profound cultural differences between white and black America had created a distinct disjunction in interpretations of Black Power. Recognising this disjunction was seldom easy, as media interpreters were enmeshed in a network of 'unquestioned racism [and] inferential assumptions ... largely invisible to those who formulate the world in its terms.'[84]

Even well-meaning attempts to address the problem were problematic. Despite A.H. Sulzberger's injunction that the media should 'report, interpret and discuss the facts and attitudes involved in race relations' the media sought definable, marketable subjects, first in the southern civil rights movement, then in the late 1960s emergence of Black Power.[85] As the 1968 report of the National Commission on Civil Disorders noted − 'the media report and write from ... a white man's world. The ills of the ghetto, the difficulties of life there, the Negro's burning sense of grievance, are seldom conveyed ... [by] ... a press that repeatedly, if unconsciously, reflects the biases, the paternalism, the indifference of white America.'[86]

Overly harsh criticism of these early attempts at assessment risks obscuring their benefits. As has been repeatedly observed, media reinforces the norms of society and cannot be looked to for critical commentary.[87] Nonetheless, at the time, useful models of collective behaviour were developed which illustrated the conceptual lenses through which militants viewed the world.[88] This was significant as, prior to the 1950s, black America was constructed as something outside of the traditional American story. As Carolyn Martindale argued 'the papers did not seem to show black Americans as part of the ordinary life of the community', which, as Simeon Booker wrote in 1956 stripped African-Americans of 'the happy feeling of belonging, the dash of dignity or a degree of self-respect'.[89]

The root of the problem was simpler still. Sustained research by scholars such as Jane Rhodes has suggested that 'the mass media were wholly unprepared to report on' the emerging movement.[90] As the Black Power slogan became a primary focus of news coverage, the media remained mired in sensationalism, although there was a growing sense of substance at the movement's core. As the *San Francisco Examiner* explained, 'The melodrama is real, the guns are real ... [the Panthers] are real revolutionaries.'[91] More precision gradually manifested in reports, but fear, as much as professionalism, drove these efforts. The implication was that the careless firing of questions would lead to the careful firing of guns.

A great deal of the media's imprecision came from a fundamental misinterpretation of the shaping strands of political Black Power. Even today, understanding the underlying ideological commitments of African-Americans who dedicated themselves to the Black Power ethos enables a deeper appreciation of the movement's cultural legacy, as the two inhabit parallel streams. In the late 1960s and early 1970s, three basic categories of ideology were offered in relation to societal protest: assimilation, pluralism and nationalism.

The first interpretation, assimilation, viewed group protest as a short-term strategy prefacing eventual integration into the cultural mainstream. Seldom concerned with altering fundamental societal values or initiating profound institutional change, assimilationists primarily sought greater participation in existing social structures. In comparison, pluralist doctrine argued that society was an amalgam of assorted ethnic groups competing for limited resources, a state of affairs acceptable so long as equal opportunities, privileges and respect were evenly accorded. Advocates argued that a cooperative coexistence of diverse groups would preserve subcultures while permitting a unified society. Ideally, given parity in influence and supported by their unique cultural roots, the groups would form a multicultural society in which each component enhanced all others.

At the far end of the spectrum lay nationalism. Its adherents distrusted claims that significantly dissimilar individuals could coexist in close proximity geographically, or socially, reasoning that one element of society would inevitably subjugate the others, eradicating cultural distinctions in the process. Seeking to avert such a catastrophe, nationalists strove to preserve group values and cultural identity while keeping the deleterious ethos of the larger society at a safe distance. Accordingly, nationalists often withdrew from the political matrix and attempted to obtain socio-cultural autonomy. Importantly, advocates of all three ideologies sought freedom of choice and power and simply practiced different approaches to obtaining it.[92] Although nationalists spurned the assimilationist approach more stridently than pluralists, both camps were generally equally representative of Black Power sentiment.

The militant's subsequent hybrid worldview can be summarised pithily: white power, enshrined in the basic apparatus of American life, was an eternal impediment to African-America's quality of life.

To shatter and disperse this repressive hegemony African-Americans had to organise militantly and collectively strive toward group empowerment. This protracted, arduous endeavour encompassed all facets of African-American life – political, economic, psychological and cultural. The end result would be invaluable, as African-America developed into an influential power bloc possessing genuine decision-making capability.[93] Whatever form it took, the new African-America, it was argued, would be an entirely novel entity, host to a culturally vibrant people possessed of a transformative power with the potential to spread its rejuvenating influence to white America.

This strategy was the converse of the established civil rights movement in some ways. Moving from a traditional civil rights approach which had primarily mobilised national campaigns to effect local change, black militants tended to utilise local campaigns to effect national change in a manner which had early echoes in the grassroots campaigns of CORE and NAACP in Mississippi.[94] This approach was intended to ensure that the much touted assimilationist trope of the melting pot would no longer smother the importance of community power in social affairs.[95] Inviolable psychological and cultural concepts undergirded these developing nationalist and pluralist ideologies, providing a core of strength for the wider movement. As William Van Deburg noted, despite their political differences, 'The varied Black Power constituents responded with remarkable unity on the issues of psychological liberation and cultural identity.'[96] Thus, a cultural perspective is one of the firmest standpoints from which to assess Black Power's legacy in American society and its historical roots prior to the political movement.

Psychological redefinition characterised the Black Power experience. A 'revolution of the mind' was considered by many militants to be a formative step in obtaining power.[97] Before African-America could hope to influence American economics or politics it first had to understand itself. Prospective militants needed to reject attempts at definition from outside the African-American experience and embark upon 'the eradication of all the western indoctrination of our people'.[98] Nationalists and pluralists alike were aware that culture held the ultimate power of identity creation. A new appreciation of the past was the prescription, a rich history distinct from Hollywood images of grinning savages and giggling buckdancing servants. Militants needed to reinherit and reassess their own histories and recreate their own myths.[99]

In the process, it was hoped African-America would develop a group consciousness and pride sufficient to support the militant struggle. This newly minted sense of black identity would act as a much needed social adhesive and steering force for the developing political Black Power movement. In this respect, it becomes abundantly clear that Black Power sought far more than the expansion of existing civil rights law. Initially however, black Americans had to be galvanised and apprised of the stark fact that success was reliant on defining themselves and their values while rejecting the cultural mores of their historical oppressors. Without this first deceptively simple step, African-American cultural consciousness would remain stagnant. Potential approaches to economic and political power would be sealed. Most unforgivably, African-Americans would continue to experience the worst form of oppression – cultural abnegation and co-optation without redress or reprieve.[100]

CHAPTER 2

WHY BLACK POWER?

For many people in the 1960s there was some confusion as to why a Black Power movement was necessary at all. Understanding the meaning and media presentations of Black Power is an important first step toward reassessing the movement's legacy, but equally critical is developing a clear vision of why many militants felt Black Power was needed within America. While most historians recognise that significant legal progress had been made with the 1964 Civil Rights Act and the Voting Rights Act of the following year, these developments obscured the fact that culturally, America was still deeply uncomfortable with its African-American presence.[1]

Despite legislative gains, observers of American culture noted that the gulf between black and white was broadening, and the bridges over that chasm seemed exceedingly thin.[2] Freedom came slowly, dragging its heels, and the longer it took, the more the African-American in the street became disillusioned with the acceptable and permissible forms of non-violent protest as long-tried patience evaporated leaving an incendiary rage simmering below the surface.[3]

As playwright and poet Larry Neal noted with satisfaction, 'The militant wing of the movement will win. The established Negro leaders are being discredited ... by the realities of brute oppression.'[4] African-Americans increasingly demanded to know the shape, form and timing of their victory over America's historically endemic prejudice. Within this context, Black Power was not simply a slogan, but a means of articulating a desire for individual and community empowerment as a step toward discarding the stigma of a historically victimised group.

Despite its prominence in our modern lexicon, Black Power, as a political term, only gained general familiarity among Americans after 16 June 1966. Speaking to activists and journalists in Greenwood, Mississippi, the young Stokely Carmichael declared, 'We been saying freedom for six years and we ain't got nothin'. What we gonna start saying now is Black Power!'[5] The 'March on Fear' begun by James Meredith started with this cry and ended in Washington ten days later, as Carmichael summarised the irrevocable shift in the tenor of the movement, shooting a white Southern Christian Leadership Conference (SCLC) staffer between the eyes with a water pistol. Non-lethal though it was, the political Black Power movement had fired its first shot.[6]

Presented by the media as a revelation, neither Carmichael's slogan nor the cultural, political and psychological concepts it encapsulated were without historical antecedents. As black studies scholar Nathan Hare noted a month after Meredith, 'The theme of "Black Power," in spite of much recent publicity, is not new on the American scene. Nor is it likely ... to come to a definite end, regardless of the outcome of the current debate.'[7] Black militancy was a pronounced theme in American culture, with a long and vibrant history. Rather than Du Bois's sorrow songs, it was Black Power which had been the 'continuing refrain in the history of the American Negro'.[8]

The militants of the late 1960s had counterparts in earlier decades, even centuries. The notion of a twin-souled America, with its distinctives expressed through conflict is a pronounced strand in generations of American historical commentary. As one writer noted, 'There are two Americas, a white one and a Black one. And they have been at "war" with each other ever since the first slaves were brought here in chains.'[9] However, this in itself is a dangerously reductionist way of perceiving the evolution of African-American militancy. Aspects of Black Power sentiment and politics were undoubtedly oppositional as both a consequence and function of their political and social climate, but the nature, form and ideals of the Black Power movement – the long history of Black Power – was derived, distilled and codified from a series of connected cultural expressions across time, which were often as creative, formative and connotative as they were oppositional, destructive or critical. The roots of the late 1960s conceptualisation of Black Power – individual responsibility, group unity and community pride – had been evidenced since the earliest days of the plantation, and to understand why the political Black Power movement arose on the long road to Washington in 1966, it is imperative first to understand the long history of black militancy in America.

When working with history and myth, particularly with regards to the long history of Black Power, there is a tension not simply between the narratives of history and mythology but between African-American narratives and those of the dominant culture. Brad Vickers, writing in *Native American Identities* noted that 'Images about Indians have traditionally precluded those by Indians' and this is similarly applicable to the African-American presence within America. America's black citizens, although not indigenous, have often seemed to offer the same sense of the alien and foreign and have, historically, been dealt with accordingly.[10]

In the replication of histories that have followed the emergence of the political Black Power movement, a new mythology lies dormant, with implications for our understanding of the long history of Black Power and African-American identity. The question of 'identity' is always inextricably bound up with history, or rather histories. Language in various forms is both a creator and a destroyer of identity, both via individual word signifiers and in the stories and histories we tell. Given the prevalence which a 'revolution of the mind' held within the constructed histories of Black Power, political Black Power rhetoric, and the longer history of Black Power, a distinction needs to be made between objective and subjective identity and the manner in which the creation and recreation of African-American identity is shaped by the contrast between stereotypes and archetypes.

Stereotypes construct identity from the outside, objectively, whereas archetypes construct identity from the inside, subjectively. Throughout their American existence, African-Americans were often the focus of both positive and negative stereotypes. From an ostensibly positive perspective, black Americans were often glamorised as the Noble Savage, as representative of a lost or dwindling human species 'deemed worthy of emulation or sustained nostalgia'.[11] The legacy of slavery also gave rise to perceptions of a harmless, childlike race 'in need of paternalistic guidance, self-improvement, education, civilisation, conversion and/or patronization.'[12]

This conception came with its own set of problems. Its black subjects were permanently consigned to an idealised past, frozen in history as artefacts which could be appreciated philosophically and aesthetically, ebony gods and folk-wise tricksters, who only became dangerous when they touched upon present political reality. The creators of these positive stereotypes feared the difference and dissidence these images suggested when not divorced from political and practical reality, and praised assimilationists who could be lauded as beneficial examples, converted and civilised by the dominant culture.

These individuals – Uncle Tom's brothers and sisters, were seen as subservient but honourable, fit to assist the 'dominant culture in the fulfilment of its destiny' realising the American dream, building America together. These constructed and rationalised individuals could only ever be of limited acceptability to the dominant culture and any deviance from their offered identity was not merely a problem, but a betrayal.

The negative stereotypes imposed on African-Americans were potentially still more insidious with regards to their effects on identity construction. Early attempts portrayed slaves as lacking 'a recognizable psychological reality' with no motivation, emotional content, coherent thought or, ultimately, soul.[13] Portraying black Americans as soulless made it an easy conceptual step to cast them as animalistic, instinctual and immoral. Mental caricature went in tandem with physical caricature to provide an image of transported black people with no historical or cultural reality, dependent on white America for their identity and judged as good or bad based on the needs of white American culture.

In contrast, archetypes emerge when identity formation and self-definition occurs as a personal, internal process.[14] This internal process can take on a multitude of forms: the intellectual deliberation so favoured by the Black Panthers, a more simple empathy with family or friends or with reference to 'heroes, oral traditions, histories. rituals, myths and cosmologies.'[15] These subjective, intuitive phenomena make challenging material for historical analysis. Archetypes, according to Jung are 'universal images that have existed since the remotest times.'[16] This book, like Jung, is concerned with the historical manifestation and transformation of African-American identities, but also with the finer gradations of evolution, adaptation, appropriation, co-optation and persistence, in a series of connected cultural expressions across time.

Jung used a process termed individuation to describe the formation of individual and cultural identity, arguing that the nature of these newly-formed identities depends on how archetypes emerge into individual consciousness. Jungian archetypes can be helpful when considering the long history of Black Power as they are antithetical in both form and function to stereotypes. Jung contends that stereotypes are projected onto the individual, while archetypes derive from either the personal or collective unconscious.

Jungian archetypes, formed in and shaped by individual consciousness, suggest a dynamic process of identity construction which is heterogeneous and diverse, and leaves space for incorporating the diverse responses to Black Power's long history. Conversely, stereotypes produce homogenous, inert identities which are both chronologically and culturally static. Both are ultimately concerned with images drawn from history and myth, but archetypes suggest 'a living, transitive and thus historically active concept of identity, one involved in "making" the world'.[17] The book seeks to trace the manifestation of these archetypes and active identities with respect to the Black Power movement and to demonstrate the manner in which they contributed to the making of the world we inhabit today.

The erosion, manipulation or elision of a race's history abnegates its opportunities to construct an active identity. Roland Barthes famously argued 'The oppressed makes the world, he has only an active, transitive (political) language; the oppressor conserves [the world], his language is plenary, intransitive, gestural, theatrical: it is Myth. The language of the former aims at transforming, of the latter at eternalizing.'[18] Yet the stark dichotomy between myth and politics that Barthes suggests falls short when looking at the long history of Black Power.

This book attempts to study the infusion of the American myth with African-American history. Moving from Barthes, Jung offers the option of two kinds of myth, both oppressive and liberating. From this Jung derives two kinds of archetypes: mythical archetypes which have 'received a specific stamp and have been handed down through long periods of time' and spontaneous archetypes '[whose] effects are felt most in our most personal life'.[19]

Mythical archetypes tend to remove things from the stream of time, eradicating their 'historical quality'.[20] Dismissed by Barthes as 'speaking corpses' these entrenched tropes, images and linguistic structures interact with his more spontaneous archetypes.[21] Jung believes the 'manifold meaning [of these spontaneous archetypes] makes any unilateral formulation impossible' but admits that although ambiguous they are 'full of half-glimpsed meanings' which represent authentic human beings.[22] In dealing with the long history of Black Power I have tried to highlight the clarification, evolution and adaptation of these 'half-glimpsed meanings' in order to show the interaction of myth and history in creating a militant African-American identity. At its most basic level, history is primarily a communally accepted narrative constructed from traces of the past and some fundamental aspects of this narrative are drawn from folklore. Accordingly, elements of what would eventually become Black Power ideology can be identified in African-American myths, legends and plantation tales.

A culture's folklore is a reflection of its deepest beliefs, codified and couched in mythic terminology, acting as a carrier for identity-forming values and a recipient of aspirational, transformative goals. People learn who they are via folktales, while simultaneously using them to express who they want to be. In this respect, African-American folklore reveals the strong militant heritage of African-Americans from the earliest days of slavery. The plantation was not, as Stanley Elkins once claimed, a concentration camp like system, churning out servile, docile Sambos.[23] On the contrary, it was the source of the earliest forms of black militancy. Beyond the obvious and oft-repeated touchstones of Nat Turner and Denmark Vesey, African-American plantation society was forging its own idealised heroes and committing to cultural memory immutable concepts of black pride, beauty and the value of direct resistance which would eventually inform the Black Power movement of the 1960s and 1970s.

The earliest iteration of these concepts was found in the story of the 'slave superhero' Big Sixteen who performed feats of strength and fortitude on the plantation. Big Sixteen may have worked for his 'Ole Massa' but he embodied African-American strength and resilience, knocking the Devil himself unconscious with a nine-pound hammer. Too powerful for heaven and too dangerous for hell, he went to raise a hell of his own out in America.[24] A mercurial figure, full of unexpected power, wandering the wooded wilderness with a 'piece of fire lookin'' for a place to go', Big Sixteen epitomised the restless desire for confrontation and change felt by many militants decades later. Despite his Herculean exploits however, empowerment in African-American folklore was not exhibited solely through physical prowess.

Folklore kept hope alive in the plantation environment and subtly elevated slaves' perceptions of themselves as superior to their white masters. Initially, tales dealt with themes of sudden unexpected liberation, an occasionally literal flight into freedom as in 'All God's Chillen Had Wings', in which a succession of mistreated slaves sprout wings to flee a malevolent driver. The catalyst for this transformative escape lies in their realization of their heritage, the knowledge that, 'Once all Africans could fly like birds'.[25] This realisation is not achieved until an old slave, representing traditional knowledge, speaks to the slaves. Promptly, 'They all ... recalled the power which had once been theirs'.[26]

'All God's Chillen' dealt with themes of identity transformation and shifting self-perception which would become a cornerstone of the Black Power movement and its emphasis on psychological transformation and self-definition. Exponents of Black Power's 'revolution of the mind' argued that this change in self-perception was an essential and historically mandated step on the road to militant consciousness.[27] Tales such as 'All God's Chillen' suggest that the mental revolution had already begun long before on the plantation. Indeed, the imagery of flight as an escape from oppressive conditions was persistent through the decades, as shown in the 1966 depiction of ghetto life, *Lenox Avenue Sunday*, where one boy notes: 'Lenox Avenue can sure make you dream ... like I'm a jet pilot zooming, zooming through space. A free bird in the universe ... everything I want to be ... I'm loose, relaxed, no strain, no pain. Everything is cool and calm; and I'm the force behind it.'[28]

This transmission of connected cultural expressions was not always a conscious act; indeed there was a distinct divide among militants concerning the worth of folklore as a tool for motivating protest. Black Arts luminary and Educational Director of the Black Panther Party Larry Neal argued passionately for 'the role of folk culture in shaping a civilisation and national consciousness', reasoning that the issue lay not with African-American folklore, but rather with the white American cultural distortions forced upon it.[29] Neal noted that 'Looming over any discussion of folklore is the spectre of American racism ... [which] ... bastardised and distorted the true beauty and elegance of the folk spirit.'[30] To clarify, if African-America was truly to define its own image, it needed to reclaim its militant heritage from white influences.

To commentators like Neal, plantation folktales presented an inspiring image of a hopeful, intelligent and culturally resistant African-American waiting to be encouraged by reconnecting to their people and heritage. In this context, slaves were spurred toward action by the very fact of their enslavement and existed in the plantation society as angry, militant and culturally active.[31]

While the consequences of uprising were often too serious for black slaves to contemplate, they talked about their hopes and desires in no uncertain terms. Whether hurling the plantation master into a fire as punishment ('Den To De Fiah') or outwitting the cruellest slave master in Southwest Texas ('A Laugh That Meant Freedom'), the protagonists of these tales triumphed by virtue of their strength, wit or intelligence. They took on the system and emerged victorious and they were victorious because they were black.[32]

Folktales were not simply stories of triumph over oppression. They were also a means of affirming moral and spiritual superiority and of confronting or subverting pervasive stereotypes. In 'Swapping Dreams', Master Jim Turner, despite being 'an unusually good master', reinforces the age-old stereotype when he tells his slave Ike: 'I dreamed I went to Nigger Heaven last night, and saw there a lot of garbage, some old torn-down houses, a few old broken-down, rotten fences, the muddiest, sloppiest streets I ever saw, and a big bunch of ragged, dirty, Negroes walking around.'[33] Without missing a beat, Ike replies, 'Yuh sho' musta et de same t'ing Ah did las' night, 'case Ah dreamed Ah went up ter de white man's paradise, an' de streets wuz all ob gol' an' silvah, and dey wuz lots o'milk an' honey dere, an' putty pearly gates, but dey wuzn't uh soul in de whole place.'[34] The implication is clear; black people may be poor, but white Americans are spiritually and morally bankrupt.

Folktales not only taught solitary resistance, but emphasised the power inherent in group action. In 'Dey's Auganized', the black coachman Ananias happily whips a lone horse fly to pieces and demolishes a bumblebee with a well-placed lash, but refuses to tackle a hornet's nest, explaining to his master that it is dangerous to bother the hornets, 'case dey's auganized'.[35] The slaves of the plantation tales were no cowering, emasculated Sambos, and neither did they rely upon divine providence to create interracial harmony. In 'Uncle Pleas's Prayer', Pleas does not ask God for succour, or fortitude to endure plantation life, but rather prays the same prayer every night, 'Oh, Lawd, kill all de white fo'ks and save all de niggahs', a blunt assertion of a very basic desire.[36]

Slaves were alert to the realities of their situation and realised that opportunities, empowerment, and ultimately freedom would be unlikely to come as a gift from their white masters. The unfairness of the system was starkly expressed in *Slave Song*, 'We peel de meat / Dey gib us de skin / And dat's de way / Dey take us in. / We skim de pot / Dey gib us the liquor, / And say dat's good enough for nigger.'[37] *Slave Song*, which the militant abolitionist Frederick Douglass described as a 'summary of the palpable injustice and fraud of slavery' demonstrated that slaves were emphatically not 'taken in'.[38] The consequences of continued deception and broken promises were darkly expressed in another plantation tale, *Promises of Freedom*. 'My ole Mistiss promise me / W'en she died, she'd set me free ... But my ole Miss, she's somehow gone, / An' she lef' "Uncle Sambo" a-hillin up co'n. / Ole Mosser lakwise promise me ... But "his papers" didn' leave me free. / A dose of pizen he'ped 'm along. /May de Devil preach 'is funer'l song.'[39]

The Black Power movement was in many ways an attempt to administer 'a dose of pizen' to white American society, to destroy a system in which there was no real hope of improving conditions over time. America was the plantation and its economic, cultural and political shackles lay heavily on the angry black Americans of the 1960s and 1970s. Any alternative seemed better than the current system and freedom, no matter the cost, was infinitely preferable to slavery, on the plantation, or in the ghetto. As the poem, *An Escaped Convict* forcefully emphasised, 'Loosed from de chains, / Wid shackles left behind me, / ... I know dere's a hard, hard road / Behind me, / An' der ain' no road in front ... I'll take my chance, brother, / I'll take my chance.'[40] With 'no road in front' African-Americans had to forge their own path into America's cultural heartland. Sustained via a series of connected cultural expressions across time, the spirit of modern day revolutionary nationalism fostered in the plantation tales was stridently evident in the intervening decades prior to Carmichael's co-opting of the Black Power slogan.

As early as 1830, Boston clothes merchant David Walker railed against the proliferation of, 'Newspapers and monthly periodicals ... in continual succession ... on the pages of which, you will scarcely ever find a paragraph on slavery, which is ten thousand times more injurious to this country than all the other evils put together.'[41] To Walker, such a blatant subsuming of black culture crippled any attempt at societal evolution. It was akin to expecting a cage deer to run as fast as its wild counterpart.[42] For Walker, as for later militants, the white gaze of the media was a millstone around the neck of the black population. Moreover, he saw white allies as lacking intimate knowledge of the situations faced by free black Americans and thus sufficient persuasive authority; 'Let no one of us suppose that the refutations ... written by our white friends are enough – they are *whites* – we are *blacks*.'[43] This echoes the argument made by one student activist decades later that 'black people organize black people more effectively than white people organize black people'.[44]

The situation was compounded by the fact that Walker stood diametrically opposite to contemporary nineteenth century opinions on violent protest, remarking in a manner which presaged Carmichael: 'The man who would not fight ... to be delivered from the most wretched, abject and servile slavery ... ought to be kept ... in chains, to be butchered by his *cruel enemies*.'[45] Yet this was not the only parallel between the militants of the nineteenth century and their later counterparts. Walker's entire philosophy centred on the belief that free black Americans would never truly escape oppression without undergoing what historian James Stewart termed 'militant self-transformation'.[46] In effect, a revolution of the mind.

Walker was not an isolated example. Charismatic, outspoken, militant African-Americans filled the antebellum years and were often recovered and reappropriated to serve the cause of 1960s Black Power, as with the iconic Henry Highland Garnet. Garnet's impassioned 'Address to the Slaves of the United States' delivered at the National Negro Convention in 1843, led to him being hailed as 'The "Young Lion" of Black Liberation' in a Black Panther pamphlet entitled *A New History of Black America*, issued in 1966.[47] Aware that Garnet's ideals formed a militant continuity, the pamphlet's authors were at pains to highlight Walker as Garnet's predecessor and stressed the importance of the 'many Black Heroes that parents and children alike can be inspired by'.[48]

While Walker and Garnet epitomised early militant responses to white American co-optation, the first few decades of the nineteenth century saw a growing sense of African-American unity, often explicitly framed in opposition to white interests. Drawing some initial inspiration from the recent triumphant establishment of the Haitian Republic in 1804, militant antebellum sentiment appears to have climbed steadily over the years. This slow but relatively steady rise was informed by the growth of the antebellum convention movement, the advocation of black military companies and a focus on community enterprise.[49] Black people getting together to discuss, defend themselves and support themselves. Huey Newton would have been proud. Yet, there was perhaps a deeper root to this upswell of militant self-reliance. One Bostonian, writing in response to Walker's death, saw the growth of militant sentiment and militant men as an inevitable consequence of an American system which had 'set the example for them for centuries, by imbruing their hands in innocent blood?'[50]

Outside of their own struggles, northern commentators looked to the rebellions of the south with a certain fervour. These urban militants recognised the impossibility of a slave-led triumph, but believed that every slave was justified in wanting to rebel against a consistently oppressive system.[51] Across the 1830s, news reports on rebellions within and without America fed the notion that black people 'like other men, have a spirit which rebels against tyranny and oppression'.[52] Indeed, by the 1840s, for some rhetoricians defending one's family became as essential a part of a respectable black identity as holding a job or keeping the Sabbath.[53]

This apparent change in perspective came during a period when continuing American industrialisation split America along both racial and class lines but was further catalysed by the passage of the draconian Fugitive Slave Bill in 1850.[54] Writing in response to the new law, free black Americans argued that only they had the necessary understanding of the black experience in America to effectively resist this new iteration of oppression. In this way, racial essentialism became a weapon, blackness was no longer a symbol of degradation, but a stamp of moral authority. A century before the Black Power movement would set the slogan free, black was not only beautiful, but potent.

Over the course of the next ten years, militant rhetoric underwent a profound distillation. In April 1850, Boston community leaders declared their intentions in the abolitionist periodical *The Liberator* to protect themselves by any means which, 'the God of Nature bestows upon us'.[55] A week later, an escaped slave named Henry Bibb warned potential pursuers that, 'when we have crossed Mason and Dixon's line, a portion of our rights has been restored to us, namely the right to self-defense'.[56]

Within a few months, rhetoric in response to the Bill had evolved into a template for later Black Panther critiques of the failing American system. Meeting at Columbus, Ohio in January 1851, the African-American assemblage declared, 'If we have no protection [under the Fugitive Slave Bill] we owe no allegiance, the amount of allegiance being graduated by the rights guaranteed and the protection afforded.'[57] The similarity in the militant language used, despite a gap of over a century between these utterances, is startling.

This was not an isolated occurrence. An article in the *Anti-Slavery Standard* of 1850 argued that, 'If the American revolutionists [sic] had excuse for shedding one drop of blood then have the American slaves for making blood to flow "even unto the horsebridles".'[58] Contrast this with the comment made by Deacon A.Z. Young of the Deacons for Defence in 1965 that, 'If blood is going to be shed, we are going to let it run down Columbia Road – all kinds, both white and black', and the continuity of militant expression becomes clear.[59] By 1890, T. Thomas Fortune, newspaper editor and founder of the National Afro-American League comfortably reasoned, 'Apathy leads to stagnation. The arsenal, the fort, the warrior, are as necessary as the school, the church, the newspapers ... it is time to begin to fight fire with fire.'[60]

Fortune embodied a distinct strand of the Black Power movement's historical heritage. Recent research suggests that many free black Americans in the nineteenth century adopted militant resistance wholeheartedly. Running contrary to established wisdom they contended that 'physical self-assertion was an authentic expression of black respectability, not a distortion of it.'[61] Walker and Garnet were joined by other prominent campaigners, including the domestic servant turned crusading journalistic activist, Maria Stewart and the editor and underground railroad operator David Ruggles. For these early Black Power advocates, respectability was predicated upon self-respect.

Such rhetoric was not solely focused on internal reconceptualisation; nineteenth century militants strove to reposition African-Americans as not merely equal, but superior, to white people. Confident in their own self-image, they argued that in comparison with white America, it was easy to discern the favoured race. As John Rock, the first black attorney admitted to the US Supreme Court bar, declared, 'when the white man was created, nature was pretty well exhausted'.[62] Or as the Reverend Samuel E. Cornish, wrote with admirable bluntness: 'We do not desire amalgamation; give US OUR LIBERTY AND OUR RIGHTS, and keep your lasses and 'YOURSELVES' to yourselves – we want none of you'.[63]

Despite the limited opportunities available for displays of cultural resistance, nineteenth century African-Americans consistently worked to communicate the sense of an alternative, empowering set of identity referents via the forms and media available to them. While Walker, Stewart, and Garnet were unusual individuals, their attitudes were reflected within black American communities. The will to resist, subvert and deconstruct became an essential part of black identity in the late nineteenth and early twentieth centuries.

This profusion of emergent, adaptive and militant identities was arguably nowhere more evident than in the Harlem 'Renaissance' – the awkward term given to the often independent artists and writers who operated in Harlem during the 1920s and 1930s. During the period, Harlem served as a site of physical and ideological reconstruction, part illicit pleasure centre, part ideological battleground where the politics of representation were debated in a mixed lingua franca which covered both race and sex. An era of both extreme experimentation and profound perception, the Renaissance offered few static perceptions of race, sex, or gender.[64]

Given that the Harlem Renaissance is consistently seen as an exercise in producing black art divorced from white 'interference' the examination of sexuality traditionally takes a back seat, but was an inherent element of many of the black identities being formed. Incorporating a more complex view of sexuality into our traditional racialised examination of the Renaissance opens previously unseen dimensions of Black Power's long history, what Alan Sinfield called 'haunting possibilities'.[65]

The Harlem of the Renaissance was a product of the mass migrations of the first two decades of the twentieth century.[66] A great many of these migrants found themselves in the streets of New York, and from there made their way to Harlem. In a virtually all-black neighbourhood, many African-Americans for the first time lived in a city which felt like their own. As Alain Locke noted, Harlem became home to 'the African, the West Indian, the Negro American ... the Negro of the North and the Negro of the South; the man from the city and the man from the town ... artist, poet, musician, adventurer, preacher and criminal, exploiter and social outcast.'[67] When Claude McKay ostentatiously branded Harlem the 'Negro Capital of the world, there was a slight truth to his words.[68]

The defining motif of African-American cultural expression in the 1920s and 1930s was a drive to reassess the African-American condition and provide an increasingly accurate, empowering and objective tableau of African-American life, thereby counterbalancing the reactionary, ahistorical and stereotypical culture forms of previous decades. Locke, author of one of the decade's defining texts, *The New Negro*, bluntly outlined the approach taken by many young artists: 'The Negro to-day wishes to be known for what he is, even in his faults ... and scorns a craven and precarious survival at the price of seeming to be what he is not.'[69] Where did this desire for raw, exposed honesty stem from? According to Locke:

> The Sociologist, the Philanthropist, the Race-leader are not unaware of the New Negro, but they are at a loss to account for him ... the younger generation is vibrant with a new psychology; the new spirit is awake in the masses, and under the very eyes of the professional observers is transforming ... contemporary Negro life.[70]

Reassessing the origins of Locke's 'new psychology' allows us to better understand both its cultural implications and its inheritance from preceding eras, placing it more precisely within the long history of Black Power. Many writers of this generation supported Locke's contention, expressing deep concerns with the malformed images of ante- and postbellum African-Americans present in mainstream American culture. It was argued that a great deal of literature surrounding African-American life originated in sentimentalised plantation and minstrel traditions and thus offered little of value.[71] Accordingly, this new generation of black writers attempted to create a novel framework for the cultural expression of African-American life.

Renaissance writers worked amid a mix of racially and political heterogeneous groups, in an environment shaped by the aims of several competing political, cultural and religious movements. Many Renaissance authors sought to tap into the long history of Black

Power presenting writers such as Charles Chesnutt, Phyllis Wheatley and Paul Laurence Dunbar as 'creative workmen ... pioneers and path-breakers in the cultural development and recognition of the Negro in the arts.'[72] Deliberately constructed works such as James Weldon Johnson's *The Book of American Negro Poetry* attempted to create cross-generational linkages, while the editors of *The Crisis* magazine, Jessie Redmon Fauset, Johnson and Locke laboured at publications which 'midwifed the so-called New Negro literature into being.'[73]

Despite Du Bois's portentous declaration in a 1920 issue of *The Crisis* that 'A renaissance in Negro American literature is due ... [and] ... only we can tell the tale and sing the song from the heart' there were several strands to the art and output of the Renaissance, which ranged blithely across class, race and gender.[74] Much of this early writing was a corrective, designed to satisfy 'a demand for a new interpretation of characters long and admittedly misunderstood.'[75] According to the art critic for the *New York Amsterdam News*, Aubrey Bowser, the situation was dire, with authors of either race presenting black Americans simply as 'reptile[s] of the underworld'.[76]

Harlem's very urban presence as a relatively novel, almost exclusively African American enclave, was both a provocation and a temptation to white America. It was 'A Strange, Exotic Island in the Heart of New York'.[77] Exploring the art of this 'island', some commentators contended, was no more than the fetishisation of a primal black sexuality. Visitors dreamt of being lost in an orgy of 'brown and black bodies' listening to songs fall from 'full lips that quickened the flesh to move', willingly subjected to a parade of 'rent parties! ... sweetbacks! ... hincty wenches! ... number runners! ... Chippies! ... Jazz Love!'[78] In short, 'Primitive Passion!' in all its forms.[79]

Images in works like Carl Van Vechten's *Nigger Heaven* risked reinforcing these delirious claims, for here was the Harlem of spitball play posters, Wallace Thurman's 'City that Never Sleeps.' For most daytrippers, Harlemites were 'too far away to be dangerous yet close enough to be exciting.'[80] From one side of this divide, the negatives seem obvious: African-America could be enjoyed without being understood, blackness could be indulged in without being engaged with. Yet, a curious inversion occurred here. In Harlem, whiteness could be a contaminant. Harlemites participated in an emergent view of African-Americans as healthy in comparison to white America, possessed of 'a pristine superiority of spirit invulnerable to the contaminating decadence of Western civilisation.'[81] Harlem itself was increasingly presented as a wholesome community whose vice was 'forced upon ... [it] ... by outsiders.'[82]

Yet the perceived exotic primitivism of the Harlem scene was not inherently detrimental. As Wayne Cooper has argued, African-American writers use of primitive imagery often constituted a repurposing of 'white stereotypes if they contained aspects of black existence vital to the black man's character and survival.'[83] In effect, it was part of the reclamation and reconstruction of black culture.

Reconstructing blackness as part of the wider American *milieu* was a slow process. In 1927 many observers still associated black identity with laziness and sloth, as Paul Guillame and Thomas Munro noted in their *Primitive Negro Sculpture* (1926), commenting that African-Americans were universally recognised for their 'passivity, lack of initiative and organisation, intellectual backwardness, [and] occasional irresponsibility of conduct'.[84] Coupling this with the danger of urban life seemed all too logical, and added a sinister class dimension to the self-condemnation of black people by black people. As George Schuyler warned readers of the *Messenger*: 'the environment in which the poorer classes vegetate in our large cities is admirably adapted for the turning out of prostitutes, perverts, criminals, drug addicts and bums.'[85]

Conversely and contemporaneously, a spirited counter-culture sought to challenge such stereotypes, perhaps best embodied by Locke's *The New Negro*, whose very title epitomised the volume's drive to refute claims that African-Americans were evolutionarily stagnant.[86] Yet if Locke was primarily concerned with demonstrating cultural parity between black and white, the situation becomes more complex when factoring in Harlem's wealth of emergent young black writers who wished to express their 'dark-skinned selves without fear or shame'.[87]

Yet, to a degree much of the Renaissance risked an existence as a middle class echo chamber in which ordinary black Americans remained to some degree an imagined audience.[88] Certainly, Du Bois's definition of the 'average Negro' was distinctly limited, imagining an 'everyday labourer attending church, lodge and movie ... as conservative as ordinary working folk everywhere.'[89] However, many writers of the Renaissance approached their task from new, provocative angles. Primarily, the idea was to make African-American culture essential to the nation as a whole. As James Weldon Johnson argued with typical *brio*, black Americans were 'the creator[s] of the only things artistic that have yet sprung from American soil and been universally acknowledged as distinctive American products.'[90] The logic ran thus: without the incorporation of art by African-Americans, America as whole would have only a hollow facsimile of a national culture. With the 'Renaissance' coming at a time when America was attempting to define its national artistic output, there was the apparent potential to make African-American art a part of the wider American milieu and so, situate African-Americans an inextricable part of the American nation. Becoming part of America, however, meant reassessing both the nation, and the place of African-Americans within it. As Wallace Thurman wrote, the output of the Renaissance was designed 'to aid in anyway possible those in revolt', but what this revolt actually entailed remained up for debate.[91] Was this to be a revolt of society, sexuality, or the mind?

For many Renaissance writers the period represented an opportunity at redefinition unlike no other, 'an opportunity ... for Negroes ... to replace their out-worn representation in fiction.'[92] The question remained though: what were these representations to be? The search for new representations took several forms, although not all advanced the cause of cultural militancy. Some attempts strove to erase the colour line, by finding similarities in black and white culture; others emphasised the perceived exotic and primitive nature of African-America, playing on the same libidinous thrills which Lester would later rage against. Importantly however, certain other culture creators, most famously Langston Hughes, Jean Toomer, Zora Neale Hurston and Sterling Brown, attempted to strip away preconceptions of what it meant to be African-American and create a new culture which would act as a guiding force for black life and a mirror for black history.

A focus on the black working class often characterised such attempts, and despite his strident refusal of brush-fuel status, Claude McKay, the 'enfant terrible of the Negro Renaissance' remains one of the foremost poetic advocates of the ordinary black man on the street.[93] Describing most black writers of the time as lost in a 'sea of shit', McKay presented a distinct image of black physicality and sexuality as immunising against corrupt, Western civilisation.[94] McKay, with typical frankness, argued that it was the black artist's duty to 'educate the black worker ... giving back to the Negro race its heritage.'[95] To inscribe these new representations of blackness, writers like McKay created a new pantheon of urban black heroes.[96]

These working-class champions allowed McKay to define his own norms – presenting a wholesome black sexuality under assault by white civilisation, 'a war joined between civilization and sex.'[97] For McKay, the Pan-African community in 1920s Harlem was surrounded by white predators, pressurising both black sexuality and black identity. In his novel *Banjo*, McKay argued that this was 'the fundamental, unconscious cause of antagonism between white and black'.[98] As simplistic as such notions of contentious sexuality appear, they would persist through to the 1970s Blaxploitation era, surfacing in Melvin Van Peebles's *Sweetback*, among others.

Similarly to Langston Hughes's satire in *The Ways of White Folks*, McKay argued that white people could study and copy blackness – but not live it.[99] Separatism threaded McKay's writing. Miscegenation was seen as undermining black strength, masculinity and working class wholesomeness. Moreover it was a moral as well as a practical concession, with the stakes being the 'identity of the black race in the Western World.'[100] Acquiescence to perverse white desires, personally or economically, was seen as inevitably corrupting black society. In this universe, white Americans are the sub-humans threating black society. It is their vices, violence and lusts which threaten to destabilise America. The separatist arguments which evolved from this reasoning would inform the models which sustained the black nationalist movement of the 1960s.

McKay was not the only lauded voice of the people. Heralded by Skip Gates as 'a representative ... of the basic black man', and more scathingly described by the *Chicago Whip* as the 'Poet Lowrate', Langston Hughes argued in 1943 that 'the function of the poet is to interpret not only his own people to the rest of the world, but to themselves.'[101] Hughes was conscious of the difficulties of Harlem life, particularly for those outside the mainstream, walking under the 'Weary sadistic eyes' of police troops looking for 'fairies' and 'Lesbian[s}.'[102] In his writing, Hughes attempted to reintegrate the excluded and unrepresented, embracing his ascribed function as an interpreter of the black masses, slipping black folk art and jazz vernacular into mainstream culture, most notably via his stories of the streetwise barfly, Jesse Semple.

Hughes was notable not only for his own cultural contributions, but for the admiration he inspired in his contemporaries. As Richard Bruce

Nugent noted in 1925, 'Hughes ... was a made-to-order Hero for me.'[103] For Nugent, Hughes was unique because he focused on giving the man in the street identity and agency, because he 'Spoke ... about the importance of the Negro's contributing his share of *himself* to a world that ... had never considered him a real person at all'.[104] As previous generations had been inspired by their own militant icons, so writers like Nugent adopted Hughes as a cultural emancipator. Nugent reminisced in 1982 that, 'Langston was like Frederick Douglass to me, the way Mother had told me Douglass had been ... like Fred Douglass – only better, because Langston was a contemporary of *mine*.'[105] All the more real and vibrant an influence for his proximity, it was Hughes who planted the seed for a defining moment in African-America's cultural production, 'when he suggested that maybe someone should start a magazine by, and for, and about the Negro to show what we could do'.[106] According to Nugent, Hughes both wrote a spiritual which inspired the publication's name, *FIRE!!* and provided its optimism of spirit, the central assurance 'that the Negro in America was like the phoenix and that some day he would rise from the fire to which America had consigned him'.[107]

In retrospect one of the most culturally significant publications to emerge from the Renaissance, the short-lived quarterly *FIRE!!* was first published in November 1926 and was beset with financial troubles from its inception, with only the first issue ever making print. Its contributors hoped to speak with an authentically black voice, and its authors saw writing about the man on the street as offering the best chance of this goal. From their perspective, *FIRE!!* had 'gone to the proletariat rather than the bourgeoisie ... to people who still retained some individual race qualities and who were not totally white American in every respect save colour of skin.'[108]

The relevancy of *FIRE!!* is apparent from its opening pages; the contents list is a roster of iconic African-American cultural producers, from the artist Aaron Douglas, to Hughes, Hurston, the oft-neglected Nugent and Wallace Thurman. These artists, gathered in the urban heart of Harlem, had been drawn from all corners of the United States and had travelled extensively. Working in concert, these young cosmopolitan African-Americans were to produce a work with militant resonance far beyond its size or longevity.

Wallace Thurman dubbed this avant-garde, unconventional group of which he was a part 'The Niggerati', a name which they embraced as fitting their definitions of themselves (and poking fun at white society).[109] As Thomas Wirth, a close friend of Nugent noted, the Niggerati saw themselves as 'clever, cultured, talented, perhaps a bit pretentious, but urbane enough ... to find their own pretense amusing'.[110] As a consequence of their diverse backgrounds, the Niggerati had insight into many aspects of the African-American cultural landscape, the genteel homes of the light-skinned Brooklyn elite, the offices of Du Bois and the NAACP, Charles S. Johnson of the Urban League (editor of the similarly revolutionary *Ebony and Topaz*) and A. Philip Randolph of the socialist *Messenger*. Their experiences encompassed A'Leila Walker's extravagant soirees, the controversial salons of Van Vechten and most importantly, the apartments of ordinary Harlemites who threw rent parties to make ends meet, low-life cabarets where Hughes's 'long-headed jazzers play [ed]' and the vibrant spirit of African-American culture flourished in earnest.[111]

Kevin Mumford dubbed these areas interzones, interracial spaces of unusual flexibility, in which rent nights and buffet flats (ad hoc, unlicensed nightclubs) blurred age and class boundaries.[112] Niggerati Manor, the affectionate term given to Thurman's boarding house, functioned as part of a gay, transnational, African-American network, offering a new matrix of support within 'an invisible, diverse community'.[113] The implications here are intriguing: 1920s Harlem arguably excited 'a tolerance for the marginalised among people with a long history of exclusion', while also providing decentralised, fluid spaces for the creation and recreation of what it meant to be black in America, by collecting African-American creators from across the country.[114]

This diversified expression inevitably proliferated out into the pages of *FIRE!!* Unjustly condemned by Bowser as a 'prostitute's directory', its perspectives on class, sex and gender were to test the limits of the allegedly bohemian Renaissance.[115] Unlike Locke's *The New Negro*, published a year before, *FIRE!!* was a collaborative creation of the finest young cultural producers of their generation. It is, as Wirth noted, 'In a real sense, the Harlem Renaissance incarnate.'[116] Financed solely by its instigators and printed *pro bono*, *FIRE!!* was liberated from the omnipresent need of most Harlem Renaissance literature to pander to patrons and publishers, who were, with few exceptions, both white and wealthy. Unlike its contemporaries, the twin colossi of the NAACP's *Crisis* and the

Urban League's *Opportunity*, *FIRE!!* entered the cultural landscape independent of sponsorship ties to organisations with domineering political and social objectives. Accordingly, its contributors saw no need to restrict its contents to material which would serve as a tool for racial 'uplift' or a goad to social progress.

The creators of *FIRE!!* revelled in this (albeit brief) freedom, to pursue excellence for its own sake via a multitude of sensibilities and styles. If any objective can be attributed to the mercurial *FIRE!!*, it was perhaps simply the desire to demonstrate the breadth and depth of talent which existed amongst the African-American literary community. This goal was achieved with undoubted aplomb and bequeathed a powerful, if subtle, militant legacy to the present. As Wirth commented, 'Their very success has obscured the magnitude of their achievement: it no longer surprises us that *FIRE!!* burns still.'[117]

Many of the pieces in *FIRE!!* bear closer analysis. Hurston's 'Sweat' is a classical folktale, its nuances rendered authentic from her long travels and conversations with the people of the American South. Steeped in the African-American experience, it also functions as a powerful commentary on the oppression of women, and an ingenious reimagining of the myth of Eve, Adam and the serpent.[118] Similarly Hughes's 'Elevator Boy' holds echoes of Dunbar's 'We Wear the Mask' in its ironic apathy, embodying the detachment from mainstream American society felt by many African-Americans.[119]

Conversely, the drawings of Aaron Douglas included in the volume are vibrant with the spirit of African-America. In particular, his iconic cover image serves as a visual statement of purpose for *FIRE!!*'s themes. Initially the images and symbols appear redolent of Africa – the lion and the sphinx, circles and chains. However, viewed as black on red, the profile of a young African-American man emerges, the circles and chains are his pierced ear, the abstract designs his eyes, nose and lips. These heavily Africanised features were in the 1920s still the subject of virulent racist caricatures in American mainstream culture and yet are represented in Douglas's art as 'a new standard of beauty'.[120] The forms in the image are elemental and strong and, so it is implied, is this young black man, a symbol of the power of African-America.[121]

Yet *FIRE!!* did not need to be complementary or traditional to be empowering. Thurman's 'Cordelia the Crude' describes a scene of Harlem life with stark frankness, but in so doing explores the shift from innocence of society to worldly awareness experienced by black Americans developing self-definition and examines the subtle class distinctions which influenced culture within the African-American community.

Perhaps the most revolutionary piece in *FIRE!!* is 'Smoke, Lilies and Jade' by Nugent who published simply as Richard Bruce, to avoid disgracing the family name. Nugent's 'Smoke' was markedly countercultural, an explicitly homosexual piece which ran entirely counter to 1920s ethics of respectability.[122] Accordingly it became a lodestone for critics. Yet, for Nugent and other members of the Niggerati alternative sexualities were increasingly acceptable topics. Here was a form of Black Power which wrote itself in lips and hips and wine, where 'sexual taboo functioned as the leading image of ... rebellion.'[123] Here, sexuality blended with other transgressive, provocative images of Harlem life.

Crucially Nugent's protagonist does little but smoke and muse on his situation, but his thoughts themselves are dangerous – the ideas he holds challenging, sexual and subversive. In retrospect, Nugent was an archetypal bohemian, a child of the counterculture born forty years before his time. One of the few artists to regularly range outside Harlem, Nugent's work incorporated references to African motifs while also embracing the work of white artists and writers.

Nugent seems to have had little interest in representing his race, or complying with the aspirations of more traditional black leadership. Living as an openly queer man, apparently at ease with his sexual identity, for Nugent contributing to *FIRE!!* was a natural reaction against the expectations of representation. Indeed it was Nugent who encapsulated the empowering nature of *FIRE!!*'s counter-cultural approach when recounting a conversation with Du Bois. Du Bois had asked Nugent, 'Why don't you write more about Negroes?' To this Nugent replied, 'I write about myself, and I'm a Negro, aren't I?'[124] What Du Bois perhaps misunderstood, was that Nugent offered a view of black manhood and gender which transcended that presented by other African-American writers and occupied a singular position as a published, openly gay, black author of homoerotic fiction. Recounting Nugent's legacy is not simple contributionism however; gay networks constituted a major structure within the Renaissance, and the creation of gay voices reflected the movement's diversity, and the challenge it offered to American society.

Even Du Bois admitted 'we are seriously crippling Negro art and literature by refusing to contemplate any but handsome heroes, unblemished heroism and flawless defenders.'[125] It was in the literature of *FIRE!!* and the stories of Hughes, Nugent et al., among the ugly, the blemished and the flawed, that the long history of Black Power continued to be most clearly shown. These writers, like their Black Power inheritors, sought a 'full and positive image of black life'.[126] Sexual dissidence was part of a strategy, as they shucked off the burden of representation, of standing *for* something, and chose to *be* something instead. This group of writers remained, unwelcome, unsettling, unclean and damned.

In this shift of emphasis, it is possible to see the extent to which *FIRE!!* embodied a revolution of the mind and an ethos of self-definition. At the heart of the publication was the idea that, 'Despite all obstacles, the artist must express the truth within himself... not for art's sake, but for his own sake, his people's sake, and for the sake of human kind... neither self, nor truth, nor art can be divided into boxes labelled "Black and White".'[127] *FIRE!!* in its own idiosyncratic manner, mandated African-American empowerment and was a physical manifestation of the agenda set forth by Hughes in *The Nation* five months earlier.

> We younger Negro artists ... intend to express our individual dark-skinned selves without fear or shame. If white people are pleased, we are glad. If they are not, it doesn't matter. We know we are beautiful. And ugly, too ... If coloured people are pleased we are glad. If they are not, their displeasure doesn't matter either. We build our temples for tomorrow, strong as we know how, and we stand on top of the mountain, free within ourselves.[128]

From on top of the mountain, the creators of *FIRE!!* and other artists of the Harlem Renaissance preached a new militant gospel. Indeed, the Renaissance produced a startling wealth of cultural material, much of it empowering in a far more diverse sense than is suggested by traditional historiography. While some of the work produced subscribed to Du Bois' notion that 'All art is propaganda', the most neglected works empowered black people in a more comprehensive sense than through narrow notions of racial uplift.[129]

The epitome of these forgotten products of the Renaissance was the self-described 'collectanea' *Ebony and Topaz*. Published once in 1927, *Ebony and Topaz* was a collection of essays, poetry and illustrations edited by Charles Spurgeon Johnson, also editor of *Opportunity*, the prestigious 'Journal of Negro Life'. Virtually ignored as a scholarly source, save for Caroline Goeser's excellent 2005 essay, *Ebony and Topaz* articulated a powerful theme of racial hybridity not only characteristic of the Harlem Renaissance, but emblematic of American culture between the wars.[130]

The militancy of *Ebony and Topaz* stems partly from the editorial style adopted by Johnson which allowed a great deal of latitude to contributors, implicitly encouraging controversial subjects elided by more traditional editors of the period, such as Du Bois. The result was a work which spurned traditional themes of racial uplift and exploded restrictive conceptions of racial identity, in the process presenting a new image of black life to the American public and advocating a new form of self-definition for its readership.

Initially published as a non-commercial extension of *Opportunity*, *Ebony and Topaz* was capable of expressing a broad range of responses to African-American culture without the restrictions of catering to the mixed tastes of a wide audience. Johnson summed up the publication's ethos when he wrote:

> It is only fair to rid this volume, at the beginning, of some of the usual pretensions ... this volume, strangely enough, does not set forth to prove a thesis, nor to plead a cause, nor, stranger still, to offer a progress report on the state of Negro letters. It is a venture in expression ... by a number of persons ... much less interested in their audience than in what they are trying to portray. This measurable freedom from the usual burden of proof has been an aid to spontaneity, and to this quality the collection makes its most serious claim.

Johnson not only sought to distance *Ebony and Topaz* from the burden of contributionism, but to liberate the cultural expression contained within its pages from both white and black preconceptions of identity. As he remarked, 'Some of our white readers will arch their brows or perhaps knit them soberly at some point before the end ... some of our Negro readers will doubtless quarrel with certain of the Negro characters who move in these pages.'[131] This did not appear to concern Johnson, who sought to gather a group of artists 'swinging free from the old and exhausted stereotypes and reading from life ... infinitely more real and honest'.[132]

Johnson eloquently pinpointed the revolution of the mind taking place among some African-Americans during the 1920s when he commented:

> The Negro writers, removed by two generations from slavery, are now much less self-consciousness, less interested in proving that they are just like white people ... care less about what white people think, or are likely to think about the race. Relief from the stifling consciousness of being a problem has brought a certain superiority to it ... The return of the Negro writers to folk material has proved a new emancipation.[133]

How did *Ebony and Topaz* articulate this 'new emancipation?' Significantly, Johnson's introduction is prefaced by an African proverb, which states 'It is better to walk/Than to grow angry with the road.'[134] The tone of progress is unmistakeable. This proverb, coupled with the fact that Johnson's introduction leads directly into a retelling of the John Henry legend, elucidates both *Ebony and Topaz*'s desire for unbounded progress and its awareness of the militant cultural tradition.[135]

The absence of Johnson's editorial presence is profoundly felt throughout the magazine, a factor which rendered the volume incomprehensible to established civil rights campaigners like Du Bois, who castigated *Ebony and Topaz* as 'a sort of big scrapbook, quite without unity, even of race'.[136] Du Bois again focused upon Johnson's decision to avoid the ideology of racial uplift, expressing his desire to see the work, 'split up into a half dozen little booklets, each with its artistic unity and clear spiritual message'.[137]

Artistic diversity may have been frowned upon by some, but arguably made *Ebony and Topaz* more representative of African-American cultural expression than those works which limited themselves to the schools of contributionism and racial uplift. The end product was a critical inquiry into the nature of the African-American identity which revealed and challenged several prevailing attitudes in America's cultural consciousness.

Ebony and Topaz encapsulated the complexities and contradiction of the movement. Some contributors like Countee Cullen were superficially conservative, but Cullen's polite, measured prose and respectable image were a fictitious, public construct which masked a more nuanced complicated persona that sought to engage with elements of a pan-African identity. Charles S. Johnson, writing in *Opportunity*, suggested that 'the spirit of the transplanted African' ran through Cullen's work and that questions of heritage figured large in his mind. Certainly, Cullen's writing shaped the images that would colour the walls and words of Black Power adherents dedicated to envisaging 'dark Gods' with 'dark rebellious hair'.[138]

These new emergent images were essential to understanding both the young firebrands of the Renaissance and their place in the connected historical expressions which would inform the long history of Black Power. Rather than representing an evolution of ideas of blackness, Hughes and his compatriots sought a confrontation, to 'burn up a lot of the old, dead, conventional Negro-white ideas of the past' for their own sake, as much for any grander edification.[139]

The parallels with the Black Power ethos become apparent when looking at the work of these young writer's as a whole. Thurman, Nugent, Hughes, Douglas, Hurston and the rest of the *enfants terrible* of the Niggerati intended to replace Locke's New Negro with a 'brand new nigger' in the process abandoning the task of racial representation, shunning the Renaissance old guard's focus on a white audience, and addressing themselves to interpreting black America.

Further echoes of the Black Power ethos were found in Thurman's editorial for the 1928 issue of *Harlem* magazine in which he urged 'the literate members of the thirteen million Negroes in the United States' to put their 'energy which they have hitherto used in moaning and groaning, into more concrete fields of actions.'[140] These concrete fields were curious pastures, with the Niggerati balancing their own individual stances with an inevitable influence on their generation.

Amidst this balance, Johnson, and the contributors to *Ebony and Topaz*, occupied a distinct position, making less strident claims than Locke, but stripped of the vitriol which marked Hughes's statement. Indeed, the political hybridity of *Ebony and Topaz* mirrors its cultural hybridity. This *laissez-faire* style held other advantages, providing access for a varied readership and most importantly, space for a plethora of racial identities, as opposed to one overarching 'New Negro' persona. This approach was not met with paternal benevolence from either Alain Locke's advocates of the white aesthetic or Du Bois's paragons of uplift. Yet this 'filth', this 'hodgepodge of punk literature' was to produce some of the most startling images in the long history of Black Power.[141]

Perhaps the most culturally militant content in *Ebony and Topaz* came from the pen of Nugent (a previous contributor to *FIRE!!*) and the young artist Charles Cullen. Scattered throughout the *Collectanea's* provocative pages, Cullen and Nugent's subversive illustrations served a dual purpose. Most obviously, these works confronted negative stereotypes of African-American identity by challenging white American conflations of dark skin and primitive behaviour. More importantly, Cullen and Nugent were subverting a persistent propensity within the African-American community to bind concepts of black identity to restrictive ideas of racial uplift, a concept which tended to ossify fixed and unrepresentative categories of race.[142] The contribution of *Ebony and Topaz* is best summarised by Johnson's closing statement; that it was a work which sought to 'touch boldly and with a striking candor some of the ancient racial foibles ... [to] ... violate the orthodoxy, but in a spirit which is neither bitterly hopeless nor resentful'.[143]

The youthful writers of the Renaissance were expressing the ultimate in Black Power by throwing off the shackles and expectations of their own race, producing art and expression unfettered by pre-existing conceptions. This was arguably just as important a contribution as those black writers who purposely sought to 'uplift' the race. Through bold, avant-garde works such as *FIRE!!* and *Ebony and Topaz*, Renaissance writers challenged established perceptions of gender, sexuality, colour and heritage, in the process inflaming the older establishment of scholars who persisted in using art as direct propaganda.

Part of the importance of works such as *FIRE!!* and *Ebony and Topaz* lies in the ire they engendered from Du Bois and other paragons of racial 'uplift'. The notions of racial diversity and sexual hybridity expressed by these two works are an equally valid but markedly neglected iteration of black empowerment. Indeed, the Renaissance served as a central moment in the continuing self-definition of African-Americans, a focal point at which many Americans redefined the way they viewed themselves and others, often becoming both culturally and politically empowered in the process. This process of redefinition was a central link between the cultural expression of the Renaissance and that of the later Black Arts and Black Power movements. The act of defining oneself – one's beliefs, sexuality, hopes, desires and relationship to the wider world – is a fundamental aspect of empowerment, and one which received clear expression during the Renaissance. In 'daring to search for beauty in things too commonplace for dignity or exaltation' these writers drew ordinary African-Americans into the nation's cultural consciousness.[144]

Crucially, the tools used to create this new empowering culture were drawn from African-American history and folklore. These young artists attacked their tasks with the same zeal that a youthful Carmichael and Newton would bring to the Black Power movement three decades later. Partially, they were following an edict similar to that set out by the poet James Weldon Johnson in 1937, when he urged African-American writers to build a cultural edifice founded on 'the American Negro's cultural background and his creative folk-art'.[145] This is in retrospect unsurprising, as many giants of 1920s literature stressed the importance of the African-American folk tradition in creating empowering artworks.[146]

These artists' attempts to create a self-conscious African-American art supported by a folk heritage foundation drew upon the work of early pioneers like Paul Laurence Dunbar and Charles W. Chesnutt. Writing at the turn of the century, these two Ohioan authors approached race and its impact on black and white Americans in a manner that anticipated later African-American writers and faced many of the problems and frustrations their 1920s counterparts would encounter. Arguably, Dunbar achieved greater public recognition; Booker T. Washington acclaimed him as 'The Poet Laureate of the Negro Race', and a number of schools, societies, and literary prizes took his name after his death in 1906.[147] Dunbar's literary career began in 1893 with a self-published collection entitled *Oak and Ivy*. It contained dialect pieces, which some interpreted as nostalgic for antebellum plantation life, along with standard English works incorporating more serious racial themes. Critics underestimated Dunbar's dialect poetry, which projected a strong sense of African-American humanity and dignity.[148] Dunbar was even more effective, though far less popular, when he moved away from dialect and celebrated black history, or addressed the psychological cost of racism, as in 'We Wear the Mask.'[149] Throughout his career however, Dunbar's dialect stories remained popular, while his attempts to seriously discuss race were largely dismissed. This seems to have done little to dissuade Dunbar, whose last novel prior to his death, *The Sport of the Gods*, examined for the first time the tribulations that accompanied migration from the rural South to the urban North, setting an early precedent for the critiques of urban squalor which dominated Black Panther rhetoric.[150]

Charles Chesnutt faced similar problems to Dunbar. His first successful work, *The Conjure Woman*, utilised dialect and featured an elderly black man, Uncle Julius McAdoo, who recited folktales about slavery in a fashion akin to Joel Chandler Harris's Uncle Remus. However, in spite of surface similarities, Julius is no Remus and Chesnutt's plantation is darker, more violent and thoroughly deromanticised. An ex-slave and 'trickster' figure *par excellence*, Julius presents a remarkably different militant view of southern life. Julius's tales, from the spells of Aunt Peggy in 'Hot Foot Hannibal' to his accounts of free black conjure men in 'The Conjurer's Revenge' and 'The Gray Wolf's Ha'nt', elucidate moments of active African-American resistance coupled with deliberate, calculated plots of revenge.[151]

With financial assistance, Chesnutt published *The Conjure Woman* in 1899, followed by a second volume, *The Wife of his Youth and Other Stories*, which dropped dialect to concentrate on race and the African-American urban elite. Chesnutt followed with three novels in quick succession, each of which addressed different racial issues and explored the social and psychological trauma of race prejudice in America. The most ambitious of these works was his second, *The Marrow of Tradition* (1901), which centred on the 1898 white supremacist coup in Wilmington, North Carolina, the first time in US history in which a local government was forcibly overthrown.[152] Chesnutt hoped to write a modern version of *Uncle Tom's Cabin* that would arouse the nation's conscience and mobilise it against the discrimination endemic in the South.

Although Chesnutt's novels took the perspective of the black bourgeoisie and his writing reflected the romanticism common to turn of the century fiction, their direct examination of race in a contemporary setting imparted a radicalism which made many white readers uncomfortable. As a result, they received a mixed critical response and declining sales.[153] However, Chesnutt remained popular among African-American readers and in recognition the NAACP awarded him the Spingarn Medal in 1928 for pioneering work in African-American literature.

The true militancy of Dunbar, Chesnutt and their later inheritors lay in their forging of a concrete ethos of African-American folklore from the morass of stereotyped plantation literature. This was a significant step towards providing connected cultural expressions in the long history of Black Power. However, it was only under the auspices of later Renaissance writers like Brown, Hurston and Hughes that systematic application of the folk tradition to contemporary African-American folk culture was undertaken.[154] Between them, these authors covered an immense diversity of African-American expression. Hughes explored the urban life of the ghetto, tenement and bar, in *The Weary Blues* (1926) and *Shakespeare in Harlem* (1942) amongst others, but also satirised white attempts to appropriate African-American lives and lifestyles for their own entertainment, in *The Ways of White Folks* (1934). Conversely, Brown, Hurston and Toomer examined the Southern cultural landscape. Of the three, Brown perhaps provided the most unique perspective, as his Washington upbringing demonstrated to him the profound disjunction between the everyday life of African-America and the distorted images portrayed by white writers like Octavus Roy Cohen.[155] In 1929, Brown commented that from the 'first treatment of the plantation, down to Dixon's rabid Ku Klux Klan propaganda, the Negro has been shown largely as an animal ... parasitical, excessively loyal, contented, irresponsible ... [or] not as faithful dogs, but as mad curs ... brutes given to rapine, treachery, bestiality and gluttony'.[156]

Brown's literary career was a focused, militant attempt to demolish these pejorative stereotypes and craft a new empowering identity. To do so, he went beyond literature and directly to the African-American south, travelling extensively and observing the daily life of its inhabitants. Locke, who dubbed Brown a 'folk-poet', commented on the importance of this grassroots approach: 'Brown has listened long and carefully to the folk in their intimate hours ... not ... as in Dunbar ... [but] when the masks of protective mimicry fall. Not only has he dared to give quiet but bold expression to this private thought and speech, but he has dared to give the Negro peasant credit for thinking.'[157]

In his peregrinations throughout the South, Brown absorbed the traditions and oral history of African-America, which in turn informed his poetry, first exhibited in *Southern Road* (1932).[158] In its pages,

Brown distilled the ethos of African-American folk culture without succumbing to the sentimental distortions of earlier writers. In this respect, he accomplished the goals set forth in the 1921 preface to Johnson's *Book of American Negro Poetry*, which argued, 'the coloured poet in the United States needs to ... find a form that will express the racial spirit by symbols from within rather than by symbols from without.'[159]

In creating these 'symbols from within' Brown utilised material directly drawn from the daily life of African-America, in particular, folksongs. Folksongs, arguably more than any other musical form, were a window into the lives of those who sang them, 'definitions of black life created by black Americans on the bloody and pine-scented Southern soil and upon the blackboard jungle of urban streets, tenement buildings, store-front churches and dim-lit bars'.[160] In *Southern Road*, the first poem in the eponymous collection, Brown produced a synthesis of the worksong and the blues, to create a poem more than the sum of its parts. The inclusion of the worksong as a shaping form is significant, because as Bruce Jackson noted in his study of Texan prison songs, worksongs *empowered* their singers, 'putting the work into the worker's framework rather than the guards'.[161]

Much as Johnson would adapt slave spirituals into a new African-American art form in *God's Trombones*, Brown shaped the humble worksong into a powerful declarative statement of rage and despair.[162] Unlike the mythological John Henry, the speaker in *Southern Road* is physically powerless, which has often led the poem to be seen as stoically accepting.[163] However, although the shackled singer of *Southern Road* is aware of the dire nature of his oppression he refuses to let his identity be sublimated or defined by the slave system.[164] For Brown, African-American responses to white oppression often maintained a clear *spirit* of revolt, even if defeat was inevitable, as seen in 'The Ballad of Joe Meek' and 'Sam Smiley'.[165] Joe Meek, described by the poem's narrator as 'soft as pie', undergoes a militant transformation after witnessing police beating a young girl. Attempting a peaceful solution, Joe, 'Walks up to the cops, / And, very polite, / Ast them ef they thought / They had done just right', and is also severely beaten for his trouble.[166]

Coming to, Joe begins a transformation worthy of Big Sixteen or John Henry. Brown writes that he, 'Went to a hockshop, / Got hisself a gun. / Felt mo' out of sorts / Than ever befo', / ... Shot his way to the station house, / Rushed right in, / Wasn't nothing but space / Where the cops had been.'[167] As in many plantation folktales, Joe continues to triumph against increasingly overpowering odds, and develops an air of mythic invulnerability, 'They called the reserves, / And the national guard ... The machine guns sputtered, / Didn't faze Joe at all – / But evvytime he fired / A cop would fall. / The tear-gas made him laugh / When they let it fly, / Laughing gas made him hang / His head an' cry. He threw the hand grenades back / With a outshoot drop, / An' evvytime he threw / They was one less cop.'[168] Ultimately, when Joe is taken down, it is not through his own failures, but through white treachery. Promising an armistice and safe passage, the Chief of Police convinces Joe to surrender, only to have him fall victim to a sniper.

Importantly, when oppressed by the police, Joe chooses to retaliate, 'Didn't lose / His shootin' eye. / Drew a cool bead / On the cop's broad head; / "I returns you yo' favor" / And the cop fell dead.'[169] Here, in the 1940s, was a clear cultural iteration of what Bobby Seale would describe in 2006 as 'putting civil rights on the edge ... saying, "If you shoot us, we'll shoot back" ... [taking] no crap from the racist-pig power structure.'[170] Brown closes by reminding his audience that, 'The very last words / He was heard to say, / Showed a different Joe talking / In a different way. / "Ef my bullets weren't gone, / An' my strength all spent – / I'd send the chief something / With a compliment." / "And we'd race to hell, / And I'd best him there, / Like I would of done here / Ef he'd played me fair".'[171] With a divide of decades on either side, Brown drew on the same tropes that animated the myth of Big Sixteen, again positing a Black Power strong enough to shake the foundations of Hell, while striking a tone remarkably similar to that created by the Panthers in their *Black Panther Intercommunal News Service* (BPINS) which declared in 1968, 'When you murder a black person in this babylon of babylons, you may as well give it up, because we will get your ass and God can't hide you.'[172] Joe Meek's closing line belies the piece's title, carrying an implicit promise of retaliation and a *caveat* to all oppressors: 'You cain't never tell / How fas' a dog can run / When you see him a-sleeping, / In the sun'.[173]

Such was the power of the poem that Brown recalled Stokely Carmichael, himself a militant icon, being extremely enthused by 'Joe Meek' when the men shared a podium at Howard University in 1973.[174] This is understandable, as Joe undergoes a psychological transformation as dramatic as the revolution of the mind demanded by Carmichael and

Hamilton in *Black Power*. However, Brown's appeal was not limited to the militant leadership; a 1966 reading of 'Joe Meek' to Howard students was attended by Amiri Baraka, Sonia Sanchez and Ossie Davis. One attendee recalled, 'By the time he finished reading "The Ballad" ... everybody in the gym was cheering.'[175] Embodying the archetype of the 'badass nigger', Joe Meek entered a line-up of folk heroes which stretched from the mythical Big Sixteen, John Henry and Stagolee, to the factual Jack Johnson and Muhammad Ali. A militant milestone on the long road to Black Power, the 'badass nigger' trope would later find its apotheosis in Van Peebles's *Sweet Sweetback* and other films of the Blaxploitation era, but has persisted to the present in films such as *Menace II Society* (1993) and *Full Clip* (2004).[176]

The militancy of Joe Meek and his fictional compatriots lies not in the characters themselves, but in the drive of their authors to present an authentic African-American culture. As Johnson noted in his introduction to *Southern Road*, Brown 'infused his poetry with genuine characteristic flavor by adopting as his medium the common, racy, living speech of the Negro in ... *real* life'.[177] Brown himself explained in interview that this empathy with African-American life imbued his poetry with a militant message, which, in the case of 'Joe Meek' was 'Don't believe the appearance of my people by the way they look ... we can take so much and then take no more.'[178]

Brown's work has occasioned much worthy scholarship, most notably from Joanne Gabbin, Mark Sanders and John Wright, but his key contribution to the development of militant culture can be summarised thus: 'Joe Meek' is the literary point at which the folk hero begins to exercise agency in the public sphere and act on behalf of the African-American community. Undergoing a revolution of the mind akin to that prescribed by Black Power adherents, Meek implies all African-Americans are heir to the legacy of John Henry and Big Sixteen. Moreover, *Southern Road*, taken as a whole, moves African-American culture onward from the ossified stereotypes of plantation imagery and urges black America to consider the limitations of its own self-image and cultural identity. In doing so, Brown's works actualise the militant power and revolutionary potential latent within African-American culture and form a part of the long history of Black Power.

Brown wrote *Southern Road* primarily out of fear that as migration from the rural South to the urbanising North intensified,

African-America's rural heritage would be eroded with a concomitant loss of autonomous culture, particularly folklore traditions.[179] Brown firmly believed, like many African-American writers of his era, that folklore buttressed African-American culture and enabled the creation and implementation of new strategies to combat oppression. Accordingly he feared urbanised African-Americans would inevitably passively consume a bigoted popular culture, or worse yet, be co-opted into producing art which abased itself before the economic demands and cultural peccadilloes of white America.

Brown's concerns were unfounded. The 1960s witnessed a surge in cultural militancy initially epitomised by a desire to reclaim the African-American historical record. In its reclamation of the African-American past, the Black Power movement was not merely reciting inspiring recollections. It was redefining history for a new generation. In the process, historical events and figures gained mythic dimensions, an air of legend which had immense resonance for the American cultural landscape and the legacy of Black Power in America. Myth has long been identified as one of the most influential cultural forms, and accordingly, the myths developed by the Black Power movement deserve careful analysis.

In David Bradley's 1981 novel *The Chaneysville Incident*, Bradley's protagonist, an African-American historian, outlines the power of myth: 'If you would bend a man ... Do not bother with psychology or diplomacy or even war ... do it with ritual.'[180] Bradley's novel, begun in 1971, is an almost literal depiction of the transfer of culture from history to myth. The protagonist John Washington gradually discards his historical, professorial narrative style for a more impassioned outlook, which culminates midway in a critique of white Western culture, as embodied in the Christian church.

To follow Bradley's, or rather Washington's, argument, to comprehend fully the ethos and impact of the Black Power movement, it is necessary to understand the myths it drew upon and created to define itself, to identify the rituals and methods by which it linked itself to African-American history and to pinpoint the new myths and culture heroes which it in turn produced. To achieve this, two concepts must be accepted. First that myth exists primarily as narrative built upon remembered historical occurrences, reinforced by ritual and repetition. Second, that cultural history is an evolution from mythology, and to understand it historians must consider what people choose to mythologise and the cultural rituals which they use to do so. Understanding this provides access to an African-American cultural heritage filled with dancers, shamans, preachers, poets, blues men and women, musicians, mackdaddies and politicians, all with a marked historical legacy.

The nature of this history and its interaction with American culture is tackled in Ralph Ellison's 1952 *Invisible Man* wherein the narrator listens to Louis Armstrong's '(What Did I Do to Be So) Black and Blue' while readying himself for retaliation against white society.[181] To understand the complexity of his American experience, Ellison plunged deeply into mythology and folklore, essential elements in the making of a people's history. Ellison's history is non-dialectical: the narrator of the novel tries to delineate his identity via his own experiences, without interference from others but is also constantly in search of a 'useable past'.[182]

Ultimately, he rejects the idea that a single ideology can constitute an entire way of being, reasoning that each individual constitutes a multitude of impulses and a society comprised of individuals necessarily mirrors this diversity. At the novel's conclusion, the narrator remains bewildered regarding his own African-American identity but determined to honour his individual complexity. As Neal noted, 'The novel attempts to construct its own universe based on its own imperatives ... the shaping of a personal vision, as in the blues and the celebration of a collective vision as represented by the living culture ... [which] with all of its shifting complexities ... constitutes the essential landscape of the novel'.[183]

Experiences cloaked in cultural ritual are no less politically significant than legislation, boycotts or rent strikes.[184] For Black Power advocates to understand cultural symbol and ritual was to connect with the African-American in the street and in doing so, to both actualise his power and give him agency. Accordingly, 'the direction of power is that of learning the meaning of the myths and symbols which abound among the Negro masses ... without this knowledge, leadership, no matter how correct its programme will fail ... the zoot suit conceals profound political meaning ... the symmetrical frenzy of the lindy-hop conceals clues to great potential powers'.[185] This was not simply excitable rhetoric. It was feared that unless militants engaged people in 'a manner demanding their most profound attention' efforts at political liberation were doomed.[186]

That attention, the fighters and writers and dreamers argued, was best gained by articulating the aspirations of a people through their daily experiences, most often expressed in the form of cultural ritual.

It has been previously argued that the cultural aspects of Black Power failed to provide sufficient support for the 1960s generation of militant African-Americans. This rather desolate view was perhaps seen most clearly in Charles Silberman's comprehensive *Criminal Violence, Criminal Justice*, wherein the author controversially suggested that black culture had failed to channel constructively the retroactive rage of black youth, as a result of what Walter Lippmann termed 'the dissolution of the ancestral order'.[187] Silberman argued that older African-Americans traditionally responsible for passing on historical and cultural experiences to the next generation had by the late 1960s either died or relinquished their function as culture bearers. Concurrently, with the 'lowering of racial barriers', middle class professionals moved to better locations, undoing the social cohesion of the African-American community.[188] Silberman, although acknowledging the immorality of segregation, contended, 'precisely because segregation was so patently and totally evil, it helped black Americans maintain a sense of community ... the dismantling of legal segregation ... swept away some of its unintended and unrecognized benefits'.[189] As a result, Silberman argued that black folklore was 'losing its power to exorcise black rage', claiming the advent of 'transistor radios, portable phonographs and tape recorders ... had a stultifying effect on performance'.[190] As he explained:

> ... listening to a recorded version of the blues or other black music – not to mention watching the omnipresent TV – is passive behaviour, in sharp contrast to the active role that spectators to a toasting session used to play. Equally important, black men have new and more effective ways of deadening ... pain ... toasts and the dozens cannot compete with heroin, cocaine or the increasingly popular ... combination of methadone and wine.[191]

Silberman suggests that without the presence of elders able to provide a link to a usable past relevant to the harsh conditions of the present, African-American youths were left to define themselves with little regard for historical lessons. Herein lay the fear which drove black militants' spirited assault upon the American cultural landscape. A delicate balancing act was required between the production of 'mojo' (cultural forms) and the exercise of 'sayso' (tangible political power).[192] Militants were not simply trying to increase African-American cultural output but to create a system of empowerment which would act as a concrete alternative to the present political order, 'a system of politics and art ... as fluid, as functional and as expansive as black music'.[193]

'Mojo', defined as the artistic and cultural presentation of the militant ethos, therefore automatically acted as a natural counter to any power which would limit its expression. Black militants found in cultural expression an avenue of attack against the American system which could not be stopped by legislation or physical violence. This avenue would likely never have opened without the strength gained from the long heritage of militancy in American history. Once catalysed by this militant heritage, African-American culture could be found 'out on every street, waiting impatiently ... to tell us how to set the sights on our intellectual arms, how to unload them of pointless ambition, and how to load them with principles and to remind us of the dog tags of our enemies'.[194] In retrospect, Silberman was patently incorrect. Folklore did not lose its power with the advent of new forms of cultural transmission but rather adapted to them, reaching a broader audience in the process. The result was an amalgam of historical event and cultural myth which held greater resonance than either taken separately, a militant synthesis of past struggle and present cultural expression.

This synthesis is epitomised in a piece by Neal entitled *Uncle Rufus Raps on the Squared Circle* in which Neal holds court with a fictional character dubbed Uncle Rufus, a reimagining and reclamation of the Uncle Remus character derived by Joel Chandler Harris from Southern plantation tales. Often seen as a pejorative stereotype, Uncle Remus rapidly entered America's cultural consciousness, first through the Br'er Rabbit stories and later with assistance from Disney in the 1946 film, *Song of the South*. The latter met with heavy criticism from civil rights activists, although this was not unanticipated by Disney. The company's publicist Vern Caldwell wrote to producer Perce Pearce that 'The negro situation is a dangerous one. Between the negro haters and the negro lovers there are many chances to run afoul of situations that could run the gamut all the way from the nasty to the controversial.'[195] Caldwell was not wrong, as *Ebony* lambasted the film as 'lily-white propaganda' designed to promote 'Uncle Tomism as the model of how Negroes should behave in white company'.[196] Animation proved a fertile medium for evolving perceptions of Remus. His legacy surfaced again in Ralph Bakshi's 1975 animated film *Coonskin*, which ranged widely through African-American culture in an attempt to satirise prevailing white racist stereotypes, as well as the Blaxploitation genre and *Song of the South*.[197]

Perhaps due to unfamiliarity with its inspirations, *Coonskin* represented as much a stereotyping of 1970s Harlem life as *Song of the South* had portrayed 'an idyllic master-slave relationship', and accordingly attracted a mixed reception.[198] Within the African-American community, CORE launched strenuous protests, with the Reverend Al Sharpton declaring, 'I don't got to see shit; I can smell shit!'[199] Conversely, the film gained a degree of support from Spike Lee (whose satire *Bamboozled* considered similar themes) and the comedian Richard Pryor, suggesting that while politically it may have been misguided, culturally it struck something of a chord.[200]

The resonance of the Remus tales is such that they were presented on film as recently as 2006 in the hip-hop influenced *Adventures of Brer Rabbit* featuring the voice of noted civil rights campaigner Danny Glover.[201] Far from being another attempt at animating animosity, the 2006 iteration excises Remus from the Br'er Rabbit stories entirely, with one reviewer condemning the film as 'A Disgrace to the African American Spirit' and another bemoaning the reduction of Harris's folktales to 'mindless pap'.[202] It seems that Remus and the rabbit, for all their controversy, have lost none of their ability to generate a conversation around race. When the evident cultural magnetism of the Uncle Remus figure is considered, Neal's *Squared Circle* recreation of Remus into Rufus to demonstrate the interplay of history and myth becomes an inspired decision. Moreover, Rufus is a truly empowering and militant creation, sharply dressed, handsome and brimming with energy. As Neal narrates, 'When Uncle Rufus bops in the door. He peacocks in a pearl gray Homburg. The coat is blue cashmere. He sports a golden-headed serpent cane; the shoes, French, Shriner and Urner, contrast exquisitely with his spats.'[203]

Settling in, Neal and his fictional counterpart share their view on the Ali-Frazier fight of the previous night. For Rufus, boxing is a metaphor for the acquisition of power, teaching a person how to handle his own body and control the movements of his opponent. Indeed, boxing is not simply a sport, but a synthesis of African-American cultural forms, almost musical in nature. As Rufus argues, 'Frazier is stomp-down blues, bacon, grits and Sunday church ... Ali is body bebop ... blues and gospel ain't his thing. Frazier can't sing, but he sings better than Ali. And that's why Frazier won.'[204]

When Neal asks Rufus who he supports, he receives a slap with the cane for his troubles, because it is the wrong question. Rufus replies that while circumstances may dictate choosing one approach or another, outside of the boxing ring, the styles of both boxers have value as legitimate responses to political and social reality. The metaphor is clear. As in sports, so in politics; to lean toward one interpretation of the militant agenda should not prevent African-Americans realising the worth of all attempts to gain black freedom. Crucially, this message becomes infinitely clearer and more accessible when seen through the lens of popular culture and sporting ritual, as opposed to the labyrinthine intricacies of the political perspective.

Observing from an inclusive cultural vantage point, black militants could appreciate the gains provided by the non-violent civil rights movement, without acceding to its ethos. One commentator remarked,

> When we cut past the bullshit, it became evident that even though the victories of the civil rights movement were legitimate, noteworthy, and necessary, they did not address themselves to the central problem of the black man in America ... simple acquisition of those rights which abstractly belong to all citizens of the United States would in no fundamental manner alter the oppressive situation in which we found ourselves.[205]

David Hilliard recently noted, 'It's important that people understand that our Black Panther Party, was the continuation ... of the then defunct Civil Rights movement. And we give credit to those movements before us.'[206] Indeed, there was a clear basic drive toward independence that linked both approaches. As King explained to Carmichael, 'The beauty of nonviolence is that you never let an outside force, nothing outside of yourself, control what you do.'[207] While African-Americans may have remained powerless despite the apparently strenuous efforts of the mainstream civil rights movement, it became apparent to militants that previous decades of nonviolent struggle had not been an exercise in gaining power so much as a prolonged period of self-definition, which had led black Americans to the unfortunate but necessary conclusion that powerlessness could not be solved through non-violent protest alone:

> We had to go through the civil rights movement to understand this. The integrationist cause championed by the NAACP, Urban League, early CORE, and SNCC represent significant watersheds in the history of the black liberation movement ... even if their concerns were not necessarily the concerns of a broad segment of the black community ... they have contributed significantly to the growth of black consciousness.[208]

Armed with a new consciousness of their situation provided by the civil rights movement, Black Power militants were able to achieve a greater unity of perspective, much as Rufus had advised Neal. Accordingly, it became apparent that, 'The freedom-rides, sit-ins, bus boycotts, Selma March, Meredith March, Harlem rebellion, Watts rebellion, Newark rebellion, school take-overs, and the explosion of black culture all grew out of a conglomerate will towards black liberation.'[209] This 'conglomerate will' had exhibited a clear and present continuity throughout the centuries prior to the political emergence of Black Power in 1966. It persisted in a history steeped in ritual, which in turn evolved into myth, creating new and potent cultural heroes for the black militant movement.

Of all the new heroes created by the Black Power movement, perhaps the most lauded is Malcolm X. Scorched into American cultural memory by virtue of his martyrdom on 21 February 1965, X has remained an iconic figure of African-American liberation. At the time, his death was an almost inconceivable event, an unreal experience, epitomised in the title of the *Rolling Stone* article on his death 'Coming At You Weird'. The very fact of X's death was an immense blow to the militant movement, as the article's author raged: 'WHAT DID MALCOLM HAVE TO SAY THAT DEMANDED HIS DEATH??? WHAT COULD SAYING (WORDS) HAVE TO DO WITH DYING?'[210]

Crucially, Malcolm's legacy appears to rest not on his political actions, but upon the cultural memories of those actions. As the *Rolling Stone* article noted, 'Memory is a bitch ... it was Malcolm who opened up most of us ... I for one can not make myself care [about] the man behind the scenes, when it was his student that finally died trying to redeem me and my people from our ignorance of ourselves.'[211] Malcolm's influence was not simply due to selective recollection however. Part of his appeal lay in his origins and his ability to relate to ordinary people, to show that he understood the struggle involved in creating a militant identity, because he too had undergone the same process. As a result, Malcolm joined the hallowed ranks of, 'prophets who lived among us who wallowed in slime and ignorance like the rest of us, who saw the light and heard the word and hipped us to what's happening'.[212]

The lesson gained was that rhetoric divorced from practical application could have no tangible effect. 'Without these messengers who enter our lives in the most concrete manner ... there will be no change'.[213] If Malcolm was idolised, it was not simply because he was charismatic, eloquent or driven. It was because the manner in which he related to the cultural rituals of everyday life in African-America gave him special resonance with his audience, enabling him to reach, 'the hidden corners of every black man's mind that pure and holy prophets cannot reach'.[214]

This resonance endeared culture heroes such as Malcolm to some members of the African-American community in a deeply personal manner which bordered on love. Importantly, this attachment was only strengthened by militants' appropriation of their long history. This combination of history and myth, some militants argued, rendered Malcolm and his associated political message extremely resistant to white cultural corruption.[215]

Within a short time, Malcolm X passed from history into cultural myth. As the *Rolling Stone* article wryly remarked, for Black Power advocates 'It's all related to Malcolm somehow.'[216] What enabled Malcolm to exert a pull on the black militant mind beyond that of the average rhetoricist? Perhaps the answer lay in his connection to African-American culture and the familiarity this appeared to lend him. Larry Neal noted:

> What I liked most about Malcolm was his sense of poetry; his speech rhythms, and his cadences that seemed to spring from the universe of black music ... I was not reared in the black church ... I did not have ready access to the rhetorical strategies of Martin

Luther King. My ears were more attuned to the music of urban black America ... Malcolm was like that music. He reminded many of us ... of Charlie Parker and John Coltrane – a music that was a central force in the emerging ethos of the black artistic consciousness. Malcolm was in the tough tradition of the urban street speaker. But there was a distinct art in his speeches, an interior logic that was highly compelling and resonant.[217]

The connection between art and the urban street highlighted by Neal would lend Black Power's cultural militancy its strength and contribute to its enduring legacy in the American cultural landscape. More importantly, this connection helps us understand the relationship between expressions of militancy over time. It was well and good for magazines, artists and authors to laud the mythic qualities of militant colossi like X, Carmichael and Newton and equally salutary for poets and polemicists to craft fictional militant icons, redolent with empowering virtues. However, these two factors had their greatest impact when taken in tandem. In creating mythical archetypes of Black Power, from Big Sixteen, through John Henry and Joe Meek, BAM and their predecessors in the Harlem Renaissance were trying to create exemplars of Black Power virtues, which the man in the street could then identify in his political leaders, like Malcolm X, Stokely Carmichael and Huey Newton.

In transferring these qualities from myth and folklore to living, breathing men, Black Power culture creators hoped to bring these empowering archetypes to a larger audience. Within the pages of *FIRE!!*, *Ebony and Topaz*, *Ebony*, *Rolling Stone* and others, the revolution of the mind appeared within reach, its virtues clear to understand, set forth in print and paint, its tenets spoken by men who walked the sidewalks, sat on the stoops and rapped with the inhabitants of African-America. The cultural output of the Black Power movement, over the long history of Black Power, strove to draw the revolution closer to the people. Arguably, this was nowhere better exemplified than in the cultural evolution of Stokely Carmichael.

For many, Carmichael was literally the poster child of the 1960s Black Power movement, a personification of its rage, eloquence, charisma and drama. Lerone Bennett, writing on Carmichael for *Ebony* in September 1966, began his elegy in Homeric terms, describing how 'the

Black Power fire he [Carmichael] ignited on the Mississippi Meredith March raged with mounting fury in all the Harlems and all the White Plains of America'.[218]

Bennett was conscious of how Carmichael utilised the media and popular culture to reach the average African-American, recalling, 'Hour in and hour out – on TV, in print media, in the slums and in the mortgaged fortresses of the black and white middle-class – men and women condemned Black Power, praised it, drew back from it in horror or embraced it with fierce hope and pride. And wherever Black Power was hailed or damned, there also Stokely Carmichael was praised or blamed.'[219]

As individuals like Carmichael and X became symbols, they became archetypes of the movement and targets for the cultural confusion it created. Arguably, no one was more divisive of public opinion than Carmichael. Was he indeed part of the militant continuity, 'a hip Malcolm X', or merely a pretender to the throne, a 'juvenile pied piper' promising little but 'black death' to any misguided enough to dance to his tune?[220] As was often the case with Black Power, the answer lay only in more questions, as *Ebony* queried, 'Who is this young man? What does he want? What does he mean by Black Power?' The view from the street was occasionally less confused, as Lewis Michaux, a Harlem book store owner told Carmichael in 1966, 'Malcolm X is still living. When you walked in, Malcolm smiled.'[221]

If Carmichael was, as he often remarked, the inheritor of the political legacy of Malcolm X, he was also, and just as importantly, the embodiment of another central tenet of cultural Black Power. The man's physical presence was undeniable, which led to SNCC colleagues affectionately dubbing him 'The Magnificent Barbarian.'[222] Neither modern nor contemporary media could decide how they wanted to portray Carmichael: was he a 'black ogre' or 'cool and very hip' exhibiting 'a disciplined wildness'? Awash in epithets, Carmichael was more than an exemplar for the philosophy of 'Black is Beautiful.'[223] Rather, he rapidly became a quasi-legendary synthesis of everything aspirational in African-American physicality, a militant avatar who 'walks like Sidney Poitier, talks like Harry Belafonte and thinks like the post-Muslim Malcolm X'.[224]

CORE field secretary Len Holt summarised the transition from history to myth occurring when he remarked, 'Stokely is the person sculptors would seek as a model for a statue of a Nubian god.'[225] Yet this strange mercurial God possessed an unusual common touch. Crucially, Carmichael's utterances catalysed self-definition. As one unnamed audience member remarked, 'He terrifies me and exalts me at the same time. He tells so much truth ... there were some things I could say in private but could not say in public until after Birmingham'.[226] Carmichael's appeal was transnational as well as local. In 1967 Obi Egbuna, the eventual founder of the United Coloured People's Association (UCPA) lauded Carmichael in still more euphoric terms – not only was Carmichael a God, but he could shape and define eras: 'Stokely's arrival was like manna from heaven ... a new phase of Black history had begun.'[227] Egbuna's veneration suggested that British militant groups formed decades later also drew on the long history of Black Power, finding inspiration, as Stephen Small noted, in 'black politics, institutions and culture, in the literature philosophies and music from African-Americans ... W.E.B. Du Bois ... Stokely Carmichael ... the Black Panthers ... the Mexico Olympics.'[228] Small's writing suggests a clear recognition of the long history of Black Power and the manner in which its articulation in connected cultural expressions across time rendered it powerful, transmissible and influential. As he concluded 'American Black culture pervades Black Britain. African-American culture reiterates itself and is transformed, in the lifestyles of black Americans in England.'[229]

The transmissibility of the Black Power ethos was often reliant on its avatars. While it might initially seem curious that Carmichael's first major speaking engagement after the controversy of Meredith was to an audience of white students at the University of California at Berkeley, as the left-field *Berkeley Barb* described, Carmichael was capable of tapping into an evolving African-American image by combining cultural forms and political pertinence: 'He uses some change of pace, some dry humor, some rhythmic repetition suggestive of poetry. But what grips his audience and frightens the phonies is his plain stark statement of exactly how this country's acts and pretensions look to a black man who refused to yield one inch to opportunism.'[230]

Sycophantic as this was, there was no doubt that mainstream media struggled to fit historically connected orators like Carmichael into their existing frames of discussion. Carmichael had little time for either the media or the social scientists scrambling to define the movement. Waving off this 'intellectual masturbation' he urged to his audience to view Black Power as a 'psychological struggle'.²³¹ According to Carmichael, to avoid the stigma and restrictions of generations of paternalism and racism black people had to 'be seen in positions of power, doing and articulating for themselves, for themselves'.²³² Most importantly, they had to see each other taking the lead.

White people's inability to deal with Black Power, according to Carmichael was an 'inability to deal with "blackness." '²³³ As he bluntly explained: 'If we had said "Negro Power" nobody would get scared. Everybody would support it. Or if we said power for coloured people, everybody'd be for that, but it is the word "Black," it is the word "Black" that bothers people in this country, and that's their problem, not mine.'²³⁴

Carmichael's rhetoric sketched the outlines of a psychological battlefield, wherein black people would achieve a psychological transformation, a revolution of the mind, becoming able to 'define their own terms, define themselves as they see fit, and organize themselves as they see it'.²³⁵ Carmichael deliberately drew on the cultural sphere to encourage this transformation. Speaking in 1967 against the Vietnam War, he told his high school audience, 'You ought to stand up like the greatest, the prettiest, Muhammad Ali. And you ought to tell them, "We are not going to fight your war."'²³⁶ In effect, Carmichael sought to turn a human reality into an emotive mythology to catalyse what he saw as a psychological revolution.²³⁷ Was this then the true face of the Black Power movement, an elegant combination of charismatic figureheads, prescribing militancy unto the eager masses? Hardly.

As fast as Black Power militancy evolved, American capitalism co-opted it. The very *Ebony* article which contained Bennett's eloquent mythologising of Carmichael also featured a number of advertisements targeted specifically, and stereotypically, at the African-American readership. A full-page spread for Campbell's Pork and Beans created a down-home image as it encouraged readers to savour the slow-cooked joys of the product.²³⁸ A scant two pages later, an alluring headshot of a pretty African-American girl proudly declared, 'Us Tareyton smokers would rather fight than switch!'²³⁹ Although the Tareyton campaign ran from 1963 to 1966, incorporating both white and African-American models, the endorsement to 'Get the filter cigarette with the taste worth fighting for!' held a peculiar resonance next to photos of Carmichael striding through Harlem.²⁴⁰ The message was loud and conflicting.

Fight the oppressive capitalist system, and buy its products as you do so. Little wonder the process of creating a militant identity could not be solved by a few new culture heroes.

Carmichael himself had suffered through the process of identity construction, dismissing southern sit-in protesters as 'Niggers [who] will do anything to get their names in the paper.'[241] As the sit-ins blossomed from state to state, Carmichael maintained, 'Niggers are like monkeys. One see, all do.'[242] Yet a week later, he joined the pickets, the psychic tipping point had been reached and a new culture hero was created. Bennett summed up the influence of men like Carmichael in his closing thoughts when he remarked: 'Black Power did not spring full-blown from the head of Stokely Carmichael ... it was in the heads and hearts of long-suffering men who had paid an enormous price for minuscule gains ... it was the genius of Stokely Carmichael to sense the mood gestating in the depths of the black psyche and to give tongue to it.'[243]

There is more to Carmichael than Bennett's assertion however. Not only was his rhetoric malleable, but it was attuned to the changing self-perceptions of his audience. As he reflected:

> I had a standard-English speech reserved for the merely affluent and curious. ...Then too I had a harder, more analytic, and ideological argument for more serious political and intellectual forums ... Then there was a down-home, nitty-gritty idiom in a style I mostly borrowed from the Harlem street corner nationalists and the Southern black preachers. This I saved for the brothers and sisters on the block. But the political message stayed the same, whatever the audience ... Only the style changed.[244]

For Carmichael, Black Power was not power with the goal of racial equality, but rather that of social equality, decent housing, jobs and a democratic decision making process. It was a clarion call to the black middle-class to set aside class distinctions and a plea to black intellectuals to re-embrace their cultural heritage. Here was the real message of the Black Power movement, directly from the lips of one of its most lauded political speakers:

> We are not culturally deprived. We are the only people who have a culture in America. We don't have to be ashamed of James Brown.

We don't have to wait for the Beatles to legitimise our culture. Black intellectuals ought to come back to the community and let the community define what intellectual is and what art is. Nothing is more artful to me than seeing a fine black woman doing the Dog.[245]

As Carmichael's comments suggest, culture, and visual art in particular, was central to the Panthers' vision of success. This perspective was reinforced by Emory Douglas, Minister of Culture for the Black Panther Party from 1967, whose revolutionary art filled the pages of the Party's widely circulated *Intercommunal News Service*. One of the few mediums completely under the Party's control, the News Service was written 'by the alienated for the alienated', helping to create an imagined community of black revolutionaries.[246] In this sense, the *Intercommunal News Service* helped ordinary black Americans become part of the long history of Black Power, including them in a collective identity which had been imagined since the early nineteenth century, creating an ideology, sense of purpose, group identity and place of action that had nothing to do with locale.

The paper's comparative success was unsurprising. The omnipresence of a simplistic mainstream narrative left a distinct gap for its countercultural stylings. As John Downing explained, 'alternative media flourish in the wastelands left by official media.'[247] This is nowhere more applicable than to the *Intercommunal News Service*, and the place of Douglas's art within it. His views were epitomised in his speech entitled 'Art for the People's Sake' delivered at Fisk University in 1972. Addressing his young audience at the historically black college, Douglas's chief target was the commercial art of mainstream America, which he perceived as 'a method of persuasion, mind control ... we go out and buy – our own oppression'.[248] For Douglas, writing from a Marxist perspective, one of the most dangerous facets of capitalist white America was that 'They have begun to analyze how to relate to Black people so that we will continue to suffer – peacefully.'[249]

Douglas's art was designed to literally give people the correct picture of the struggle and its appeal, at least to his mind, was clear. He reflected, 'People loved those pictures. Our art, our paper was reflective of the community.'[250] The art was more than reflective, however. It was constructive, designed to create a new identity in which carrying a gun was an essential understandable part of daily life, and in which the opposition of the state was visible, farcical and destructible. The *Intercommunal News Service* became a weekly act of cultural resistance.

As Douglas argued, cultural subjugation required cultural retaliation, 'we have to take that structure of commercial art and add a brand-new content to it ... that will serve the interests of Black people'.[251] Moreover, he was under no illusions as to his core audience, declaring that, 'art is for the masses of Black people; we must bombard the masses with art. We cannot do this in an art gallery, because our people do not go to art galleries ... We have to put our art all over the United States, wherever Black people are.'[252]

Rather quixotically, Douglas and many other Panthers viewed the omnipresent cultural commercialism of mainstream America as a potential tool in the fight for empowerment, a structure which could be adapted to feed the vitality of African-American militant protest, if utilised appropriately. Once again part of the challenge lay in self-definition, in establishing the meaning, purpose and audience of militant art. For Douglas, 'art is defined by the people, because the people are the ones who make art'.[253] Speaking in 1972, he might have been describing Sterling Brown's tour of the Deep South, when he argued, 'No artist can sit in an ivory tower ... The artist has to be down on the ground; he has to hear the sounds of the people, the cries of the people, the suffering of the people, the laughter of the people – the dark side and the bright side of our lives.'[254]

What then was the proposed output of this artistic union with the black community? The answer was two-fold – an uplifting of African-American pride and self-esteem, linked to a scathing critique of the mainstream American system. Both of these objectives were encapsulated in stark, vibrant art, which reached thousands via the *Intercommunal News Service*. As Douglas concluded, 'we praise the people in relationship to art. We show them as the heroes; we put them on the stage. We make characters of our people (around the idea of what they know life should be about.).'[255]

Douglas's exalting of ordinary people through art was coupled with attempts to use the language of the street as an organising tool. It became a point of pride with many Party members: 'No element of the

Panthers' culture was more prized than the leader's ability to engage in righteous rapping, to combine street vernacular with social theory' an intellectualised mix of anger, intelligence and eloquence designed to appeal to the same individuals the young Panthers had grown up with, fought with and shared the streets with.[256] As Seale claimed with customary ebullience, 'once you organise those brothers, you get niggers, you get black men, you get revolutionaries who are too much'.[257] Panther politics were pragmatic – rallies drew crowds selling barbecue and potato salad for a dollar, portraying identifiable, empathisable, understandable images to the American people. As Gilbert Moore, one of *Life's* first black reporters noted: 'These ... weren't tennis playing niggers ... not slick cocktail niggers ... these weren't smooth talking niggers ... there were the cats off the block ... the bad motherfuckers, who came up hustling and pimping and taking numbers and kickin' ass just to stay alive because they didn't know how to do anything else'.[258]

Whereas the pulpit preacher style of the nonviolent movement had resonated with elite audiences the Panthers seemed to appeal more to the man in the street.[259] The rhetoric of Black Power, articulated via and shaped by the long of history of Black Power, was designed to speak broadly to the black community.[260] As Hilliard proudly noted, 'We have attracted a cross section of our generation – political activists, warriors, intellectuals.'[261] This did not come without problems, as Cleaver recollected, 'We knew who the Panthers were, but in order to maximize the number of people we pulled in, we did not argue with people if they put on a black leather jacket or black berets, or said that they were Panthers'.[262] New recruits drawn by mass mediated constructions chose style over substance, 'many ... fatally confused ... [the Panthers'] ... flamboyant tactics with the substance of their goals ... few ... understood that the theatrical actions were ... only the initial step in organising ... social change.'[263]

Despite these claims, Douglas, in common with many Panthers, did not see art or culture as the supreme factor in the movement. Politics retained primacy, or as Douglas explained: 'A picture can express a thousand words, but action is supreme.'[264] However, the perspective taken by an activist in 1972 and that available to an historian over four decades later is markedly distinct, and casts the role of cultural forms within the movement in a different light. The overt political emphasis in Panther rhetoric often ignored the motive force provided by popular culture expression, focusing exclusively on the political causes.²⁶⁵ However, the majority of Panther sources available to historians come from those luminaries – Newton, Hilliard, Carmichael et al. – who dwelt in the movement's political heart. Accordingly it seems questionable whether ordinary people gave the same degree of weighting to the forces of politics and culture in developing militancy and identity, as that implied by the rhetoric of the Panther's iconic figures. As *New York Times* reporter Earl Caldwell recalled, for many ordinary supporters, Panther art 'was nothing short of shooting a gun ... it became a signature thing.'²⁶⁶

Regardless of the relative perspective on the primacy of art or politics in the mind of the audience, the transference of influence ran both ways. As art could stimulate politics, and by extension militancy, so too could politics become art. Douglas's own title, Minister for *Culture*, embodies this dichotomous, symbiotic relationship. The Panthers' struggles to alleviate the economic hardships of urban African-America, from the 'Free Breakfast' programmes, through sickle cell anaemia and housing relief efforts, fed back into the artistic consciousness movement and inspired its cultural producers to greater heights. Consequently, the art produced inevitably gained greater resonance and began to radiate outwards into mainstream American consciousness. The long history of Black Power, transmitted via cultural forms, both shaped and was shaped by the political movement.

Douglas acknowledged the symbiotic relationship between political protest, economic campaigning and cultural militancy when he wrote: 'the artist must begin to interpret the hungry stomach, bad housing, all of these things and transform these things into something that would raise the consciousness of black people.'²⁶⁷ What Douglas realised was that in drawing close to the people for whom they struggled, the Panthers were producing a unique brand of folk art, iconic imagery and identity-forming values. Accordingly, the Panthers' Minister for Culture stressed the need for the man in the street and the cultural producer to grow closer, arguing:

> If we, as artists, do not understand our role and relationship to the society, to the political situation and the survival of Black people,

then how can we create art that will project survival? ... When the artist begins to love the people ... we can begin to interpret and project into our art ... Freedom, justice, liberation: all those things that we could not apply to our art before.[268]

This love for the people, this fundamental drawing close to the roots of struggle, was the same approach taken by Brown, Hurston and Hughes in the 1920s. It was the ethos that informed the work of Chesnutt and Dunbar and the underlying spirit of those plantation tales which were to find modern expressions in Malcolm X, Stokely Carmichael and Muhammad Ali.

The art of the Panthers then was the latest iteration of a strong line of continuity running throughout African-American history, a deep river of militant sentiment which continually proposed a closeness with its subjects — the suffering, struggling and defiant. Douglas, in the 1970s, followed this tradition in creating an art which corresponded to the community's daily life, designed to elevate the consciousness and shape the identity of the man in the street. Douglas's art fed on politics and resulted in iconic cultural imagery which in turn provided further impetus to militant political struggle and economic action. The long history of Black Power had created a militant cultural legacy deeply rooted in everyday African-American life. What remained was to see how the men and women in the streets of America would respond to this potent cultural force and how it would manifest in their own lives, popular and political, economic and international.

To understand this response, it is necessary to consider the organisations and institutions which carried the tradition of cultural militancy into the American public sphere and then to analyse how not only African-America, but also white America, reacted to this dramatic legacy which was permanently to alter the cultural landscape of the United States. In the process, it will become apparent that the long tradition of African-American cultural militancy, distilled across the decades, always emerged at the intersections of the realities of African-American life and the possibilities of African-American thought. By taking the clear continuity of militant cultural expression highlighted previously and examining how it interacted with the peculiar practical realities of late twentieth century America it becomes possible to understand the pragmatic responses of Americans of all creeds and colours from a new, chronologically extended perspective. From this vantage, the specific distinctions which emerge in response to Black Power enable the repositioning of the movement within historical discourse in a manner which presents it as a phenomenon thoroughly integrated with the broad span of American history.

CHAPTER 3

A NATION OF MILITANTS?

As a result of its long evolution, the myriad definitions of Black Power were given myriad applications linked to the circumstances of their growth on the American streets. To connect with the people, the concept of Black Power and its attendant ethos of militancy and self-definition had to be communicated via practical programmes undertaken in a diverse variety of social contexts, many initially resistant to outside intrusion, particularly from this menacing band of hotheads, demagogues and subversives. Yet, this seemingly daunting endeavour was essential to both the movement's political survival and to its subsequent cultural legacy. If practical plans were not implemented, decades spent distilling the ethos of Black Power from a militant heritage would have proven worthless.[1] A group's strategy for obtaining power was dictated as much by its temporal and spatial role within the community as by its political ethos. In relating to their community and reaching outwards from it, the cultural sphere in which militant activists chose to ground their campaigns and the attendant problems of its inhabitants were profoundly influential.

To understand the relationship between Black Power and the American people, it is essential to consider the manner in which these diverse cultural-political community units interacted, where militancy flourished in American society and how it marshalled and defined its forces. Providing an exhaustive list of the points of cultural expression which sustained militant sentiment is a gargantuan task, but a coherent picture can be constructed by examining the American scene via the most basic questions which had greeted the political movement's emergence. Who were these people? What did they want? And why did they want it?

Every Black Power group, to varying degrees, exhibited a profound interplay between cultural communication and political agitation. The long history of Black Power shaped which forms of ideology their beliefs rested upon, conditioned the manner in which they sought to express those beliefs and provided opportunities for them to adapt, reconstruct and alter their identities in accordance with the world they wanted to see. During the late 1960s to mid-1970s period traditionally seen as the zenith of cultural militancy in the United States, militant sentiment multiplied through a plethora of organisations; on American campuses, both black and white, on its playing fields and in its stadiums, and in its total institutions, behind bars and under fire.

So intimidating was the leviathan web which emerged from this multitude of organisations that historians have often found it more than a little challenging to perceive the precise structure of the Black Power movement within its sprawling history.[2] This historiographical concern was mirrored among contemporaries of the militant movement. In November 1967, *Esquire* magazine published an article entitled 'The Black Power Establishment' which aspired to show 'Who's who in the powerhouse'.[3] Compiled by the African-American journalist William Worthy, the article bore the caveat that it was 'a chart guaranteed to be out-of-date in six months'.[4] From an historical perspective the chart is illuminating, being organised not chronologically, but according to perceived degrees of militancy. Divided into five degrees of activism, *Esquire's* chart significantly organised itself along colour lines noting that, 'Black, at the top, is the most militant; white, at the bottom, the most moderate.'[5] Three intermediate gradients existed and their content distils the historical perspectives held by many late 1960s militants. In the dark brown section Worthy placed 'politically important supporters of Black Power and anti-colonial struggles'.[6] However, he was at pains to note that he preferred to focus on those who expressed the 'concern that guns and phobias rather than ideas and self-confidence might dominate'.[7]

For the obviously sympathetic Worthy, as for many militant activists, and contrary to the bulk of media images, the revolution of the mind preceded that of the gun. Thus in the dark brown section lay Langston Hughes, hailed as 'the Tolstoy of the black revolution'.[8] According to

Worthy, Hughes's sole failing was that, 'Unlike LeRoi Jones, he was a never a poet of the barricades.'[9] Below Hughes lay the tan band, home to the 'old-line fighters ... and black bourgeoisie'.[10] Worthy's assessment here speaks volumes, describing the tan members as 'torn between secret satisfaction with Stokely Carmichael and their mortgages'.[11] The choice of Carmichael as Black Power's iconic pole again reflects the man's quasi-mythic status and cultural impact, but more intriguing still is the remainder of Worthy's complex chart. Completing the colour gradation were those in the off-white band, whom Worthy termed 'moderates and responsibles'.[12] Sub-divided into categories ranging from 'Negro Dropouts' to 'Their Bark is Blacker Than Their Bite' this section epitomised Worthy's thematic approach to categorising Black Power.[13] Herein could be viewed Martin Luther King's climb from off-white (1965 and Selma) to deep black (speaking in 1967 on Vietnam). Worthy's striated attempts to chart personal transformation were undeniably intriguing, but the shifting colours of his chart only begin to examine the reasons behind these changes in politics, polemic and perspective.

Worthy was clearly aware of Black Power's long history, or at least that charted by its iconic figureheads. Paul Laurence Dunbar occupied the blackest section of the 'Black Humour' column, while W.E.B. Du Bois sat next to Robert Williams, Stokely Carmichael and H. Rap Brown in 'Champions of Self-Defense'.[14] '(Dead but not forgotten)' heralded a continuity from Spartacus, through Toussaint L'Ouverture, John Brown, Nat Turner and Denmark Vesey, taking in Harriet Tubman, Sojourner Truth and Marcus Garvey, before terminating with Malcolm X and Medgar Evers.[15] Meanwhile, the 'Required Reading' section traced a similarly notable trajectory, placing Herbert Aptheker's *American Negro Slave Revolts*, David Walker's *Appeal* and Du Bois's *Souls of Black Folk* at the top of the list.[16]

The connected cultural expressions which undergirded the movement were implicit here, but were made explicit when Worthy dedicated a substantial, completely black section of his chart to 'The Cultural Revolution' accurately noting: '(It preceded the action on the streets).'[17] Here lies an essential concept behind the militant explosion. The revolution of the mind always preceded that of the gun. Cultural and personal change was a necessary catalyst for political change and not merely its resultant product. Throughout Worthy's article, the chart is peppered with pictures of badges regularly worn by activists occupying a particular section. Not merely adornments, buttons and badges communicated the militant message at street level via a highly graphic medium, when other more traditional avenues of communication were colonised by the white media. As Worthy commented, 'buttons have become a means of communicating in the face of *de facto* censorship'.[18] Distilled visual messages of empowerment sold at street level, requiring little education to interpret; their presence was indicative of the way that grassroots cultural developments affected national media and politics.

The chart itself made an undignified entry to the debate. A clumsy, sensationalist *Boston Globe* advert inverted Worthy's arguments completely. In stentorian tones, the advert trumpeted warnings of 'Growing Dangers In the Black Power Movement', ranging from 'subversion by Communist-backed reactionaries' to a 'definite Black Power link with North Vietnam', ending in an 'international non-white pact – the hottest new powder keg of all.'[19] In Worthy's view a culturally sedated public, black and white, were only now realising the full implications of their political and social situation. Yet, as he ruefully recollected in a later column, appropriately titled, 'Aftermath', trying to report on the political and cultural shifts in African-America was a forgone conclusion 'it was like wartime: nobody wanted to hear it.'[20] Yet ignoring the sound of matches being struck only made the detonation seem that much more startling. The resulting explosion in militant African-American organisations was an attempt to redress a long overdue balance, nowhere more dramatically evidenced than on the university campus.

Renowned cultural historian Sterling Stuckey wrote in 1971 that 'Black people have met with as great injustices from American scholarship as they have from American life ... colleges and universities have long paved the way for confusion and ignorance, arrogance and presumptuousness, violence and bloodshed in black-white relations.'[21] The dissident presence of African-Americans in education had been evident far earlier than Seale and Newton selling copies of Mao Tse-Tung's *Little Red Book* in Sproul Plaza, where Mario Savio took his first, shoeless steps towards Free Speech.

Historically, the American educational system often acted as a crucible for the volatile blending of cultural expression and militant protest. Initially, lack of education had been considered the chief impediment to empowerment. A corollary to this was the notion that African-America would be empowered not by mass action, but by a select few chosen, educated apostles – 'The Talented Tenth'. As W.E.B. Du Bois, who coined the phrase, remarked in September 1903, 'The negro race ... is going to be saved by its exceptional men.'[22] To prove his point, Du Bois drew on Black Power's long history to construct a litany of exemplary African-Americans who had 'passed into forgetfulness'.[23] Yet for Du Bois, the vast majority of these early exemplars were 'voice[s] crying in the Wilderness'.[24] What sustained these doughty mental pioneers? The answer, according to Du Bois, lay in 'their own hard experiences and well wrought culture'.[25] If historians subscribe to Du Bois's view, their triumph was particularly impressive 'Because for three long centuries this people lynched Negroes who dared to be brave, raped black women who dared to be virtuous, crushed dark-hued youth who dared to be ambitious, and encouraged ... servility and lewdness and apathy.'[26]

However, the impact of Du Bois's views for conceptions of African-American agency and educational aspiration are profoundly limiting. Du Bois questioned his readers: 'Was there ever a nation ... civilised from the bottom upward? Never; it is, ever was and ever will be from the top downward that culture filters. The Talented Tenth rises and pulls all that are worth the saving up to their vantage ground.'[27] This view removes from history the broader spectrum of students, academics and their families who sustained militant protest within the grounds of the American academies. When considering the place of campus protest within Black Power's cultural legacy, historians should note the paradigm shift from the notion of elite saviours to the idolising of mass action it occasioned.

Du Bois rightly observed that the University was a unique agent of cultural transmission, 'a human invention for the transmission of knowledge and culture from generation to generation ... and for this work no other ... will suffice'.[28] Key to the impact of the universities were their students, who carried forth newly acquired cultural modes and knowledge into the community. Du Bois himself noted, 'the college-bred Negro ... is ... the group leader, the man who sets the ideals of the community ... directs its thoughts and heads its social movements.'[29]

During the zenith of the Black Power movement, this cultural conveyance was not the measured, steady process Du Bois had envisaged, but was rather manifested in a series of explosive demonstrations which swept the nation's campuses. Regardless of the efficacy of its individual goals, or the responses of specific administrations, campus protest was a way of creating new cultural frameworks for personal identity construction and interpretation. Conversely, however, these emergent clubs, groups and movements of idealistic, energetic and impatient young people presented a fertile hunting-ground for the ongoing process of media manipulation.

The campus's identity forming role was all the more formative for the clear positions held by either side. Most obviously, student protestors presented a clear, and often inflexible range of demands, backed up by militant action. Even a small sampling of the multitude of protests that convulsed the campuses of America shows this evolution, and its attendant establishment response. During the 1968 and 1969 protest at San Francisco State College which centred upon 'non-negotiable' demands by the African-American Black Student Union (BSU) for the creation of a black studies faculty and open admission, students not only boycotted classes and picketed campus buildings, but undertook a sustained campaign of sabotage, demolition and arson, culminating in a major clash with the San Francisco Police Department.[30] Whether physically or academically, it seems likely that this particular generation felt increasingly confident in codifying and defending their terms of engagement.

The San Francisco strike, like many across the period, garnered a mixed response which did not always fall neatly within the expected racial lines. One young African-American student commented when asked if he agreed with the BSU's demands: 'Some of them aren't logical, like the demand that all black students be let in here whether they're qualified or not.'[31] Conversely, a secretary who had witnessed the vandalisation of her office was moved to remark: 'I can't help but feel that in a sense the white man is asking for it. Four hundred years of subtle slavery does weird things to people. I don't like violence ... but the black Americans are reacting. Most of their demands are right.'[32]

San Francisco State was not an isolated occurrence. Over two thousand miles to the north-east, at Wisconsin State University-Oshkosh, students strode into the office of president Roger Guiles and presented a list of demands encompassing equality in housing, financial aid and curriculum provision. Faced with stonewalling from Guiles, the students quickly realised a different approach was needed. Simply making the administration aware of their grievances was not sufficient: the students had to engage with the reality that enthusiasm and conviction seldom translate into results in the face of racism, expediency or simple economics. As sophomore Sandra McCreary noted, 'We were going to have to face the consequences of having made the decision ... to get an education in a little white town in 1968 that did not want us and wasn't ready for us.'[33]

In Oshkosh, a sustained protest campaign followed apparent administrative intransigence. Ultimately, 94 of the 114 African-American students on campus were expelled. Many of these students did not enter the protest expecting it to progress far, but in the process of the demonstration, catalysed by administrative indifference and persecution from portions of the white student body, they underwent the revolution of the mind advocated by Carmichael.[34] Freshmen Milton Mitchell recalled the palpable shift in consciousness: 'When we came in with our list of demands and they were not listened to, we were walking out. And someone in the crowd said, "no, we're not leaving till these demands are addressed".'[35] Another expelled student, Henry Brown, recollected: 'We said wait a minute, we better go back, and then the idea hit us, we're in Oshkosh, and we just crossed the line.'[36]

Crossing the line, whether physically or conceptually, required confidence, persistence and personal resilience, and it is these transitions, these individual decisions to articulate dissent, regardless of the success of that articulation, that show the increasing presence of militant sentiment in campus protest and the manner in which it shaped the identities of many protestors. Recalling the events of Oshkosh on their fortieth anniversary in 2008, McCreary described them as 'an insurrection and revolt' which had profoundly affected the way she thought.[37] Part of the importance of student campus demonstrations lay in the way they exposed long simmering racial prejudice, and in so doing, instigated a change in the way African-Americans not only perceived themselves, but the wider American society surrounding them. As McCreary recalled, 'Every unaddressed insult, every sidelong glance, every bottle hurled at us ... every scream in the night, everything we had experienced and kept quiet about – it was all out there.'[38]

The historical context of these protests is significant. The febrile days of 1968 found America mired in an exhausting foreign war and reeling from the assassinations of the Kennedys and Martin Luther King Jr. The milieu in which the campus rebellions of the late 1960s occurred was possibly the most emotionally turbulent yet seen by a battered black populace. As Tom Jones, founder of Cornell University's Afro-American Society (AAS), recalled:

> ... there were riots in major cities throughout the country. There was a division within the Black community of whether to pursue the kind of non-violent system ... that Dr. King represented ... or the more ... militant activism represented by the Black Panthers ... And Malcolm X who talked about armed revolution and self-defense ... The country was in turmoil over resistance to the Vietnam War ... there was a real question if America was going to erupt, socially ... That same historical context was reflected on campus.[39]

Absorbing the atmosphere and arriving in Oshkosh was a vastly increased student body, far beyond expectations. While enrolment had been predicted to reach 5,000 by 1970, in reality it soared from 2,048 in 1959 to nearly 11,000 by 1968.[40] This massive expansion, mirrored in other American universities, instigated two significant developments within the University administration: a drive to recruit African-American students and a subsequent failure to provide all the facilities and personnel required for their equal education. As John Schuh, an assistant head resident at Fletcher in 1968, commented, it was impossible to 'find anywhere in the institutional leadership of that time ... any people of colour ... anyone who would've had an alternative point of view'.[41] Schuh's remarks are pertinent. To an extent, the clashes on campus were so intense because the cultural divide spanned not only race, but generation. Administrators often simply closed ranks in the face of sweeping, impractical demands, which only exacerbated the sense of division. The drive for immediate change created by the Black Power movement meant, 'Young people wanted things to happen a lot faster'.[42]

Perhaps what truly angered students was not simply the pace of change, but the disparate rate of change across the educational system.

As McCreary recalled, many students 'had come from high schools where, for the first time, there was a black student union, was the expression of "black pride", and when they stepped off the train into Oshkosh, they stepped back in time'.[43] Change, whether instigated by the established civil rights movement, or the long militant history of Black Power, did not sweep America in an all-consuming wave. The dynamics of local politics, alongside economic and most importantly cultural norms, could speed or slow the pace of militant empowerment dramatically.

In the case of Oshkosh, the gulf of generational alienation between the administration and the students was arguably as significant as racial differences, with the two factors compounding and exacerbating each other. The Oshkosh protest was an amalgamation of myriad converging concerns, from incidents of racism, through lack of financial aid and a shortage of housing. Yet intellectual deprivation remained a key issue, manifesting in a lack of literature and classes representative of the black cultural experience. Students rebelling against the educational system were not simply seeking programme reform, but taking the last action left to an ostracised group marooned in what seemed culturally 'hostile territory'.[44] The Oshkosh rebellion ended in severe repression, with so many students arrested that the excess were taken to jail in rented trucks.[45] As McCreary recalled, 'it was just like seeing our dreams go up in smoke'.[46] Yet the smoke rising from Oshkosh was soon joined by other fires of student rebellion which cast a pall over the nation.

Across the continent at Cornell University, the sight of a flaming cross on the lawn of the African-American Wari House cooperative for female students on 18 April 1969 signalled an especially militant episode in the war for the campus. The next morning, members of the university's Afro-American Society occupied Willard Straight Hall, setting in motion events which were to instigate decades of social and cultural change.[47] A few hours later, a number of white students from the Delta Upsilon fraternity invaded the Straight and clashed with AAS members before being summarily repulsed. Fearing further violence, the black students took the next step toward militant resistance and brought guns into 'the Straight'. That evening, members of Students for a Democratic Society (SDS) encircled the building to lend support to the AAS protestors. Shortly thereafter, ten thousand white students took over Barton Hall in a gesture of interracial solidarity, which took some AAS members by surprise. As Jones, chief spokesman for the AAS noted, 'White students who could have said, "This isn't my fight"... [instead] said, "This is our fight too and we are not going to let the black students be isolated".'[48] Once again, campus divisions took greater heed of generational, rather than racial lines.

The drama of the SDS gesture, coupled with the scale and speed of the protest, was a cultural shock to many white observers. George Taber, a junior police officer stationed on campus, recalled that the event felt like 'a whirlwind. One thing after another ... I had no idea what was going on'.[49] Within hours, police deputies had swarmed through New York State and assembled in downtown Ithaca. The potential for violence was immense, but crucially, the Cornell occupation remained both armed and peaceful. As Taber commented, 'It could have made Kent State and Jackson State look like the teddy bears' picnic.'[50]

On Sunday 20 April, after hours of heated consultation, the AAS students emerged from the hall, rifles held loosely and bandoliers slung across their bodies. The subsequent Pulitzer Prize winning photo, snapped by Associated Press (AP) photographer Steve Starr, took the cover of *Newsweek*, fronting the incendiary article, 'Universities Under the Gun.'[51] Like many militant protests of the era, the Straight Takeover was defined by the presence of firearms and the AP photograph, provocatively titled 'Guns on Campus,' focused public attention exclusively on the terror aroused by the arrival of guns on a college campus.[52] In Starr's image, everything is subordinate to the iconography of the gun. While the two protesters flanking AAS member Eric Evans hold their guns in a relaxed, confident posture, the camera dwells on Evans and his upraised weapon. Seemingly deliberately, Starr ensures an armed student, instead of a welcome banner, takes centre stage, in the process excluding a great deal of context from the image.[53] Crucially, Starr's photo also removed the effect of movement. As one commentator noted, 'Amidst a field of chaos, Evans wasn't running, screaming or holding up his fist; instead, he simply walked, heavily and calmly with militant stiffness, holding his chin and rifle high with a chilling grace.'[54]

Uncritical commentary on Evan's protest represented a greater focus on obsession with the gun. In much commentary on protests of the era, both on and off campus, Panthers were almost always 'gun-toting', little more than ambulatory 'black uniforms ... lugging pistols, rifles and shotguns around in public'.[55] Above all guns came to shape what media scholar Jane Rhodes defined as the 'fear frame' – offering stark and profitable contrast with the previous non-violent movement.[56] As Rhodes explained, 'The visual field is not a blank slate but is itself a racial formation. These photographic representations enabled a racialised and politicised reading of the Panthers that merged the coon figures of minstrelsy origins ... with the black brute and the civil rights demonstrator.'[57]

Even now, in the 40th anniversary coverage of the protest, fetishisation of the gun and the media's obsession with the potential for violence remains paramount. Writing for the *Cornell Sun* on 16 April 2009, columnist Lucy Li lingered heavily on classic tropes of the gun obsession, commenting of Evans:

> A dark strap of bullets capable of massacre slashes across the contrasting whiteness of his clothing. Even though his facial expressions are intelligible ... behind the glare of his glasses, his presence and what he represented were powerful and terrifying ... the disturbing ease with which a deadly bullet strap wraps over a benign schoolboy sweater, the militant appearance of an Ivy League gentleman in a bullet vest instead of a bullet-proof vest, and the reality that armed violence had permeated from inner cities and the jungles of Vietnam to picturesque college campuses ... saturated the image with fear and shock.[58]

'Saturated ... with fear', is an apt phrase to describe the predominantly white cultural perceptions articulated in contemporary coverage of campus protest and this saturation lingers in both modern media and modern scholarship. A concerning majority of the recent commemorations on the fortieth anniversary of 1968, and the succession of smaller exercises in public memory in subsequent years, exist primarily in a conflicted knot of nostalgia, iconography and uncritical commentary.[59]

If analysing Black Power in its present moment was a problematic challenge, then memorialising and analysing its legacy offers an even more thorny challenge. Capturing the qualia of the movement and conveying it within and to any particular generation represents a significant challenge. The contemporary media's attempts to do so were themselves cultural products indicative of immediate and long-seated anxieties alike.

The end result of this obscuring cultural tangle is to elide the complexity inherent in militant protest, of which Cornell is a key example. Marilynne Starr recalled of her husband, 'For Steve, [the photograph] was not about black Americans wanting equal treatment as much as a photo that told in shorthand the lengths students would go to get the attention of the administration.'[60] Starr himself summarised the narrow approach taken by the AP when he remarked, 'we believed Cornell was an exploding story from '68 [that foreshadowed] a steady progression of increasing violence. [This] is why we jumped on the story so hard'.[61] Starr's comments should be cautionary. Too often absent from commentary, both modern and historical, are the motive factors behind protests such as the occupation of Willard Straight. In looking so closely at African-American hands clutching the gun, historians have occasionally lost sight of the reasons why African-America felt obliged to raise it in the first place.

Coverage of events like Cornell tends toward the predominantly negative. Readers are often reminded that, a year later, those iconic guns appeared again on the Kent State campus and of the subsequent loss of life. Alternatively, the media often adopts the theme of the 'deep psychological scars burned into the minds of many'.[62] The current of cultural memory carries us back to the gates of Elkins's concentration camp and we are obliged to sit without reprieve through another parade of traumatised African-America, with no thought for the protesters' agency, no mention of the empowering aspects of protest, or the revolution of the mind required to take steps toward confronting the system.

Four decades later, the importance of events like Cornell risks being lost through oversimplification. Recently it has been argued that, far from being a catalyst for dramatic social change, the Cornell occupation was merely a violent occurrence on a campus where institutional change was already underway.[63] However, it is possible to acknowledge the steps taken by the administration and the constraints on faculty, while simultaneously realising that the protest itself was symptomatic of a wider generational awakening, a group process of identity construction which would leave a clearer legacy than individual campus reforms. For many in this generation, it seemed that change was best effected at the points where identity transformation and educational reform intersected, a sentiment which would animate and inspire the growth of the black studies movement.

Cornell provided ample evidence of the developing gulf between the dramatic change demanded by militant African-Americans seeking greater attention to black studies and the limited ability of the established system to address their concerns, whether through intransigence, opposition or simple pragmatic limitations. The increasing drive toward black studies was spurred by the growing understanding held by African-Americans of how much their own history and input had been expunged from conventional narratives. Here lay the root of the clarion call for a fundamental reform of the American higher education system. To protest against the state of society was one thing, but to be removed from the history of that same society seemed deeply offensive to militants increasingly aware of Black Power's long history. Jones, as well-informed as any, recalled: 'None of the curriculum said anything at all ... about our history or the fight for freedom that we had undertaken in terms of slave rebellions ... We were simply saying that the full story needs to be told.'[64]

Jones clearly felt the Willard Straight invasion was a significant chapter in that story, and in the broader narrative of empowerment. For Jones, part of the triumph of Cornell lay in the 'dose of pizen' it administered to the American public via the watchful lenses of the media. As he reflected, he had hoped that 'The symbolism ... the cumulative impact of these events ... would ... shock America and say that we were going to become a different kind of country ... for people to see what looked like the specter of armed revolution.'[65] With rather typical youthful confidence, Jones confidently declaimed, 'because you know it's never the peasants that lead a revolution, it's always the intelligentsia.'[66]

Strongly echoing Du Bois's belief in the power of the educated minority, it is unsurprising that for Jones the Black Power movement's legacy was never in doubt. As he proudly declared, 'The takeover was one of the events that made that chain of history that led directly to Barack Obama being elected.'[67] While the veracity of Jones's statement is debatable, the confidence with which he articulates his perception of the militant legacy is undeniable.

In the present, over four decades from the political zenith of Black Power and removed from the thunderous events of the late 1960s, we can both acknowledge that the opinions of the militant protesters have changed over time and appreciate how hindsight lends greater credence to an increasingly complex view of the cultural legacy of the Black Power movement and its interaction with the utopian reconfiguration of black academia. This emergent perspective needs to give due weight to the contributions of not only African-Americans, but also of their opposition, in the administrations and frat houses of the American campuses.

In retrospect, Cornell appears an entangled battleground, with lines being drawn between generations and between white and black. Yet white America, as demonstrated through the actions of SDS, was far from homogenous in its reaction to militant protest, the spectre of armed revolution and the shadow of the gun. If protesters' perspectives of themselves have changed, historiographical perspective must evolve accordingly. Steps must be taken to remove the iconography of violence from its position of dominance and place it into context. By stepping out from the long shadow of the gun, it becomes possible to see the militancy of the Black Power movement in a new light, gaining a richer understanding of the movement's cultural legacy and its development across temporal, racial and generational lines.

As David Hilliard trenchantly noted in 2008, 'The revolution ... was never about the guns'.[68] Behind the smoke and noise of protests like Cornell and Oshkosh, another revolution was taking place, perhaps less photogenic, but no less militant for its silence. The drama and iconography of these events appeared to lend credence to the sentiment behind the graffiti outside Finley Hall on the City College of New York's Campus: 'HONKIES: ATTENTION/YOUR TIME HAS COME.'[69] Yet more revealing was an exchange of graffiti at Northwestern which began 'BLACK IS BEAUTIFUL' occasioning the response 'WHITE AIN'T SO BAD' to which the reply was 'BLACK IS *STILL* BEAUTIFUL'.[70]

The revolution on campus was as much a matter of perception as politics; perception shaped by cultural forces and historical inheritance. As Lerone Bennett noted, 'A black cultural revolution is convulsing the campuses of America [which] ... pits students against administrators, the young against the old, "Negroes" against "Blacks," and "Negroes" and "Blacks" against whites. From one end of the country to the other, the revolution rages.'[71] As senior editor of *Ebony*, Bennett was ideally placed to watch events unfold and was certain as to the motive force behind campus rebellion, remarking: 'This is a new kind of war – a war for the mind. But for all that, it is a real war with real battles and real casualties.'[72]

For Bennett, the campus revolution was a 'remarkable cultural cataclysm' powered by a narrow span of enterprises, 'Afro-American student unions on white campuses and Black Power-oriented student organizations on black campuses'.[73] However, the political existence and practical actions of these groups was not their sole relevant factor. As Bennett noted, 'On one level ... students are demanding a relevant black education with in-depth studies of Afro-American history and culture ... on another level, they are engaged in a painful and necessary labor of self-discovery, self-legitimization and self-definition ... both levels ... make a deeper thrust against ... racist society and the racist education institutions which perpetuate that society.'[74]

African-American militant protest evolved alongside the wider student protest culture, inheriting its techniques and refining its methods. Protest thus was a cultural endeavour. First, because it necessitated adopting an iconoclastic approach to traditional values, coupled with a resilience to the previously assumed authority of institutional elites. Alongside this, campus protest mandated the creation of both an individual and a collective identity that complemented and informed the young activists' developing social and political beliefs. Many of the elements of this identity were naturally drawn from previous examples of struggle and expression. The result was a highly motivated, culturally and historically aware group with an influence upon and activity within the sphere of academic protest beyond its actual numerical presence.

According to one study, despite the fact that African-American students formed only 6 per cent of the nation's college enrolment, of the 292 college protests recorded in 1969, the major issue in 49 per cent of them was 'black recognition', in contrast to prevailing popular assumptions that the bones of contention remained Vietnam and the draft (which accounted for 2.0 and 0.3 per cent of perceived major issues, respectively).[75] A 1969 Urban Research Corporation study conducted across 232 campuses found that while 60 per cent of all protest petitions were denied, African-American demands were acquiesced to twice as often as those of white protesters and that African-American protest often exhibited a different tenor and independence.[76] African-Americans organised and led over three-quarters of all protests on racial issues, and of these, 76 per cent 'resulted in no violence or destruction' albeit, as one *Jet* journalist noted, 'despite the impression left by pictures and accounts ... at Cornell'.[77]

If African-American students of the late 1960s generation truly possessed a power to affect the academic establishment disproportionate to their numbers, it raises questions as to what made a conventionally restrained group place both their careers and their convictions on the line. Earlier precedents in the 1964 Free Speech movement and the subsequent Vietnam protests do not adequately explain the differing goals sought by young African-American scholars. Rather it seems far more likely that rebellion in America's urban heart was the chief spark which catalysed divergence and proliferation in African-American student protest. The summer of violence which raged across the northern ghettos had stimulated national debate on the omnipresence of discrimination and the endemic racism in American institutions. A 1967 proposal noted: 'Black high school students are more and more conscious of themselves as black people, chiefly because of the racial unrest of recent years.'[78] As a new generation of African-Americans entered American higher education, observers such as historian and journalist Ernest Dunbar claimed they brought the political perspective and culture of the streets into the classroom, 'tracking Watts and Newark into the fastidious halls of many of the nation's most hallowed institutions of higher learning'.[79]

Travel was no longer necessary to articulate discontent. In this new militant protest schema, addressing discrimination in the immediate environment usually took top priority. Between 1967 and 1968, over 90 per cent of sit-ins instigated by African-American students occurred on campus.[80] The majority of these demonstrations focused on the premise that 'for a black student the typical liberal education ... is a destructive one'.[81] Existing in a system ill-designed to accommodate or empower them, African-American students remained restricted by the nature of their curriculum. As one commentator observed, 'There is no such thing as an integrated institution when the educational process is geared toward one group of students.'[82]

As an extension of this fundamental critique, the nation's major universities were often accused of seeking to diffuse tensions by courting non-white students, creating, so one proposal committee claimed, 'a segregated institution with black pupils to give the college liberal visibility'.[83] It was alleged that the established administration hoped to maintain its intellectual hegemony by luring increased numbers of inner city African-Americans to white campuses, tacitly encouraging familiarity with, and acquiescence to, the dominant socio-cultural paradigm. The practical logic underlying this belief argued that an expanded African-American middle-class would be invested in social stability and would accordingly act as a palliative force on the concerns of disillusioned urbanites.[84]

Attempts at reform by the administration, it was argued, were not only misguided, but harmful. As a San Francisco State Black Institute proposal commented, 'Even the most liberal reforms on this campus are at least irrelevant and at most destructive to black students.'[85] The proposal urged readers to consider the hypocrisy in forcing African-American students to endure lectures on capitalism and the 'American Way' before returning 'home ... to face [the] rats, cockroaches, and cops of the real America'.[86] Why, it was asked, should African-Americans exposed to liberal professors haranguing the stagnation of white America and the Vietnam War be criticised when they expressed no wish to 'become integrated into such a decadent society'?[87]

Regardless of the truth of such allegations, the militancy of the new college generation made assimilation seem hopelessly unattainable. The demands of African-America's youth culture were energetic, optimistic and uncompromising. Aggregate visions of African-American empowerment ran the gamut from unqualified admission for minority group applicants to mandatory sensitivity training for white sorority and fraternity officers, from the hiring of black physicians to an increased variety of African-American oriented products in student union shops.[88] Primarily however, African-American students demanded the ability to control their educational experience. Quite literally, knowledge *was* power and the campuses of America were, as Van Deburg explained, 'academic jousting fields upon which key social power relations were decided'.[89]

To lose the battle over the campus, campaigners believed, was to lose control over the future of African-America and to cede the transmission of cultural, social and political values to a dominant power group which had an historically proven record of the most profound abuse. Heeding Malcolm X's injunction that 'Education ... is the means to help our children and our people rediscover their identity ... our passport to the future', Black Studies advocates warned of a future generation 'so dulled, stunted, and humiliated by this fascist liberal education that they ... succumb to the vacuous, secular religions of western civilization'.[90] Education by extension would be at best an end unto itself, at worst a means of cultural suppression, rather than a tool to reshape the American social landscape.[91]

Why then should a prospective militant risk submersion in the culturally oppressive atmosphere of the white campus? John Killens argued, 'the "militant" student should be the best student on campus' but warned prospective enrolees: 'much of what you learn will not be relevant to your black thing. Learn it anyhow. Learn everything ... in order to beat Charlie's game you've got to know his system.'[92]

Study at a predominantly white university, by its nature, bequeathed a better understanding of the workings of the ivory tower to any participating African-Americans. It was argued that this understanding could then be used to seek chinks in its institutional and administrative armour, which would aid the wider drive for African-American empowerment.[93] For student protesters of the late 1960s, education and empowerment were, inevitably intrinsically linked. For these young men and women, the existing university may have been both a soulless machine and a corporate shill, but, with one eye on Du Bois they argued that a reformed university would lead to a reformed America. However, as S.E. Anderson warned in a 1967 *Negro Digest* article, African-American students needed to adjust their perceptions and paradigm in a profound manner to effect this educational reform: 'The Afro-American student must THINK ... to be black is not enough. And to be bitter is not enough. To know of our magnificent black heritage is still not enough. We must become dedicated militant human beings constantly questioning the roots of society.'[94]

For Anderson, key to bringing a 'black' cultural perception into one's life was a pragmatic acknowledgement of the potential need for violence in response to America's historical predilection for force as a solution. As shown in the AP photos of the Cornell protest, America was culturally encouraged to dwell upon violence and the gun. As Anderson explained, 'America has instituted violence to the extent that it is strategically generated by and *through* its culture.'[95] For African-American students to succeed on campus, their perceptions of their place within a culture defined by force had to change and survival would only be assured in numbers. If mainstream American culture was robust and militant, then African-American responses had to be nurtured accordingly.

Across the country, perceptions of the educational system were indeed changing. Ernest Dunbar wryly remarked: 'Time was when the occasional Negro accepted at an Ivy League school felt so happy to squeak in that he worked fanatically to become what he imagined was a proper college gentleman. Today a new breed of black cat is tearing up white campuses, poking holes in some ivy-covered notions about integration.'[96] This new influx of fresh young minds encountered a system which through either choice or inertia obscured their cultural development and stifled empowerment. As one black studies proposal raged, 'What happens to a black high school student, conscious of his world, mentally prepared to struggle to function as a human being? ... Where are the courses dealing with Black psychology, Black history, African history, African languages, Black arts?'[97]

The very framework of the educational establishment appeared discriminatory. A student could find 'courses which analyse racism from every perspective from Marxian [sic] to Conservative but ... none which break down racism from a Black perspective'.[98] The only apparent solution for a struggling young black person was to gather with people who felt the same way, for 'With what or whom can he relate other than other black students who are oppressed by the same sins of omission?'[99] However, as in all walks of life, people did not simply band together because they were angry. The protest groups formed on campus became crucibles for identity formation and reflection on what it meant to be black in America. The formation of militant groups bound by ties of common grievance and shared cultural interests was the inevitable consequence.

Meeting in late 1962, eight African-American undergraduates at Columbia University discussed their experiences on a predominantly white campus. One of the group, Hilton Clark, son of Dr. Kenneth Clark, first African-American president of the American Psychological Association, recollected, 'We felt we were lost, mentally, in a white college. I realise the words "identity crisis", have become a cliché, but we really didn't know who we were and we were trying to become something we could not be.'[100]

Clark argued that the chief problem was that 'The average black sought to ... join some company and be the "corporation's nigger."... While he was at Columbia ... There was Harlem all around him, but not only did he refuse to talk about it or exert any of his energies ... toward solving Harlem's problems, he took the same attitude toward Harlem that many whites have ... "These people are not making it because they are lazy."'[101] Clark's eight person group subsequently expanded to include approximately 32 African-American students attending Columbia who formed the core of Columbia's Students' Afro-American Society (SAS). At approximately the same time as the SAS was being formed, the Association of American and Afro-American Students (AAAS) was founded at Harvard and Radcliffe. Both organisations arose from a prevailing mood of discontent, encapsulated by Dunbar as 'a feeling of isolation, of having to conform to standards and values that held little meaning ... for Negroes, and an awareness of losing something valuable ... as they attempted to fit in. Equally important was a desire somehow to funnel some of their talent into the local black ghetto, even while they were still in school'.[102]

Both Columbia's SAS and Harvard's AAAS were symptomatic of a phenomenon spreading through white colleges in the late 1960s; the emergence of focused African-American clubs and societies or 'Afro groups' which, Dunbar observed, caused 'considerable headscratching among university officials, consternation in some faculties and reaction ranging from apprehension to puzzlement from white students'.[103] The core rationale behind the formation of these groups was a quest for identity and an awareness of the historical poverty of white culture. As a spokesperson for San Francisco State's BSU explained, 'All of us feel that black people should be aware of their own identity ... a lack of identity in the last fifty years among whites have [sic] given rise to despotism all over Europe and America.'[104] Insufficiently attuned to the revolution of the mind occurring on campus, and – according to African-American militants – historically suffering from a deleterious lack of identity, the white administration's confusion was often palpable. However, it is deceptively easy to see the bewilderment engendered by the emergence of these groups as representing clear divisions between white and black, student and faculty, which were not always so stark in actuality. As early as December 1966 a regional conference of Afrogroups held at Columbia boasted three hundred delegates from 30 Northeastern schools. The majority of students in attendance had been financed by their schools' administrators in response to a plea by the conference's organisers.[105] The campus may have been a battleground, but the divisions between the sides were seldom as clear-cut as either militant rhetoric or media portrayals suggested.

The 1966 Conference was representative of the challenge posed to university administrations by the revolution of the mind occurring on campus. Many activists believed that 'White liberal professors and administrators have a long history of paying lip service to understanding ... a growing black consciousness.'[106] This was, at best, a reductionist perspective. Beneath this common assertion lay the unspoken issue that the process of self-definition was confusing for observers and participants alike. As Clark explained, 'The administration had a hard time forming an attitude toward our group because they didn't know what the group was going to do. Hell, *we* didn't even know!'[107] Several white observers proved more perspicacious than Clark's opinion, or the historiographical record, might suggest. As Columbia's Vice-President David B. Truman explained:

> These students do not, on the whole, act from a policy of deliberate separatism. They want to associate together because they wish to avoid being lost in the white majority, to which they do not want to be compelled to assimilate totally, and partly because they do not wish to dissociate themselves from the Negro community outside the University. These are reasonable and understandable purposes.[108]

If tensions between the administration and the students were considerably more complex than often presented, were the racial lines within the student body a more significant divisive factor? One Negro sophomore remarked: 'When you start talking about "my black brothers," these white cats can't relate.'[109] Afrogroups were often constitutionally and linguistically exclusive, prohibiting white students from membership, but this was primarily a consequence of their founding rationale and the militant goals they held sacred. Many of these groups sought to redress the elimination of the long history of

African-America from the historical record. White students, it was argued, could never fully engage with this quest due to their differing cultural background. As Francille Rusan, an officer of Wellesley College's Ethos (a campus organisation for African-American women) explained, black students' priorities were profoundly different: 'There are a lot of white girls here ... whose families have money. Their very expectations about life are quite different from ours. Being a Negro is sometimes incidental, but at other times, it's fundamental, and we wanted to explore the fundamental aspect.'[110]

Ethos was the product of an energetic taxi-cab conversation between five African-American Wellesley College students returning from the Columbia University conference in December 1966, and exemplifies the goals and militancy of many contemporary groups and the difficulties faced by African-American students on a white campus. The very name of the group emphasised its belief in the centrality of culture to empowerment and in aiding resistance to assimilation. Having 'realized that there were no existing organizations ... that adequately represented the needs and obligations of the Black student on a white campus[,] Ethos[,] ... defined as "the pervasive characteristic that distinguishes a group of culture" was formed'.[111] Like many of its sibling organisations, Ethos was optimistic, confident and militant, reiterating the awareness of Black Power's long history and its close connection to the community consistently evidenced throughout cultural militant discourse. As the organisation's *Newsletter* noted, 'Our objectives are manifold: to serve as a common and effective voice on matters that concern Black students on and off campus; to establish and maintain a meaningful relationship with the Black Community; to study our own history and traditions and to prepare ourselves, as Black women, to approach the challenges of a crucial era.'[112] Tired of a college where black students seemed like nothing more than an opportunity to fathom 'the secret workings of a black chick's mind', Ethos members put forward a programme of recommendations to introduce black administrators, professors and student recruiters, while placing Afro-American history on the school's curricula. When they were initially rebuffed, a blunt threat of a hunger strike in front of major press outlets led the administration to capitulate with surprising speed.[113]

The assertive tone forwarded by culturally militant groups such as Ethos was a consequence of a growing militancy amongst

African-American students who increasingly saw education as a tool for community improvement as opposed to 'a passport out of the more oppressive regions of race'.[114] These groups represented a shifting cultural perspective, a realisation of identity and a growing recognition by students of their place in a social and historical context. As Dr. Clark noted, 'They are saying ... the privilege of going to these schools must be paid for with commitment and concern for the greater black community'.[115]

Afrogroups such as AAAS, SAS and Ethos strove to achieve more than simply uniting African-American students on white campuses. Improvement in the available education remit and separation from the white system was the ultimate goal. As San Francisco State's BSU explained, 'black students spend much of their time justifying their blackness to white people ... one of the purposes is to eliminate that process and allow black students to get the best possible education ... to serve the entire community'.[116] The implementation of practical approaches to change was paramount, from seminars on Negro politics held at Harvard's John F. Kennedy institute to a black history course organised by AAAS member Robert Hall at Norfolk state prison, Massachusetts.[117]

Maintaining locally focused protests while gaining closer ties with the ghetto necessitated a delicate balancing act. The demographic shift toward increased African-American enrolment meant an 'infusion of blunt-talking, ghetto-bred youngsters turned up by special university talent searchers'.[118] The arrival of these young men and women not only challenged white collegians on campus, but was a profound culture shock for many African-American students. As Tom Williamson Jr., a well-heeled Harvard senior, noted, 'I don't believe in romanticising the ghetto, but part of the cost of living in the kind of environment I came from is not to have had the broadening experiences of knowing other Negroes ... Soon after I got here, I grew up. I had to revise some of my basic assumptions.'[119]

The revision of assumptions highlighted by Williamson was shorthand for the development of a new, more empowered African-American identity. Assimilation and incorporation were no longer desirable goals. The best strategy for survival within the university environment was to embrace cultural and racial differences. As Williamson recollected, 'There's no end to the contest if you're just a black man trying to excel so thoroughly that people will forget you are black. I began to see that as a fruitless struggle and sought to develop a sense of individuality. Part of that individuality is being a Negro.'[120] Exploring this individuality opened the playing field to a much broader spectrum of young men and women, as identity construction was not directly tied to physical confrontation. Personal empowerment was possible without being militant. A mental revolution could take place without a physical component. In this respect, the campus students had emerged from the shadow of the gun. Williamson held reservations, particularly as he had a white girlfriend. From this perspective the policies of the AAAS seemed 'negative, keyed to exclusiveness', but, like many others, he admitted, 'I don't like the idea of people telling me that black people can't do something by themselves.'[121] Williamson's divided approach highlights the fact that the revolution of the mind was seldom as complete or as simple as its militant advocates wished. However, this does not mean partial or failed revolutions held no significance. Each recognition of a positive aspect of the African-American experience, every step toward a greater acknowledgement of Black Power's long history was changing the cultural vista of not only the campus, but its surrounding communities.

Such progress was hard won. The African-American student population on the white campus was subject to the same cultural tensions affecting America as a whole. The increasing consciousness of history occasioned by the Black Power movement's search for inspirational and structural cultural expressions fed into the changing self-perceptions of these young people, and raised new, speculative avenues of change, resistance and confrontation. Burgeoning militancy amongst students heightened already pronounced racial divisions. Archie Epps III, assistant dean at Harvard and the only African-American in the administration, observed 'An increasing militancy among the Negro students ... they become hostile to white faculty persons and grow more hostile as time goes on. Some faculty ... have ... difficulty communicating with their black students.'[122] Militants argued that this impasse was not always a conscious decision on the part of the white administration, but rather a brute fact of the cultural-historical perspectives created by the American system, reasoning: 'It is not only a sense of awareness which qualifies one to understand and deal effectively with the lives of black students. There are ... many whites who are sensitive and aware and deeply concerned.

But there has been a[n] ... enforced separation – of histories of blacks and whites in America ... a result of that separation has been the creation of two separate standards, perspectives and realities.'[123]

Communication across the colour divide was further hampered by perceived exclusivity in African-American cultural expression on campus, exemplified by the creation of a 'Soul Table' in Harvard's dining hall. AAAS president Jeff Howard highlighted the hypocrisy of these accusations when he remarked, 'The cats from Andover eat together, the cats from Exeter eat together, the football types eat together and nobody sees that as exclusiveness. When we eat together, whites somehow feel threatened!'[124]

What white observers perhaps failed to understand was that the cultural revolution occurring on campus fostered a need for African-American students to congregate as part of the identity-forming process. As one campus document explained, 'The fundamental realities which all black people have in common (though they may differ in standards and perspectives) ... draw black people together ... leaving out ... most others.'[125] Events such as Yale's 'Spook Weekends', gatherings designed to help black undergraduates from different universities meet, party and debate were signal examples of the realigning social strata on campus.[126] Likewise, although exhibiting disparate political beliefs, a niche, but vibrant range of campus periodicals contended that black culture was thriving and, importantly, superior, to that offered by white society.[127] As one student noted with satisfaction '[White students] are talking about the Beatles and we are digging James Brown. They are doing dances Harlem was doing five months ago, and we are doing dances Harlem is doing now.'[128]

Afrogroups, by promoting unity and recognition of cultural positives, acted as a sustaining force, a framework upon which new students could construct an African-American identity and subsequently use that new empowered identity to define the shape they wanted their education to take. Educational reform followed from personal and cultural change. Barbara Butler, a freshman at Northwestern, summarised the process when she commented: 'This group reaffirmed my identity ... my reality as a black person. And now it's like ... my life blood.'[129] By drawing African-American students into unified Afrogroups, campus militants aided the process of self-definition, but also increased delineations between black and white on campus.

As Harry Edwards commented, 'We must have the chance to appreciate our own kind and our own culture ... you can't do this if, every time you turn around you are faced with a room full of "crackers".'[130]

As always, cultural division had political repercussions, notably in increasing divisions between black and white activists on the political Left. Many Afrogroups drew members from organisations like SDS, luring recruits with explicitly Black Power oriented programmes. As San Francisco State's Jimmy Garrett argued, 'SDS has all the Marx and the rhetoric, but hell, I've studied Marx too, so I blow that right back on them! We want *them* to go out and organise *white* people to reform this society; until they've done that, all this talk of theirs is irrelevant!'[131]

More contentious still than the relationship between black and white was that between campus and ghetto. As Dunbar perceptively noted, 'Many well-to-do black Americans run into the same kind of scepticism from slum inhabitants that well-meaning whites encounter ... born of decades of manipulation in the guise of charity ... for the wealthier black Americans ... the trip to the ghetto is a longer voyage than the actual distance on a map'.[132] Despite a number of notable successes, as with the campaign by San Francisco State's BSU to elect the young militant Ron Dellums to city council, the conflict between academic protest and ghetto activism, set to the backdrop of a changing cultural mind-set, placed incredible stresses upon young activists and the administration, even if sometimes well-intentioned, was ill-equipped to support them. As Harvard Dean John Monro noted, 'A Negro kid feels he's here in this sort of frivolous atmosphere while over in Roxbury black people are being oppressed, and his conscience asks him if he shouldn't be over there. But once he gets involved over there, his grades start to fall here ... and he's pulled apart ... who around here does he turn to ... the Negroes on the faculty ... and there aren't many'.[133]

Discontent among students, or 'the Harvard Blues', rose sharply during the late 1960s, particularly amongst students from disadvantaged backgrounds. A growing awareness of Black Power's long history and its elision from campus caused increasing anger which often affected academic performance. Donald R. Hopkins, assistant to Berkeley's executive vice-chancellor noted, 'Our most angry and articulate black students are not doing well. Many see their professors as racists for assigning them to read ... Hemingway and Faulkner instead of Alain

Locke or ... other good Negro authors ... some of our best students have left for this reason'.[134] However, the awareness which led to so much anger amongst young students was also the catalyst for a transformative revolution of the mind. Hopkins, who also served as a student counsellor, remarked in an address to young African-American students:

> Many black people are coming to an awareness of their essential worthiness ... during the freshman and sophomore years. They see the evils and injustices that exist in this society, and want desperately to do something about it. They seek their allies among the young, and you will be sought out. The same powers of critical analysis you develop by studying Greek civilisation will be of critical importance in making an independent analysis of this one ... many young black revolutionaries are turning their back on that critical fact and ... crippling their chances of ever being capable or effective reconstructors.[135]

The message was clear. Students could only build a new society if they had the correct tools, and for that, an education was needed, focused on African-American values, history and culture, but incorporating other aspects of learning.

Calls for a structured programme of black studies on campus often took an holistic approach with a clear cultural focus, as in the 1966 proposal for a combined black youth workshop at San Francisco State which appealed for 'The creation of a programme of black value commitment by combining the resources of our brothers and sisters in the black churches ... and ... in the arts ... to create a programme that operates regularly to bring Black artists in front of Black youth'.[136]

The goals of San Francisco State's BSU were epitomised in a statement by its chairman, Jimmy Garrett. The militant tone of its opening amply demonstrated the students' inheritance from Black Power's long history, and the current charged cultural environment. Garrett argued that the BSU:

> ... has as its purpose to aid in further developing, politically, economically and culturally the revolutionary black consciousness of black people both on and off campus. As black students, as black

people, we are being exploited to the fullest extent in this racist white America and we are therefore preparing ourselves and our people for a prolonged struggle.[137]

San Francisco's BSU emphasised a profound duality in the African-American student experience which combined a desire for closeness with the local community with a growing awareness of the international context of the liberation struggle. The statement claimed: 'We are a third world organisation. We adhere to the struggles in Asia, Africa, and Latin America. Ideologically, spiritually and culturally.'[138] Garrett and the other BSU activists sought to remind the administration and America that many students' aspirations were neither esoteric nor unattainable, that their primary goal was 'simply to function as human beings, to control our own destinies'.[139] The chief obstacles to the realisation of this goal were the cultural perceptions of mainstream America and the predilections inherent in its social mythology. As Garrett explained, 'Following the myth of the American Dream ... we have learned ... it is impossible for black people to function as human beings in a racist society in which black is synonymous with enemy, no matter what the educational attainment.'[140] The solution seemed clear; if the very basic premise of mainstream America was an obstacle, power could only be gained in an alternative paradigm. Accordingly, Garrett and other BSU members declared their intent to 'fuse ourselves with the masses of black people and ... collectively control our own destinies'.[141]

Paramount to framing and informing this new paradigm was an awareness of Black Power's historical legacy, which required development and encouragement via a systematic educational programme. Garrett promoted 'a programme and department of Black Studies ... where black students can come to draw on their own historical references ... which are basically different from those of western civilisation'.[142]

The zenith of this structured approach was demonstrated in the creation of a Black Communications Project (BCP) on the San Francisco campus. Under the aegis of LeRoi Jones, the BCP amalgamated resources from on and off campus 'to produce, black plays, dance, art, films – all created and recreated by black people'.[143] The result was a body of cultural work designed to foster a revolution of the mind and empower its audience. Constructed by the community, it was hoped it would accordingly resonate more deeply with their concerns, the end result being 'Black Art with an ethic and an aesthetic ... drawn from the people ... a means not only to recreate the lives of black people but to guide those lives in a revolutionary direction'.[144]

An evolution from the postbellum Harlem Renaissance perspective of art without agenda, the art produced on campus nonetheless shared a basic commonalty with its predecessors; it was a catalyst for change and a productive force which stemmed from African-America's roots. Garrett explained: 'Black Art is a means by which change is realised – not as an end – because so long as there are black people, Black Art has no end'.[145] The emphasis on continuity and interconnectivity inherent to the campus perception of culture led to closer relations with the local community. In the case of San Francisco's BSU, the establishment of black history and culture discussion groups in Bay Area high schools was a major step in forging direct links between African-American high school and college students.[146] At San Francisco State at least, militant culture proved an invaluable tool in crossing the divide between campus and community.

An increased involvement in community affairs also meant BSU had a platform from which to articulate its anti-war sentiments and to spread the militant message within the community, initially on a local and then on a national level. Following this format the creation of a National Union of Black Students was posited as the ultimate goal. Unsurprisingly, Garrett firmly believed that change would emanate from the campus, remarking that 'further organising of Black Students' groups is now a necessary part in the overall rise of the consciousness of the Black Community'.[147]

In retrospect, this approach again recalls Du Bois's Talented Tenth theory of African-American enlightenment, with the educated on campus inspiring those in the ghetto. However, the situation on campus was complex. The 'Tenth' were now far greater in number and represented a mix of backgrounds, from the ghetto to trust fund. Issues of race, gender, politics and generation all influenced the identity transformation occurring on campus, resulting in conflicted, evolving, enthusiastic young men and women, undertaking a revolution of the mind, at their own speeds, within their own historical and cultural contexts. The ability to distil practical programmes from this morass of ideological revolution was a profound achievement which bequeathed a significant legacy to the American educational system. Garret summed up the pragmatism of BSU and other student groups' approaches when he concluded: 'we offer a positive programme of Blackness. Our programmes are work programmes. Our direction is revolutionary. Our method is organization. Our goal is Black Power.'[148]

Building on Garrett's rhetoric, prominent figures in African-American education argued that if campus revolution was to have any hope of transforming American higher education, classroom instruction at a basic level had to foster institutional reform, 'by all means necessary'.[149] As a result, student militants argued vociferously for the instigation of not just Black Studies programmes but departments.[150] While Afrogroups and student unions on campus provided cultural and ideological vitality for the campus revolution, academic campaigning was necessary to create connections with the campus power structure. It was argued that poised between the public, the student body and the administrations, Black Studies facilities would serve as intermediary transmission points for values of African-American empowerment.

In a fundamental shift, it was hoped that, although subject to an oppressive administration, African-American faculty members could still offer empowering lessons by encouraging students to place greater value on the cultural expression of African-America.[151] Whereas the old guard of the United Negro College Fund had merrily circulated jokes suggesting Black Studies graduates were fit only to pick cotton, a new generation of African-American educators saw Black Studies as a fundamental statement of African-American identity capable of challenging the institutional and cultural underpinnings of American racism.[152] Dubbing their predecessors 'Bledsoes' after the autocratic, servile college president in Ellison's *Invisible Man*, who colluded with the white administration in destroying the spirit and emasculating the consciousness of his students, these new academics sought to engineer an environment in which white America would no longer constrain African-American intellectual expression. The chief method of doing so, as students had also realised, was the creation of a separate paradigm within which the white cultural sphere was just one among many and not the qualitative measure of all experience.[153] Ultimately, it was hoped that this campus crusade would remove white cultural hegemony, initially on, and then off campus, placing African-Americans as equal intellectual operators within society.[154]

As the drive toward Black Studies spread across America after 1966, it became apparent that the end result of these competing expectations would leave all parties unsatisfied. From the administration's perspective more concessions had been made than was desirable, with no guarantee that militant agitation would abate even if Black Studies programmes were implemented. Those courses which did arise were often financially and intellectually impoverished, staffed by 'practically anyone who looks black or has mentioned Negroes in an article, book or seminar paper'.[155]

It was doubtful whether this disparate band of new academic enterprises would have either the numbers or intellectual clout to influence the American educational system. Change seemed imperative however; the stress amongst African-American faculty members teaching integrated classes was evident, with Harry Edwards remarking 'Teaching crackers is like trying to kick your way through a steel door with boots of Jello.'[156] However, it is debatable whether 'teaching crackers' was as consistently oppressive as Edwards claimed. As his Department Head at San Francisco State, Dr. Harold Hodges, happily remarked, 'From the start, Harry showed a unique ability to empathise with students ... black and white. Even those initially hostile were won over.'[157] Edwards's classes on minorities and 'Youth Problems Today' had eight hundred enrolees and were so popular that they were transferred to larger classrooms.

Salutary precedents already appeared to have been established in the work of existing African-American colleges such as Georgia's Morehouse College. Larry Neal's diary recalled how one of his lessons incorporated a 1968 Morehouse poetry festival recording – alongside a Bob Dylan single and tracks from LeRoi Jones and the Jihad singers – to emphasise the importance of poetry and art in responding to practical contemporary circumstances, and thus, its utility as another tool for the revolution of the mind.[158]

Yet as lenses, hearts and minds increasingly focus on the campus struggle, it seemed that neither historically black colleges, nor revamped curricula would achieve the synthesis of community integration, historical consciousness, self-definition and cultural emancipation which increasingly resonated as the key tenets of black studies activists. The proposed solution was the creation of a Black University. As one advocate explained, 'in the evolving concept of the Black University, *community* is the essential constant ... It is to serve the interests of the community that the Black University will exist.'[159] Activists envisaged the Black University as a large-scale iteration of the self-definition process occurring amongst students on campus, ultimately coalescing in a new image for African-American education. Supported by an admixture of federal funding and charitable donation, with living costs ameliorated by work programmes designed to immerse students in the African-American community, a self-sufficient African-American university would, it was hoped, act as a lodestone for disenchanted militant academics across the nation who would feel honoured to help construct a nationally credible black institute.[160]

In an environment where education was more than a means of advancement in white society, this new, hip, faculty would focus on aiding the transition to an empowered self-image.[161] In the process, they themselves would be emancipated from the traditional academic structure. A practical goal underwrote such conceptual dreaming. Many activists wanted to demonstrate convincingly that higher education and African-American empowerment were not mutually exclusive.[162] If it could be implemented, the Black University would be 'the brain of the movement, that builds the engine, that puts the movement into motion.'[163] In this scenario there was 'no contradiction between the cultural revolution and the Black Liberation'.[164] In fact, the two were intrinsically linked, as eloquently summarised by Vincent Harding, when he argued 'the search for the Black University is really a part of our larger search for a sense of direction and life in the new, black-oriented time that is now upon us.'[165]

Ultimately, the Black University remained primarily a conceptual model, but the very drive and fervor of the arguments put forward in its favour epitomise the changing *zeitgeist* on campus, the genuine belief that if the correct sacrifices were made, the American educational system could be reoriented to embrace black aspirations and black culture.[166] However, the concept was most closely incarnated in the Institute of the Black World formed in 1969 as the second element of the Martin Luther King, Jr. Memorial Center, with Harding himself at the helm. The IBW's formation was a direct response to the confusion surrounding the increasingly sprawling black studies movement, proposing a new focus which, as Coretta Scott King reasoned at the dedication of the Institute's Martin Luther King memorial center, would 'emerge proudly out of the heart of the black experience in America ... [and] ... meet with uncompromising insistence the problems and needs which face black people today'.[167]

Subsequently evolving into an expansive independent establishment, the Institute strove to become, according to Harding, 'the major black educational creation of this generation'.[168] Established as an international center with a focus on research, the IBW tackled the emergent and controversial field of Black Studies using several basic premises. Firstly, the Institute contended that the new discipline was undergoing continual evolution and was 'really a field still being born'.[169] As a corollary to this, it was argued that this evolution was fundamentally altering the American education system, catalysing 'a profound mining of the black experience [which] challenges and transforms the basic educational structures of the nation'.[170]

The IBW's existence was undeniable evidence that Black Power conformed to no concrete pattern, but instead was capable of cannibalising and adapting existing institutional apparatuses to meet the demands of African-American empowerment.[171] As protest swept the white and black campus, the ideology of Black Power, its cultural expressions and its educational goals evolved to mesh with local concerns. The result was a 'Black University' which, as contemporaries noted, existed on street corners, in rehab facilities, in the cheap seats of community theatres and on the chalkboards of political action groups, in effect 'within the minds of all black people'.[172]

Further, the IBW expanded on the community focus central to Afrogroups on white campuses, reasoning that any subsequent programmes should be African-American constructions, as 'the field of Black Studies stands logically as a task and a challenge for black people in America ... the initiative must be ours'.[173] Reform of the educational apparatus was itself an empowering opportunity, enabling African-America to take the lead in defining its educational goals and aspirations.

As a consequence, organisations such as the IBW were seen as salutary examples for further work, being 'in an excellent position to play a central role in defining the field and creating some of the models so urgently required'.[174] Not merely examples, such institutes would help synthesise the energy and ideas created by African-America's revolution of the mind, 'combining the thought and activities of those black persons throughout the nation who are working at the Black Studies task'.[175] Expanding upon the need for unity to resist white cultural sublimation, the IBW declared: 'a unified, rather than a[n] ... academic, discipline-bound approach to the creation of Black Studies is not only desirable but absolutely necessary'.[176] Moreover, it was recognised that the endeavour was a long-term revolution which would be 'the task of years and not a make-shift programme for a few persons to do in several weeks or months'.[177] What made the IBW's historical legacy significant was the pragmatic application of these basic assumptions. Implementing the desired programme of profound change on a national scale over a period of years was no small task, but the IBW, drawing on Black Power's long history, believed itself more than prepared.

Founded on the historical legacy of the struggle for empowerment, buttressed by 'the older hopes and dreams of such predecessors as W.E.B. Du Bois, Charles S. Johnson, Ralph Bunche and Alain Locke', the IBW approached its task aware that history and culture were inseparable.[178] Accordingly, two of its paramount goals were 'Serious research in many areas of historical and contemporary black existence which have either been ignored, or only superficially explored' and 'encouragement of those creative artists ... searching for the meaning of a black aesthetic, who are now trying to define and build the basic ground out of which black creativity may flow'.[179] Aware of the necessity of cultural self-definition alongside historical rediscovery, the IBW's emphasis on the symbiosis between history and culture defined its militant educational programme. Accordingly, the Institute advanced its pragmatic measures under the fundamental injunction that, 'Encounter[s] among ... artists on the one hand, and scholars, activists, and students on the other must be constant'.[180]

What was the expected output of this intermingling of contemporary militant culture and historical legacy? Far from being disconnected from practical application, the IBW saw its historical-cultural programmes undergirding 'Continuous research on those contemporary political, economic and social policies which now shape the life of the black community in America and ... determine its future.'[181] By bringing together struggles past and present, a plan for the future, it was argued, could be devised. However, to tie this plan closely to the community, the concept of Black Studies needed to be culturally fluid and as universally applicable as possible. The IBW therefore called for 'Constant experimentation with the meaning of Black Studies for the surrounding black community, and openness to the possible input of that community into the creation of Black Studies.'[182] Gone was the notion that the 'Talented Tenth' would save African-America. The IBW instead wished to foster a 'communiversity', where dialogue between academics and those outside the ivory tower was freely available, noting: 'The two-wayness of the experience is essential and must be encouraged.'[183]

Not content with a free dialogue between campus and ghetto, the IBW also sought a truly international audience via 'the constant interaction of black students and faculty on northern and southern campuses [and] ... the encouragement and development of contacts among black students, scholars, political leaders and artists from various parts of the world'.[184] In uniting North and South, and in linking African-America to the wider world, the IBW endeavoured to imbue Black Studies with a sense of cultural ownership and unity, arguing: 'Black Studies cannot really be developed unless we understand more fully both the unique and the common elements of our experience in the black diaspora.'[185]

The IBW strove to create not simply a reformed iteration of the white American educational system, but an entirely distinct educational apparatus, informed by the international African cultural experience and sustained by its own system of academic resources and scholarly publications. In achieving this, a new type of practical education reform, it was believed, could be realised – the construction of a culturally empowering system in which 'Black Studies programmes will not be palliatives, but significant pathways to the redefinition of American education and of the Black Experience.'[186] The implied goal was clear. If African-America had begun by defining itself, it now wished to define its educational system free from white influence, to dramatically alter both the place of African-Americans within America and the basic educational structure of the nation.

Crucially, this strand of Black Power played to an entirely different audience than the incendiary conflicts of the early 1960s. Its militancy came from its emphasis on history, identity and culture, rather than the media-magnet seizure of campus buildings, or the appearance of guns and bullets in halls that had previously prized busts and books. Accordingly, the coverage of the debate around the black university's existence was carried on by and with the African-American community and the African-American media itself, most notably in a three year series of *Negro Digest* special issues. In the process, these educators, students and administrators attempted to take control not only of their educations, but their past, their future and the discourse surrounding both. In the process, they moved the war of the campus out of the 'fear frame' and into the hands and hearts of those it truly affected.

The revolution and evolution of the African-American presence within higher education was an essential step toward self-definition and empowerment. However, the campus was not the only avenue for change. The young campus radicals were well aware that beyond the borders of the United States other revolutions had been catalysed by student unrest, but had spread far beyond the narrow remit of education.[187] Thus, both consciously and unconsciously, these young militants brought the revolution back into their own worlds, to the streets and stoops, the sports bar and living room, inexorably politicising their community.[188] The militant values of the campus, inspired and sustained by Black Power's long history, and forged in the cultural crucible of campus struggle, were spreading across the generation gap and beyond the academy to the street. However, this was a two-pronged assault. As the campus brought its message home, the militant manifesto was entering the apartments of African-America, fired from the greatest of all cultural weapons, the cathode ray tube. On the TV screens of America, on the race track in Mexico City and in the boxing ring, a different brand of cultural empowerment was reaching African-America and changing its cultural assumptions forever.

CHAPTER 4

'DRAMAS-OF-AGGRESSION': BLACK POWER IN SPORTS

Even as the drama of campus protest was exposing the cracks in the American educational system, the provocative images, ideas and tropes drawn from the long history of Black Power were finding other potent vectors into the American imagination, perhaps nowhere more so than through its sporting heroes. In the burgeoning American sports industry, white capitalist America had cultivated an extremely profitable enterprise wielding immense cultural influence and for many Americans sports had become a popular culture religion. On weekends, a substantial portion of the country was either in a stadium or in front of a television, providing a unique means of influencing mainstream America's cultural landscape. These at-home viewers experienced the sporting spectacle, and the changing presentations of African-America, in ways that their bleacher-bound counterparts could not.[1]

During the twentieth century, technological advance and commercial innovation inexorably led to the sporting spectacle becoming increasingly grand, engrossing and culturally prevalent. Instant replay, slow-motion and a slew of sidebars, stats and additional arcana increasingly presented sporting matches as 'sets of spectacular happenings occurring off as well as on the field.'[2] By the mid-60s, the sports and entertainment industry had become a cultural arbiter, offering a new and ever-changing pantheon of cultural heroes to the American public. The result was a fundamentally imbalanced power relationship which attempted to strictly mediate the way in which black athletes were presented to the white masses. As African-Americans proliferated on the national sporting stage, the oppression occasioned by this imbalance became increasingly evident.

Initially, the statistics of African-American participation belie the anger felt by militant activists. By 1968, African-Americans comprised nearly 25 per cent of Major League baseball players, a third of professional American football players and just over half of all professional basketball players.[3] This demographic slice featured some of the most famous names in sports, receiving equally notable salaries.

Inclusion did not guarantee equality however and African-American athletes increasingly took issue with the vagaries of the sporting enterprise. The unbalanced division of rewards originated in the entrenched cultural stereotype of the 'Negro ballplayer' claimed John Henry Johnson, a running back in the National Football League (NFL).[4] Ironically for John Henry, the roots of the stereotype led back to the plantation, specifically the persistent assumption that African-Americans were athletically gifted, but intellectually deprived.[5] Added to this traditional castigation was the claim that African-American sportsmen buckled under stress and were unable to motivate white players. Less athletes and more entertainers, African-Americans were often excluded, consciously or otherwise, from assuming guiding roles in the sports which dominated the American cultural landscape.[6] This was most clearly evidenced in the NFL, which was hamstrung by the persistent assumption that African-Americans could not fill the iconic position of quarterback, due to their inability to function in 'thinking' roles.[7] However, despite this, and many other instances of entrenched opposition, sports were an ideal tool for communicating the ideas and images of a new, more empowered African-American cultural presence and one with great precedent in Black Power's long history.

As the twentieth century progressed, the sporting world became a crucial battleground in the contest over African-America's developing racial identity. Sport was a tool for the social construction and comprehension of race, for identity formation and militant cultural expression. In a modern context, sports institutions tend to be portrayed as benevolent purveyors of a colour-blind, opportunity-rich vision of America. This image is reinforced by popular culture recollections of African-American sporting heroes and within this pantheon few of these sporting colossi are remembered as reverentially as Major League baseball's Jackie Robinson.

In *Jazzing the Basepaths*, Montye Fuse and Keith Miller argued that Jackie Robinson's distinctive style resulted from a year-long apprenticeship in the Negro Leagues, concealed to present Robinson as a 'storybook individualist instead of a product of distinctly African American-styled baseball'.[8] Introduced to the sport in 1946 by Brooklyn Dodgers manager Branch Rickey, Robinson was initially cast as an exceptional African-American guided by a patriarchal white benefactor, to the extent that sports journalist Grantland Rice was moved to declare, 'Next to Abraham Lincoln, the biggest white benefactor of the Negro has been Branch Rickey.'[9]

Save for Fuse and Miller's *Jazzing* and Jules Tygiel's *Baseball's Great Experiment*, historians have generally accepted Robinson and Rickey's interpretation.[10] However, the development of Robinson's distinctive style in the Negro Leagues merits closer attention. At the time, African-American baseball appeared to have reached its zenith in the careers of iconic players like Robinson, Cool Papa Bell and Satchel Paige. From this triumvirate, Robinson is history's most enduring scion because, while his style of play was informed by his Negro League predecessors, his person epitomised the romantic individualism lauded by the white sporting establishment.[11]

Players such as Paige, Bell and Robinson confronted and confounded America's dominant cultural constructions in the same manner as Ellison, Hughes or Hurston. As African-American writers offered a militant challenge to American society through literature, so did the Negro League athletes who humbled Major League stars on the field, none more so than Robinson. African-America's early presence in baseball has been elided because white contemporaries gave little credence to the Negro Leagues, an omission mirrored in much current historiography. Historians have variously dismissed the Negro Leagues as a 'lost American society' and the League's players as 'invisible men'.[12] If the players were 'invisible', they were only so in the manner Ellison used the term. Drawing crowds of thousands during the summer, African-American games remained a ghostly echo in the white sporting media. As one Negro League veteran recalled, 'people didn't know the Negro Leagues existed before Jackie Robinson signed with the Brooklyn Dodgers'.[13]

Despite Ted Williams's 1966 induction speech wish that 'some day Satchel Paige and Josh Gibson will be voted into the Hall of Fame as symbols of the great Negro players who are not here only because they weren't given the chance', the reclamation of African-American baseball primarily began in the 1970s with a scattering of dedicated historians and ex-Negro League players.[14] These individuals created an oral history and autobiographical record which highlighted the differences between African-American baseball and that beloved of white America. This increase in documentation was paralleled by an increase in recognition, as from 1971 to 1977, under the aegis of the Negro League Committee, a steady trickle of Negro League players were inducted into the Cooperstown, NY Hall of Fame.[15]

As with plantation folktales, the lauded attributes were cunning, flair, speed and intelligence. Revelling in 'a whole lot of trickeration', players like Larry Brown delighted in the sense of superiority and skill conveyed by their athletic prowess, remarking of the Major Leagues, 'They just play. We used to do everything.'[16] Cool Papa Bell, when congratulated on his phenomenal speed, remarked of his opponents, 'they're just slow in thinking.'[17] The bravado and cadence with which these tales were told also recalled folkloric staples, as when Satchel Paige boasted of his pitching style, 'I got bloopers, loopers and droopers. I got a jump ball, a bee ball, a screw ball ... and a bat dodger.'[18]

With such ostensibly talented players, the absence of African-Americans in early baseball seems incongruous until the influence of the media and the sporting establishment are considered. Sports reporters seldom bothered to cover Negro League games – as one player, Buck Leonard, recollected: '[The reporter would] ... show up in the third inning and ask ... "What happened"?'[19] Sloppy coverage was compounded by the baseball establishment's obsession with tabulated statistics. The cultural impact of whites' adoration of numbers was highlighted when a committee member campaigning to add black stars to the Hall of Fame was told: 'If only you could prove these things, if only you had the figures.'[20]

The outcome was a sporting apparatus which would not recognise African-Americans without statistical proof, and which had little interest in garnering proof from players who were African-Americans. Conceptually limited, baseball's racial bottleneck was compounded by economic factors. As Connie Mack, owner of the Philadelphia Athletics, commented when asked if he would sign an African-American player, 'It would have taken too many jobs away from the white boys.'[21] Excluding African-American players not only damaged the cause of racial equality, but also of baseball itself, denying the big leagues an influx of Negro League talent.

By turning in bravura barnstorming performances against Major League teams headed by luminaries such as Babe Ruth, Ty Cobb, Walter Johnson and Bob Feller, Bell and his cohorts highlighted the inherent weakness of Major League baseball's restricted approach.[22] Of these interracial tussles, 268 were chalked up as African-American victories, with white teams claiming 100 fewer.[23] Pragmatic economics initially drove these interactions, with both black and white teams seeking extra barnstorming dates after the season's end. As Lincoln Giants' shortstop Frank 'Strangler' Forbes noted, 'we would clean up in October. They didn't allow Negroes in the [major] league, but we were very attractive to them in October. Hell, we would practically get more games... than we could play.'[24]

However, if economics laid the groundwork for these match-ups, the interaction of personalities and skills they engendered created a complex and unusual dynamic. Forbes crowed: 'We would win 60 per cent of our games against the big leaguers... The Yankees were nothing... hell, they were no competition... we beat 'em — we beat everybody.'[25] On the other side of the fence, Jay 'Dizzy' Dean admitted: 'I have played against a Negro All-Star team that was so good, we didn't think we had an even chance against them.'[26] The statistics seem to support Forbes's and Dean's claims. Consistently and dramatically outperforming their white opponents, African-American players gave the lie to embedded notions of white superiority, but also provided a proving ground for white players. As the Philadelphia Stars' Stanley Glenn explained:

> The black players will tell you those games proved how good the black Americans were. I say it proved to the white players how good they were. A star in the majors might hit .330 for the season and play a twelve game barn-storming tour against black players. On that tour, against top black pitchers, he might hit .250. He's going to say to himself, perhaps I wouldn't have that high average if I had to hit these guys all the time. A guy like Jimmy Foxx or

Lou Gehrig would hit just as well against us as against the whites, so he knew ... that he was a good ball player. We kind of proved things.[27]

The performance and presence of some Negro League stars was such that they developed as much an air of mythic invulnerability as their folkloric predecessors and their Major League counterparts. The Indianapolis ABCs' Oscar Charleston was feted as 'Fast enough to stand behind second base and outrun the longest line-drive ... powerful enough to loosen the baseball's cover with one hand ... fearless enough to snatch the hood off a Ku Klux Klansman'.[28] Charleston was venerated to the degree that Major League manager John McGraw was reported to have backhandedly bemoaned: 'If only I could calcimine him'.[29] However, despite their vivification of culturally established avatars, an empowering image was not the only tool in the Negro League's arsenal.[30]

What sustained the consistent triumph of African-American athletes over their white opposition? Negro League veteran Eugene Benson believed that African-American players 'were all so unorthodox ... [whites] went by the book'.[31] Ultimately, the conflict of play styles was a conflict of sporting ideologies. As the influx of ghetto youngsters into the campus environment had brought new minds into play, so did the clash of the Negro and Major Leagues. As Bell succinctly explained, 'That's why we beat the Major Leagues so many times ... They'd go by "written baseball." But there's so much "unwritten baseball."'[32] The showmanship occasioned by 'unwritten baseball' often made a mockery of white opponents; Bell recalled he was admonished by an umpire after a particularly bravura performance, 'Look, you just don't do that against a big league team.'[33]

As Frank A. Young, the iconic *Chicago Defender* sports editor, wrote, the substantial biracial crowds attracted by Negro League games 'proved once and for all that America's baseball fandom want to see a ball game regardless of race, colour or creed of the performers ... while the White Sox were taking a 14 to 9 licking [at] Comiskey Park, here was Satchel Paige, Hilton Smith and the Monarchs performing in big league style but denied the right to play in the big leagues because of their colour'.[34] Through the simple act of watching these teams play, America exposed itself to a changing set of historical and contemporary images of blackness.

By deploying a different set of semiotics, placing emphasis on cunning, 'trickeration', skill, bravado and flair at the expense of adherence to accepted standards, Negro League players exposed the cultural myth offered to the American public by the baseball industry.

Part of this process was countering the exoticising of African-Americans within baseball. Racial stereotyping of African-Americans as light relief was sufficiently pronounced that many Negro League teams featured a designated 'clown' on their roster during the 1930s and 1940s. Signal examples included the Brooklyn Royal Giants' Ralph 'Country' Brown who knelt while batting and Lloyd 'Pepper' Bassett who played catcher sitting in a rocking chair.[35] Although evidently skilled, by their very inclusion these players participated in a disempowering endeavour, ensuring the focus remained on their humorous antics and not their athletic ability. The trend reached its apotheosis in two all-clown teams, both orchestrated by New York promoter Syd Pollock.

The first, the Zulu Cannibal Giants Baseball Tribe, wore grass skirts and pseudo-African tribal paint and, despite attracting heavy criticism from other Negro League teams, were extremely popular with audiences, perhaps because the ridiculous nature of their costumes sapped some of the inherent threat from their obvious athleticism and competence. The same could not be said for Pollock's second team, the Indianapolis Clowns. Predominantly African-American or Cuban, the Clowns also featured a cast of 'entertaining' characters but were a more complex proposition than the Cannibal Giants. The value of the Clowns is relatively absent from the historical record despite their combining theatrics and skill in a manner akin to the Harlem Globetrotters. Most importantly, their ability to sell tickets and play excellent baseball brought African-American athletes before a large audience. Jim Cohen, a player from 1946 until 1952, recalled, 'The acts we put on guaranteed that no matter what the local economy was like that particular week, we'd draw. But ... sandwiched in between all the ... jokes was some very good baseball.'[36]

Such an approach was a double-edged sword. As in other mediums, it was difficult to present a comedic spectacle while retaining an empowering identity. Comedy might have bred attention, but it seldom fostered respect. Nelson Stroch observed that, 'Going to see the Clowns was like going ... to see a Laurel and Hardy film ... You knew you were off to a great show and you got it. They played good baseball, of course. But it was the show, from batting practice through the last pitch, that drew the fans.'[37] However, as Othello Renfroe noted, the Clowns' ability to draw a crowd had wider repercussions: 'They paid the salary for the league, because any team able to barnstorm with the Clowns made money. They packed them in.'[38] Tickets meant money. Money, arguably, equalled influence. In helping to sustain the League, the Clowns fed a tradition of black athleticism, skill and innovation which was to become a powerful thread in the heartland of America's favourite sport.

Outwith their economic pull, the Indianapolis Clowns occupied a unique place in American baseball. Arguably, by attracting white audiences with their theatrics, they created an opportunity to earn respect through their sporting prowess and thereby present a more empowering conception of African-American baseball players. However, this approach highlighted the problematic cultural perception afflicting baseball. White America still categorised African-America as the 'other', an exotic curiosity to be appreciated not for its barnstorming skill in interracial games, but for its strange and alien allure. Thus, it was all the more significant that players such as Bell, Benson and later, Robinson were to challenge the received image of American baseball.

At the time, Robinson was entering a vitriolic world, the pressures of which might have been ameliorated had Rickey provided him with company in the form of other gifted players.[39] However, it seems Rickey deliberately chose to isolate Robinson in order to preserve the cultural image he wanted to portray to the American public, that of a lower-class man succeeding with the paternal assistance of a wealthy sponsor. By depicting Robinson as a lone hero striving to integrate, Rickey presented his white American audience with a quandary. They could either change their perspective on racial integration, or set themselves up as opponents of the American dream.

In the process of his ascent to fame, Robinson was moulded by Rickey to refute other, more culturally dangerous, sporting predecessors such as the boxer Jack Johnson. Robinson biographer Carl Rowan suggests Rickey bore in mind the racially iconoclastic 'image of Jack Johnson and his three white wives' and instead strove for 'a clean-living family man whose character was above reproach'.[40] Johnson's unconventional lifestyle had directly challenged entrenched white cultural norms.

In contrast, Robinson seemed to promise everything that Rickey desired, being 'mature (28), stable, (married), psychologically solid, articulate and famous.'[41] A walking investment, Robinson was to be permitted no Johnson-esque conflict with the establishment under Rickey's guidance. Meek and mild, he was instructed to 'turn the other cheek' in the face of racist audiences.[42] Often portrayed as a barely independent actor, Robinson himself seemed to believe he was little without Rickey, declaiming: 'It was Mr. Rickey's drama ... I was only the principle actor'.[43] Although this litany of the rough black urchin guided to greatness resurfaces in almost all Robinson biographies, his Negro League heritage suggests he was dependent on a wider group than merely Rickey for his rise to fame. As Sug Cornelius pointedly remarked, 'Had there not been a Kansas City Monarch ball club, Robinson wouldn't have been in ... baseball'.[44] Initially dismissed as a 'benchwarmer' on the Monarch's 1945 Venezuela tour, Robinson developed a style and skill which was honed during his time in the crucible of the Negro Leagues.[45]

Robinson's Major League performance stemmed from his Negro League apprenticeship, which bequeathed an improvisational style that shocked audiences and players alike.[46] Red Barber recalled, 'People who hadn't seen Jackie ... could hardly believe the testimony of their own startled eyes.'[47] Robinson's significance partially lies in his introduction of African-American improvisation to the Major League game. The stylistic approach and distinctive skills in base running and footwork he deployed in the Major Leagues were, so players like Bell claimed, a direct result of their tuition. Bell and many others argued that the Robinson who joined the Kansas City Monarchs as an awkward, ill-placed shortstop was a distinctly inferior player to the man who arrived in Ebbets Field. As Bell bluntly claimed, 'the kinds of tricks he did in the majors, he learned them from me'.[48]

The players of the Negro Leagues stood in stark contrast to the rigid structure of Major League baseball in America, bequeathing a legacy to Robinson which turned him into the 'Bojangles of the Basepaths'.[49] Pitted against a colossal number of white players, who according to received cultural wisdom were innately superior to African-Americans, Robinson, argued award-winning journalist Roger Kahn, 'humiliated a legion'.[50] In deflating the mythical supremacy of white Major League baseball, Robinson, despite his own denials, opened the way for historical and social consideration of the Negro Leagues' cultural legacy.

Moreover, at least some of the people who saw him play gradually began to adjust their perception of African-Americans, and themselves. As one Dodgers fan remarked, 'Did I feel uncomfortable when the black fans descended on Ebbets [explain stadium] when Jackie Robinson came up? ... I felt uncomfortable in the first game and a little awkward in the second ... by the third ... we were all cheering wildly together ... by May there weren't any black fans and white fans, just Dodger fans.'[51]

Although Robinson was no archetype of militancy, he was the carrier for a brand of African-American athleticism which was to alter audiences' perceptions of the game. When set against the skill of the Negro Leaguers, white sportsmen appeared neither athletically superior, nor theatrically more entertaining. In this respect, African-American baseball was a subtle step toward empowerment, an episode of cultural 'trickeration' which provided an unavoidable contrast to traditional perceptions of black-white power relations. It increasingly seems as though Robinson has been commemorated for the wrong reasons – we should look to the Negro Leagues, to Bell and Benson as well as Robinson, to gain a more comprehensive picture of African-American baseball's enduring cultural legacy.

The transition of Robinson from the Negro to Major Leagues suggests a far broader inheritance than the solo rise to fame promulgated by Robinson and Rickey. If Robinson was, as is often claimed, a 'five-tool player', then the recollections of other Negro League players suggest that the other tools in his repertoire were acquired in the Negro Leagues and reemphasise the fact that Robinson was not a unique example of charismatic, talented, athleticism, but existed amidst a community of skilled individuals whose unorthodox approach to the game both contrasted with and challenged their white counterparts. Likewise, the massive commercial and cultural appeal of 'clown' teams such as the Indianapolis Clowns, coupled with the inter-racial appeal of Negro League games, indicate that the American love for baseball is founded on a broader and richer basis than that reinforced by popular recollection.

If baseball exhibited subtle militancy, American boxing delivered the message of African-American empowerment with all the finesse of a vicious right hook. The importance of the sport is hinted at in a précis created by Larry Neal for his work entitled *Black Boxing* which sought to highlight the role of 'Boxing in American & Black American History.'[52]

Focusing on boxing's mystique and oral history, Neal argued that it served as a physical cultural extension of a civilisation's discontent.[53] From this perspective, boxing was not merely entertainment, but vital cultural catharsis.[54] America needed 'the drama-of-aggression just to keep from undoing itself'.[55] Recognising the entrenched presence of boxing in American folklore, Neal's précis contended that 'There cannot be a "great-champion" unless he has a "great-drama" to enact.'[56]

Neal was correct; as the twentieth century progressed, the great drama occurring across America's political landscape was mirrored and informed by an equal drama in the ring. For Neal, there were three great champions, each with their own attendant psychomachia which played out in the American soul: 'Jack Johnson – The Othello Drama, Joe Louis – The Drama of David Vs. Goliath, Muhammad Ali – The Drama of the Antichrist.'[57] A committed Black Power ideologue, Neal's selection of this trinity of culture heroes and his ascription of their dramatic expressions is as reflective of the 1960s Black Arts Movement's (BAM) aspirations as of the historical reality of these sportsmen.

Johnson, in part, represented America after the civil war, as divisions healed and steps were taken toward a more unified national culture. A 'vaudeville villain out of Tom Sowyer [sic] ... who could ... beat all of the baddest dogs around and do it all with a style ... charming and fascinating to see', Johnson was a mirror for America's self-image; robust, hearty, defiant and new.[58] The first black heavyweight champion at a time when the notion of an African-American champion profoundly unnerved a large sector of the American population, Johnson's sporting prowess made him conspicuous, but his existence challenged established cultural perceptions.[59] He was, for Black Arts militants reflecting on the period, 'the first American "bad-nigger" ... in his being he foreshadowed both the birth and death of America'.[60]

As Johnson scholar Al-Tony Gilmore explained, to be a 'bad-nigger' was to exhibit 'the personality type who adamantly refuses to accept the place given to black Americans in American society, and ... frequently challenges the outer perimeters of expected behaviour'.[61] In this respect, later boxers like Muhammad Ali have been represented as a cultural progression from Johnson, with Neal himself hailing Ali as a distilled image of African-American empowerment, 'broader and more complex ... a "badder-nigger", a black man so "bad" that he proves in his being the possibility and eventual advent of a greater avatar ... a much more serious prophet, a much clearer image.'[62]

Neal underestimated Johnson somewhat, his opinions inevitably coloured by the late 1960s militant perspective. Conversely, the Reverend Junius Caesar Austin, writing in the 1977, saw each pugilist as existing within an historical continuity, commenting 'If we hadn't had a Jack Johnson, we wouldn't have had a Joe Louis now.'[63] Former boxer turned psychologist Nathan Hare concurred, contending: 'Without a Joe Louis and a Sugar Ray Robinson ... we wouldn't have a Muhammad Ali.'[64] For both Austin and Hare, these athletes existed in connected historical moments across time, each influencing the other technically, culturally and ideologically. As Hare noted, Johnson was, 'incomparable[,] ... the first of the great "psyche-while-you-fight" heavyweights ... Muhammad Ali would later predict the round in which he would knock out an opponent. Jack Johnson could predict each blow, saying he was going to hit you in the eye ... in the mouth, then do it.'[65] Given the admission of Johnson's prowess, what did it mean to be a 'much more serious prophet' within the boxing world and what gospel fell from these prophets' lips?

Neal, in highlighting Ali's 'much clearer image', provides a clue. Part of the power of these figures lay in the image they projected into not only American, but international, media. Johnson's sheer physicality and presence as 'The lean-flanked, cat-footed jaguar of Reno' was a challenge to white supremacy and an incarnation of oft-repeated Black Power tropes.[66] In his broad frame and impressive stature could be sketched the indomitable will of John Henry and the raw power of Big Sixteen. Conversely, Ali presented the evolution and distillation of Black Power's long history in a form not indistinct from the panther which stalked across picket lines in Oakland, California.[67]

Between these poles of empowerment lay Joe Louis, tellingly hailed by *Ebony* as 'the first authentic black folk hero'.[68] World heavyweight champion from 1937 to 1949, Louis was 'An "American" at a time when a great-American-champ was needed'.[69] Something in this poor-boy done good, with his apparently humble demeanour and generous spirit appealed to Americans on an instinctual level in a time of crisis. Indeed, cultural critic Gerald Early recalled Louis as 'the greatest, the most expansive and mythical blues hero in twentieth century America'.[70] Early's claim was not without substance, evidenced in the hundreds of fan letters Louis received every day and the numerous children who grew up bearing his name.[71] As historian Thomas Sowell noted, 'How he fared in the ring mattered more to black Americans than the fate of any other athlete ... before or since. *He was all we had.*'[72] Sugar Ray Robinson put things more prosaically, recollecting that he believed in the unassailable power of two things: 'God and Joe Louis'.[73]

Louis's appeal was culturally broad, embodying the reciprocal nature of African-American cultural empowerment. Pioneering jazz trumpeter Dizzy Gillespie was conscious of Louis's place in the long history of black empowerment, remarking that 'Black people appreciate my playing in the same way I looked up to Paul Robeson, or Joe Louis. When Joe would knock out someone ... [I] ... felt like I'd scored a knockout ... because he's black like me.'[74] Not only an individual inspiration, but a link in the chain of cultural revolution, Louis and other black boxers were ideally positioned to communicate Black Power values through the medium of sport. An avatar of both national and community empowerment, Louis made for great copy. Al Monroe wrote in the *Chicago Defender* of 1936: 'Make way for the king ... And everybody does. Along Route 2 ... you see thousands of people scattered ... all straining for one purpose – to see Joe Louis ... Soon you begin to think ... Joe Louis must be a hero.'[75] Working with rather more brevity, Richard Wright, author of *Native Son*, succinctly summarised Louis's importance when he remarked: 'Joe was ... the concentrated essence of black triumph over white.'[76]

If Johnson had represented the formative stages of America engaging with its African-American aspect, Louis embodied the cultural evolution of America's image as a world power. The defining conflict which cast Louis as the all-American hero was his 19 June 1936 fight against Max Schmeling. Schmeling was a particular focus of hatred for some sections of the African-American community, a 'fascist Goliath [who] represented a Third Reich ... dedicated to recreating the ... aryan race'.[77] Louis lost in the first clash with Schmeling and expectations were raised as the drama moved from a sporting conflict to an international clash of ideologies. Functioning as embodiments of their respective nations' fundamental creeds, both fighters were drawn into the upper political echelons – Louis was the guest of President Roosevelt at the White House, while Schmeling's spouse was invited by Adolf Hitler to hear the fight live in his personal residence.[78]

In the midst of this international posturing, Louis, like no other boxer before, came to exemplify the virtues of the American image when set against Schmeling's Aryan colossus and accordingly he received heavy support from a substantial subsection of the American public who might never have cheered Johnson, or Ali. His victory in their second clash on 22 June 1938 elevated Louis from national hope to American scion. As the *Chicago Defender* explained: 'white Americans who ordinarily find no reason to celebrate a race victory let go a few whoops for Joe – because the Bomber, even if black, is an American, and his victory was not one for his race alone, but for millions of Americans.'[79] Such was the revulsion felt for the fascist regime in Germany and the approbation for Louis as an America champion that 'by the time of their second meeting Louis was the champion of the free world while Schmeling was Hitler's champion, the champion of the Philistines, Goliath'.[80] The biblical overtones of the conflict made Louis's triumph all the more symbolic. To BAM commentators looking back, Louis's success was 'to foreshadow the drama of the second world war with almost "ritualistic-precision"'.[81] Having guided African-Americans through the horror of the Great Depression in the style of a plantation folk hero, Louis seemed ideally positioned to stand against the horror of war in the American imagination. Media coverage appeared to reflect his cultural standing. A survey of the front pages of the *Chicago Defender* between 1933 and 1938 found Louis received more front page space than any other African-American leader, including the Emperor of Ethiopia, Haile Selassie and fellow Chicagoan Oscar De Priest, the first African-American elected Congressman since 1901.[82]

The arrival of the war with the attack on Pearl Harbour created, according to Neal, a new 'ultimate-bad-nigger' in the spectre of fascism.[83] Reeling from the cataclysm in world politics, America's perception of its African-American sportsmen shifted. Louis found he embodied a new empowered archetype, supported by a white establishment which wanted him to contest the championship; he had become, 'a righteous-black-American'.[84]

Yet, Louis's acceptance by white America did not preclude a similar acknowledgement by African-America. As Neal reflected, 'He was always first a righteous *black man*. As he once said: "If I ever let my people down, I hope to die"'.[85] Moreover, Louis's marriage to 'the best dressed woman in America', Harlem socialite and model Marva Trotter, cemented his apparent commitment to a 'black is beautiful' ethic, long before such cultural sentiment was formally articulated.[86] The permanence of Louis in cultural memory is highly unusual and stems from the manner in which he transcended the limits of both his sport and his own life, becoming a *point fixe* in the connected cultural expressions which comprise the long history of Black Power. This was epitomised by Louis's sixtieth birthday celebrations in 1973 which brought a host of tributes, summarised by an *Ebony* article which declared 'Louis ... was ... more than a great fighter ... he became a symbol, a living legend ... the consummate hero'.[87]

Importantly, Louis, the consummate hero, made the transformation from 'bad-nigger' to 'righteous-black-man' in the eyes of white America. As black militant activists underwent the process of self-definition, so too was America readjusting to the presence of African-Americans in its midst. Sometimes rapidly, often glacially, America was recognising the full spectrum of its population on the cultural stage, adjusting to a new set of emergent dynamics between Black Power and the American people. The iconic presence of these African-American boxers was a crucial step in this recognition, finding its zenith in Muhammad Ali.

Competing at amateur level aged twelve, the young Ali heard his father enthusiastically boast, 'Got another Joe Louis here', an early allusion to the fact that Ali was seen to be inspired by those sporting culture heroes who preceded him.[88] Ali recalled, 'I grew to love the Jack Johnson image. I wanted to be rough, tough, arrogant, the nigger the whitefolks didn't like.'[89] This is hardly surprising. Johnson had never really left the African-American imagination, his stolid ghost looming large on the fringes, coaxed into the light by writers, playwrights and actors. On the 21st anniversary of Johnson's death, playwright Howard Sackler reintroduced Jack Johnson to America, not the flawed reality of the man, but the culture hero crafted by two decades of calculated memorialisation. Sackler's magnum opus, *The Great White Hope*, premiered in December 1967 and incorporated almost 250 speaking parts spanning five continents over 21 scenes.[90] Constructed around the quasi-biographical story of an African-American boxer named Jack Jefferson, driven to exile after spurious charges are filed concerning an interracial affair, the tale virtually mirrors Johnson's own life.[91] James Earl Jones, then relatively unknown, recollected that he portrayed Jefferson/Johnson as he hoped the boxer would have seen himself; in the words of Johnson biographer Randy Roberts, as 'heroic, honest, passionate, intelligent, and a moral force for his generation'.[92]

By summer 1968, following extended critical acclaim, the play's growing audience included Muhammad Ali.[93] Embroiled in controversy over his religious objections to the Vietnam War draft, Ali was immensely drawn to the play. As he commented to Jones, 'That's my story ... take out the issue of white women and replace it with the issue of religion. That's my story!'[94] Such was the connection Ali felt that his cornerman, Drew 'Bundini' Brown, would conjure the historical legacy of Johnson to inspire Ali to greater feats in the ring. While Ali battled Jerry Quarry in his 1971 comeback fight, Bundini chanted, 'Jack Johnson here. Ghost in the house.'[95] The ghost appeared to lend his strength not just to Ali, but the series of connected cultural expressions of which he was perceived to be a part. Apparently strengthened by a clear awareness of his own position within Black Power's long history, Ali appeared a Nietzschean figure to BAM observers, embodying 'The feeling that power is *growing*, that resistance is overcome!'[96]

Such observers felt that Ali's rise presaged the downfall of the American empire, along with its attendant corruption and discrimination. America, it was argued 'trembles at the brink of fascism; Ali, the glorious barbarian, speaks to them of their decline and fall'.[97] The dubbing of Ali as 'the glorious barbarian' signified the perceived resurgence of the 'Magnificent Barbarian' cultural archetype previously embodied by Stokely Carmichael. That Ali, only intermittently glorious, proved to be a mercurial, opportunistic individual, given to brutality physically in the ring and verbally outside it, had little effect on his mythologising by Black Power devotees.

The subsequent veneration of the Ali myth was not merely the self-congratulatory activity of a militant cult, but had broad repercussions for the transmission of Black Power concepts of identity. The ideal of an empowered, virile, self-confident individual was easily applicable to the high drama of the boxing ring and extended the visibility of this archetype of empowerment beyond the political arena.

What did this mean in practical terms? Firstly, it enabled a militant rationalisation of Ali's opposition to the *bête noire* of the time, the

Vietnam War, using boxing as a frame of reference and an historical precedent, thereby arguing 'Like Joe Louis, Ali is on the side of God when he says that he has nothing against his yellow brother.'[98] For Black Arts militants like Neal, increasing empowerment created a sensation of the acceleration of history, events unfolding in a continuity which culminated in 'the rise of a new consciousness, a third-world-consciousness, the consciousness of one who has seen himself called barbarian and slave. The consciousness of the guerrilla'.[99]

The musing of a Black Arts luminary such as Neal might seem divorced from the reality of African-American life, but Neal subsequently expanded his *Black Boxing* précis in an outline for *Boxing as Drama*, a projected work with Seymour Gray, which drew figurative concepts of empowerment closer to the street, utilising established folkloric tradition to create 'An extended tall-tale beginning at a bar called "My Bar", but elaborated upon at Harlem notoriety joints, a fine hotel and a boxer's training camp.'[100] Both a parody of and an abstraction from American history, the work rapidly assumes the dimensions and tenor of a folk-fable filled with, 'barroom drunks and dreamers, utopian nationalists, Marxists, vaudeville comics, ex-boxers, tap-dancers and reformed lunatics'.[101] Uncle Rufus, Neal's hip, empowered evolution of Uncle Remus, returns to conjure empathy with past empowerment in the guise of 'a blues bard commenting on the human condition ... and nostalgic narratives of time long gone'.[102]

Neal's and Gray's narrative begins with Neal and Rufus discussing the Ali-Frazier fight of 1971. It is unsurprising that this clash, dubbed the 'Fight of the Century', opens the book, as the conflict was as noted for its societal undertones as for its sporting drama. Described as 'the greatest, one-shot, pure cash moneymaker in history', selling 1,500,000 closed circuit seats within America alone, reaching a foreign audience of millions via new satellite technology and auctioning commercials for $4,000,000 a minute, the fight had an immense cultural presence.[103]

Circling this behemoth spectacle, the media polarized around the fighters, with *Ebony* correspondent Lacy Banks crowing, 'Ali connotes anti-establishment. He is black pride out-loud, its fury unleashed in a salvo of fistic lightning ... poetry and dramatic antics.'[104] Politics and culture merged in the ring as Ali, a Nation of Islam member who had vociferously refused the draft, faced Frazier, adopted by certain sections of the mainstream press and castigated as an 'Uncle Tom' by Ali as a result.[105] Frazier himself was dismissive of Ali's racial branding, commenting, 'Clay and his followers ... have labelled me an "Uncle Tom" and "the Great White Hope" because I don't go around and make a lot of racial speeches ... and say that I am fighting in the ring for black people ... I'm nobody's but my own hope ... I'm fighting for my five kids, my wife and myself.'[106] Frazier's frankness may have highlighted the caustic nature of Ali's approach, however such cultural labelling was indicative of the unique place boxing and sports played in mediating the relationship between America and African-America.

Serving as a bridge, sport could unite the country behind a cultural archetype, as with Joe Louis. Conversely, it was the perfect stage from which militant African-Americans could display their confidence to a nation ill-equipped to absorb the shock. Most dangerously, sport was an elegant tool for the creation and dissemination of myth. Frazier recollected: 'Clay's saying that he is fighting for black people has much to do with what people believe ... even if I don't go around saying that I am fighting for my black brothers and sisters, that doesn't mean I'm not helping my black brothers and sisters whenever I can.'[107] As honest as Frazier's statement was, it was too late. The juggernaut of the Ali myth, once it had gained sufficient momentum, steamrollered all inconvenient historical truth, as the human nature of the men involved was subsumed beneath the glory of the ring. Ultimately, it is unsurprising that Neal and Gray's précis ends with a focus on 'the historical-affect [sic] of boxing'.[108]

Sports, therefore, always functioned on a dual level. On the one hand, it served as a theatre for America and African-America to play out the evolution of their mutual relationship, for archetypes of militancy, 'magnificent barbarians' to confront pillars of the establishment, 'Great White Hopes', be they white or, as with Frazier, black.[109] At the same time, sport mirrored practical, political concerns, domestic and international. This profound and essential duality of perception is best illustrated by reconsidering the 1971 Madison Square Garden clash.

On one level, the event was characterised by the international conflict in Vietnam, with the constructed image of the two boxers being presented as a collision of political and cultural polar opposites.[110] Thus, militants alleged, Ali's fall to Frazier in the fifteenth round resonated with his fans, because it was as if he had been 'slain by ... the hero of the white man'.[111] The irony and tragedy inherent in this rebranding of Frazier is inescapable. As he reflected incredulously, 'The trouble with me having whipped Cassius Clay is that some people still don't believe it ... I whipped him in front of four million people ... and still ... people ... don't believe it'.[112] The selective nature of cultural recollection doomed Frazier, a man who, *Thriller in Manila* director John Dower noted, was far closer to Martin Luther King than Ali, who had revelled in his appearance at a Ku Klux Klan rally in 1975.[113] Set against this, Frazier's claim that 'I'm giving black brothers a break ... without doing a lot of whooping and hollering about it. We have fought much too hard for integration to want separation now' seems more representative of what many African-Americans appeared to be striving towards.[114] However, Frazier, a man who frequently assisted Ali both financially and professionally, appeared to have been irrevocably replaced in the African-American imagination.[115] As one member of the public, Layding Lumumba Kaliba, commented in *Jet* after the fight, 'Joe has already lost a fight. He lost a decision to Uncle Sam (white America) when he thought he could be a black champion without first being a black man.'[116] The nebulous quality of being a 'black man', and the insinuation that this had somehow escaped Frazier, infuriated him. He raged:

> ... people are hung up on Clay telling them how black he is and what a Tom I am ... his blackness is as phony as a three-dollar bill. How can they believe he's so black? ... He's got a white trainer hasn't he? ... Clay talks about how much he hates the white man ... yet every time I see him on TV ... I see him with some white folks, including white women.[117]

On one level, the Black Power movement's cultural campaign had succeeded: from this perspective, Ali would always be triumphant, because he apparently embodied the revolution of the mind advocated by black militants, presenting the pricelessly adaptable image of a fearless man, strongly wedded to his convictions, a 'more aggressive prophet' indeed. The quiet empowerment and dignity exhibited by Frazier remains comparatively unsung, insufficiently incendiary to grab the headlines. As he mused sarcastically, 'Whenever I go into the ghetto, instead of making racial speeches, I give the kids autographs and pictures ... not like Clay who comes into the ghetto and *sells* the kids pictures.'[118]

The reality of the contrast between Ali and Frazier casts African-American cultural and identity politics in a new light. Prior to the Manila fight, Ali rolled out a favoured tactic, animalising his opponents. As Hare explained, 'Ali ... seeks to depersonalize an opponent ... Ali will look for a quality in which [he believes] he outstrips his opponent, then personalizes (or animalizes) that shortcoming.'[119] Whereas previous opponents had by turns been rabbits or bears, Frazier became 'The Gorilla'. Delightedly waving a small rubber ape to cameras, Ali grinningly declared it be the soul of Joe Frazier.[120] While partially youthful grandstanding, Ali's behaviour demonstrates two negative aspects of militant rhetoric – its willingness to turn racial epithets on African-Americans perceived as collaborating (as Robert Williams would do with soldiers in Vietnam) and its predisposition toward an audience, preferably the white media. The rhetoric of revolution was profoundly dangerous for African-Americans who did not benefit from the shroud of celebrity. As Frazier noted perceptively, 'black racists, like Ali, go into the ghetto and preach their race hate about Whitey. They get the brothers all worked up and then they go to their fine luxurious homes far away ... while the cops beat on the poor misguided black Americans who thought they could take things into their own hands'.[121] Frazier's remarks highlighted the danger of sport as a conduit for militant rhetoric. Images and words were easy and ephemeral, pragmatic applications thereof significantly harder.

Frazier viewed boxing as essential to cultural communication, in much the same manner that Neal advocated via Uncle Rufus, but was less convinced of their efficacy. As William Wiggins highlighted when reassessing Louis, fights were like speeches, a solid impetus to action and reflection, but a poor substitute for practical effort. Frazier elaborated on this to an *Ebony* reporter, explaining: 'the heavyweight champion of the world holds a position of influence ... I believe in using whatever influence I have to help my black brothers and sisters ... I don't really think it is fair for athletes to get involved in politics unless they really understand what it's all about.'[122] Moreover, performance on the sporting stage had a dangerous tendency to shape athletes into representations of the audience's expectations, rather than revealing the men they actually were. As Frazier complained, 'People always want me to be what the hell I ain't ... You always are representing something'.[123] The ability of athletes to 'represent something' however, was exactly the quality which was to propel militancy to prominence on the international stage.

Catalysed by the growing political movement, the late 1960s and early 1970s saw a new wave of sporting militancy, epitomised in the unprecedented campaign by Harry Edwards to boycott the 1968 Mexico City Olympics. Always a nexus for discontent, the late 1960s saw Mexico City become a forum for the airing of America's troubled racial conscience. In 1967, Edwards, a sociology instructor at San Jose State, declared 'You do not accrue prestige when you go the Olympics because when you come back you're still a nigger.'[124] The sentiment behind this particular brand of cultural militancy was first evidenced in Edwards's 1967 attempt to prevent San Jose's opening season football game from being played, in protest at the treatment of the school's African-American athletes. Declaring his intent to raze the stadium if his demands were not met, Edwards was denounced by California Governor Ronald Reagan as unfit to teach and threatened with the National Guard.[125] Edwards's protest was successful, but more importantly, once again demonstrated the cultural and political weight of sports as a protest medium. San Jose State was the first significant educational institution in America to cancel an athletic event as a result of African-American protest and subsequently instituted concrete reforms of its sporting curriculum to accommodate the majority of demands.[126]

The Olympics was no stranger to political protest, As early as 1936 boycotts of the Berlin Games gave rise to an alternative People's Olympics in Spain. Two decades later, the 1956 Melbourne Games was shunned by the Dutch, Swiss and Spanish teams to protest the Soviet Union's invasion of Hungary. Alongside immediate boycotts, the power of sustained activism on the Olympic stage was epitomised in the struggles of the South African Sports Association (SASA) between 1959 and 1964 to expel South Africa from the Tokyo games. The success of SASA's protests was paralleled by early expressions of African-American Olympic activism, perhaps most notably in the efforts by 1948 champion Mal Whitfield to encourage an American boycott of the 1964 Tokyo ceremonies.[127]

Edwards's campaign in 1968 was qualitatively different. Rather than international pressure from without, the 1968 protest was an internal revolution, a confrontation of a nation by its own athletes. Providing America with sporting glory for decades, African-American athletes were, according to Edwards, 'hailed before the world as symbols of American equality – equality that has never existed'.[128] In a year steeped in international and domestic violence, the Olympics became a focal point for an internationally displayed critique of American society.

In public memory, and much historical scholarship, the Olympic protest survives as a single iconic image. In 1968, Edwards saw two of his students, Tommie Smith and John Carlos, triumph in the two hundred meters. Rose-tinted myth holds that prior to the podium ceremony, both athletes donned a specific and symbolic choice of apparel and struck a studied pose. Smith claimed, 'My raised right hand stood for the power in black America. Carlos' raised left hand stood for the unity of black America ... they formed an arch of unity and power. The black scarf around my neck stood for black pride. The black [dress] socks with no shoes ... for black poverty'.[129]

The truth is slightly more prosaic. Smith and Carlos only had one pair of gloves between them. 'I had gotten my wife to send them from California, though I didn't know how I was going to use them', Smith recalled. 'Then ... I had to get off the victory stand and get the heck out of Dodge'.[130] A curious mix of spontaneity and forethought, the Olympic podium apparel was as much reflective of the men involved as their message. As Smith remarked, 'John is a very strong academic type person also, and he had his own mind what he wanted to do.'[131] Carlos has remained relatively taciturn, remarking to a *Time* reporter in 2012, 'The demonstration said what it needed to say. If you're still interviewing about it 44 years later, it must have hit the nail on the head.'[132] For Carlos, the symbol seems to have been message. In contrast, the meaning which Smith later chose to ascribe to events speaks volumes of his perception of his protest and his desire to place it specifically in a militant continuity, as another legend for the burgeoning mythology of Black Power.

According to Smith, this symbolism was not designed to forward any 'official' militant agenda. He claimed: 'We were embracing those who had no other platform but the streets. My silent gestures were designed to speak volumes.'[133] Communicating visually to the African-American masses tuned in to the Games, both athletes (supported on the podium by Australian sprinter Peter Norman) ensured the iconography of the protest reached the widest audience possible. As the strains of the national anthem swelled, both athletes bowed their heads and raised their fists in the now iconic Black Power salute. The effect on participants and observers alike was electric. As Smith recalled, 'The totality of our effort was the regaining of black dignity.'[134] For observers at home, that dignity was not simply regained, but projected in contrast to the state of American society. Edwards, who watched events unfold onscreen, believed that 'If these athletes, who have made it to the apex of their sport, stand on a podium and say there are things in sport and in America that are terribly wrong, everybody has to pay attention, whether they agree with them or not.'[135] His opinion carries historical weight. Robert Lipsyte of the *New York Times* dubbed Edwards 'the most important sports activist of our lifetime', and he remains a vociferous and committed commentator on the relationship between sporting protest and the American people[136]

Primarily, Edwards's perspective was a product of his early college experience, coupled with sustained exposure to the realities of protest, both within the Panther party and on campus.[137] 'Edwards is an angry man, and his anger reveals his humanity', Maya Angelou commented in 1980.[138] Shaped by his experiences in San Jose, Edwards's studies increasingly focused upon the interaction of race and society.[139] During the course of his education, he frequently commuted from Ithaca to New York to hear Malcolm X speak.[140] After hearing white students rejoicing to the news of Malcolm's assassination, Edwards lamented the cultural divide between campus and ghetto, concluding that 'the reality and implications of Watts had utterly failed to penetrate the pastoral, ivory-tower milieu of Cornell'.[141] For Edwards, as for many contemporary students, politics and cultural concerns were profoundly intertwined, a view not shared by the older generation of American educators. Edwards recalled many of his professors 'were hostile to the very idea of any attempt ... to synthesize my political and social concerns with my scholarly interests. But theory and life had become fused into a single unity for me.'[142]

Eventually returning to teach at San Jose State, Edwards increasingly saw the sporting world as the best avenue for increased political influence, recognising 'the power to be gained by exploiting the white man's economic and almost religious involvement in athletics'.[143] This realisation led to the 1968 formation of the Olympic Project for Human

Rights (OPHR) and the subsequent boycott of the Mexico City Games. Led by Edwards, OPHR compiled extensive demands ranging from the removal of International Olympic Committee (IOC) chairman Avery Brundage, whom Edwards considered 'a devout ... anti-Negro personality', to broader goals encompassing the censure of South Africa and Rhodesia's teams and the return of Muhammad Ali's titles, stripped as a result of his refusal to serve in Vietnam.[144] Importantly, alongside the removal of obstacles to equality, OPHR sought a broadening of African-American participation, including the addition of two African-American coaches to the Olympic team and two black members to the US Olympic Committee.[145] Mainstream America's sporting culture was not being refuted wholesale by militants, but adapted.

Much like Carmichael, Edwards represented an aspirational cultural archetype – 'Nat Turner, Malcolm X, and Paul Robeson all rolled into one' – but this magnetism viewed from a white perspective meant that, as OPHR's campaign gathered momentum, Edwards increasingly became a focal point for retaliation.[146] Intimidation at the local level – the scratching of 'KKK' on his car, and the slaying of his pet dogs – was mirrored by media headlines which blared: 'Negro Hothead Threatens Games Boycott.'[147] Dubbed 'a fanatic revolutionary' by Hoover, Edwards, through his coruscating rhetoric, seemed to justify his place on the FBI's Rabble Rouser index.[148] Proclaiming in the *Saturday Evening Post* that any African-American athlete who failed to endorse the boycott was 'a cop-out and a traitor to his race', Edwards even endorsed the creation of a separatist African Games.[149] Blasé declarations such as 'Let whitey run his own Olympics' fed the sensationalist headlines surrounding the protest, but these inflammatory pronouncements had benefits as well as drawbacks.[150] Described by Edwards as the 'necessary stridency of the era', it achieved tangible results earlier in the year at the Madison Square Garden protests against the New York Athletic Club's track meet and the subsequent attendance of only a few African-American athletes.[151] Edwards and the five hundred or so other African-Americans who took part in OPHR's protest outside Madison Square were representative of the growing presence of African-American militancy on the international sporting stage.

Edwards declared in 1969 that, 'the black athlete has left the facade of locker room equality ... to take his long vacant place as a primary participant in the black revolution'.[152] Was this indeed the case?

Some contemporaries certainly concurred. *Sports Illustrated* devoted a five-part series to the Olympic protest which concluded: 'Like it or not, face up to it or not, condemn it or not, Harry Edwards is right.'[153] Edwards's support amongst the African-American sporting elite was far from unanimous however, with athletes such as Willie Davenport questioning how exactly returning as Olympic champion could be disempowering.[154] Ultimately, although OPHR's demands received little political attention, with the boycott itself failing to materialise, Edwards's primary goal – to turn the cultural spotlight on the obstacles facing African-Americans in sport, and by extension society – was powerfully realised.

The planned Olympic boycott did not fade from the scene, but took on a more personal component, representative of the revolution of the mind being experienced by each individual athlete. A series of individual protests were planned, culminating in the iconic podium salute made by Carlos and Smith. These contrasted sharply with a number of more conventionally patriotic gestures from African-American athletes, most notably George Foreman who quietly waved an American flag after his match against the Soviet Union's Ionas Chepulis. Foreman reflected morosely in 2006 on the mixed reaction his protest achieved, 'People seemed to like it, applause began, but the newspapers twisted it all wrong: they wrote that George Foreman had demonstrated support for the government and opposition to Carlos and Smith, while I was just showing the colours of our team.'[155] Despite the ambivalent reaction amongst African-Americans and the approbation by whites, Foreman had an extremely clear rationale for his actions. As he explained, 'Two or three years before I had been lying in the street, from head to toes in shit, hiding from the dogs, and here I was, with a job, with three meals a day, with some money to send back home, with basic education and even with an opportunity to learn boxing, and all that thanks to that very US government. I was naturally proud of where I come from. Many did not like it ... but I feel no remorse.'[156]

Yet Foreman was equally proud of his teammates: 'I'll never forget seeing John Carlos walk past the dormitory when he was sent packing with all these cameras following him around and I saw the most sad look on his face. This was a proud man who always walked with his head high, and he looked shook. That hurt me and it made us all mad. Forget about the flag. This was our teammate.'[157] As on the campus, identification and empathy with the Olympic protest was shaped by a multitude of factors.

The response to the podium protest, in America and internationally, was instantaneous and opinionated. The IOC immediately revoked the sprinters' medals on the grounds that the demonstration 'violated the basic principle of the Olympic games that politics play no part whatsoever'.[158] Bob Kane, then secretary of the US Olympic Committee, described the two protesters as 'Embarrassing exhibitionists ... [who] ... had used one of the genuine peaceful forums of the world to demonstrate against an internal problem'.[159] On the other side of the fence, athletes like Lee Evans were left 'in a trembling rage'.[160] The sprinter recalled he was 'too shook to eat breakfast' and lashed out at an IOC representative for greeting him in the morning, 'I grabbed him and shoved him so he almost fell down, "Mother, don't even speak to me after what you done to my partners!" ... I was cryin'. I went to the elevator and started beatin' on it with my fist.'[161]

Suspended from the Olympic team and summarily dismissed, Carlos and Smith faced the court of public opinion on their return, dismissed by the *Los Angeles Times* as purveyors of a 'Nazi-like salute' and branded 'black-skinned storm-troopers' by the *Chicago American*.[162] The nadir of media coverage was reached in a *Time* article which replaced the Olympic motto 'Faster, Higher, Stronger' with 'Angrier, Nastier, Uglier' in response to 'A public display of petulance that sparked one of the most unpleasant controversies in Olympic history and turned the high drama of the games into theater of the absurd.'[163] Despite dismissing the demonstration as petty, *Time* nonetheless conceded that 'As a way of calling attention to racial strife in the US, the demonstration was undeniably effective.'[164]

At Smith and Carlos's home college of San Jose State, President Robert D. Clark's response to the controversy encapsulated the ability of sporting protest profoundly to affect American observers at home, challenging cultural assumptions on and off campus. Clark wrote:

> We ... are proud of the achievements of Tommie Smith and John Carlos ... All Americans should be proud of their achievements ... Millions of Americans must have seen Tommie Smith on

television, as I did, explaining the symbolism of his and John Carlos' gestures ... The message he conveyed should be of real concern to all Americans ... They do not return home in disgrace, but as the honorable young men they are, dedicated to the cause of justice.[165]

For Clark, a scholar keenly aware of the relationship between sports and patriotism, the failure lay not with Carlos and Smith, but with America's own cultural resistance to accepting all members of its society, epitomised in the media abhorrence of Smith's and Carlos's perceived airing of America's 'dirty laundry' on the international stage.[166]

Smith's and Carlos's demonstration was merely the first step toward increasingly militant protest in the Olympic arena. The 1972 Munich Olympics was defined by Palestinian activism while the 1976 Montreal Games were a focus of anti-apartheid dissent. The culmination of the interaction between sporting culture and militant politics started by Edwards came in 1980, with President Carter's boycott of the Moscow Games. As Edwards remarked, 'I find it rather ironic that twelve years after I was denounced for calling for a boycott of the Olympics, the president of the United States has called a boycott – proving unequivocally that sports are indeed political.'[167] Yet simply proving sports were political was only part of the point. More pertinent was that the sporting arena was to produce some of the most significant and influential cultural expressions across the long history of Black Power. The American people were tuned into the unfolding drama of their chosen warriors and entertainers, and their perceptions of these pay-per-view parables would engage on them levels beyond the traditional political paraphernalia of the Black Power movement.

On returning to Cornell in April 1969, Edwards continued to explore the cultural impact of sport in society, in an attempt to move beyond 'the fiery, but shallow and ephemeral, rhetoric of activist politics'.[168] Arriving in Ithaca, he witnessed the Straight takeover and advised participants, 'I would arm myself. If there's going to be shooting, I would be doing some of it.'[169] Rather impressively concluding a PhD in the midst of the controversy, Edwards produced *The Sociology of Sport*, a text which would define his life's work, as he subsequently went on to lecture at Berkeley for thirty-one years. Edwards, like many activists of the time, has become part of the system he once railed against, serving as a diversity awareness consultant for the FBI. The ability of Edwards to assume a place within the system is testament to the change effected by cultural protests such as Carlos's and Smith's salute. As he explains, 'I'm saying essentially the same things now that I was saying then, only now they don't call me a revolutionary and a radical ... they call me a consultant'.[170]

When considered as part of Black Power's long history, the Olympic protest becomes not an isolated icon, but an enduring image from a period of significant cultural evolution in America, the legacy of which persists today. The changing patterns of American sport were to have tangible effects: as African-American sportsmen increasingly harmonised with the growing militant mood of the 1960s, boundaries were pushed, tested and redefined.

From Jackie Robinson's shattering of the colour barrier in 1947 to Curt Flood's self-destructive challenging of Major League baseball's reserve clause in 1969, the increasing willingness of African-America to not only use the sporting industry as a protest tool, but to defy its basic structure, opened the way for a culture of individualism and idolisation which culminated in Ali's 1975 zenith at the 'Thrilla in Manila'.

However, the long history of Black Power did more than create a pantheon of new militant figureheads. By exposing the deep heritage of America's favourite sport beyond the bright lights of the Major League diamond and providing an historical context for the drama of the boxing ring, cultural Black Power placed these sportsmen and their audiences into an historical continuity, lending humanity to these figureheads and direction to their fans as sports opened up new avenues of communication and new means of embedding Black Power tropes in the public consciousness.

In retrospect, the IOC's insistence that politics played no part in the Olympics rings hollow. The 1968 Olympic protest was the result of a profound change in the way African-American athletes viewed their cultural place within America, and an equally significant change in how America and African-America presented itself on the international stage. As Tommy Smith reflected in 1993:

> I never felt such a rush of pride. Even hearing the Star-Spangled Banner was pride, even though it didn't totally represent me.

> But it was the anthem which represented the country I represented ... They say we demeaned the flag ... no way man ... that's the American flag and I'm an American. But I couldn't salute it in the accepted manner, because it didn't represent me fully; only to the extent of asking me to be great on the running track, then obliging me to come home and be just another nigger.[171]

To come home and be just another nigger was no longer an option for many American sportsmen and women, nor was it for a significant portion of students returning to the ghetto from Cornell, Oshkosh and San José State and neither was it tenable for some of those African-Americans fighting abroad in Vietnam. As will be seen in the next chapter, these GIs were also redefining their relationship to the American flag they fought under, and their steady return throughout the 1970s was to change permanently the American cultural landscape.

CHAPTER 5

BEHIND BARS AND UNDER FIRE

Time correspondent Wallace Terry II noted in 1970 that 'Black soldiers, schooled in the violent arts of guerrilla war ... are returning home from Southeast Asia, fed up with dying in a war they believe is white man's folly and determined to earn their share of American opportunities even if that means becoming Black Panthers or turning to guns.'[1] Surveying 833 servicemen, black and white, from a variety of units and locations between May and September 1969, exhibiting what he claimed was a 'significant trend in GI attitudes', Terry concluded that returning servicemen 'could add significantly to the racial problem in the United States'.[2] It was perhaps inevitable that he would take this perspective, having been heavily embedded in Vietnam from 1967–1969 and having witnessed the deaths of compatriots and friends.[3] However, Terry's article was indicative of a growing concern in the American psyche. When the great quagmire of Vietnam finally subsided, what would its brutalised survivors make of the situation in the country which they had fought for?

Surveys such as Terry's centred on the contention that many African-American soldiers no longer wished to risk death for an America which denied their basic rights. Arguing that the true battle lay at home, 31 per cent of respondents in Terry's *Black Scholar* poll, compiled over two years of interviews in Vietnam, expressed a definite desire to join a militant group such as the Panthers or SDS on their return, with a further 17 per cent acknowledging the possibility.[4] Moreover, Terry claimed 45 per cent of African-American troops expressed a willingness to riot and take up arms once repatriated to 'get the rights they have been deprived of at home'.[5]

The degree to which these militant proclamations appear to have been followed through is unclear, and it seems likely that the majority of GIs latched onto the machismo and power of the Black Panther image as a means to sustain and reinforce their identity while away from home. However, at least some of these bold claims were substantiated. Sergeant Major Edgar Huff, who had fought at Da Nang, reminisced about his childhood terror of the Klan in Alabama and reflected on how his perspective had changed. He mused, 'Whenever the Ku Kluxers would come, I would be terrified ... And I thought about that many times when I was overseas, and I had those beautiful machine guns. I just wish to hell I had somethin' like that back in Alabama when those sonofabitches came through there. I would have laid them out like I did those damn Congs. The same way.'[6] Paratrooper Gene Woodley was one of the confirmed few who enrolled with the Panthers on returning, and was clear on his reasons for doing so – the allure of the party's violent image. As he frankly explained, 'Rifles, guns. I joined the Black Panthers basically because it was a warlike group. With the Panthers we started givin' out free milk and other community help things. But I was thinkin' we needed a revolution. A physical revolution. And I was thinkin' about Vietnam. All the time.'[7]

In 1969 Captain Alexander Benjamin, an African-American personnel management officer interviewed in Dong Tam, remarked, 'Young black soldiers are much more hostile than ever before ... we are probably building a recruiting base for militant groups in America.'[8] Captain Benjamin's fears were likely somewhat inflated. The nature of army life constrained the cultural modes through which discontent was expressed. Under fire, a facade of unity often prevailed, however, back at barracks, as army discipline deteriorated, African-American soldiers were increasingly undergoing a process of self-definition and cultural expression which took its referents from the long history of Black Power.

American entry into Vietnam marked the beginning of a protracted and draining conflict which catalysed a profound reassessment of what it meant to be American and what values America held dear. What was changing was not American culture itself, but African-America's realisation of its place within the American system. As Navy Lt. Owen Heggs explained, 'White people haven't changed ... What has changed is the black population. As the military represents in microcosm the society we live in, black people today in the lower ranks represent the young black movement in our country.'⁹ African-Americans' disapproval of the conflict escalated sharply between 1966 and 1969, as two perceptions came to dominate – the credible belief that the war drained funds better spent at home, and the less easily substantiated but powerful conviction that young African-Americans were suffering disproportionately as the conflict dragged on.¹⁰ From an activist perspective, militants were increasingly harsh in their criticism of GIs whom they perceived as having failed to undergo the revolution of the mind, declaiming: 'You niggers have your minds all messed up about Black organizations, or you wouldn't be the flunkies for the White organization–the USA–for whom you have picked up the gun.'¹¹ As Eldridge Cleaver reasoned, 'Your own People ... are ... fighting for their freedom against the very same pigs who have you over there doing their dirty work.'¹²

The stridency of political rhetoric such as that offered by Cleaver obscured the common aspects of anti-war protest. Divorced from Cleaver's political perspective, GIs on the ground often took a more holistic view of their place in the struggle for freedom, defined by their culture and culture heroes as much as by their political beliefs. As G.I. Larry Burton wrote while on tour, 'Although the Black Panthers are for violence ... and the NAACP or SCLC non-violence, you can't denounce either ... they are all basically for the same thing ... I love all my black leaders, Rap Brown, Stokely Carmichael, Coretta, King, Eldridge Cleaver, Jesse Jackson, Muhammad Ali ... they are all my black brothers and sisters.'¹³

Central to African-America's opposition to the war was the apparent hypocrisy in the white government's demand that African-Americans fight and die for the Vietnamese. Militants argued that federal efforts would be better directed to ensuring enfranchisement and feeding the starving in the northern ghettos, than crusading for the rights of a foreign people. As a 1966 SNCC position paper pointedly enquired: 'Where is the draft for the Freedom fight in the United States?'¹⁴

From this perspective, attempts to encourage African-American enlistment by appealingly to a nebulously defined patriotism rang hollow. Increasingly it seemed apparent that it was 'time to turn the guns the other way'.¹⁵ Reports of alleged atrocities committed by American soldiers appeared to foreshadow increased violence against the nation's African-American citizens. These rumours emerged alongside works such as Samuel Yette's *The Choice*, which predicted the coming obsolescence of the African-American race and warned of 'a concerted effort in this country to re-enslave, perhaps even to wipe out, its black population'.[16] Such reports, coupled with the perceived high proportion of African-American GIs serving on the front lines, raised the paranoid spectre of a government-endorsed eradication programme. In this nightmare scenario, the 'cream of black youth', would perish in Southeast Asia.[17] The rewards for service seemed ephemeral, the practical costs incredibly high. As a poster for the Vietnam Solidarity Campaign sarcastically trumpeted: 'Become a member of the world's highest paid black mercenary army! Support White Power – travel to Viet Nam, you might get a medal! Fight for Freedom ... (in Viet Nam) Receive valuable training in the skills of killing off other oppressed people! (Die Nigger Die – you can't die fast enough in the ghettos.)'[18]

Militants' claims of disproportionate sacrifice among young black soldiers are often disputed in current scholarship on Vietnam. Despite historians' assertions to the contrary, US. Army statistics suggest these claims had solid grounding in fact.[19] Between 1961 and 1966, young African-Americans comprised around 11 per cent of the American population between nineteen and twenty-one, but accounted for over 20 per cent of Army combat deaths.[20] The years 1965 and 1966 were the deadliest, with black casualties composing 20.7 and 20.8 per cent of Army casualties respectively.[21] While it is important to remember that this mortality rate was roughly proportional to the number of black Americans in combat brigades, there remains a statistical kernel of truth which would rapidly evolve into Stokely Carmichael's hyperbolic claim that 'the [white] man is moving to get rid of black people in the ghettoes'.[22]

The February 1967 release of the National Advisory Commission on Selective Service's report seemed to validate militant concerns. The commission, which sought to ensure that wartime responsibilities borne by an ethnic group were proportional to its per centage in the population, cited evidence of the 'Negro's over representation in combat'.[23] In response to the high tolls of 1965 and 1966 Pentagon policy changed drastically. As one Army General explained. 'We deliberately spread out Negroes in component units at a ratio pretty much according to the division total. We don't want to risk having a platoon or company that has more Negroes than whites overrun or wiped out.'[24]

As a result of the reorganisation, combat fatalities amongst African-Americans dropped sharply in 1967 and continued to decline until the cessation of hostilities. This resulted in black Americans compromising 13.1 per cent of combat deaths across the war period (1961–1972), the figure commonly used by historians in dismissing militant claims of disproportionate suffering, as it was slightly above the per centage of Army eligible black Americans in the population and almost the exact per centage of black Americans enlisted in the Army.[25] As can be seen from the bloody years of 1965 and 1966 however, militants' claims of an African-American blood tithe were not wholly unjustified, but escalated into a fear which rose far beyond the facts.[26]

From a militant perspective, refusal to participate in the war was a calculated move toward garnering international support in the domestic struggle. It was alleged that the Vietnamese saw dissenters as 'brothers, friends, and natural allies', who would, in time, aid African-America's own struggle.[27] Consistently, Black Power advocates told African-American G.Is their priorities were the result of systematic and sustained cultural brainwashing. As Williams attempted to explain, 'The Viet Cong is not going to follow you to the ghetto to oppress, terrorize and dehumanize you, but that big burly smiling hypocrite of a cracker commanding you is.'[28] According to activists, a process of sustained cultural resistance was required to escape this insidious indoctrination. From a militant perspective it was not simply desirable but essential that African-American GIs be culturally stimulated to turn their guns the other way. Militants believed that, once armed and trained, the youth and anger of these combatants would make them 'natural soldiers'.[29] The dynamite in the ghetto, heated by the jungles of Vietnam, seemed the ideal target for recruitment.

Opposition to the war was not limited to African-Americans who refused to participate. Whether volunteers or conscripts, African-American GIs were often vocally militant in a culturally alien environment. As military control deteriorated and black confidence increased, young militants felt secure enough to critique a previously terrifying situation. As one commentator wryly remarked, 'Saigon is a wild scene ... but it ain't quite Lenox Avenue.'[30] These vocal converts argued that segregation and racism were as endemic in the barracks and basecamp as in the cities back home. It seemed to them that, 'Even in war-torn Saigon, the crackers don't want no nigger in the ritz joints where they hang out.'³¹

Faced with accusations of collusion from militants back home and subjected to consistent indoctrination in the field, many black soldiers found themselves unsure of their place in the war effort. Any G.I. who encountered the heavily distributed Worker's World pamphlet entitled *Listen, Brother!* was faced with Robert Williams's accusation that 'Now, you are the brutal cop. The man with the gun. The licensed killer in the coloured ghetto.'³² African-American GIs could have been forgiven for thinking they had few allies on either side of the colour line. The old refrains of the traditional civil rights movement rang increasingly hollow as the war stretched out and Black Power rhetoricians seized upon the unease it created. Williams's pamphlet mused: 'CHANGE IS GONNA COME ... Now really, is it? Black men have been thinking this since ... Crispus Attucks ... fell in Boston Common. The theme is heartening, but the related facts are cold and dismal ... you are at war, cannon fodder and trained killer dogs in a white man's crusade.'³³ Alleged trained killers for white interests, brutal thugs equivalent to the ghetto cops of folkloric horror, how could the GIs of Williams's doom-laden refrain express any militant resistance? The answer, activists contended, lay in their cultural expression, in the revolution of the mind occurring beneath the helmet. As Williams conceded, 'The big white daddies in Washington are bragging about the good showing of their loyal "Nigras" in Vietnam ... The man doesn't know what's on your mind. He doesn't know what you feel in your heart.'³⁴ Williams suggested that GIs should turn to their cultural and sporting heroes for inspiration, commenting: 'Take Mohammed [sic] Ali, he's a solid black man. He's not about to let no peckerwood dictate who he must hate and kill.'³⁵

Whether they took Williams' advice or not, discontent seemed prevalent among black soldiers. A six-month study at 15 bases found many African-Americans felt persecuted on both a cultural and physical level, deprived of African-American oriented products at base exchanges and subjected to harassment by military police.³⁶ The strictures of the military environment, once relatively unquestioned, now seemed a ripe target for dissension as discipline eroded and militancy gained a foothold. As one mixed race air force human relations team commented, 'Unless Air Force commanders are willing to stop gambling with festering frustrations their options will most probably be pre-empted by the eruption of violence and the emergence of hard-core black militancy within the ranks.'[37] Tellingly prominent among the objections raised was the allegedly inappropriate use of base security police in maintaining standards on base. The report noted that, as in the ghetto, cultural stereotypes quickly came into force: 'Security police are often thought of by the black man as ... the "personal bodyguard" of "the man" ... We must get the S.P. away from the "pig" and "Gestapo" image.'[38] Concluding their report with a quote from James Baldwin, the team warned that unless more culturally aware measures were developed there would indeed be 'fire next time'.[39] As official control of the Vietnam situation ebbed, African-American soldiers felt increasingly confident in articulating their grievances – real, or imagined.

Few African-American troops were born militants. Indeed, for many black GIs military service seemed the ideal arena to demonstrate African-American competence. The cultural perception of Vietnam as a proving ground from which respect could be carried home was so prevalent that many African-Americans not only volunteered, but returned for repeated tours.[40] However, once on the battlefield, African-Americans found that their achievements were defined by pre-existing cultural stereotypes, specifically that of the accomplished warrior.[41] General Westmoreland in particular was vocal about the combat prowess of the African-American G.I.[42] Such praise combined with sustained media attention, which persistently reiterated pejorative stereotypes of the loyal African-American warrior. As *Ebony* ruefully remarked, 'that Southeast Asia battlefield was again the place where the black man's violence was heralded'.[43]

The military prowess of African-America was quickly appropriated by civil rights organisations such as the National Urban League, who in 1966 drew analogies between the Vietnam War and the American civil rights struggle. Praise of black warrior's combat ability was not confined to the African-America media; seizing on quotes such as that by one Pentagon spokesman that high casualty rates demonstrated, 'the valor of the Negro in combat', major magazines such as *Life* increasingly participated in the 'valorization of suffering'.[44] Yet this culture of group sacrifice came into increasingly regular conflict with a burgeoning sense of African-American individuality.

As Major General Michael P. Ryan of Camp Lejeune commented in December 1969, African-American recruits were arriving into the armed forces 'more aware of what their rights are'.[45] The cultural legacy of black militancy, fed by a series of connected cultural expressions across time, was fundamental in shaping these new soldiers. A 1972 US Marine Corps study noted that recruits were moulded by:

> Charismatic black leaders ... an overall heightened black consciousness ... everywhere apparent in demands for instruction in black history and culture in the public schools, in cultivation of certain aspects of African life in dress, music, and hair styling, and in a recognition of the values of a separate black life style best expressed in the phrase 'black is beautiful'.[46]

Serving within a white-dominated institution, African-American GIs existed in an environment which challenged increasingly highly developed expectations of the ability for cultural expression, experiencing similar disconnections to those of the student protesters on campus. Facilities such as Camp Lejeune, some troops argued, felt less like a military complex and more akin to 'small country clubs for the elite', dominated by a pronounced generation gap and facilities geared toward the officer corps and the over 30s.[47] Some African-American troops maintained that the officer corps was thus inevitably distanced from both white and black soldiers and accordingly, less attuned to their concerns and beliefs. As one African-American private dryly remarked, 'You don't see many of the brothers out on the skeet range.'[48] Although these accusations had little grounding in reality, they demonstrated the changing perspectives and expectations of some young African-Americans. This alleged generation gap underwrote and exacerbated the lack of respect and discipline spreading through certain quarters of the military and added another layer of tension to the complexity of cultural and mental development within the army. As the composition of the armed forces changed, this was to become an increasingly fraught issue.

Under the aegis of Project One Hundred Thousand, from October 1966 to June 1969 a disproportionately high number of African-Americans were inducted into service, not by virtue of their skin colour, but as a result of their economic status. Of the 246,000 recruits,

40 per cent were black and 50 per cent were poor southern white.[49] 47 per cent of the total were draftees, and amongst these draftees roughly 16 per cent were African-American, approximately 5 per cent higher than black representation in the general population.[50] Looking back at the figures, militant claims that large numbers of African-American youths were being led to their deaths were hyperbolic, but not entirely unfounded. Assigned by automated processing methods, the majority of new troops found themselves in combat roles and over half of those present in the Army and Marine Corps eventually arrived in Vietnam.[51] Although drafted via economic, rather than racial, discrimination these individuals found themselves in a profoundly alien environment, where to be African-American was to be on the fringes of a large and dangerous machine.

Despite the Army's attempts at 'blackenizing' its bases, the military remained culturally white and accordingly resistant to African-American cultural expression.[52] As Steven Morris commented when surveying a Marine Corps basecamp for *Ebony*: 'A visitor ... could have gotten the impression ... that the "integration" order had never gone through. In base barber shops he would have seen black barbers but, among the pictures ... that show acceptable haircuts, no pictures of black Americans. In the mess halls there were no pictures of black medal of honor winners.'[53] The situation was pithily summarised by the first African-American to command a battalion in the Marine Corps, Lt. Col. Hurdle L. Maxwell: 'The Corps says it treats all men just one way-as a marine. What it actually has done is treat everybody like a white Marine.'[54]

In this world of guns, death and bloodshed, the importance of soul music, Afro hair or familiar food might not be immediately obvious, but as *Ebony* explained, 'Grooming rules and entertainment facilities ... are touchstones of the serviceman's non-combat world, important to him ... as affirmations of his importance in the organization that forms ... the inescapable framework of his life'.[55] Although initially muted by the stricture of military discipline, the degradation of the military command structure as the war dragged on provided increased avenues for personal expression, which many African-American GIs now seemed to consider a right, rather than a privilege.

Part of the problem with greater cultural expression in the Marines was in the nature of their role. One article commented: 'The job of the Marines is to ... bomb and maul and explode and mutilate and kill'.[56]

The change in mind-set mandated by military training clashed not only with the life some recruits had known previously, as one former art teacher noted, but also with the life they were to return to once discharged.[57] This anxiety manifested itself in criticisms of the system, which, while generally factually inaccurate, were passionately articulated. Rumours were spread and disseminated rapidly within and between facilities with high personnel turnovers such as Lejeune, which processed 3,750 Marines a month on average.[58]

Not all troops caught the malaise. Army work, both in combat and non-combat positions, offered valuable opportunities and training. Some soldiers even saw service as a tool for empowerment. Sergeant Willie E. Burney Jr. regarded army life as training to fight racism in America, while gunship pilot Wesley C. Wilson summarised the thoughts of a significant number when he remarked: 'the thing that you leave with is a sense of assertiveness – a sense of self-esteem – that's very important'.[59] Nonetheless, it was commonly assumed that the talents learned on the Vietnam battlefield did little to help young African-Americans find their place in American life once discharged. As one Chicago-based private queried about his return home, 'Where am I going to go to blow up a bridge?'[60] The entrenched military chain of authority exacerbated this feeling of powerlessness. A G.I. from Detroit explained: 'Your commander can do anything. He has absolute power over you.'[61] Outraged that cars both at home and in Vietnam could freely fly Confederate flags while gestures as small as a sign on the inside door of a wall locker reading 'Black is Beautiful' could be forcibly removed, African-American GIs were eager to seize on alleged injustices as grounds for violent action. Each rumour of past discrimination was a 'rankling wound' and a lodestone for black soldiers feeling alienated, repressed and censured.[62]

Despite and in some cases, as a result of, perceived systematic discrimination on base, many militant African-Americans used culture as a weapon for self-expression. In 1972, Captain Raymond Hopkins, an African-American officer stationed in Aberdeen, MD, was acquitted of disobeying a direct order to wear a hat. Speaking in his defence, Hopkins attacked the Army establishment, accusing his superior officers of trying to 'emasculate, depersonalize and dehumanize a Black Soldier who wears a natural and identifies with Black culture'.[63] In arguing his case, Hopkins highlighted an essential problem in America's cultural perception of its

African-American citizens – while legislation might change with relative speed, stereotypes were slow to alter. The army expected African-American enlistees not merely to conform to regulations, but to fit the traditional historical stereotypes bequeathed by mainstream American culture. As Hopkins saw it, 'They refuse to accommodate the black man as he is today. They insist that we black Americans act out their images of Black men, the short cropped and the "yes siring" all the time. We are not allowed to express ourselves as Black people.'[64]

Hopkins's trial was significant, as during the proceedings the Captain not only countercharged seven white officers with racial conspiracy, but cited the commanding General of the First Army for dereliction of duty for failing to support his case. From his arrival at the Aberdeen Proving Grounds in January, Hopkins claimed that he had been constantly harassed regarding his hair and his refusal to wear a hat, but, as he elaborated, 'the issue ... was much deeper than the length of my hair, and if I should wear a hat outdoors ... the Dept. Of Defense ... approved the natural for Black soldiers but no one came to my defense'.[65] Narrowly avoiding conviction, a substantial fine and a bad conduct discharge, Hopkins concluded: 'Today's Army is not the place for the Black man ... they are not sincere about their own policies.'[66] Undoubtedly, Hopkins was not alone, the growing tension between the cultural expression desired by many African-American soldiers, and the suppression of individuality mandated by the military, made the armed forces seem an increasingly alien environment to a growing minority of militants. In this instance, an awareness of the connected cultural expressions which had fed the long history of Black Power was a bitter pill. Many young soldiers faced a profound dichotomy between attempting to assert their humanity, and desiring to serve their country. This was compounded by the fact that African-American protest in the armed forces ran counter to another accepted narrative in American society. As media coverage of the Black Power movement increased, it became customary for an increasingly disapproving journalistic corps to place images of black protest next to harrowing images of American sacrifice abroad, attempting to highlight the assumed hypocrisy of the militant struggle when contrasted with pictures of fallen marines and wounded soldiers.[67] When those same marines attempted to adopt the Black Power ethos they fitted neither the narrative provided by the army nor the entrenched expectations of the American public.

If the American military appeared inhospitable to some African-Americans, its restrictions paled in comparison to the stresses placed upon militant inmates within the country's penitentiaries. While the battlefields of Vietnam represented a more visceral threat, the prisons of America were archetypal total institutions apparently possessed of all the dehumanising aspects of Elkins's psychological concentration camps. However, the blossoming of culture militancy behind bars provided a signal lesson in the psychological importance of Black Power.

The African-American militant campaign within the prisons was unique, as many of its spokesmen had either spent time within penitentiary walls or remained there still. Cultural figureheads and firebrands such as George Jackson and H. Rap Brown provided a magnetic focus for prison protest, but of more significance to Black Power's growing presence within the American psyche was the struggle of everyday African-American prisoners to resist the psychological oppression of the prison regime.

As former prison guard Leo Carroll's 1970–1 study of an anonymous 'Eastern Correctional Institution' (ECI) concluded, 'analysis of race relations in the prison shows prisons to be a reflection of the society they serve'.[68] As he explained, 'A humanization of American corrections thus presumes a humanization of American society.'[69] This was not simply wishful thinking on Carroll's part; the growth and development of Black Power within the penitentiary had significant repercussions for understanding its manifestations the outside world.

Prison, despite its hardships, was also a crucible for self-definition. Militant activists believed it presented an opportunity for mental growth and political education.[70] As Carroll noted, 'It is probably no accident that revolutionary leaders such as Malcolm X, Eldridge Cleaver, and George Jackson developed in prison. The ideology of black revolution would appear to have immediate relevance for the black convict. Subjected to a series of ... debasements that destroy their sense of self, all inmates face the problem of constructing a new identity.'[71] However, for many African-American prisoners, incarceration initially seemed another iteration of continuing white attempts to deprive African-America of freedom of expression, justice and power.[72] By the late 1960s, America's judicial system was a subtle tool of control with the tools of peremptory jury dismissal, pre-trial detention and plea bargaining at its disposal.

Upon conviction, African-American inmates often experienced marked disparity in their treatment. Whether this discrimination was expressed in substandard accommodation and inferior rehabilitation programmes or in physical intimidation from prison officers, the effect was the same: a sustained assault on those values black prisoners held dear. In this aggressive environment, the chief appeal of Black Power ideology lay in its ability to offer inmates an alternative identity to that of the 'convict', laced with empowering imagery and intoxicating history, which enabled prisoners to reassess their place in society. As Carroll argued, 'viewing themselves from the perspective of nationalism, black prisoners are able to integrate their role as a prisoner with their role as a black man in a way which places them in the vanguard of a worldwide movement against colonial oppression'.[73]

With clear exemplars in individuals such as Eldridge Cleaver and George Jackson, many ECI prisoners, as Carroll documented, 'developed a collective definition of themselves as political prisoners'.[74] This was not without certain disturbing implications. Most obviously, it became possible for many inmates to interpret their crimes as political acts, a factor which was undoubtedly part of the initial appeal of militant rhetoric. Crimes committed against white people were justified as acts of revolution or redress, crimes against black Americans as evidence of a white plot.[75] As one interviewee remarked, 'You read that book *Black Rage* ... Then you can see there ain't no telling why a black man's doing something. Even raping a black woman's probably cause of the brainwashing white society done on him.'[76] The power of militant rhetoric to shift perspectives in such a blatant manner was a relatively new phenomenon which found fertile ground in the hothouse prison environment.

The rise of cultural militancy within the prisons was primarily a result of the confluence of two factors – the shift from a custodial to a rehabilitational perspective and the rapid growth of civil rights movements in the latter half of the twentieth century. As perceptions of race and racial identity clarified, they became a significant factor within the penitentiary. Initially, the proliferation within the prison of new interest groups, both cultural and political, was partly catalysed by the success of African-American inmates in persuading prison authorities to permit the Black Muslims as a religion, with appropriate first amendment rights.[77] This specific initial triumph resulted in a proliferation of prison groups, religious, secular and specifically cultural, which bequeathed new structures and cadences to prison life.[78]

This proliferation is seldom discussed in historiography, but is essential for understanding the growth of cultural Black Power within the prisons and its capability for transforming inmates' perceptions of themselves and their place within the system. As Carroll explained, 'once established, such groups serve as a base for the importation into the prison of perspectives having their origins outside the prison, and ... articulating these perspectives in a manner giving new meaning to imprisonment.'[79] In short, these groups helped to mediate the relationship between Black Power and the American people, within and without the penitentiary.

Militant critiques of the prison system centred on the propensity of the administration to categorise many militant activists as alleged political prisoners. Branded as enemies of white society, militants claimed these inmates were judged not on their crimes, but on their beliefs and cultural world view. As Huey P. Newton argued, militants were 'sent to prison for what they did, but ... kept in prison for what they believe'.[80] According to Newton, prison was a modern iteration of the plantation and the slave camp, wherein the African-American was likewise subjected to total disempowerment by authority.[81]

In this oppressive atmosphere, how were inmates to find any form of free expression? Newton noted: 'Jail is an odd place to find freedom, but that was the place I found mine.'[82] For Newton, as repeatedly documented in Panther memoirs, it was cultural communication within the penitentiary which led to the formulation of his theory of 'Revolutionary Suicide', inspired by an article in a May 1970 copy of *Ebony* slipped under his door.[83] From a Black Power perspective, this was no rarefied transformation; according to militants, mental liberation was available to all inmates.[84] Initially, prisoners were urged to immerse themselves in revolutionary writing, analysing notable texts by Mao, Marx, Lenin, Nkrumah, Che and Ho Chi Minh.[85] The ideological impact of such study is debatable. As Lester Jackson, father of George Jackson, remarked in *Ebony* after his son's death, 'Any programme for action must pay considerably more attention to practical implementation.'[86] The prospect of physical confrontation or revolution within the prison environment seemed ludicrous to Lester, who spoke for many outside observers when he commented: 'The very idea of violence

... is the same as suggesting that an inmate ... handcuffed ... shackled with irons could defend himself in a locked prison cell against guards with pick handles, rifles and pistols.'[87]

Nonetheless, some ECI inmates who undertook such ideological reading programmes apparently saw a very practical goal for their efforts. Coupled with enrolment in vocational training programmes, these convicts managed to combine a play for speedy parole, preparation for employment and, they claimed, the acquisition of all the skills 'necessary in the event of the formation of a black state'.[88] Digging beneath such optimistic statements, it becomes apparent that the chief benefit of these exhortations to political study lay in the contacts forged with outside militant groups, most obviously the Panthers. Liberation of prisoners was a key concern of the Panthers, featuring as one of the ten points in the Party's October 1966 platform.[89] Ultimately it was hoped that with a new political awareness linking them to the world outside, African-American inmates would begin to undergo the revolution of the mind necessary to resistance. To do so, prisoners had to realise that the power of the total institution was not explicitly total.

While physical resistance was a deadly and frightening prospect, the possibility of mental resistance was accessible to the majority of inmates. From the initial day of imprisonment, prisoners experienced a system designed to alter and codify their cultural values and political ideologies. African-American prison militants conversely contended that such attempts at 'rehabilitation' were predicated on false assumptions and that what the administration saw as flaws to be corrected were often calculated choices to refute the authority of the prison system. Much as early social science surveys had castigated black Americans for being trapped in a pathological cycle of laziness, duplicity and indolence, it appeared that the prison system viewed militant resistance in similar terms, as a barrier to returning to society.[90]

From a militant perspective, the goal was to enable prisoners to retain dignity and self-definition. The alternative, acquiescence to the administration, would have been a tragedy for self-empowerment, 'a death of the spirit rather than of the flesh'.[91] If inmates could achieve this mental resistance and maintain the integrity of their beliefs, it was argued that their minds could remain free, even if their bodies were imprisoned. Resistance to external control was itself, militants argued, a valuable form of empowerment.[92] However, for the militant's political message to be disseminated, it needed a practical, reliable method of transmission within penitentiary walls.

As with Black Power outside the prisons, it was African-American cultural expression which facilitated the movement and implementation of political concepts within penitentiary walls. Silberman, who had previously lamented the death of traditional culture, lauded its persistence in the penitentiaries, while folklorist Bruce Jackson noted oral traditions such as toasts (dramatically performed narratives of urban myth and streetwise heroism) survived and were 'told in county jails more than anywhere else' as a result of the abundant lower-class African-American population and, rather inevitably, a profound need to kill time.[93] This was not some quaint legacy – toasts, rapping and signifying were concrete tools in establishing dominance and power relationships within the prison hierarchy.[94]

This persistence of cultural tradition and cultural expression was supported by the structure of prison life. Fitting the conventions of existing rehabilitation schemes, African-American historical groups, cultural gatherings and theatre workshops were often permitted and occasionally fostered by prison authorities. Carroll noted that participation in African-American orientated prison groups caused increased politicisation of convicts, but 'even prisoners who never become formal members of the groups ... come to define themselves as political'.[95] George Jackson's claim that such groups represented an effort to 'transform the black criminal mentality into a black revolutionary mentality' was validated to an extent, but not in the overtly political way Jackson perceived.[96]

Programmes such as Colorado State Penitentiary's Black Cultural Development Society (BCDS), one of the first African-American prison groups, created an environment in which prisoners were able to wear tikis and dashikis they had produced as they took classes in Swahili and African-American history.[97] An outpost of cultural empowerment in a traditionally oppressive environment, BCDS was, as one inmate explained, 'The most revolutionary thing to hit any prison since striped uniforms were done away with!'[98]

The creation of BCDS was a practical exercise in empowerment, planned and orchestrated by African-American inmates, before belatedly gaining the consent of the administration.[99] As L.C. Hurd, President of BCDS explained, 'There really wasn't any big trouble once the brothers got themselves together ... we were revolting against the old way of looking at ourselves and one another. Luckily the administration was with us.'[100] BCDS, like the campus Afrogroups before it, connected with the community, inviting local leaders and academics to speak at its meetings.[101] BCDS member Stick Williams summarised the power of this connection pithily: 'The kids dig talking to the brothers and the brothers dig talking to them.'[102] For these inmates attempting to look at both themselves and their community through different eyes, the chief tool for their cultural reconstruction was Black Power's long history, its 'historical roots, cultural past and spiritual destiny'.[103] Empowerment came from a consciousness of connected expressions of empowerment across time; the realisation that, as Hurd put it, 'we all ain't been hangin' from the trees all our lives'.[104] BCDS's African-American history class rapidly became the most popular of the prison's twenty-two self-help groups. Perhaps as a result of this historical consciousness, BCDS, while culturally militant, were not separatist, noting: 'Too many black cats can't fight Whitey on his own terms. We gotta prepare men ... to talk back and speak up.'[105] Ultimately, BCDS and similar organisations were exercises in permitting the revolution of the mind to continue behind prison bars and in providing empowerment within a traditionally powerless arena. Hurd explained to a reporter, 'We'll always be ex-cons and we'll always be black, but at least we can learn to look at ourselves differently and not feel ashamed.'[106] This process would have been inestimably more challenging without the reference points provided by Black Power's long history.

The success of BCDS was mirrored in other institutions. At ECI, Carroll noted, 'Nearly the entire black prisoner population are members of the Afro-American Society, the purpose of which is "to attain and maintain unity among the black brothers and to uplift our standards of dignity".'[107] Being African-American increasingly became the focal point for inmates, as opposed to merely being a convict. This was supported by the increasing permeability of the prison system which these new cultural and historical groups permitted. Carroll observed, 'As a result of their interaction within the Afro-American Society, the black prisoners have been able to import into the prison perspectives having their origin in an external black culture, and to adapt and specify these perspectives to the context of confinement.'[108]

Convicts' responses to the new cultural influences entering the prisons were far from homogenous however. Divergent interpretations can be discerned between those inmates who focused upon the cultural aspects of Black Power and those who dwelt upon its political side. Cultural Black Power was most evident within the prison in the form of 'soul'. As Ulf Hannerz iconic study of ghetto culture *Soulside* (1969) explained, survival in the face of uncontrollable circumstances was generally considered 'soulful' amongst the ghetto black Americans who comprised a large proportion of the prison population.[109]

Carroll aptly defined the distinction between the various levels of militancy operating in the prisons when he noted, 'The "soul" movement is a collective involvement with personal emotions as opposed to a personal involvement with collective problems.'[110] Unlike white inmates, the majority of black prisoners were united in some form of solidarity, grounded in either the cultural or the political aspects of Black Power, both of which infiltrated the prison environment via the work of groups such as the ECI's Afro-American Society and the BCDS. However, prisoners were conflicted as a result of the tension between the 'soul' movement's celebration of historic culture and the black militant drive toward a liberated future.[111] It was apparently easier for prisoners to look backward than forward when seeking touchstones for their identity.

The tension between these two strands of Black Power led to increased complexity in the way inmates perceived one another. An overarching network of brotherhood, couched in nationalist argot and embodying the recognition of a shared fate at the hands of a common oppressor, alongside the expectance of mutual aid in the face of oppression, formed the superstructure of interactions. These tenets were embodied in programmes such as ECI's 'Uptight Programme' in which the Afro-American Society maintained a supply of essential items for newly arrived black convicts.[112]

Brotherhood implied neither friendship nor trust however, and was primarily constructed through membership in African-American prison groups.[113] Undergirding this formal structure were relationships built on trust, love, friendship or familial ties. As a result, black convicts found themselves possessing multiple identities and enmeshed in complex patterns of cultural and political responsibility. Carroll observed: 'nearly the entire black population is bound together in an interlocking structure of diffuse relationships'.[114] Even collaborators with the prison administration, 'Toms', had their place in this byzantine scheme, serving as a negative example.[115] Inmates believed 'Toms' reinforced white officers' stereotypes of black prison behaviour, polarising perceptions to the degree that 'behavior which in the eyes of the black prisoners is merely "being a man" [is perceived] as militant and threatening, and therefore more likely to be penalized'.[116]

Thus, while many contemporary observers and many subsequent historians regarded black prisoners as being a single cultural group, the profound tensions between cultural and political Black Power require a more nuanced understanding of cultural militancy in the prison to do justice to the changing perspectives of convicts.[117] Whereas some inmates, albeit a small proportion, were bona-fide revolutionaries in the George Jackson or Huey Newton mould, it is important to consider those individuals who adopted aspects of the movement's message but focused primarily on its cultural meaning and its message of empowerment and independent identity.

Termed 'halfsteppers' by Carroll, these inmates did not maintain the stoic drug and sex free existence exhibited by a minority of prison activists, or venerated by many Black Power demagogues. Flawed and fallible, these inmates used Black Power's long history in no less militant a manner. Although accused by more hardcore inmates of 'talking the talk' without the walk, by adopting revolutionary language, style and rhetoric, they still managed to craft a new place for themselves within the system.[118] The approach of these prisoners was seen by many convicts as a more attainable goal and it was these convicts who were often most successful at transferring militant ideals into the wider prison population, replacing earlier, more militant revolutionaries deemed too dictatorial or dogmatic. As the new president incumbent of ECI's Afro-American group explained in his first speech, 'what's the harm if a man scores a little dope ... now and then. He's still black ain't he? He can still be working for the revolution can't he? ... He can still think black, he can still act black, and he can still be there when the shit goes down. And that's what counts, "brothers".'[119] Accessible avatars wielded greater potential transformative power than remote, unattainable icons.

Working from the common ground of Afro-American societies, cultural groups and history education classes, many inmates on both sides of the ideological divide eventually felt empowered and defined enough to promote militant activism and guide their fellow prisoners toward liberation. The cultural output of these mentally liberated individuals became a chronicle of the flowering of African-American expression and the progress of the militant cause.

Epitomised by Etheridge Knight's 1968 poem 'Hard Rock Returns to Prison from the Hospital for the Criminal Insane', this literature featured convicts 'known not to take no shit from nobody', battered and scarred but proudly sporting a 'thick/ Canopy of kinky hair'.[120] These inmates, embodied by Hard Rock, were violent, strong individuals, capable of taking on eight guards simultaneously and poisoning them with 'syphilitic spit'.[121] A metaphor for resistance within the system, Hard Rock is eventually lobotomised, turned into a 'gelded stallion' and the other prisoners lament the passing of their 'Destroyer, the doer of things we dreamed of doing'.[122] Knight wrote in the tradition of African-American folklore, crafting a tale with the same cadence and themes of physical retribution and eventual destruction as Joe Meek and Big Sixteen. Moreover, it is evident that Knight's poetry was broadly grounded in an awareness of Black Power's long history, an ethos distilled in the poem 'The Idea of Ancestry'.[123] What legacy then was bequeathed by this apparent sense of cultural connectivity, catalysed by history and steeped in politics? Knight summarised the prison movement's impact when he recalled the August 1968 arrival of youthful militants to the penitentiary, noting that they 'shook up the joint with their blackness and their boldness'.[124] He described how the prisoners, entering shackled together, had their hair styled in natural designs, wore tiki charms around their necks and strode through the gate with cuffed hands raised in a Black Power salute as they smiled and called to the other prisoners.[125] When one older convict commented 'Somebody oughta talk to them niggers so's they don't make it hard for all of us', another inmate replied, 'What are you talking about, muthafucka? . . . I'm glad they're here 'cause them young niggers just ain't gonna take the shit we took'.[126]

Regardless of initial concerns, Knight recollected that as time passed he observed a 'lifting of the shoulders' among the African-American inmates.[127] Citing the increasing presence of an 'air of pride' among African-American prisoners, Knight claims conflict between black inmates lessened and gangs formed to protect younger black Americans from the most abusive inmates.[128] He noted tellingly that the population's desire to absorb African-American culture and history was sufficient to raise the gaol price of a copy of Lerone Bennett's *Before the Mayflower* to an exorbitant ten cigarette cartons.[129] In the face of such evidence, it is hard to deny that cultural militancy flourished within Indiana State Penitentiary. As with African-American GIs, militant African-American prisoners contended that the yard, the cooler and the cells represented in microcosm American society as a whole.[130] All three were extremely difficult environments in which to achieve self-definition, empowerment and liberated cultural expression. Each in their own way resisted, socially, legally and culturally, the notion of empowerment. Ultimately, however, none of these institutions were to succeed in obviating black cultural militancy. Thus, not merely the survival, but the growth of African-American cultural expression within the total institutions was testament to the capacity of African-American culture to convey militant ideals throughout American society. Both the army and the prisons created African-American martyrs, offering new images of heroic sacrifice to the man in the street. Disseminated via print, poetry, television and radio, how did these cultural images interact with the African-American in the street? How was African-America to respond to the growing militant expression of black culture?

The development of cultural Black Power within the army and the prisons demonstrated the power of militant rhetoric to change the way in which a person perceived the system and his place within it. Chains of ideology, image and rhetoric were created and sustained in incredibly inimical environments, reinforced by converts drawing upon the resources of history, myth and popular belief available to them. In the process, soldiers and inmates alike affirmed the importance of Black Power's long history in creating and defining identity and in providing cultural touchstones. These points of reference served as building blocks for identity construction and keys to understanding oneself and one's place within the wider world. The resulting constructions could be ultimately positive, providing a sense of purpose and place, but they could equally lead to strife, stress and mental anxiety, setting a confused individual against enemies and slights as often imagined as real. Volatile hothouse environments, these total institutions demonstrated the varied symptoms of Black Power's cultural legacy with clarity and power. However, similar changes and developments were taking place in more genteel surroundings, where the fences were not barbed wire, but white painted wood, although, in retrospect, the stresses and challenges faced by these allegedly more liberated individuals were no less pronounced.

CHAPTER 6

CHARIOTS TO THE STARS

In 1930, Robert Johnson sold his soul to the Devil for the secret of the blues. Or so the story goes. As time went on, and African-American thinkers, music critics and culture creators turned their minds to the stars, a new idea was born. Johnson, it was suggested with a certain wry humour, had traded his own immortal soul, for 'a black secret technology.'[1] Understanding the power of music within the long history of Black Power helps explain both why Johnson's trade seemed so threatening, and so arcane.

Music is often implicated in the reinforcement and the reproduction of hegemony. The charts offer a sanitised version of the world which promotes conformity, normality and compliance in accordance with Western, usually white, norms. Music can also serve as a means of resistance against that same hegemony, allowing a space for self-definition in which a person can articulate their history and local identity in a particular voice. The simple act of music appreciation – going to gigs, listening alone or together, generates social relations and experiences which can act as the foundation for new cultures and new perspectives. Put simply, music can impose the identities of the dominant society, but it can also create spaces for identity construction and act as a catalyst for the proliferation of new identities throughout society. As Tsutomu Noda noted, 'Music is a pleasure everyone can engage in, an outlet for emotional emancipation outside the loop of production and consumption. Therein lies its danger.'[2] Johnson's crossroad deal placed him as part of a number of black culture creators who stepped outside of their accepted and understood confines, via the medium of music.

Johnson himself had mythic qualities. As Martin Scorsese noted in the introduction to Alan Greenberg's screenplay *Love in Vain* 'The thing about Robert Johnson was that he only existed on his records. He was pure legend'.[3] The reality of the legend was academic. Larry Neal's admonition on the power of myth held equal weight in the musical realm.[4] Although journalist Chuck Klosterman acerbically noted 'Johnson ... met the devil about as many times as Jimmy Paige, King Diamond and Marilyn Manson did, which is to say never' he conceded the power of the myth, remarking, 'the fact that people still like to pretend a young black male could become Lucifer's ninja on the back roads of Coahoma County (and then employ his demonic perversity through *music*) makes Johnson's bargain as real as his talent.'[5] Klosterman's article evidences the Johnson myth's integration with historical reality, as the blues singer's metaphysical trade is discussed along with the more prosaic demises of Lynyrd Skynyrd, Elvis Presley and Jeff Buckley. Johnson, black and devilish though he was, has entrenched himself in our musical pantheon.

The Johnson legend persists today. Sherman Alexie's *Reservation Blues* presents it in its simplest form. In this tale the devil is a constant anonymous companion for the bluesman, with Johnson remarking to his Spokane Indian companion, Thomas Builds-the-Fire, 'I ain't gonna tell y'all his name. The Gentleman might hear and come runnin'. He gets into the strings, you hear?'[6] America certainly heard. Johnson now figures large in a wealth of novels, documentaries, scholarship and slightly lurid journalistic copy.[7]

Of all the modern interpretations of his legacy, Greenberg's *Love in Vain* perhaps comes closest to articulating the power of the Johnson myth. In his introduction to the screenplay Scorsese visualises Johnson as a 'haunted prophet who must go into the desert to find his voice, and who plays his music not out of choice but because he has no choice; he has become possessed by the spirit of the blues.'[8] Johnson certainly undertook a prophet's journey and spent his time in the wilderness (for somewhere between six months and two years) returning much changed from the allegedly terrible guitarist who left the juke joints of Robinsonville, but seeking a metaphysical explanation for his talent obscures a more complex relationship.

In historical recollections this quasi-divine aspect blends with the prosaic facts of Johnson's life, but neither loses their vitality. One of his girlfriends, Queen Elizabeth Thomas noted '*of course* Robert Johnson sold his soul to the devil, that was why he *had* to play', explaining that all blues singers, driven to sing the blues, have in some ways sold their soul to the devil.[9] From this perspective, the devil was the song itself. The compulsion to give voice to the blues.

With skills sufficient to wow Son House the possibility of an actual demonic trade did not seem implausible to some.[10] Wandering through the Delta, Johnson not only encountered blues virtuosos like Ike Zinermon but exposed himself to a technology, neither explicitly secret, nor explicitly black, but fundamental to his improvement – the phonograph.[11] Opening Johnson to a world of musical influences beyond the immediate locale, the phonograph's impact was enhanced by Johnson's talent for mimicry – once he heard a tune, he could play it.[12] Simple hard work undoubtedly factored in to Johnson's prowess, but many musicians, then and now, claimed to sense something indefinable at the core of Johnson's playing and his changed personality.[13]

Johnson's acquaintance with a diabolically talented mentor has many origins. Son House remarked on the curious tale, but Johnson himself was happy to propagate the legend. This is unsurprising. Blues had been 'the devil's music' since Baptist ministers castigated it for encouraging face to face dancing.[14] Others reached further back – Reverend Booker Miller claimed that the idea of soul-selling stemmed from 'those old slavery times.'[15] With their origins in the slave songs of the plantation, blues tunes drew on a repertoire of secular dissent. As James Cone noted, 'these early tunes 'were "non-religious", occasionally anti-religious, and were often called "devil songs" by religious folk. The "seculars" expressed the skepticism of black slaves who found it difficult to take seriously anything suggesting the religious faith of white preachers.'[16] As this music evolved and moved from the hot earth of the Deep South plantation to the cool smoky haze of roadside juke joints, it lost none of its sacrilegious quality. Yet despite religious disapprobation, many musicians were happy to be seen dancing with the devil. Peetie Wheatstraw sold himself as the 'Devil's Son-in-Law', Tommy Johnson cheerily told his brother that 'a big black man' imbued his guitar with power at a crossroads and Ike Zinermon darkly claimed he had learned to play guitar 'while sitting on tombstones at midnight in graveyards.'[17]

The thrill of the supernatural might have sent delicious shivers along listeners' spines, but it was no more esoteric than the tactics used by the modern music industry. As blues historian Gayle Wardlow noted, 'Today we could call such devilment "hype".'[18] Yet there was a mystique to this hype absent from modern accountings, a combination of the mystical and the practical. As Honeyboy Edwards recollected, Robert Johnson 'told me about going to the crossroads ... I come there ... get me a bottle of whiskey, half a pint and I sit there play the blues at night, until the sun shine ... but I never met a man! Robert was a big bullshitter.'[19] Here lies the appeal of recasting Johnson's deal as a trade for 'black secret technology'. Drawing on the past, black musicians recognised the bullshit, or more charitably, the artifice in the legends, but also acknowledged the power of the myth itself, the allure of chasing an indefinable black spirit, which could potentially be gleaned by sifting the songs of the blues and other artefacts of African-American culture from the connected musical expressions present in the long history of Black Power.

The Johnson legend still holds power today and the notion of a diabolic trade is still redolent with meaning. The man himself allegedly appeared to the writer Gerhard Kubik in 1999 as he was struggling to finish *Africa and the Blues*, noting he 'had better sign up with the devil'.[20] Hip-hop luminary Nelson George prominently featured Johnson in his lauding of the heroes of *Hip Hop America* while drum and bass pioneer A Guy Called Gerald titled his 1995 magnum opus *Black Secret Technology*.[21] Stranger comparisons existed. *Tennis* magazine's April 1990 issue saw a strong connection between Johnson and the tennis star John McEnroe, with 'each selling his soul to the devil in order to make violently graceful black magic with his instrument.'[22]

Reporting on the 1991 case to find an heir to the blues singer, the *New York Times* reminisced 'The legend was that if you touched Robert Johnson you could feel the talent running though him, like heat put there by the devil on a dark delta crossroad in exchange for his soul.'[23] The very title of the article demonstrated how the myth of Johnson had utterly supplanted the historical reality as the *Times* dubbed him the 'Father of Blues'.[24] The new 'father of the blues', unceremoniously supplanting W.C. Handy, represented a much deeper tradition in African-American culture than most of these articles acknowledge. As people of African descent living within America, for many black Americans the concept of the African devil was conflated with that provided by Western religion. Lying at the intersection of Western religion and African rhythm, the blues demon was a hybrid spirit of peculiar power.

The Western devil arrived through the church of the deep south, its Faustian bargains an inheritance from sixteenth century Germany, in which musical genius was one of the demon's many gifts.[25] The Puritan tradition nourished this burgeoning fiend, which waxed fat on concepts of sin that stemmed from the Great Awakening of the eighteenth century 'an explosion of dread and piety that Southern whites passed on to their slaves and that black Americans ultimately fashioned into their own religion.'[26] Crucially, as scholar Greil Marcus noted, the blues singers 'accepted the dread but refused the piety.'[27]

The snake-tongued, horned and hoofed figure of Christianity was not alone in the Delta, working many of his greatest deals with an African partner, a version of the devil-as-trickster, stemming from the vodou lwa Esu-Elegbara, Papa LaBas or Legba, the guardian of gateways and crossroads.[28] Importantly, in voudoun, Legba not only guards the boundary between the profane and the sacred but the boundary between creativity and reality, as a lord of the cultural arts, both in music and poetry.[29] Possessed of a 'mordant sense of humour' and deep 'delight in chaos', Legba was easily conflated with the devil, although sin and damnation do not fall within his purview.[30] In a complex manner, Legba was neither exclusively good nor evil, but could be either or neither as the situation required.[31] Helpful and spiteful in equal measure, the mercurial loa did not fit well with a Christian theology which sought binary oppositions. As a result his 'synchronous duplicity' saw him rapidly shoehorned into the space of the devil.[32] An African-Atlantic presence, insinuated into the mythology and narrative of African-America, Legba's presence ranged through the songs of the blues and across some of the most iconic twentieth century works of African-American writing.[33] Evolving along with transatlantic African identities, the Legba of the Deep South was a different creature to that which had embarked from the West African coast.[34]

Fuelled by the spirit of Legba, the blues was castigated for its hoodoo associations and its connection to an atavistic African memory, but the power of the Johnson myth is as much futuristic as it is atavistic.[35] At its simplest level, Johnson trades something indefinable for access to a new universe of skill or talent, be that a devil-tuned guitar or some more nebulous 'black secret technology'. Johnson himself represents startling progress, sometimes inexplicable, but always capable of challenging, shattering and realigning the boundaries of the society. This perhaps explains why African-American bluesmen and white social scientists alike, despite their differing perceptions of culture, are comparatively equally split in their acceptance or dismissal of the Johnson legend. Both groups recognise the power of the myth and the possibilities afforded by its mysterious change. Johnson is the creative leap. The step beyond assumed boundaries. The blending of Baptist hellfire and vodou trickery. The combination of an African past with an American musical future.

It is perhaps unsurprising then, to find Johnson at the roots of a strange phenomenon which emerged in the 1990s, generated by black cultural luminaries sifting the artefacts of history in an attempt to create a proactive vision for the future of black creation. The ethos of Afrofuturism epitomised the combination of heritage and progress that Johnson embodied and turned to him, understandably, as its first and most cryptic signifier. Johnson was a suitable sinner turned saint, as the emergence of Afrofuturist thinking in the late 1990s was itself something of a mystery. The term was an attempt to give a name to a search which had been on-going since at least the 1970s. Afrofuturism was, from one perspective, a sifting of the past to find directions for the future of black culture. At its heart lay the contention that the black experience in America, was fundamentally one of alienation. In his now-iconic essay, 'Black to the Future' culture critic Mark Dery defined this ethos, when he wrote, 'African Americans, in a very real sense, are the descendants of alien abductees; they inhabit a sci-fi nightmare in which unseen but no less impassable force fields of intolerance frustrate their movements; official histories undo what has been done and technology is too often brought to bear on black bodies'.[36]

For historians, Afrofuturism is a particularly pertinent concept. As Ytasha Womack explained, it exists at 'the intersection between black culture, technology, liberation and the imagination'.[37] In essence, it offers both historians and artists 'a way of bridging the future and the past and essentially helping to reimagine the experience of people of colour'.[38] To understand the revolution of the mind offered by Black Power, we must also understand the futuristic intersections which it drew upon and emerged from. Afrofuturism, like most other vectors of African-American identity conception, drew heavily on the historical and cultural expressions which had preceded it. Most obviously, the movement was strongly rooted in the pioneering African-American science fiction which emerged during the 1920s, which arguably reached its zenith in W.E.B. Du Bois's *Darkwater*.[39] Of all the pieces in *Darkwater*, it is Du Bois's *The Comet* which truly stands out as being clearly science fiction and expressing perhaps the most powerful viewpoint in the book.[40] On the surface, 'The Comet' adopts a classic motif of the sci-fi genre, an apocalypse which leaves only two survivors, a man and a woman, in a manner akin to Adam and Eve. Within this framework however, Du Bois begins to explore themes of race, class and gender. His story begins with New York City awaiting the passage of the titular comet in close proximity to the planet. Although Earth escapes a direct impact, the gas from the comet's tail kills almost everyone on the planet, save for a single lucky black bank clerk, Jim, deep underground in a secret vault and a young white woman, Julia, preserved in a photography dark room.[41] Sent to vaults 'too dangerous for more valuable men' it is ironically this discrimination that protects Jim.[42] Symbolically removed from society, he descends to another, alien, world: 'Down ... beneath Broadway, where the dim light filtered through the feet of hurrying men; down to the dark basement beneath; down into the blackness and silence beneath that lowest cavern ... in the bowels of the earth, under the world.'[43] Eventually emerging from his subjugated place under the world, Jim sees horrific scenes of death and devastation as the gas poisons hundreds. He comes to the logical conclusion that 'The comet had swept the earth and this was the end.'[44]

There is a liberation that comes with this realisation. The death of white society opens up its pleasures to Jim who walks the 'gorgeous, ghost-haunted halls' of a Fifth Avenue restaurant, raids its food and reflects 'Yesterday, they would not have served me' but still struggles to choke the delicacies down.[45] He continues to avail himself of the quintessential pleasures of the American dream, stealing a Ford from its unlucky owner. Yet even this joy is short-lived. As Jim drives he notices that 'Everywhere stood, leaned, lounged, and lay the dead, in grim and awful silence ... an automobile, wrecked and overturned ... a gay party whose smiles yet lingered on their death-struck lips; on past crowds and groups of cars, pausing by dead policemen.'[46] It is only this 'dead congestion' that leads to the discovery of Julia, whose panicked cries from a high window sound in his ears 'like the voice of God.'[47] Travelling to Harlem together, Jim realises he has lost his whole family.

In an attempt to avoid the same fate for Julia, the pair engage in a frantic hunt for her family which leads them past the 'dark and lined dead of Harlem' and towards the Metropolitan Tower. Everywhere the couple find only 'silence and death – death and silence.'[48]

Apparently utterly alone and cut off from communication with the outside world, the two survivors find a commonality not just in their survival but in the disintegration of the rigid segregation laws and subconscious social conventions that had separated black from white.[49] Jim and Julia, Du Bois suggests, are now simply equal participants in the unfolding crisis with an equal stake in the survival of the human race. In this simple metaphor, he not only summarises one of the basic tenets of *Darkwater*, but addresses the foundation of his wider thinking on racial issues. As with other African-American science fiction, to be alien and to be black are one and the same. From Du Bois's perspective, Jim has always existed outside of society: 'Few noticed him. Few ever noticed him save in a way that stung. He was outside the world.'[50] It is only the destruction of society which permits him to make a proper, equal contact with another human. The initial shock Julia experiences on meeting Jim encapsulates this tension:

> They stared a moment in silence. She had not noticed before that he was a Negro. He had not thought of her as white. She was a woman of perhaps twenty-five – rarely beautiful and richly gowned, with darkly-golden hair, and jewels. Yesterday, he thought with bitterness, she would scarcely have looked at him twice. He would have been dirt beneath her silken feet. She stared at him. Of all the sorts of men she had pictured as coming to her rescue she had not dreamed of one like him. Not that he was not human, but he dwelt in a world so far from hers, so infinitely far, that he seldom even entered her thoughts.

This awkwardness lasts only a moment. Jim's alien nature is shed with speed until he seems 'quite commonplace and usual.'[51] Julia later reflects, 'He did not look like men, as she had always pictured men; but he acted like one and she was content.[52] Jim and Julia have both emerged from darkness, physically and figuratively, shedding their preconceptions and undergoing a revolution of the mind.[53] This seems more difficult for Julia who occasionally lapses into the same stereotyped fear of black men which Julius Lester had sarcastically criticised in *Look Out Whitey!* but Du Bois adds to this terror a fear of the profoundly alien nature of black people. At one point, Julia panics as she realises that she is 'alone in the world with a stranger, with something more than a stranger, – with a man alien in blood and culture – unknown, perhaps unknowable.'[54]

Yet, Julia rapidly overcomes her fears, spurred by the same knowledge of basic divinity which undergirded Du Bois's own world view on the shared divinity of humanity. His characters muse that, rich and poor alike, 'The Lord is the Maker of them all.'[55] However, there is more to the story than simply Christian inspiration. A predecessor of the revolution of the mind mandated by Black Power adherents lies at its heart; a fundamental change for both Jim and Julia. As he explains to her, 'I was not – human, yesterday, ... And your people were not my people, she said; but today – .'[56] From the roof of the Metropolitan Tower, Julia's epiphany is somewhat more grandiose, as she realises she is:

> no mere woman. She was neither high nor low, white nor black, rich nor poor. She was primal woman; mighty mother of all men to come and Bride of Life. She looked upon the man beside her and forgot all else but his manhood, his strong, vigorous manhood – his sorrow and sacrifice. She saw him glorified. He was no longer a thing apart, a creature below, a strange outcast of another clime and blood, but her Brother Humanity incarnate, Son of God and great All – Father of the race to be.'[57]

Both survivors, black and white, are freed from societal convention by tragedy. As they set off fireworks on the roof of an abandoned skyscraper, the sight of a bright white star, echoing the North Star of slave narratives, catalyses an even greater transformation in Jim, as he becomes almost an avatar for the classic, mythical tropes of African-American strength and beauty. Du Bois writes that: 'The shackles seemed to rattle and fall from his soul. Up from the crass and crushing and cringing of his caste leaped the lone majesty of kings long dead. He arose within the shadows, tall, straight, and stern, with power in his eyes and ghostly scepters hovering to his grasp. It was as though some mighty Pharaoh lived again, or curled Assyrian lord.'[58] For a brief moment, entwined together, Jim and Julia are utterly equal, 'Their souls lay naked to the night. It was not lust; it was not love – it was some vaster, mightier thing that needed neither touch of body nor thrill of soul. It was a thought divine, splendid.'[59]

Yet it is here that Du Bois orchestrates his grand reveal. Just as they come to the realisation of their equality, a car horn sounds and Julia is met by her retuning father and her young suitor, Fred.[60] The father, as paternalistically as any slave owner, recoils at the realisation that Jim is 'a nigger!', but gives him money for 'saving' his daughter and then quickly whisks her away.[61] As other people emerge from the once silent streets, Jim hears the familiar racial epithets fill the clearing air once again and narrowly escapes a lynching.[62] The world turns, and comes to rest at its point of origin. Du Bois's final vision is bleak. Although the comet kills millions, hatred, prejudice and discrimination survive unchanged. At the story's end, Jim meets his wife, who clutches their dead child to her breast. In his closing lines, Du Bois literally and irrevocably kills all hope for the future.

Via its post-apocalyptic trappings, *The Comet* echoed growing frustrations with the slow process of iterative political reform and hinted at the desire in much anti-colonial rhetoric to see the corrupt American empire tumble. As Reiland Rabaka explained:

> ['The Comet'] suggests that more radical measures than mere piecemeal socio-political reform ... are needed to make the system an authentic multicultural democracy ... There is a sense in which 'The Comet' can be read as a racially oppressed and poverty-stricken person's dream come true ... in terms of the oppressed desperately desiring to see their oppressors and the oppressive system they imperially invented toppled. The story is also Fanonian in the sense that there is room for racial reconciliation and redemption if–and this is an extremely important 'if' that cannot be over-emphasized– if they both free themselves from the social conventions, vices, and vulgarities of the former white supremacist world.[63]

In his earlier 1903 essay *The Souls of Black Folk* Du Bois remarked on his school days with white children that he felt 'shut out from their world by a vast veil.'[64] Ultimately, Du Bois uses science fiction as a means to discard the veil of race from our way of looking at the world, and to meditate on how we might relate to each other in a world free from such constraints. Widely read and gloriously creative, Du Bois's science fiction offered a new avenue from which to communicate the black experience in America to the American people. In this respect, *The Comet* is a profoundly militant piece, a work, which as Sundstrom writes: 'saw through the pathology and absurdity of "race", and sought to display the sickness of the American "racial" politic.'[65]

Du Bois's proposed solution to this sickness again lies in his earlier writing, specifically the idea that African-Americans suffer from a double consciousness, being both American and black. Each of these facts bequeaths an historical inheritance and a perspective on the past that cannot be seen from without the race. The notion that any African-American must eventually 'merge his double self into a better and truer self' without losing either of his cultural inheritances receives a clear expression in *The Comet*, when Jim finally becomes, albeit briefly, more significant for being a *living* man than a *black* man.

Du Bois was somewhat ahead of his time however. Turn of the century science fiction tended to portray an ethnically pure future, as in Fritz Lang's 1927 *Metropolis*. Much of this early racism was somewhat unconscious, present in science fiction primarily because it was 'long rife in popular fiction of all kinds'.[66] As the science-fiction scholar Samuel Moskowitz reflected, 'it was indeed fortunate that early writers of teenage science fiction exercised personal responsibility or they could have infected white youths with an even greater virus of colour hate.'[67] While some works, such as the 1930s Flash Gordon series, featured evil Asian antagonists, ethnic minorities were often utterly absent. This trend did not dissipate as the twentieth century progressed. Some of the most prominent fiction of the 1980s cyberpunk era, from Gibson's *Neuromancer* (1984) to Ridley Scott's epic *Blade Runner* (1982) tapped into the fear of sinister Eastern influences.

Post-World War II, as the nonviolent Civil Rights Movement developed, science fiction began to advocate a more peaceful coexistence of the races, a perspective which rapidly became central to the genre. By the 1970s, African-American authors had begun to make a clear impact on the field, many of them setting the stage for the emergence of the Afrofuturist movement in the 1990s – producing fiction that married the issues of race and the evolution of science and technology. In particular, the 1970s saw the rise of two pioneers of the Afrofuturist movement in Samuel R. Delany and Octavia E. Butler. Delany and

Butler, although varied in their style and approach, shared a number of common points of reference: race was integral to their writing and utterly integrated with their plots and protagonists who themselves were often possessed of not merely narrative agency, but tremendous shaping power. Following their footsteps, within the last few decades, racially aware science fiction has exploded in scope and approach. Afrofuturism continues to set the bounds of these new cosmic fables, and African-American voices sound strongly in the void of space, although works of Latino science fiction and stories dealing with race in a more abstract fashion are beginning to emerge.[68]

Samuel R. Delany was not only one of science fiction's first black authors, but a luminary in the 'New Wave' movement, a name used to unify a disparate group of science fiction authors who produced highly experimental writing, both in form and in content and who saw science fiction not merely as pulp entertainment but as a literary art form.[69] Retelling familiar stories in new forms which questioned evolving personal identities, many of these works focused on soft, rather than hard science fiction, exploring the ideas and philosophies suggested by futuristic thinking and new technology, without going into precise details as to the nature and functioning of that technology. Delany's *Dhalgren* epitomises this approach, using fractured, stream of consciousness narratives, looping perspectives and poetic asides to frame a story that is itself revolutionary, challenging static notions of gender and race, while introducing shifting perspectives not simply on race and gender relationships but on reality itself.[70]

The novel begins when its anonymous, amnesiac main character, eventually dubbed Kidd, travels into the blasted, writhing ruins of the city of Bellona, its shattered post-apocalyptic streets marked by twin moons and stalked by shifting hologram gangs and red-eyed dogs. While the rest of American life proceeds as normal outwith Bellona, within the city's warped, mercurial interior, a new set of societal rules on life, sex, race and war emerge. Violence is a constant counterpart, reflected in the deadly 'orchid' that Kidd carries with him, a brutal iron flower of interlocking blades which cannot seem to be left behind, and always reappears heavy with menace. An inescapable piece of arcane technology, the orchid presages the Afrofuturist movement's focus on perception changing devices and opens the gates for Delany to warp the settings and assumptions of his characters.

Delany pushes readers to challenge the binaries of American culture, using his dark skinned, bisexual protagonist to twist notions of white vs. black, gay vs. straight, male vs. female or even the formative distinction of sanity vs. insanity. Bellona itself is a contradiction: it is apocalyptic, but it is not a disaster zone and it is undeniably affecting to its inhabitants, but it may not be real. Writing fresh from the social turmoil of the 1960s, Delany frames Bellona's upheaval in a manner which challenges ingrained perceptions of social structures, suggesting that even our surroundings speak to our cultural values, and that flux itself is no negative thing.

As the 1970s progressed, the apocalyptic tone of black science fiction strengthened. Sun Ra's 1974 space odyssey *Space is the Place* begins with the plaintive refrain 'It's after the end of the world, don't you know that yet?'[71] In the blood-soaked, smoke-stained shadow of the 1960s, the dire warnings of the genre seemed not dissimilar to the reality of much African-American life at the time, and often, there appeared to be a distinct closeness between African-American science fiction and the reality of black life in America.

As Greg Tate argued, 'Black existence and science-fiction are one and the same'.[72] There is some truth to this statement. In much black science fiction from Samuel Delany's *Dhalgren* to Du Bois's *The Comet* there is usually a protagonist who is at odds with the apparatus of power and whose profound experience is one of estrangement from the society in which they find themselves. *Dhalgren* is particularly significant as it marks the first time that black characters are not merely protagonists but change the entire terms of the story.

Similarly to Delany, Octavia E. Butler, one of the first African-American female science fiction authors, brought the New Wave ethos into her stories by retelling old science fiction tales from novel perspectives and used those perspectives to discuss her favoured themes of identity, gender and race. Arguably, Butler's most famous work is *Kindred*, published in 1988, which takes one of the oldest science fiction tropes, time travel, and uses it to present a complex and racially charged history in which the novel's protagonist, Dana, is flung back in time against her will.[73] Rather than being spirited forth by benevolent technology, Dana's odyssey is involuntary, and she finds herself torn from modern day California to land in the harsh confines of the nineteenth century antebellum South. Via this simple conceit, Butler forcibly inserts present racial reality into the connected historical expressions which have informed the black experience in America.

In her new situation, Dana is endangered by both her race and her gender, pushing her to reconceptualise her identity, undergoing a revolution of the mind which is made all the starker when her white husband adapts to the antebellum setting with enthusiasm, even as the chains of a slave's life way ever heavier on Dana. Ultimately, the brutal reality of the African-American situation, and the origins of Africans in America are hammered home when Dana is obliged to save a white child to ensure her own future birth, and must help him orchestrate the rape of her own great-grandmother to guarantee her own survival. In the process, Butler not only uses time travel as a means to juxtapose the attitudes of the antebellum South with modern America, but shows the inescapable continuities which defined history on a personal level for many African-Americans, and the difficulties in remembering a history that, as techno artist Mike Banks explained 'we're not past. We're told to forget.'[74]

While it gets much of its content from the historical lived experiences of the black diaspora, structurally, Afrofuturism also owes a debt to the filmmaking legacy of the 1980s. This cinematic evolution effectively began with the first Havana film festival on December 3, 1979, an event that sought to more profoundly integrate the politics of movie makers with the aesthetics of their work.[75] At the turn of the decade, Cuba not only symbolised an alternative way of perceiving the world, but seemed to suggest practical steps towards achieving concrete change. One such step was taken in 1982 by John Akomfrah, one of the founding members of Black Audio Films, a collective venture designed to provide a voice for black concerns, producing documentaries shaped by the prevailing cultural and political agendas of the time. This was epitomised by Akomfrah's first film, *Handsworth Songs* which studied the 1985 Brixton and Handsworth riots through meditative photographic and filmic montages.[76]

As in America, early 1980s Britain seethed with racial antagonisms, but filmmakers like Akomfrah perceived the media as failing fundamentally to provide a clear perspective on the changes in perception being undergone by black protestors and the reasons for their anger. As he argued, 'Television is very amnesiac... We saw a connection between the events of 1985 and events 30 years earlier... We tried to provide the urban unrest with a memory and a history.'[77] This approach, which focused on connecting contemporary dissent with historical experience, characterised the efforts of a number of black filmmakers during the decade, and gave transatlantic significance to the connected cultural expressions which formed the long history of Black Power.[78] With his emphasis on signs and symbolism, Akomfrah was ideally placed to relate the martyr-heroes of African-American history to his own British reality.

Arguably the most readily available repository of symbolism in African-American history is religious, and so when Akomfrah produced *Seven Songs for Malcolm X* and *Martin Luther King – Days of Hope* he used the tension inherent in sacred iconography to present two very contrasting portraits which evoked the relationship between these iconic avatars of protest and the American people, and explored the way in which their image was conveyed transatlantically.[79] He recalled, 'With Seven Songs for Malcolm X, I thought we could speak through the image, the icon, because most people never met him in his life and he came to us as a sanctified image, while people remember King for his legacy.'[80]

Consequently, *Seven Songs* offered a broad spectrum of commentary on the image of Malcolm X, which echoed the manner in which his memory came to dominate both the Black Arts Movement and the Harlem community after his assassination. Conversely, Akomfrah's portrayal of Martin Luther King literally straddles the line between light and dark, using shifting patterns of illumination to show King's changing place in the freedom struggle, in a manner reminiscent of William Worthy's *Esquire* chart, which moved King on a sliding scale from white to black, in order to demonstrate his perceived militancy and dedication to civil rights issues across time.[81]

On another level, Akomfrah's use of lighting resonates with the emotional appeal of King as an icon first, and a man second. This combination of emotion, stylisation and agenda defines much modern black film-making, which questions our current assumptions on race, alienation and identity, but does not necessarily push a dogmatic political line.[82] As Akomfrah noted, 'What I learned from these cinemas is that to make something new you have to question the premises of the mainstream. In this I have a cultural and a political agenda but I don't have a "way"'.[83]

Like his American counterparts, in relating memory and reality, Akomfrah necessarily engaged with the African diaspora, connecting fragments of the black world, adrift in the deep and turbulent waters of Paul Gilroy's *Black Atlantic*.[84] It is perhaps unsurprising that Akomfrah turned to science fiction for this task, seen in his film *The Last Angel of History* where science fiction themes are mirrored in the interaction of contemporary black life and the legacy of the African diaspora. As he explained, 'The interest in science-fiction for me has to do with the encounter between Africans and Modernity. Science-fiction narratives are usually about alienation, abduction and transportation and that is a very powerful narrative for understanding the transportation and displacing of African people across the world.'[85]

This powerful narrative runs through *The Last Angel of History*. The film casts the reconstruction of a modern black culture as a literal process in which the titular *Last Angel* is in fact a 'data thief' who acts as a combination of prospector and archaeologist, extracting techno-fossils from the heritage of black history and culture. To the data thief, the internet is a valuable tool from which fragments of black culture can be gleaned as black cultural forms and aesthetics infiltrate the popular consciousness. In the process of this gleaning, the thief becomes something more: 'an angel ... the angel of history.'[86] This syncretic and symbiotic approach to the past defines Afrofuturism and marks it as a significant phase in the long history of Black Power. More importantly, it also provides signal new strands for Black Power history and memory to enter the American cultural conscious.

In his 1995 essay, Dery described Afrofuturism as absorbing, consuming and reproducing 'images of technology and a prosthetically-enhanced future.'[87] At its most fundamental level, early Afrofuturism was a way for black people and artists to move beyond the limits of their present day situation and to place African-Americans in new, often provocative, usually iconoclastic, situations. To many writers and musicians in the 1990s the limitless terrain of space and the imaginative possibilities of sci-fi seemed to offer a link between Africa as a lost continent in the past and Africa as an alien future.

Arguably, the 'first touch of sci-fi came when Africans began playing drums to cover distance'. Certainly it is common to conceptualise music as both a warning device and its own language of resistance. From calypso, through Fela Kuti and Gil Scott-Heron, protest and sound have a close relationship, but the black musical tradition received its first heavy infusion of science fiction via the recordings of Lee Perry's Black Ark Studios and the Sun Ra Arkestra.[88] These groups produced what Ishmael Reed referred to in reverent terms as 'a mirror of the universe.'[89] Technology was not always a unifying force for African-Americans. As aural and visual theorist Kodwo Eshun noted, 'Computer tech started out in the military sphere ... [providing] ways to create sonic worlds that will secede and are antagonistic.'[90] It was here that Eshun gave birth to the concept of 'sonic warfare': the use of sound and music as a subversive device. Sonic warfare, its exponents argued, was a weapon for the colonised, whether in Africa or in America, to challenge the boundaries set by their colonisers.

One of the foremost exponents of this new style of auditory activism was the Detroit techno collective Underground Resistance (UR). In one version of their story, UR portray themselves as a high-tech guerrilla troop, fighters in a 'war against the programmers dominating the world.'[91] In the other, more prosaic version, Mike Banks and Jeff Mills formed Underground Resistance in 1989, as the Detroit techno scene was proliferating out into a global world and returning with European influences.[92] In its current incarnation, UR is both a record label and a pseudonym for a loose collective of musicians, with an ethos based around reciprocal artistic and social support.[93] The group exists both on a local level, with established, explicit connections to the Detroit community and on a transnational level as part of a global electronic music scene. In addition, the reality of Underground Resistance and the fiction offered by their self-created mythology of resistance overlaps frequently, and with little respect for traditional boundaries between artist, performer, audience and environment. Drawing on the connected historical expressions of black militant sentiment, this emergent urban mythology is both critical and aspirational, dissident and constructive. There are few groups active in America today that demonstrate as complex a relationship between urban space and electronic sound inhabiting a genre of music that is one-part electronic dream and one-part struggle for survival.[94]

Techno existed prior to Underground Resistance, beamed down into the Belleville suburbs by Juan Atkins, Derrick May and Kevin Saunderson. This early Detroit techno was a musical form that recognised its African-American heritage, but also rejected any limiting notions of what that heritage entailed.[95] Consequently, when early techno engaged with Detroit, it did not do so directly, but rather by telling science-fiction stories about the city. However, in UR's music, the condition of the city remains the ultimate reference point, both as a catalyst for a transformative vision of black life and as the place where the *vision should become reality*.

Traditionally, science-fiction narratives were adopted for their escapist potential, offering their readers a chance of participating in Sun Ra's 'interplanetary emigrationist movement', but Detroit techno's science-fiction fables, like the political rhetoric of many Black Power adherents, stress the transformation of existing urban society, beyond the limitations and prejudices of the inner-city environment.[96] Ultimately, science fiction opens up the possibility of identity formation spaces which are not necessarily tied to previous racialising or ethnic narratives. Thus, the emergence of UR's own particular brand of inner-city identification merits analysis. As a musical form and a mythological matrix, UR, in contrast, were not representative of Detroit city's entire population in the 1980s and 1990s but they do speak to one way of viewing the problems in its urban heart. Techno artists prior to UR neither sided with, nor identified with the urban poor but rather, created utopian visions of alternative societies within urban spaces.[97] For most of these artists, and contrary to our usual way of thinking about identity politics, the connection between identity and social location was not that important. UR in contrast, clearly seek to place themselves as fundamentally rooted in their community, as part of a black radical tradition, and a concomitant black radical mythology; but they also promote a set of dissident identities that are not explicitly tied to race.

In the dystopia of their mythology, UR's music surfaces across a soundscape pockmarked by the concrete shells of decaying leviathans – houses, factories and complexes left unoccupied since the 1967 riots and further hollowed out by the hungry teeth of the 80s economic downturn. Wracked by deindustrialisation and suburbanisation, the final nail in the coffin for mid-twentieth century Detroit seemed to be the relocation of Motown to Los Angeles in 1972.[98]

In contrast with its contemporary fortunes, post-war Detroit was a symbol of America's modern industrial achievement. Its workers were portrayed as heroes regardless of race and its murals hinted at the reconstructive, sci-fi dreams which would inform UR's rhetoric, proclaiming: 'We dream of a world to meet our individual and communal needs ... as the world changes, we invent new tools ... [and] fashion a world closer to our ends, invested with meanings and purposes of our own creation'.[99]

Yet by the latter part of the twentieth century Jerry Herron felt confident in declaring 'Detroit stands for an America that is over.'[100] Perhaps there was something to this. General Motors, Ford and Chrysler had fallen like slain giants, their rebar bones littering the inner city. After the riots of July 1967, a large-scale flight to the suburbs hollowed out Detroit, rendering a city that had been 70 per cent white, 80 per cent black.[101] As the city emptied of material and people, Detroit arguably lost a broader sense of belonging.

In this post-fiscal apocalypse, UR saw themselves as vinyl guerrillas hacking the programmatic audio narratives pushed by the mainstream music industry.[102] As John Wraight recollected, 'Among the guns and ammunition of the city's pawn shops they chose discarded instruments as their weapons of choice.'[103] This embattled Detroit, with its reputation for violence and urban decay, seemed to offer easy ciphers describing the group's agenda and appearance, but the reality is far more complex.

It is increasingly evident that post-crash Detroit has a scene all of its own.[104] Echoing descriptions of 1920s Harlem, journalists such as Tsutomu Noda recall a city where 'cabaret parties proliferate at night while the city streets fill with the smell of burning rubber as Motor-city engineers of all creeds, colours and generations pitch their wits against each other (and the police)'. After some time in the city, Noda concluded that 'Optically [Detroit's] much more than the desolate (dis)illusion so often depicted.'[105] Sonically, things were also changing profoundly. For UR, Detroit was an optimistic, techno-futuristic warzone, and in that warzone music was a weapon and music was medicine. It was both aggressive and curative. As part of DJ culture, UR's soundtrack was mobile, both physically and conceptually: 'a dynamic weapon ... a force that disturbs through its detachment from the visual or knowable, symbolically acting on the imagination, infiltrating and destabilising power.'[106] In UR's universe, new tracks 'ambush and replace old ones'.[107] UR itself has no musicians, only 'sonic commandos'.[108] Their language is ruthless, the implications Darwinian.

Yet the Detroit music scene also holds purifying properties, its embedded journalists spitting forth a sea of biological metaphors describing the manner in which 'bass DJs sonically inject vaccines into house parties ... [and] ... MCs guide the antigens through the body until the receptors are burning, grinding and twisting on the dance floor.'[109] The net effect is to argue for a sense of unity within the music and by extension, the community: the 'hood' we are told 'entertains its own.'[110] Yet the hood, for UR, represents something very different to the ghetto of contemporary hip-hop. One of the key distinctions is that, along with a strong sense of space, UR's techno identity politics are heavily intertwined with a creative, often sci-fi mythology that twists, alters and reconstructs the reality of their contemporary urban spaces. As Thomas Meinecke writes in *Hellblau*, techno is an 'effectively invisible city [which] has almost no streets, [and] no street credibility, [it exists] ... far beyond any myths of social reality [but] appears nevertheless as a radically dissident political medium.'[111]

Whereas hip-hop emphasises the place of the ghetto as something to be defended and venerated, techno emphasises the home-space of the 'hood', as a place of creation and resistance which exists both figuratively and literally. For UR, the hood is one of many reference points, but one which inflects their music significantly. Of still more interest to their mythology is the imaginative capacity of the people *within* the hood, the desire to create and recreate, to move beyond the accepted, 'electrifying the inner city with hi tech thoughts and dreams'.[112] In the process of this electrification, UR transforms notions of techno's relationship to black culture and positions Detroit as part of wider global flows, its music neither essentially African-American nor European. Popular music scholars John Connell and Chris Gibson have argued that 'Cities are nodes in international mediascapes' and this is particularly applicable to Detroit.[113]

As Sean Albiez explained: 'Techno is African-American music that casts its eyes and ears elsewhere than the urban ghetto, the church and the street.'[114] As techno is produced transnationally and interculturally, it does not seem to qualify as black music because it does not function as black music is expected to, compositionally, lyrically or socially.

Consequently, black techno artists and white electronic musicians were involved in an imagined community in the 1980s and 1990s, existing as part of a shared transnational sonic futurescape, making music without reference to borders, heavily inflected with science-fiction components.[115] As these artists were working interculturally and beyond localities music historians don't talk much about the racial dimensions of techno, but for UR, race inexorably inflects their music and mythology.[116] The group sees itself as grounded in a black radical historical tradition, and deliberately situates itself in that tradition via the myths it creates.

This mythology is grounded in the character of the Unknown Writer, who dispenses grave aphorisms on the liner notes of each release. 'While you feel safe and sleep – beware by night we fly', he warns on UR 36.[117] 'Resistance can be perceived as righteousness when what one resists is evil' cautions UR 45.[118] 'Only together will we win', he sermonises on UR 20.[119] Taken as a whole, the Writer's pronouncements echo the declarations of solidarity and promises of retribution that characterised the 1960s Black Power movement, but present them through an anonymous mythological avatar who lives in the liner notes.

There is a clear appeal to this romanticised fiction of rebellion, which allows listeners and producers alike to position themselves as part of a militant subversive legacy. The Writer, whomever he may be, styles himself 'an urban commentator who uses the city of Detroit and the centre labels of UR vinyl as a notebook in which to inscribe the need for empowerment, struggle and resistance.'[120] In toto, the Writer's messages act as a hypnotic pseudopoem, whispering messages of subversion, while the narrative he creates becomes a modern urban mythology of 'wandering souls created by injustice who will eternally haunt mankind', unless their grievances are addressed.[121]

Despite the intervening years, The Unknown Writer, as a commentator, is not dissimilar from many other iconic figures of black dissidence from Ellison's Invisible Man, through Bradley's John Washington, Neal's Uncle Rufus, Clinton's Starchile or Monae's Archandroid.[122] The Writer *knows* this. He presents his existence as part of a series of connected expressions across the long history of Black Power. As he reflects and cautions on the memorial to Detroit steelworker Malice Green: 'We are helped to remember our right to be here/We are helped to remember our responsibilities/We create our justice daily.'[123]

The repetition of 'we remember', turns liner notes into litany. From the connection the Writer draws to the past there is a powerful assertion of equality in the present, and his language evidences the same sense of personal responsibility and action that undergirded the ideology of groups such as the Black Panthers. His declaration that 'We are helped to remember' implies a connection with the past that is not simply a reliance born from repetition but a strength derived through historical understanding.

The character of the Writer emphasises that UR were under no illusion that their music, like their politics, was darker and harder-edged than its predecessors, a progression from the religious stoicism of civil rights into something more subversive. As Mike Banks explained 'Our people have consistently only had music as a voice. Whether it was Field Work songs, or coded shit like "Wading in the Water" ... music has been one of our few tools to access mainstream media within the USA.'[124]

Listen to the group's *Interstellar Fugitives* and that voice takes form: 'The day-time praise and fellowship of gospel gives way to a shift in frequencies as soon as twilight begins to tarnish the sky. Then begin the coded transmissions from the nocturbulous.'[125] *Fugitives* is an incredibly complex work that discusses maroon slave communities, Afrogermanic identities, broadcasts from a lost civilisation of advanced Atlantean-Americans and the 'negative evolution' of western society, all within one vinyl record. Yet the diversity of UR's voice and vision has been virtually ignored by historians. Partially the blame for this lies with Stuart Cosgrove, who warned in the liner notes for Virgin's 1988 *Techno!* Collection that 'The new grandmasters of Detroit techno hate history ... Detroit refutes the past ... it prefers tomorrow's technology to yesterday's heroes ... it says nothing to the Lord but speaks volumes on the dancefloor.'[126]

The work of UR shows that this could not be further from the truth. Working under the mandate that 'Man must know his past before challenging the future' these coded transmissions made explicit connections with nineteenth century resistance, grounding myths that lay centuries apart in the same geographical hub.[127] Listeners were reminded that 'Travelling along an elaborate trans-state escape route known as the Underground Railroad, 19th Century fugitive slaves fled the south in search of the freedom of Canada ... Last stop, the 2nd Baptist church, last stop Detroit ... code-name Midnight.'[128] The implication was that Detroit was the home of UR and the final resting place of decades of rebellion.

This sense of history could not be any clearer than in Suburban Knight's 'Maroon', the second track on *Interstellar Fugitives*. Taking its inspiration from the name given to freed slave communities, the track prominently features a distorted voice which declares: 'I am a voice from the past/Standing in the future/To forever haunt you/You should never have done this to us/Because now we can never rest/we are/black electric/ strong electric.'[129]

In a few lines, the distant past of slave rebellions is connected powerfully to the electric modernity of the present and the interstellar promise of the future. There is a deeper resonance here, between the reality of history and the imagery that the electronic musicians of Detroit wanted to construct for themselves in the twentieth and twenty-first centuries. The liner notes for *Interstellar Fugitives* take pains to make explicit connections with the long history of Black Power and black empowerment, referencing Paul Robeson, Rosa Parks, Coleman Young (Detroit's first black mayor), Joe Louis, James Baldwin and Huey Newton, alongside the slightly less orthodox choice of William Wallace, the thirteenth century Scottish rebel. These luminaries are juxtaposed with ordinary warriors of both genders, the regular Detroit citizens who have suffered at the hands of the police and are presented as street level casualties in the urban war of oppression. The end goal is to situate the black community firmly in the past in order to create a more empowering identity in the present, and thereby drive change in the future. Whereas early techno offered 'little in the way of overt critical or social commentary', UR's music relies on it.[130] As Banks explained, each release could serve a different purpose 'to help listeners through tuff times ... [as] ... coded directives to the swarm and necessary movements to protect the hive ... [or they could be] ... reflections of necessity, imagination, environment, emotion ... soundtracks to events which are far from positive.'[131]

This community aspect has meant that up until as recently as 2006, UR has been identified as black nationalist techno.[132] This is a gross oversimplification. UR's mythology, via the Unknown Writer, functions as part of a network of allusions, part of what Cedric Robinson called 'the continuing development of a collective consciousness informed by the historical struggle for liberation.'[133] In this sense, the group taps into a series of connected cultural expressions across time, producing a complex set of identities devoid of Nationalist essentialism. Banks recalled: 'We wanted a label and a sound that depicted brothers in a different darkness and a different light.'[134]

UR's mythology sidesteps black essentialism to provides opportunities for identity formation that range beyond the established restrictive reference points, and so becomes part of a radical tradition which is simultaneously about personal identity construction *and* collective social liberation. UR, as the purveyors of this shifting set of identity referents become part of their own myth, 'wharf-rat individuals seizing on the most up-to-date technology, to combat some ever more monolithic globally interlinked InfoTec state ... cyberpunk come to life, by turns grindingly bleak (as harbingers of the present) and deliriously optimistic (as harbingers of the future.)'[135] Interestingly for scholars of black history, the end product of this post-modern scavenging is 'a blackness that is defined by a radical fluidity ... across genders, sexualities, ethnicities, generations [and] socio-economic positions'.[136]

Due to its globally inflected nature, this audio assault took place in a new conceptual space of 'transnational cultural construction' defined by Paul Gilroy as the 'Black Atlantic.'[137] By the late 1990s, the Black Atlantic had come to symbolise a 'nexus of black musical expression, historical oppression, and urban dystopia' which was at the heart of UR's emergent dystopian identity.[138]

The creation of that identity was itself a radicalising process, which inevitably changed its participants. As Banks noted, 'I'm not a friendly native no more. I've been modified into some different shit.'[139] This difference was expressed through music, communicated via sound to a much broader audience. Identity formation took place beyond natural coordinates, within and around the music. The music was both the conduit and the context. The identities produced were hybrid, globalised *and* localised creating 'environmentally evolved young sonic mutants ... an exciting blend of man and machine'.[140]

Quantifying the actual influence of these new spaces for identity creation is challenging. This is partially because connecting techno to young Detroit men and women isn't easy, as Banks noted 'the only thing they respect ... [is] ... something that can physically dominate or scare them, because they ain't too scared of anything, because of the environment.'[141] However, the globalisation which UR brings – the expansion of that possibility space, might have a very real effect on the identities of young Americans.[142]

Banks recollected '[our] sax player is 19, one of the keyboard players is 22 ... one of the dancers never flew on an airplane before. So ... what UR has been in the city, is a hope, and the young people, it's a great opportunity for them ... they might know the local drug dealer but my man right there he just back from Norway, you ain't even been to Colombia where they make the cocaine. It diminishes their power, and gives someone doing something positive more power.'[143]

Music critic Simon Reynolds believed that these forms of urban music exposed the reality of city life, acting as 'mirrors to late capitalist reality, stripping away the façade of free enterprise to reveal the war of all against all: a neo-Medieval paranoiascape of robber barons, pirate corporations, covert operations and conspiratorial cabals.'[144] From this perspective, Reynolds argued, solidarity and militancy were the only escape. As he explained, 'In the terrordome of capitalist anarchy, the underclass can only survive by taking on the mobilisation techniques and the psychology of warfare forming blood-brotherhoods and warrior-clans, and individually, by transforming the self into a fortress, a one- man army on perpetual alert.'[145] In Reynolds's plan for the transformation of the self lie aspects of the Black Power movement's demand for a revolution of the mind, for the creation of a self-identity sufficient to withstand a city which remained 'a treacherous terrain of snipers, man- traps and ambushes.'[146]

Reynolds's lurid prose, like all fiction, pushes beyond the edges of historical truth, but his concerns echo our own fears of the polarising of urban dystopias, the split of our cities, and eventually our world, into two binary parts, the core and periphery, the developed and the developing, the haves and the have-nots. This was a dichotomy first academically articulated by Immanuel Wallerstein.[147] Within our modern cities, the periphery often counterintuitively exists within the heart of the core itself. It has become, once again, as social scientists and governmental officials once claimed, a cancer to be excised from the healthy body of the city.[148] Sociologist Mike Davis's recent works warn against the creation of these impoverished urban enclaves which exist within otherwise vital cities, colonised once again by the spread of technology.[149] It is here at the matrix of urban poverty, racial oppression and technological influence that the real hints of what motivates Afrofuturism might be found by historians.

Defining the current state of Afrofuturism in any technical sense is challenging. On one level, it marks the meeting point between the soaring exploration of black science fiction – the blasted cities of Samuel Delany, the strange new races of Octavia Butler and the febrile fables of Ishmael Reed – with the cultural theorising of Greg Tate and the technological and theoretical evolution of black electronic music. These sounds followed a neon route through the jazz of Sun Ra, the dub of Lee Perry and the funk of George Clinton, through to more modern pioneers in the Detroit techno and UK drum 'n' bass and jungle scenes.

Taken together, these seemingly disparate elements constitute what John Akomfrah terms a 'digitised diaspora'.[150] From an Afrofuturist perspective, this was not as anachronistic as it might seem, as futuristic elements were present from the very earliest stages of African-American life. John Corbett contended that artists such as Ra, Perry and Clinton drew on a shared set of historically produced mythology and icons, while Kodwo Eshun extended the reach of this historical inheritance, arguing that 'In the eighteenth century slaves like David Walker read poetry to prove they were human, to prove they weren't robots' and concluding accordingly that 'a sense of cybernetics has already been applied to slaves in eighteenth century America.'[151] For Afrofuturists, the connected cultural expressions which informed the long history of the Black Power movement held an almost prophetic clarity. By treating slaves like automata, Afrofuturists argued, the plantation masters took the first steps towards creating a science-fiction existence for Africans in America.

Afrofuturism confuses some observers because it simultaneously embraces progress toward a technological emancipation and a certain gleeful iconoclasm. By suggesting that the line between social reality and science fiction is an optical illusion, it opens another avenue for the revolution of the mind, what techno pioneer Juan Atkins termed a 'technological revolution' designed to infiltrate 'the mind, the electro mind'.[152] At its roots, part of the appeal of Afrofuturism lay in its ability to envision a better future, in which modern society assisted the development of black culture and consciousness. As Eshun saw it, 'Afrofuturism studies the appeals that black artists, musicians, critics, and writers have made to the future, in moments where any future was made difficult for them to imagine.'[153] These appeals, these fragments of protest existing as connected cultural expressions across time are what Akomfrah's Data Thief, and this book, seek to retrieve.

Assembling fragments of memory and history to create a new communal historical record has strong parallels with the new approach to music that evolved in the late twentieth and early twenty-first centuries, engagingly and anarchically recounted in the hip-hop documentary

Scratch. In this interpretation, disc jockeys became the data thieves, gleaning fragments from musical history to create a new sound and vision of the future. As Greg Tate, hailed by *The Source* magazine as one of the 'Godfathers of Hip-hop Journalism' argued 'sampling allows musicians to concentrate all eras of black music onto a chip.'[154] Operating in a manner fundamentally analogous to the same selection from previous eras undertaken by Black Power adherents, both polemical and digital sampling creates an arena in which the practical process of historical selection affects our recollections and perceptions of that same history. When applied to musical sampling, the net effect, Afrofuturists argued, was the 'creation of digitised race memory'.[155] The creation of this memory blurred the boundaries between science fiction and historical reality. As the jungle artist Goldie explained, because 'Technology can take from any era, time is irrelevant.'[156] Accordingly, the techno movement softened the boundaries of periods and chronologies. The distillation of an era melded with the evocation of an era, particularly in jungle music, which used technological means to evoke traditional drumbeats and rhythms.

The role of the DJ inevitably lends itself to this amalgamation of past and present as their fundamental approach is to construct something new from fragments of previously extant tracks. The archaeological finds of old albums, samples drawn from the era of blues and gospel, combine with older symbols and samples drawn from African mythology, religion and cosmology. From this composite of past elements, a more futuristic sound can emerge, one which manipulates time in its acceleration and deceleration, punctuated by scratches, which not only introduce powerful rhythms, but originate in a tool which was not intended to be used as an instrument. Previously everyday objects assume new significances and purposes. Swathed in electronic sound, this music inevitably interfaced with science fiction. Mix Master Mike claimed his music could summon visitors from other worlds, while the iconography of sci-fi became a common trapping of many modern DJ sets. Some musicians, such as George Clinton more prosaically noted, 'I wanted to land a UFO on top of the track', but even this bold statement hinted at a deeper goal, what Derrick May saw as 'man and machine intertwined to take technology to the level of the human instinct.'[157]

In the late twentieth century Ishmael Reed lamented of black America, 'We are not believed, we are like aliens'.[158] Greg Tate pushes the contention one step further, arguing that black Americans are not merely akin to aliens, but exist in a world defined by alienation, living 'the estrangement that science fiction writers imagine'.[159] As Kodwo Eshun wryly noted, if you are black in America, 'it doesn't get more alien.'[160] Nona Hendryx from funk group Labelle put things more bluntly, wryly remarking on her childhood, 'New Jersey is some kind of outer space'.[161]

This alien aspect to American life echoed both the back to Africa movement of the late nineteenth century and the subsequent 1960s rhetoric of the Black Panther Party which presented African-Americans as a colonised nation within America. As Reed explained, 'We are considered as outsiders ... as not part of the American experience ... we are always aliens ... send us back to the planet of our origin.'[162] This sentiment received a chilling contemporary interpretation in Derrick Bell's *The Space Traders*.[163]

In Bell's grim tale, a messianic alien race arrives in the skies above America and promises solutions to all of the country's fiscal, economic and ecological problems in exchange for all of America's black citizens, to be delivered on 17 January, Martin Luther King day. As Bell unfolds his parable, he exposes a rapacious eagerness on the part of white people to sell the black Americans in their midst. In Bell's universe, African-Americans have degenerated far below their current standards of existence. Echoing Wallerstein, the majority of the population live in inner-city ghettos which exist within the body of larger, functioning cities, like cysts upon an otherwise healthy patient. The gains of the civil rights movement have been lost, its legislation repealed. The solution, the white actors in Bell's story suggest, is to excise these burdens like a cancer. While the other American minorities, the Hispanics, Asians, and Jews, protest the expulsion of the African-Americans, they do so only from self-interest. One rabbi fears an upsurge of anti-Semitic hate, reflecting, 'In the absence of black Americans, Jews could become the scapegoats for a system so reliant on an identifiable group on whose heads less-well-off whites can discharge their hate and frustrations.'[164] Similarly, big business joins in the fight to keep African-Americans who, Bell astutely and cynically points out, comprise much of the capitalist system's profits, spending more per capita and engaging fully with the decadent American apparatus. Yet even these corporate protests are insufficient. Following the wishes of the President himself, America willingly trades its entire African-American population for another century of prosperity, at the expense Bell suggests, of the moral and political gains of the last two hundred years.

Conversely, John Sayles's *The Brother from Another Planet* offers a rather more optimistic perspective on changing race relations.[165] The titular brother is, in fact, a runaway slave from beyond the stars, pursued by two sinister men who are as much stereotypical Men in Black as angry slave owners. Crashlanding in Harlem, the Brother survives with the help of the community who form an impromptu intergalactic underground railroad, which interfaces, both literally and visually with the New York subway. In this manner, Sayles deftly transposes one of the most profound aspects of the slave narrative, the railway to freedom, into the modern present, directly acknowledging the continuity of this historical trope.

Despite being utterly mute, the Brother manages to recruit a raft of interracial allies, from a white woman who takes him in as a tenant, to a Hispanic work colleague. As Roger Ebert reflected, 'by using a central character who cannot talk, [Sayles] is ... able to explore the kinds of scenes that haven't been possible since the death of silent film ... most of them with a quiet little bite, a way of causing us to look at our society'.[166] In contrast to *The Space Traders*, Sayles presents a welcoming, inclusive America, which although not free from racial tension exhibits a community spirit and a willingness to help the underdog. Whereas almost every white person in *The Space Traders* will willingly turn over every single black person in the country, in Sayles's vision of the future, the inhabitants of New York refuse to sacrifice a single man to his intergalactic hunters.

While the optimism provided in science fiction signposted a more equitable future, the very presence of space seemed to highlight the disparity and incongruity of the African-American situation. The intrepid Albert II was the first monkey in space in 1949, followed by the 1957 Sputnik flight and Yuri Gagarin's 1961 orbit of the earth. Success in exploring the edges of the cosmos seemed to suggest an unbroken chain of progress in the fortunes of the United States. This sentiment reached its apogee in Kennedy's 1961 speech to Congress on 25 May which declared 'We go into space because whatever mankind must undertake, free men must fully share.'[167] To many black Americans, still mired in the hardships of the civil rights struggle, Kennedy's notion of sharing must have seemed quaint at best.

In fact, for some African-American observers like George Clinton, space exploration was not a discovery, but a reunion. As he somewhat cryptically remarked, 'Space for black people is not something new ... the essence of all mankind is striving to return there.'[168] The appeal of space and the notion of 'Black people out exploring space' was not always so esoteric.[169] Bernard Harris, an ex-NASA astronaut who described himself as 'one of the original trekkies' and was the first African-American to perform an EVA simply recalled that 'When I saw the first human being walk on the moon, I was hooked.'[170]

It is telling that many Americans when asked to name significant black space explorers, first reference Nichelle Nichols, who played Lieutenant Uhura on *Star Trek*. Martin Luther King, himself a *Star Trek* fan, recognised the show's potential when he told Nichols, 'This show is changing the ways in which people see us, and see themselves. And the manner in which they're seeing the world'.[171] Harris certainly concurred, flying a flag on his first mission which was designed to represent all the countries of Africa, buoyed by the Afrocentric notion 'that black people were the first mathematicians and astronomers in this world.'[172] Uhura's adventures aboard the Enterprise hardly seemed less aspirational. As a representative of the futuristic United States of Africa, Nichols may have been the immediately recognisable point of contact on American TV screens, but NASA was itself a progressive environment. As Nichols noticed when she toured the facility she saw 'men and women of all colours working at every level', 'women, black Americans, browns and yellows, working in every level of the agency.'[173] In part, NASA felt and seemed representative because it embodied visions of a science-fiction future. It looked 'like Star Trek'.[174] Nichols drew on this in her first address as a National Space Society board member, imploring NASA decision makers to 'come down from your ivory tower ... because the next Einstein might have a black face, and she's female.'[175] Nichols address, 'New Opportunities for the Humanisation of Space' was aptly subtitled 'Space: What's in it for me?'[176]

It was easier to envisage solutions off the earth than on it. The brute fact that African-Americans still lacked such basic rights as the electoral franchise tended to take a back seat to the inspirational nature of space-based science-fiction. Nona Hendryx recalled: 'We hadn't been in any of the shows I grew up on ... I was fascinated by space travel.'[177] For the young Nona, in the stellar future, progress was a given: 'Freedom, equality ... that didn't particularly cross my mind ... I assumed I would be going.'[178] Touring across America gave her a different perspective, which fitted more closely with Tate's views on alienation. Hendryx noticed, 'When we travelled in the South ... that's when I felt like being an alien on a different planet.'[179]

In general however, the notional possibilities of space seems to have engendered a strong sense of optimism. George Clinton recollected, 'As far as civil rights, I felt like I was better than most people myself ... from the first time seeing [*Star Trek*] ... I knew there were different realities in other's people minds than on the planet.'[180] These different realities, distant though they were, could be expressed in very simple ways. Before he became Dr. Funkenstein, the young Clinton styled Nona Hendryx's hair, among others, and his approach to fashion quickly combined the aesthetic of the street with the optimistic unity that sci-fi promoted. As he explained 'It didn't matter to me what we looked like ... the garbage man on Saturday eve, the pimps, the preachers, everybody looked [cool], everyone looked the same when we were done with them.'[181]

As always, however, the establishment of a unified, hip image for African-America also meant its co-optation. Clinton remarked in 2011 that 'Black itself had become commercial', a factor which had historically spurred the search for novel avenues for Afrofuturist expression.[182] If Earth was a slave to marketing, Afrofuturists reasoned that African-American identities had to take root elsewhere. As Clinton explained, 'I had to find another place for black people to be. And space was that place.'[183] Indeed, while the Afrofuturist aesthetic had a long and varied heritage, with musicians like Sun Ra and Lee Perry laying the foundations for its approach, but it was arguably Clinton and Parliament Funkadelic (P-Funk) who introduced Afrofuturism to everyday Americans and who gave Afrofuturist artists much of the iconography and concepts they still use today.

Much of this imagery came from Pedro Bell, aka Sir Lleb of Funkedelia, who joined P-Funk in the early 1970s and was given the job of translating George Clinton's ideas into reality.[184] Bell's liner notes often parodied overly pretentious approaches to African-American culture, providing satirical sermons and faux-political polemics describing the tracks they encased. Exhibiting the trickster élan which Dery saw as defining most Afrofuturistic work, Bell created a 'slanguage' all his own. 'Zeepspeak' was the tongue of P-Funk's alien world, rife with 'neegroid protoplasm' fit to combat the ominous presence of 'babymasturbating nixonharpies'.[185] Bell's images matched his words, producing 'high-density cyber-porn' art which captured the sexuality and futuristic optimism in Parliament's neon funk.[186] In his work, Afrocentric history and pop psychedelia merged to create 'cover art saturated with an Afrofuturistic perspective.'[187] Combining style and message, Parliament's album covers not only defined the 1970s funk scene but offered a significant challenge to the mainstream American image, when Clinton's 'weird twilight zone stories' were filtered through the lens of Overton Loyd and Pedro Bell's art.[188] As Emory Douglas had argued and as Clinton noted, art was a weapon: 'you can do some of the harshest shit if it's illustrated'.[189] For Parliament, this ethos reached its zenith in the 1972 *America Eats Its Young* which featured a monstrous Statue of Liberty devouring armfuls of multi-ethnic babies on a livid green dollar.[190] Bell, along with Clinton, was instrumental in connecting this subversive aesthetic to the hip-hop generation which followed. His 1996 liner notes for P-Funk's greatest hit collection again showed his flair for satire, parodying the east coast, west coast conflict as 'Two tribes of Hip Hounds ... engaged in a conflict noted as Woof War I' locked in a battle 'over the shortage of sample bytes, an essential auditory war of this sound driven planet.'[191] In Bell's fiction the return of Clintonesque aliens to the planet reinvigorates the moribund war as they descend 'spewing boxes of Funk Munchies to the sample starved landscape' uniting the community in an orgy of 'thunderous licks, loops and bassactivism.'[192] Bell's parody retained its hard edge, as he queried, 'Will you still be alive after this album?'[193] Despite his critique, Bell seemed to acknowledge that the hip-hop generation, in an often anarchic, sometimes inept manner sought a revitalisation of the fundamental dreams of the 1960s freedom movement.[194]

As with Underground Resistance, P-Funk's mythology evolved alongside their popularity, creating an easily recognisable brand which fans could interact with and relate to. This imagery was seldom prescriptive. Fans were allowed to interpret the art as they saw fit, in relation to their own circumstances. However, several of the central tropes of Afrofuturism can be seen in P-Funk's lurid, erotic, pan-galactic world; ideas of transportation and escape, concepts of alienation and notions of a shared hybrid identity.

Images of transportation are predominant in African-American culture from the depictions of flight that characterised 'All God's Chillen' and Lenox Avenue Sunday, to the fabled Midnight Special train which promised freedom for slaves fleeing North; which Larry Neal saw, 'haulassing through' America to the sound of 'a lonesome woman wailing.'[195] Yet the ultimate avatar of transportation was the ship, both terrestrial and interstellar. Ships were most obviously present historically during the Middle Passage, the name given to the gruelling transatlantic voyage suffered by slaves being brought to America. This historical presence often melded with a second layer of biblical imagery, drawn from plantation spirituals which promised the arrival of sweet chariots to bear the suffering away from their troubles.[196]

Parliament saw the same chariots coming to offer salvation, although they originated in the stars, rather than in heaven, and their pilots were somewhat more avant-garde than a few stately seraphim. Yet the group's music straddled the line between past and future, memory and possibility. The giant thrusting shapes of the craft on the cover of *The Electric Spanking of War Babies* may have delivered a payload of naked women that challenged Christian sensibilities as late as 1981, but Star Child (aka Clinton) still sings the old refrain on *Mothership Connection* 'Swing down, sweet chariot, stop and let me ride.'[197] In some respects, the framing changes, but the song stays the same.

From an Afrofuturist perspective spaceships, as John Corbett noted, became literal 'vehicles for subversion'.[198] In his work for Parliament, Bell drew from literature and art as much as from lust, referencing H.G. Wells's tripods on the cover of *Hardcore Jollies* and providing a Grecian hero rendered with Dali-esque verve on the cover for *Standing on the Verge of Getting On*. However, he reached the zenith of his creation in the eponymous Mothership which first invaded American airspace on the cover of the 1975 *The Mothership Connection*. The shape of the Mothership shows Bell's influences, it is half-guitar dial, half the nipple of the *Cosmic Slop's* galactic goddess, combining the sleek lines of sci-fi with the tricked out glitz of the custom car movement which fascinated Bell during the mid-1970s.[199]

Around these ships, Clinton and Bell created a universe which took the alienation of black people from mainstream American culture and upended it. Funk, these neon prophets whispered, had been carried to the planet by benevolent beings on a mission to make our booties shake. This notion originated as a gentle critique of similar ideas, more terrestrially bound ideas of African exceptionalism espoused by the Nation of Islam and other Afrocentric thinkers. Africa might as well have been outer space to many Americans, so Clinton took the concept literally. In 1970, Parliament released *Mommy, What's a Funkadelic?*, its title echoing Fuller's 'What is Black Power, Daddy?'. Both texts sought to define an esoteric new way of thinking about the black condition within America. In the song's licks, Clinton provides an introduction to the benevolent effect of an alien identity, singing: 'my name is Funk/I am not of your world/Hold still, baby, I don't do you no harm/I think I'll be good to you.'[200]

In the artwork for *Mommy* Bell expanded on Clinton's ethos, presenting the band as an invasion force and giving them cosmic makeovers in a variety of shapes, sizes and colours. When Bell depicted P-Funk members their ethnicity was disregarded as they became avatars of funk. More importantly, this same transformation was offered to the P-Funk concert audience who could, however briefly, transcend the limitations of their colour by moving to an alien world, much like Jim in Du Bois's *The Comet*. This almost physical liberation, paired with an equally powerful mental liberation, would become a central theme in Afrofuturist literature.

Parliament's own mythology went beyond even these twentieth century constructions, harking back to the plantation tales of Big Sixteen, as the band played at being virile trickster figures simply too large for the world to contain them. Clinton manifested as Starchile, who like Sayles's character is a *Brother From Another Planet*. Starchile however, is no fugitive, rather he has been sent by his mentor, the great Dr. Funkenstein, to bring Funk to humanity in a cosmic battle against his nemesis Sir Nose D'void of Funk. In a manner strikingly similar to Sun Ra's *Space is the Place* and with an attitude similar to the 1930s contributors to *FIRE!!*, Funkadelic's avatars glorified African-American features and physicality, taking the field in 'Egypto-glam-space-pimp-wear'.[201]

Exploring similar ideas to those in Erich von Däniken's 1968 book, *Chariot of the Gods*, P-Funk gave a futuristic twist to the black diaspora, arguing that aliens had jump started Egyptian civilisation, and that the Egyptians in turn had given African civilisation to the world.[202]

Although aliens and alienation are central aspects of much Afrofuturist writing, Bell's extra-terrestrials are unique in that they do not separate their ordinary audience from the world, but offer a new place in galactic mythology where colour is irrelevant, where listeners can be at one with the universe and where the beat ain't so heavy.

The serenity of space could not last forever. By 1978, the Electric Light Orchestra and *Close Encounters of the Third Kind* had sucked the funk out of interstellar life. ELO's *Out of the Blue* offered an air-brushed, glossy, vacuous vision of space that neither swam with the cosmic slop nor played host to a firm-breasted galactic goddess. Funk had not died however. It had simply landed in the American heartland and then burrowed deep underground.

The music that Clinton and Parliament Funkadelic produced was lauded by Wondaland Arts Society producer Chuck Lightning as 'probably the best music for race relations that ever was.'[203] Certainly, P-Funk's music was the logical culmination of the collision between the broad, brash, sexualisation of the Blaxploitation era and the emerging sci-fi aesthetic of black America's twentieth century. Gospel and arrogant swagger merged in a transformative cacophony. As Hendryx noted: 'What would be noise [in other bands], he [Clinton] took it to church.'[204] Changing with the times, the religious aspects of P-Funk's music took a back seat to a more secular heaven populated by pulsating motherships piloted by befeathered men in giant nappies.

Much of this lurid aesthetic was the work of Larry LeGaspi, a costume designer who not only attired both Hendryx and Clinton, but ran his own store called Moonstone, described by contemporary observers as an almost literal moonscape.[205] LeGaspi's work not only defined the look of the Hendryx-fronted funk-rock pioneers Labelle, but had a significant presence in the wider fashion sphere which relied upon Afrofuturist notions of transformation. As he reflected, the idea of space was a means of pushing things forward and achieving tangible progress. In a world which seemed prosaically limited, 'Space seemed the only direction for me to go, because the seventies just seem[ed] to be a repeat of the thirties through the sixties.'[206] LeGaspi's designs famously tended to excess, so that while 'Cher [was] wearing aluminium ... we' Hendryx recalled with pride, 'were spending money on silver and gold.'[207] Spending on psychedelic confections was itself a statement; a refusal by black musicians to be defined sartorially or economically by mainstream

American society. The gaudy excess of P-Funk and Labelle was one indicator of progress, but the LeGaspi glitz concealed other narratives beneath the surface. As Clinton put it, 'Our thing was to make you think.'[208]

As their career progressed, playing devil's advocate, writing songs 'from the bad side of a thing' became an important part of the P-Funk repertoire, although they tended to return with regularity to the boundless optimism and promise of space.[209] This approach was not without its drawbacks. Clinton modestly explained, 'When you start being positive, you got a responsibility. People start looking up to you like god.'[210] Mercifully, the rickety construction of Parliament's own plywood Mothership stopped Clinton short of hubris, as he reflected 'I got a perfect excuse to fall from here if I'm God.'[211]

Despite these brief acknowledgements of mortality, on stage, P-Funk were an anarchic, iconic superhero team come to life. A riot of star-shaped shades, odd wigs, combat boots, angel wings and outsize diapers. This unbounded expression was a lot of fun, but was not just an explosion of sound and colour. In their performances, P-Funk introduced African-Americans to places they had never been before. The expansion of the possibilities suggested by their futurist visions excited both audiences and later scholars, to the extent that historians such as Rickey Vincent believe that the experimentation and anarchy of P-Funk represented the culmination of the freedoms gained by the civil rights movement: 'They were celebrating the intellectual breadth of the black experience and giving people a grand space to celebrate all that they had become. Sly Stone said, "I Want to Take You Higher." George Clinton said, "Yeah, and I got the Mothership to take you there." In a sense, he was doing what black folks had wanted to do for generations: Take themselves up.'[212] Vincent's contention is plausible, but benefits significantly from hindsight. Whether P-Funk and Clinton himself intended this at time is significantly more dubious. As he reflected raucously 'We were higher than anyone else!'[213]

George Clinton's swaggering persona was not alone in dominating the 1970s charts. The African-American music of the 1970s produced empowering images for men and women alike. Nona Hendryx's Labelle were not only the first black female group to feature on the cover of *Rolling Stone* magazine, but had a string hits throughout the decade.[214] Although Patti LaBelle sang that 'Tomorrow's a dream, running out of steam', Labelle's dream proved extremely durable.[215] The trio were the first African-American female group to play the New York Metropolitan Opera in 1970 and marshalled an army of ardent, argent devotees for the event, including a legion of nuns in silver and a horse and carriage.

The subsequent performance was the epitome of Hendryx's belief that 'To get the attention of people you ... give them something they can take and make their own.'[216] Labelle's opening night at the Met was sufficiently steeped in sci-fi that one commentator later remarked that 'The Metropolitan Opera House in New York was invaded by aliens on Sunday, Oct. 6, 1974'.[217] The atmosphere inside was simultaneously egalitarian and futuristic as 'West Village drag queens sat next to Puerto Rican couples and Black Power glam rockers from uptown.'[218] This eclectic audience was swept up in 'a swirl of gospel, rock and soul' as Labelle almost literally descended from the heavens, albeit on wires.[219] The very presence of Labelle changed the notion of what pop groups and women singers in 'girl groups' were capable of, connecting music to the reality of ordinary American lives. As Patti LaBelle recollected: 'People were looking for three outrageous women who might sing and say anything. The idea was for artists to sing what they live and write the songs they live ... And that did allow for different things to be said.'[220] The group's dramatic transformation from Patti LaBelle and the Bluebelles was made all the more startling by the fact that they had spent the previous decade in sharp wigs and satin gloves. Adopting the combination of Larry LeGaspi's futuristic designs and Hendryx's politically forthright and sexually loaded lyrics transformed the group into 'a stage show that was part gospel revival, part circus, part love-in.'[221]

Tapping into the same optimism and desire for progress coupled with societal critique that coloured the science fiction of the 1970s, Labelle attacked the popular music of the day, hammering Cat Stevens's *Moonshadow* into a slick gospel footstomper, opening for The Who and recording with Laura Nyro in 1971. Throughout, the band offered emotive performances coupled with militant momentum. As the group's manager Vicky Wickham recollected, 'It wasn't really accepted that black girls could sing these songs. A lot of Nona's songs had double entendres, it wasn't like radio was going to jump on it. The time really wasn't right, but ... we were so big on doing it live and having great audiences that nobody really said, "Hang on a second, you need to have something that goes on radio."'[222]

Labelle's legacy endures in artists from Gnarls Barkley to Santigold and Lenny Kravitz, who identified with their struggle remarking: 'In America more than other places, when you don't put something in a nice, neat box and label it and put a ribbon on it, it's hard for people to grasp. All the years I was trying to get a record deal I kept hearing, "It's not black enough" or "It's not white enough".'[223] A binary racial identity did not appear to fit the futuristic vision Labelle sought and they defied easy categorisation, partly because African-Americans in general were beginning to test the boundaries of their assigned identities. The Nyro collaboration, according to Patti LaBelle's childhood friend Kenneth Gamble, was indicative of a wider change in self-perception: 'People were really starting to feel free to respect themselves more. Labelle was part of that transition.'[224] The revolution of the mind had found a new beat to groove to.

Labelle's success partially rested on Nona Hendryx's ability to draw on musicians and Black Power politicians in equal measure. Hendryx cited a wide range of influences from the yogic spiritualist Ram Dass, author of the 1971 *Be Here Now*, the novelist and artist Henry Miller, to the two colossi of socially connected 1960s and 1970s music, Nina Simone and Gil Scott-Heron. This musical heritage was complemented by a political and feminist inheritance, embodied in the feminist and activist Angela Davis and the Black Panther Party's Nikki Giovanni.[225]

If Hendryx turned to Black Power politics to craft an empowering vision of the future, P-Funk went a step further, using an actual Mothership as a lyrical metaphor for their new future funk perspective, offering audiences someone: 'Black coming from space, pimp-like, just coming in cool.'[226] The Mothership itself is an excellent metaphor for the impact of Afrofuturism. Its bombastic appearances received a rapturous response and embodied the boundless possibility inherent in the futuristic outlook of post-civil rights 1970s America, but its presence evoked tropes of liberation which ran through connected cultural expressions across time, right back to the plantation.

As the Smithsonian's Music and Performing Arts curator, Dwandalyn R. Reece, noted in 2011, 'With large iconic objects like this, we can tap into ... themes of movement and liberation that are a constant in African-American culture. The Mothership as this mode of transport really fits into this musical trope in African American culture about travel and transit.'[227] Much as the slaves' drums carried rhythms across the sea, for many concert attendees, the Mothership brought a certain optimism down from space.

The Mothership's first landing was in New Orleans at the municipal auditorium on 27 October 1976. Recalling the ship's reception a year later in Washington, Darryl Brooks, the organiser of the Funkadelic's tour production company, noted how Clinton offered a fervour and optimism that was absent from much African-American music at the time: 'Here's a guy coming out of a Mothership with a mink coat and platform shoes. *And* a cane? And a fur hat? C'mon, man. Black folks been down so long ... It was jubilation.'[228] The euphoria was not solely dependent on the costumes. At the Capital Center on April 25 1981, Clinton paraded out of the Mothership, utterly naked except for a golden cape slung over one shoulder, embodying the 'black is beautiful' ethos as much as Stokely Carmichael or Muhammad Ali.

Journalists tend to get very excited about the Mothership, described by *Washington Post* reporter Chris Richards as 'the most awe-inspiring stage prop in the history of American music'.[229] In particular, the myths surrounding the Mothership's recent disappearance are as lurid as the album covers it featured on: 'It burned in a fire. It was disassembled. It was stolen. Scrapped. Kidnapped. Thrown in the woods. Chained to a truck by a drug dealer and dragged to funk-knows-where. The band's most devoted followers say it flew off into space.'[230]

The Mothership last touched down in Detroit in 1981, wreathed in dry-ice and the fading splendour of the civil rights movement. By Spring 1982, as Richards pithily put it 'Parliament-Funkadelic frontman George Clinton and his bandmates were battling debt, drug addiction and each other.'[231] The Mothership was pawned to pay the band's debts, ironically consigned to anonymity in a junkyard behind a petrol station on the Martin Luther King Jr. highway.

For some historians, such as Thomas Stanley, the myth of the ship is more powerful than the reality. Put simply, it is 'much more satisfying to imagine this sacred artefact bound firmly in the bosom of the strong black communities that straddle the D.C. line between Suitland and Seat Pleasant ... It is very important', he argues, 'that we not seek truth at the expense of myth. Music and Myth are, after all, P-Funk's most enduring legacy.'[232] While Stanley is perhaps romantically reductionist, there is some truth to his claim. The Mothership offered a tangible reminder of a brief and glorious optimism that removed mental barriers for many ordinary people in the audience. Now exhibited alongside the iconic brass of Louis Armstrong's trumpet, the peacock power of James Brown's stage costumes and the studied elegance of Lena Horne's evening gowns. Reece believes that the silver voyager, 'definitely fits in', because, 'Funk is not just a good groove, it was its own kind of social protest movement.'[233]

Funk was indeed its own kind of protest movement, and it lay at the roots of Afrofuturism, so it is unsurprising that its luminaries, when looking back, feel so strongly about its power. Clinton believed that 'Afrofuturism was the word that gave me the key to understanding how I felt about black Americans in the future.'[234] Echoing the joy felt by Van Peebles's audiences, he recollected, 'every so often I would see a (sci-fi) film where a brother or a sister would live to the end ... then you see this music and black people aren't just surviving the movie, they're running, they're owning the movie.'[235] While black ownership of the silver screen may have begun in the 1970s, Afrofuturism moved beyond this Blaxploitation aesthetic to a realm of more complex possibilities.

While Clinton stressed the positivity of the ethos, Nona Hendryx emphasised the importance of technology in Afrofuturism, commenting, 'As far as I'm concerned it just means that black people have a future ... without tech you're not in the future.'[236] Ultimately however, for both luminaries, Afrofuturism and science fiction provided a catalyst for the revolution of the mind. Clinton remarked recently 'Maybe I might need to build a ship to get there ... to learn the tools ... the soul is the most outrageous space you can travel in, to get to know your own mind ... The planet is small, technology is something we need to get our heads on.'[237] By the end of the 1970s, for some black Americans space had become the soul, and the soul was to be found in space. Even today, Janelle Monae, perhaps the most authentic inheritor of the P-Funk legacy, acknowledges that 'sci-fi opened my mind to a world of limitless possibility' and pairs that optimism with the same pragmatic frankness expressed by Nona Hendryx, reflecting 'There's always going to be somebody in the room who says "who gives a fuck", so I throw it up in the air and see who catches it.'[238]

African-American music and science-fiction were not pessimistic by default. At a basic level, they were often a motive force for change by creating a significant distance from the present. As Samuel Delany explained, 'we ... look at what we see around us and say how can the world be different.'[239] Essentially, science fiction also connected the present to the past. Monae, a Wondaland artist and self-described 'Archandroid' works in an environment inspired by aesthetics from the Twilight Zone to Fritz Lang's *Metropolis*, using music videos to provide a multi-layered commentary on influences both historical and futuristic. In the video for 'Many Moons' as androids line up for a futuristic slave auction, Monae's voice intones a litany of suffering African-American suffering, pinpointing key moments in the long history of Black Power and civil rights, while her black and white attire echoes the manual labour dress of generations gone before. Consciously stylised to a high degree, the presentation of Monae's music itself stems from a long tradition of black cultural creation, and draws heavily on its historical expressions through time.

As Chuck Lightning, one of the founding members of the Wondaland Arts Society, noted: '[Our] stylisation was a reaction against hip-hop ... we decided we would go in that direction because no one else was doing it.'[240] Wondaland grew out of the Dark Tower Project which Lightning founded at the historically black Morehouse College, notably selecting a name for his new organization which echoed the 1928 literary salon and nightclub established by A'Leila Walker in Harlem; itself named after Countee Cullen's regular column in *Opportunity* magazine.[241]

Much as Lightning seeks a tangible connection with the past, the dominant themes of Afrofuturism retain their relevance in the modern day. In Cauleen Smith and Salim Akil's 1998 *Drylongso*, the traditional discourse of alienation meets the emasculation of Du Bois's *The Comet* when a young woman begins photographing what she deems 'America's most endangered species,' African-American males, in order to preserve them for posterity.[242]

Yet as much as alienation is a pronounced theme in Afrofuturism, the rhetoric and fiction of colonialism has now evolved to form our modern postcolonial discourse. This is most eloquently expressed in Nisi Shawl's short story 'Deep End', published in 2010 as part of an anthology entitled *So Long Been Dreaming: Postcolonial Science Fiction & Fantasy*.[243] Set on board a prison ship, 'Deep End' introduces as its protagonists a cargo of convicts intended as colonists for a new planet, prophetically named Amends. Shawl implicitly suggests that Amends is the 'New World' renewed, but demolishes the traditional Western narrative of colonisation by making her characters prisoners. Initially Amends appears less America, more Australia.

Shawl subverts this rhetoric when she reveals that her protagonists are people of colour whose consciousness has been transplanted into the cloned bodies of the same wealthy white magnates they revolted against. They have the opportunity to create a new world, but one which will be fundamentally white, peopled by white children, in which they themselves live a hybrid existence, victim to a profound and cruel version of Du Bois's double consciousness.

As the book progresses, Shawl crafts a futuristic slave narrative in which the ship's AI Dr. Ops administers punishment like 'the lash of a whip' and wherein the Afrofuturist theme of abduction looms large.[244] Ultimately though, many of the colonists discard their old friendships, accepting their new white bodies and their new white existence. Shawl's story is deceptive however, as in writing it, she not only questions the very acceptance she discusses, but brings together an amalgam of issues to debate our changing self-perceptions. Within the confines of her spaceship, Shawl explores the permanence or transience of the revolution of the mind so beloved of Black Power adherents, the importance of the icons we inherit from the past and the degree to which our inheritance, historical, cultural and genetic, can shape the society we find ourselves in. In closing, she suggests that the themes which Afrofuturism has drawn to the surface – alienation, transportation, abduction and colonisation – are now not merely concepts to be studied, but tools to be used in the construction of a modern hybrid identity.

In his foundational essay, Dery appropriated William Gibson's cyberpunk mantra that 'The street finds its own uses for things' in order to argue that African-American culture was essentially adaptive.[245] Almost a decade later, the ships of science-fiction have carried us into a far more complex world which exists beyond national boundaries. From our current historical perspective, the shores that border the Black Atlantic seem drawn ever closer together, pulled by transnational tectonics, framing a space far larger than the street, an endless shifting ocean into which the writers, authors and culture creators of today slip their neon nets, questing for the silverfish fragments of a shared black past, drawing into the light the potent and persistent legacies of the long history of Black Power.

CHAPTER 7

CULTURE FROM THE MIDNIGHT HOUR

'We bear witness to a profound change in the way we now see ourselves and the world ... an ongoing change', wrote Larry Neal in 1969. He perceived 'A steady, certain march toward a collective sense of who we are, and what we must now be about to liberate ourselves'.[1] Certainly, African-America's self-perception was irrevocably changing, as the man in the street responded to an increasingly broad and provocative array of Black Power images and tropes being articulated through television, film, theatre and oratory. In an era wracked by tumultuous political and social transformation, marked by a devastating war and witness to a dramatic shift in the goals of the civil rights struggle, the emergence of Black Power cultural forms developed over decades of connected cultural expressions would redefine the interaction of African-Americans with American society and rearrange the bounds of the American cultural landscape. Echoing Fuller and Carmichael, Neal argued: 'Black Power, in its most fundamental sense, stands for the principles of Self-Definition and Self-Determination ... This was the gut essence of the Black Power philosophy before the political butchers and the civil rights hustlers got into the game.'[2] Examining how Black Power militants conveyed this message to the American people helps explain both the response to and the influence of Black Power rhetoric.

In a manner akin to many of his contemporaries, Neal stressed that not only was culture an essential facet of the contemporary struggle, with the Black Arts Movement (BAM) developing alongside its political counterpart, but, more importantly, that Black Arts and black culture as a whole far antedated the contemporary movement. For Neal, the BAM was an organisation which sought to express 'the Soul of the Black Nation' and in so doing 'define the world of art and culture in its own terms', providing a fusion of forms which would 'link, in a highly conscious manner, art and politics in order to assist in the liberation of Black people'.[3] How was this to be achieved? Black Arts militants argued that the connected cultural expressions present in Black Power's long history were an essential motive force and any 'linking must take place along lines ... rooted in the Afro-American and Third World historical and cultural sensibility'.[4] As Neal summarised, a clearer image of African-American culture and its relation to not only the white world, but also the freedom struggle, was needed. Accordingly, 'Black artists' found themselves 'concerned with the development, for lack of a better term, of a "Black Esthetic"'.[5] The bounds of this aesthetic can be defined by analysing manifestations of African-American culture in everyday life – changing patterns of thought in art and literature, the interaction between history and myth exhibited in the work of BAM and expressions of empowerment and identity in contemporary style and fashion. Examining the place of music and theatre in identity construction and the ability of television and film to shape peoples' perceptions of their place in relation to the struggle for empowerment reveals that a profound change was occurring in African-Americans' self-perception. The degree to which the African-American community accepted these new cultural manifestations and the consequences of this acceptance were to change the American cultural landscape and the relationship between Black Power and the American people. An analysis of the manner in which Neal's 'Black Esthetic' was created, promulgated and sustained illuminates a level of the Black Power experience heretofore seldom discussed.

The development of an aesthetic was itself a militant act, an affirmation of the vibrancy of African-American culture in comparison to the oppressive tropes offered by mainstream America. Black Arts members contended that an awareness of Black Power's long history led to the realisation that 'What the Western white mass calls an "esthetic" is fundamentally a dry assembly of dead ideas based on a dead people ... found meaningless in light of contemporary history.'[6] White culture was 'a cold, lifeless corpse ... the emanations of a dead world';

African-American militants were 'witness to the moral and philosophical decay of a corrupt civilisation'.[7]

It was argued that white America was a parasite which absorbed and distorted African-Americans' received self-image, offering only stereotypes perfected over the centuries. Neal raged: 'we are constantly forced to see ourselves through white eyes ... in the process, we do ourselves great spiritual and psychological harm'.[8] A cultural counterweight was needed, a means to counteract what Du Bois had termed double consciousness, the 'sense of always looking at one's self through the eyes of others, of measuring one's soul by the tape of a world that looks on in amused contempt and pity'.[9] The result was a concerted effort by African-American militants in the closing years of the 1960s to communicate Black Power ideals to ordinary black Americans. As Neal explained in stentorian terms, 'In 1969, Du Bois' sons and daughters in the Black Arts Movement go forth to destroy the Double Consciousness to merge these "warring ideals" into One Committed Soul.'[10]

For all Neal's fiery rhetoric, his choice of words suggest that he was well aware that the BAM originated in an earlier series of historical expressions. The trick, for Neal, was to imbue these expressions with contemporary relevancy, and vibrancy. In the process, the images and ideologies of Black Power would be recognised as an intrinsic part of the American experience.

No clearer manifesto could be found than in his passionate assertion that: 'The Black Arts Movement strives for ... intimacy with the people ... to be a movement ... rooted in the fundamental experience of the nation'.[11] This historically grounded perspective influenced the Black Arts' selection of its chosen media. 'Contemporary Black music and the living folklore of the people are ... the most obvious examples of the Black esthetic', Neal argued, drawing heavily on the connected cultural expressions which informed the movement, 'the truest expressions of our pain, aspirations and group wisdom. These elements', he concluded, 'decidedly constitute a culture'.[12]

Working from this interpretation of culture and history the BAM became not simply an artistic venture but a concerted attack on persistent mainstream white values and prescribed cultural stereotypes. It was 'more than the process of making art, of telling stories, of writing poems, of performing plays'.[13] Fundamentally, movement members sought 'the destruction ... of white ways of looking at the world'.[14]

This destruction was to be achieved, indeed, could *only* be achieved, via the cooperation and comprehension of ordinary black people. Repeatedly, movement activists reiterated that they were not 'speaking of "protest" art' but of 'an art that addresses itself directly to Black people ... that validates the positive aspects of our life style'.[15]

Movement members envisaged a progressive art with pragmatic applications, which 'makes us understand our condition and each other in a more profound manner; that unites us'.[16] Liberation, it was argued, mandated clear communication. Clarity of communication, in turn, was assured by maintaining fidelity to African-America's historic culture. As Neal summarised, 'Black poets dig the blues and Black music in order to find in them the means of making their address to Black America more understandable.'[17] Understanding, in turn, prepared the population for revolutionary discourse. From a Black Power perspective, culture was an essential foundation for advancing political goals, offerings the keys and codicils into the hearts of the American people. The wise artist studied 'Afro-American culture, history and politics and use[d] their secrets to open the way for the brother with the heavy and necessary political rap'.[18]

Activists were aware that the relationship between art and politics was symbiotic and that both were necessary in the militant struggle. Neal admitted that 'Art alone will not liberate us ... culture as an abstract thing within itself will not give us Self-Determination and Nationhood.'[19] Thus, cultural expression needed to be tied closely to the community, situated at the roots of revolution. A political triumph at the price of cultural distortion, it was argued, would be worthless. The success of political Black Power was intimately connected with the daily lives of black Americans. As Neal phrased it, 'A cultureless revolution is a bullshit tip ... a revolution without culture would destroy the very thing that now unites us and makes it more possible for us ... to do whatever is necessary to liberate ourselves.'[20]

The key to genuine liberation lay in African-American militancy embracing African-American culture. From Neal's perspective, not only average African-Americans, but many militants had failed to do so, falling instead for the blandishments of folk-pop America. He argued that 'A revolution that would have Leonard Bernstein, Bobby Dylan, or the Beatles at the top of its cultural hierarchy would mean that in the process of making the revolution, the so-called revolutionaries had spiritually murdered Black people.'[21] The alternative to this spiritual murder was the careful selection of a new range of cultural referents, drawn from the long history of Black Power. If, as movement supporters such as Neal contended, black culture creators 'represent our various identities ... [and] ... link us to the deepest, most profound aspects of our ancestry', then the culture heroes chosen by the movement speak volumes about the identity it wished to bestow upon African-America.[22]

In seeking this identity, movement artists interwove history and myth to create a new African-American mythology and a novel pantheon of culture heroes, which ranged from Malcolm X and Martin Luther King, through Renaissance luminaries, postbellum scholars, slave agitators and finally to the folkloric roots of Stagalee, Shine and the Signifying Monkey.[23] LeRoi Jones perhaps best clarified the purpose of this eclectic melding when he wrote in *Black Art*: 'We want a black poem. And a Black world. Let the world be a Black Poem.'[24] A new mythology and a greater sense of history, it was argued, could create a greater sense of unity and by extension a drive towards an African-American nation.

Historians do not have to look far for practical evidence of this belief: the 1967 James Brown hit 'There Was A Time' effectively traces the history of African-America through dance, while Gylan Kain's *Shalimar* lauds the strength found in a world where 'alligator shoes/leopard skins/ funny kind of hats that slant/downward and sideward/ ... in some funny kind of way/become ultra-hip/ the voodoo, who do/ what you don't dare do people.'[25]

In a similar manner, Carolyn Brown demanded 'a poem that don't be cryin/or scream/preachin/rappin/for the end of scream/preachin/rappin/ or protestin for the cause of protestin/or lyin for the white pigs, I want a mean poem/uh cool muthafucka poem/uh we all black & love each otha poem.'[26] This convivial, communal attitude was prevalent amongst BAM members and was dramatically distilled by the poet Ed Spriggs, who described ghetto inhabitants as culture-heroes of riot and revolt, 'cats in hero bones/[who] shoot your shit from starless roof[s]'.[27]

This was not poetry from the middle-class worlds of the civil rights establishment or the art community, but rather cultural expression penned by the man in the street, militant words which throbbed with the 'tenement radiator pulse'.[28] Independence was the key refrain.

As Arthur Pfister spat in the rap rhythm of the street, 'Mouths ain't guns/& tongues ain't missiles ... Poems ain't knives, or grenades to sling/but dig me brother, we gon' do our thing'.[29] Much as The Roots, Flobots and Saul Williams would emulate decades later, this was the language of the street used to deliver a stark warning to white America.

On the page and on the air, the sentiment was clearly articulated; Smokey Robinson warned, 'if there's a smile on my face/It's only there trying to fool the public'.[30] The rhetoric of frustration battled that of liberation on the page and on the stereo. Even as Jerry Butler informed his listeners that 'Only the Strong Survive', bands such as The Last Poets produced lyrical hits redolent with 'Black Love ... and Black Liberation'.[31] Formed on 19 May 1968 (Malcolm X's birthday) by Gylan Kain along with Felipe Luciano and David Nelson, the Poets took their name from a piece by Keorapetse 'Willie' Kgositsile articulating his belief that he was living in the last age of art before the age of the gun began.[32] Indeed, Kgositsile passionately summarised the contentious relationship between reality and art when he wrote: 'What does my hunger have to do with a gawdamn poem? ... WHEN THE MOMENT HATCHES ... THERE WILL BE NO ART TALK. THE ONLY POEM YOU WILL HEAR WILL BE THE SPEARPOINT PIVOTED IN THE PUNCTURED MARROW OF THE VILLAIN'.[33]

Perhaps hoping to galvanise, rather than terrify their audience the Poets preached a less apocalyptic gospel to that of their inspiration, urging, 'Niggers are scared of revolution/ but niggers shouldn't be scared of revolution/ because revolution is nothing but change/ and all niggers do is change.'[34] Ultimately, the BAM's challenge was to structure these sentiments and offer black Americans a 'culture [which] gives us a revolutionary moral vision and a system of values and methodology around which to shape the political movement'.[35] The culture thus created was not solely based on artistic forms but rather, 'the values, the life styles, and ... feelings of the people expressed in every day life'.[36]

Neal claimed that 'It is the task of the Black artist to ... go beyond merely reflecting ... oppression and the conditions engendered by oppression.'[37] Artists had to alter the world around them, and resonate with its concerns. Amiri Baraka recalled, 'We wanted a *mass art*. An art that could "Monkey" out the libraries and "Boogaloo" down the street in tune with popular revolution.'[38] This was nowhere more important than in that most communicable of mediums, popular music. As with other artists, musicians were urged to take 'Black culture, its life styles, its rhythms, its energy and direct that ... toward the liberation of Black people.' The maxim was simple: 'Respect and understand the culture don't exploit it.'[39]

Beyond its artistic representation, the survival of that culture required practical implementation via 'Meaningful institutions ... run and controlled by Black People with a vision'.[40] Several such institutions were established during the period, from Amiri Baraka's efforts in Newark, to the battles of Clarence Reed and the young members of the Harlem Youth Federation. The foundation of the National Black Theater by Barbara Ann Teer in 1966 and Gaston Neal's New School for Afro-American Thought in Washington D.C. in the same year was followed by the establishment of the East Wind poetry workshop in inner Harlem in 1969, which in turn fostered grassroots support for theatres like the New Lafayette, while in the educational sphere A.B. Spellman and Vincent Harding continued to strive to establish an African-American university.[41] These institutions, activists felt, were the soul and sinew which animated any emergent new black consciousness. Neal explained: 'These attempts at building Black Institutions are finally about the physical and spiritual survival of Black America. In the context of our struggle ... they are as important as the gun.'[42] From a BAM perspective, cultural expression was a necessary preparation for impending conflict. After all, adherents quizzed listeners, 'If de war comes, and dis being America, it probably will – whose images and songs will flicker on the film of your brains: Billie Holiday's or Janis Joplin's?'[43]

Despite the short lifetime of many of its projects and the operational and political difficulties its members faced, much of the BAM underwrote the political facets of African-American militancy, supplying, 'an arsenal of feelings and images, and myths'.[44] Self-definition was a difficult process which needed these reference points. The matrix of cultural touchstones which emerged was drawn from Black Power's long history and was not simply a matter of stylistic choice. The complex evolution of African-American militancy could not be delineated within the bounds of an Afro or dashiki. As Neal preached, 'Everybody ... knows that this thing goes beyond hair styles and African clothing. The most brainwashed brother on the street is hip to that. That's why some of the meanest, most potentially revolutionary niggers still wear processes.'[45]

This was not to deny the signal importance of apparently superficial forms of cultural expression. For some militants, 'The new references of clothing and hair' were 'essentially visions of ourselves perfected ... sign posts on the road to eventual Self-Determination.'[46] The process of crafting the new self-image mandated by Black Power's central revolution of the mind was, more often than not, entirely literal. For African-American women in particular, adopting new, non-Western hairstyles was presented as a fundamental step. A new hairstyle was not merely a fashion statement, but a personal statement. Put simply, 'For a Sister to wear her hair natural asserts the sacred ... nature of her body. The natural ... symbolises the Sister's willingness to determine her own destiny. It is an act of love for herself and her people.'[47] By adopting a physical cultural change, movement activists argued, the woman in the street brought herself closer to African-America and by extension, to militant politics: 'The natural helps psychologically ... liberate the sister. It prepares her for the message of a Rap Brown, a Robert Williams, a Huey Newton, a Maulana Karenga. The Sister's natural helps to destroy the "Double Consciousness" Du Bois spoke of.'[48]

Beyond the striking example of liberated hair, the notion of increased authenticity through cultural expression permeated street culture. As Jeff Donaldson, chair of Harvard's art department and co-founder of the African Commune of Bad Relevant Artists (AFRICOBRA), commented in *Black World*, he was interested in the creation of 'Superreal images for SUPER-REAL people'.[49] AFRICOBRA's work combined the atmosphere and style of the ghetto with the deeper mythological images Neal and his associates had been so keen to promote. As Donaldson explained in a litany of enthusiasm, 'We want the things to shine, to have the rich lustre of a just-washed 'Fro, of spit-shined shoes, of de-ashened elbows and knees and noses, The Shine who escaped the titanic, the "li'l light of mine", patent leather, Dixie Peach, Bar-BQ. Fried fish, cars, *ad shineum!*'[50] Donaldson's enthusiasm translated into activism; he was instrumental in creating Chicago's 'Wall of Respect' in 1967, which would in time become an iconic site for both the cultural and political Black Power movement. This initial project inspired myriad grassroots urban mural movements which proliferated across America in the 1970s, becoming a 'statement about the importance of both political struggle and artistic creation to the Afro-American community'.[51] In the words of Don L. Lee, 'the Wall' was the voice not of elevated demagogues, but everyday people, 'brothers & sisters screaming "picasso ain't got shit on us/send him back to art school"'.[52]

The adoption of BAM's language and message by prominent African-Americans like Donaldson was significant, as it illustrated the apparent fulfilment of the goals set by Neal and his associates. The acceptance of the alternative black culture promulgated and promoted by BAM was seen as an essential step in surviving within American society. As Neal warned, 'If Black Revolutionary Cultural Consciousness is perverted by jive Negro hustlers and Madison Avenue freaks, it is our job to illustrate how that very perversion is consistent with the nature of the capitalistic, colonialistic, and imperialistic monsters that now rule the planet.'[53]

In short, knowing the nature of the monsters, or more prosaically, understanding oppression, meant understanding the cultural domination of white America and subsequently resisting it by adopting varied forms of African-American cultural production, something which the militant political wing of African-America could not achieve alone. Startling as it might seem to those born and burned in the heart of the civil rights struggle, the campaigns for legal equality and economic parity were insufficient to achieve true liberation. As Neal explained, 'To merely point out to Black people the economic and political nature of our oppression is not enough ... because people are more than just the sum total of economic and political factors.'[54]

Movement activists sought 'the death of the white lie ... of the double-consciousness' in order to convince African-Americans that: 'You are Black Art. You are the poem, as Amiri Baraka teaches us. You are Dahomey smile. You are slave ship and field holler. You are Blues and Gospel and Be-Bop and New Music ... you are both memory and flesh.'[55] Militants contended that Black Art, as 'memory and flesh', as the combination of cultural inheritance and contemporary practical reality, could be found amongst everyone. It was the product of Black Power's long history, created by generations of 'Visionaries and warriors ... Niggers and Toms ... mean Poppa Stoppas ... pimps and prostitutes ... railroadmen and mackdaddys ... college presidents and porters ... mucked-up intellectuals and exploited workers, gun-toting ministers, and lollygagging mommas ... numbers runners ... shuffling waiters and drifters'.[56] If the roots of Black Art lay in the community, it was that community's acceptance of African-American culture which would decide the enterprise's success or failure.

In the late twentieth century, the beating, evolving heart of the black community remained firmly buried in the concrete ribs of the ghetto, at the nexus of historical and contemporary identity formation. For the civil rights activist Robert Williams, the ghetto simultaneously symbolised the oppression of white America and the cultural heritage of African-America, 'You hate it, and yet, your roots are buried there ... it reflects the soul of an oppressed but dauntless people.'[57] In a similar vein, Black Arts founder David Henderson (described by biographer Terry Joseph Cole as 'the literary heir of Langston Hughes') spoke of the ghetto as an occupied country, a deep forest thrumming with the music of African-America, but saturated in white American cultural presence.[58] Henderson's *Keep on Pushing*, written in 1964 and published in 1969, took its name from a hit of the same year by Curtis Mayfield and the Impressions. Whereas Mayfield had sung 'maybe some day'/I'll reach that higher goal/I know that I can make it/With just a little bit of soul' in a manner reminiscent of the civil rights movement's nonviolent anthems, Henderson depicted a country at war with itself, wherein 'Police Commissioner Murphy can/muster five hundred cops in fifteen minutes/ ... for harlem/reinforcements come from the Bronx/ ... a shot a cry a rumor/can muster five hundred Negroes/from idle and strategic street corners.'[59]

In this riven America, conflict was not solely physical; deprivation was endemic, structural and environmental. Henderson recalled that 'I see the store owners ... − all white/and I see ... /The white Police in the white helmets/and the white proprietors in their white shirts' while in the same street toil 'Negro handymen put to work because of the riots/ boarding up smashed storefronts' using freshly hewn pine and sparkling new nails. Henderson muses that 'pine boards are the nearest Lenox Avenue will ever have to trees'.[60]

African-America, Henderson reminds his readers, is not white America, and should not share its perceptions or its cultural mores. As he queries, 'Am I in the 1940's? Am I in Asia? Battista's Havana?/ ... when are we going to have the plebescite [sic]?' An alien land, upon which white culture and capitalism intrudes with sinister intent, the ghetto is inhabited by 'children/ ... like no other children anywhere ... unpopular foreign/as if in the midst of New York existed a cryptic and closed society'.⁶¹ Into this foreign country, white America sends its forces of subjugation, 'grim champions of the free world/Trucks dispensing Hershey Bars and Pall Malls'.⁶²

Like his BAM contemporaries, Henderson sees resistance only in the ghetto's acceptance of African-American culture, noting that 'At night Harlem sings and dances' and exhorting the inhabitants to 'Come out of your windows/dancehalls, bars and grills Monkey Dog in the streets/like Martha and the Vandellas ... 'cause you got soul/Everybody knows ... / Keep on Pushin'.'⁶³ In this universe, the mundane becomes militant. He presents his readers with a world where Fish and Chip shack proprietors talk of 'ammunition and violence'.⁶⁴ Conflict is integrated with perceptions of daily life. The white media is vampiric, salivating lasciviously over the trauma of the riots, promising 'The Face of Violence – the most striking Close-ups' while lecturing on the 'fruits of Democracy' and reminding ghetto citizens that 'violence only hurts'.⁶⁵ Conversely, 'the radio station that serves/the Negro Community/tools along on its rhythm and blues vehicle' as the announcers 'declare themselves "the most soulful station in the nation"'.⁶⁶ Ultimately when these two cultures clash, the result is violence. As Henderson concludes, 'There will be no Passover this night/ ... the gunfire high/in the air death static over everything.'⁶⁷ Yet in the silence after the destruction Henderson hears the refrain of American capitalism continue, as the radio whispers '"Tension? ... take Compoz!"/ Headache? – Take Aspirin.'⁶⁸

There are fundamental truths buried in the morass of Henderson's dystopia. In contrast to the prescriptive sounds of mainstream radio, live performances in the community could provide an avenue of escape from the daily grind of ghetto life. Playwright Clay Goss recalled, 'I was a very young dude back then ... my older cousin Luther would take me to the shows where I would really go to clean out my mind.'⁶⁹ For Goss, live gigs were a means of 'learning about life and soul and rhythm and blues ... blues peoples and black people'.⁷⁰ As he would later understand, gigs themselves were examples of the slow process of self-definition, where minds changed faster than fashions: 'the mean "jitterboppers" wore processes then without realising they were showboating self hate commercials'.⁷¹ Goss believed that the artists of the day, such as Dave 'Baby' Cortez, Dee Clark and the Chantels connected profoundly with their audience, to the extent that 'the hoodlums in de place would secretly slip gang war scarred hands deep into their multi-coloured gang jackets pinching their rib cages to see if they wasn't really dreaming'.[72] Worshipping in a secular temple, Goss recalled how the dancehall's light would 'change the performing groups' suits to lovely shades of lost African Easter Sundays'.[73] Songs such as Donny Elbert and the Vibra-Harps 'Hear My Plea' held meaning because 'everybody in the house was in some kind of misery'.[74]

Music may have fostered a sense of a broad, shared identity but bands like Lee Andrews and the Hearts particularly appealed to the Philadelphia-born Goss due to their local roots.[75] Even later luminaries like James Brown and His Famous Flames brought a vibrancy and militancy to everyday music 'in their Red and Yellow suits, white shoes and out of sight dance steps, before they became millionaires and shouted "SAY IT LOUD – I'M BLACK AND I'M PROUD" but they were still Boss Kings back then'.[76] Even when viewed from a purely pragmatic perspective music was an excellent communicator of the modern African-American cultural aesthetic, with songs like The Drifters' 'There Goes My Baby' penetrating deep into Mississippi with impressive sales figures.[77] Music united the community with peculiar intensity, bringing together 'Jive dudes and hip mommas, mailmen and dayworkers, young teens and warlords, everybody ... up on their feet and singing along'.[78] Moreover, it was hugely popular amongst many white listeners who not only accepted this aspect of black culture on its own terms, but helped to sustain and promote it.

The impact of live music on its listeners emphasised that the politics of the street and the Black Power movement's cultural legacy were not distinct forces, but interrelated parts of a greater whole, each informing and driving the other, joined via the synapses of connected cultural expressions across time. This unique ethic, wherein politics took its strength from a community's culture, thereby enabling that community to engage to a greater degree with politics, found one of its clearest iterations not in the urban North but in the rural South, as young African-Americans, fired by the culture of the Northern BAM, travelled South to spread its legacy amidst the silt, shotguns and suspicion of the Mississippi Delta.

The evolution of the Free Southern Theater (FST) from humble beginnings in 1963 embodies the often overlooked inter-relationship between the cultural elements of the northern and southern civil rights struggle and the manner in which that struggle was shaped by the people it sought to aid. During the course of its existence, the Theater became a cultural focal point and an invaluable tool for cultural communication between otherwise disparate elements of black America.

Historically, the northern urbanised sections of the African-American militant movement were separated, to varying degrees depending on their ideology, from the Southern movement. The result was an insular community ill-suited to the transmission of novel ideas, tropes and cultural expressions of resistance and empowerment. Potentially transformative concepts were, according to contemporary observers like Neal, 'locked up in tight clusters of persons who hold already similar ideas about the ... problems affecting black people'.[79] This echo chamber effect, compounded by the north/south geographical divide meant empowerment occurred sporadically on a regional basis with little coordination between the cultural messages forwarded by disparate militant groups. While numerous efforts were made to bridge this gap, the emergence of a small, spontaneous theatre group initially seemed an unlikely candidate for drawing black empowerment closer to the American people.

The emergence of the FST represented an expression of African-American militancy markedly different from that igniting the streets of Watts and Detroit, namely the creation of a community-orientated and culturally grounded African-American theatre in the American South. Several of its key members, including Len Holt, Gilbert Moses and John O'Neal, had close ties to the Student Non-Violent Coordinating Committee (SNCC), one of the chief motive forces in the Southern civil rights movement. As part of their organisational ethos, SNCC members frequently buttressed their position by living with the people they sought to empower. Neal noted that 'They even went so far as to adopt the dress and the speech of the regions they hope[d] to politically affect.'[80] What may initially seem a trivial gesture was in fact a calculated decision. By adopting familiar methods of cultural expression and talking to the community on their own terms, SNCC activists were able to communicate to an audience of hundreds of thousands of rural African-Americans in a significantly more accessible manner. In turn, the increased sense of community created by deploying familiar cultural forms served as a foundation for the construction of a political message.

Accordingly, many of the strategies adopted by SNCC in the South were designed to use familiar cultural media to ameliorate fears of white aggression. The African-American South, and Mississippi in particular, had long been devoid of any established formal theatrical presence. Importantly however, popular culture gatherings remained a staple of daily life. Music, sports and the church drew consistent, attentive audiences. The church in particular presented an ideal format, combining theatre, ritual and audience participation in regular gatherings. By targeting these pre-established audiences, SNCC and subsequently the FST found an avenue which enabled them to present a novel vision of African-American history to the black South utilising existing social structures.

By coordinating from a church base, SNCC activists were able to involve local ministers and their parishioners in the campaign process. More importantly, the adoption of gospels and spirituals as freedom songs for the movement represented a hugely significant appropriation of African-American cultural expression for the purposes of the civil rights struggle.[81] 'This was a natural result of working in the South', Neal commented, 'It was also a fantastic leap in black cultural consciousness on the part of black activists.'[82]

As a consequence of their religious, gospel and spiritual base, SNCC activists developed a political campaigning style which had its origins in historical African-American cultural forms, shaped by a framework of response and interaction in a manner analogous to the call-and-response styles of southern church and earlier slave spirituals. However, despite the formative role of cultural expression in many militant political programmes, cultural forms (with the sole exception of freedom songs) were never formally deployed as tools for empowerment in the civil rights movement's political campaigns. Cultural expression nevertheless permeated the Southern movement's political discourse, although it was chiefly articulated unconsciously, 'by default instead of by design'.[83]

From this perspective, the FST represents one of the most daring endeavours in civil rights history. As a committed African-American theatre, operating formally within the larger civil rights movement, it had the potential to be a focal point for developing personal and organisational identities. The theatre was certainly formed with such a goal in mind, namely to unite and strengthen the communities in which it found itself, to 'validate the positive aspects of black life styles, of the living culture'.[84] The manner in which it did so and the difficulties it experienced in the process shed light on the historical development and subsequent legacy of African-American cultural militancy.

In 1964, an FST report claimed: 'The ... Theater is as much a product of "the movement" as voter registration, community centres or the Mississippi Freedom Democratic Party [MFDP].'[85] However, although it emerged from the same societal context, the goals of the FST were distinct from the political endeavours which it presented as familiar reference points. Unlike these purely political efforts, the theatre primarily sought to provide programmes which would help African-Americans in their struggle for equality by simultaneously incorporating art and politics. This approach was embodied by its founders, one of whom, John O'Neal, remarked that 'the most profound poetry is the poetry of action'.[86]

Perceiving itself as both a political and cultural organisation, the Theatre strove to dramatise the reality of the black freedom struggle at protest events throughout the rural South. Working regionally, the FST engaged members of the community in all aspects of theatrical production from writing to directing and producing. In the process, it challenged ordinary African-Americans to reassess received interpretations of their history and cultural experience in order to confront white-imposed stereotypes and to evolve new ways of challenging oppression. The methods and approaches taken by the FST set a precedent for other grass-roots theatre groups such as Luis Valdez' Teatro Campesino (TC) who, two years after FST's foundation, would provide *agitprop* morality plays to illiterate farmworkers from a flatbed truck in the fields of Delano, California.[87] Formed on the picket lines of the Delano Grape Strike in 1965, TC persists to this day, utilising the combination of community involvement and radical militant politics pioneered by the FST.[88] Yet the FST was as relevant for its immediate impact as its legacy. Under the group's guidance, for some Americans theatre became not only a catalyst to practical action, but an impetus to critical analysis of the cultural sphere. In the process, the Theater provided cultural roots for the wider political movement sweeping the South. In a manner analogous to the approach taken by Emory Douglas, the Panther Minister of Culture, FST members argued that political action was pointless if unsupported by an attempt to fill the southern cultural vacuum and combat the information deprivation and educational neglect suffered by the South. The aim was 'to take ... [the] ... structure of commercial art and add a brand-new content to it ... that will serve the interests of Black people'.[89]

The defining text on the Free Southern Theater, an eponymously titled book by several of its founders – Thomas C. Dent, Richard Schechner and the originally uncredited Gil Moses – was as much a study of the development of a militant, nationalist perspective among civil rights activists of the mid-1960s as it was a narrative of the Theater's formation. From an FST perspective, the theatre was not simply a theatre, but a forum. After each show, vociferous debates encouraged a free exchange of opinions. This direct dialogue with the community enabled the FST to craft a programme relevant to its audience and to establish a dialectical discourse which would produce new locally grounded cultural forms. In effect, the FST was driven, sustained and furthered by its southern black audience. Accordingly, its persistent aim was to cultivate that audience and provide constant stimuli for the involvement of ordinary black Americans. It primarily did so by organising tours of the American South, under the pragmatic rationale that if black Americans were unable to come to the theatre, then the theatre must go to them.

Larry Neal acknowledged the importance of the community sentiment this approach created when he argued that the FST and its successors in the BAM both strove to 'shape out of the materials of black people, black culture, black sensibility, black emotions, black history and black mythology an artistic form that acts to spiritually liberate us'.[90] In its formative General Prospectus, FST contended that 'within the Southern situation a theatrical form and style can be developed that is as unique to the Negro people as the origin of blues and jazz'.[91] Crucially, in attempting to establish close ties with its community, the FST ensured that local African-Americans would be both the producers and audience for their works, resulting in 'plays written for a Negro audience, which relate to the problems within the Negro himself and within the Negro community'.[92] Ultimately, the FST saw theatre both as a tool for assisting in the quest for self-definition being undertaken by Southern black Americans and as a device which would bring cultural expression to the forefront as a political weapon. The prospectus boldly concluded: 'we think to open a new area of protest. One that permits the development of playwrights and actors ... the growth and self-knowledge of a Negro audience, one that supplements the present struggle for freedom'.[93]

As a result, the FST made a conscious decision to perform plays produced by southern black Americans and inspired by local history. Through workshop projects, it strove to create a new body of work that accurately represented the depth, vitality and complexity of being black in America. From the FST's perspective, the only way to overcome American society's inherent racism was to actualise the potential present among its black audience, to write in a manner which addressed the black experience, in an idiom which complemented that audience's African-American heritage. In the process, the line separating art and propaganda was redrawn to the point where 'The artist can speak quite sharply to a specific cultural situation without sacrificing to propaganda.' Rather portentously, the FST contended that the black artist 'operates at the vanguard of man's cultural consciousness ... his responsibility is to inform judgements: from this principle he derives aesthetic license.'[94] In making this statement, FST not only ascribed itself a great deal of cultural responsibility, but explicitly contradicted Du Bois's oft-repeated maxim, that 'All art is propaganda.' In contrast, the young men and women of FST appeared to hold similar sentiments to those expressed by Johnson, Hughes, Hurston and those other Renaissance firebrands who had situated themselves as the guiding lights of everyday black American audiences seeking a more authentic existence.[95]

Unlike the aesthetes of the Renaissance, the FST placed its art directly on the frontlines of American segregation. In common with SNCC and CORE on the political front, the FST had selected Mississippi as it initial base of operations, to directly challenge white bigotry in the heartland of American racism.[96] Seen as both culturally bereft and political riven, the Magnolia State was increasingly presented as the location which would most immediately benefit from a programme to enrich African-American cultural life and historical consciousness.[97] Yet the FST sought confrontation not only in its locations, but also in its methodology. A large degree of the contemporary enthusiasm surrounding the Theater's initial efforts stemmed from its perceived radical approach to integration within not only the Deep South, but also the ivory confines of American theatre. Thus, from its inception, FST, like its Harlem Renaissance forebears, faced a dichotomy – although attempting to create a distinctly African-American theatre, informed by African-American people, the group also strove to present an integrated company, which relied on pre-existing, unequal, power structures.

The difficulty in reconciling these opposing goals was seen in the protracted delay in the FST's production of a theatre which addressed itself to the African-Americans of the Deep South. As Neal pithily explained, several years were devoted to simply 'hacking away the deadwood of American liberal and aesthetic ideas'.[98] The end result of this prolonged endeavour was neither as militant nor as radical as the group's initial prospectus suggested. The explanations for this dilution were rooted in received cultural stereotypes, namely traditional theatre's adherence to 'classic' or, rather, white, productions. Validity beyond the bounds of accepted plays and playwrights was difficult to find. In attempting to rewrite America and the American people, FST removed both the limitations of traditional theatre, but also the legitimacy which it could provide.

Despite FST's talent for combining both venue and audience into performance, the diverse African-American communities in the South did not respond as a single homogenous entity and were not instantly favourable to the concept of radical, militant theatre. Vast cultural differences existed between rural and urban black Americans and there was a similar class divide between middle-class and working-class groups.

The voices of the people were proving too varied and too dissonant to capture on the page. Struggling with conflicting audience expectations and beset by financial and logistical problems, the FST transferred to New Orleans in November 1964. The Big Easy was to prove anything but. In the course of the move, the FST removed itself from the established movement milieu, and from the framework and impetus it provided.[99] In comparison to Mississippi, the FST's work in Louisiana had less obvious relevance to the problems of local black Americans and the fact that the FST chose to site itself in New Orleans did not automatically make the community receptive to its political message, nor did it lead local people to choose the FST over more commercial entertainment. As Dent explained, 'The Movement idea, the integration, the disrespect for social conventions in dress and behaviour, left a bad taste in the mouths of New Orleans black Americans, who of course did not consider themselves black.'[100]

Shortly after its arrival however, the FST changed the Louisiana environment irrevocably, establishing a radical newspaper, *The Plain Truth*, and offering an array of free cultural services to the local community. 'People just walked in', FST member Chakula Cha Jua recollected; 'the kids came back every night, they knew the lines to all the plays – it was really a community thing. We had so much going on in that little raggedy building ... poetry readings ... coffee shops ... midnight jazz.'[101] The loud noise from that little building represented the first stages of the FST's integration with the New Orleans community.

From its inception, the FST had maintained that it 'expressed the will and supported the interests of the common people', a belief enhanced by its conviction that the artist was an integral part of the wider community, 'responsible and accountable for the political as well as the aesthetic consequences of his efforts'.[102] Resolving to become an African-American theatre in its entirety, the FST permanently established itself in the impoverished Desire district of New Orleans, reasoning that in the heart of the community African-American involvement would be easier to procure. As Dent explained, it strove to fill a void in an area traditionally neglected, a ghetto wherein 'no voice speaks for the needs of the people ... against the fact that they are forgotten by the City of New Orleans'.[103] Once it found a way to tap into the vibrant cultural atmosphere provided by the Louisiana scene, which exhibited an intricate network of social and ethnic relationships, the FST again found avenues in which cultural production could spur political action.

Most radically, in an attempt to establish greater confidence in theatre and community alike, a redefinition of the group's art and aesthetics was suggested. Much as African-Americans were redefining their own identity, so too did the FST reformulate its approach to art. This change began with the suggestion that the theatre experience and perceptions of that experience were fundamentally different for black and white audiences, and consequently, only black Americans could define the meaning of their art. Accordingly, art could not be separated from the black struggle for equality; oppression became by cultural definition, white. Echoing Du Bois's 1903 musings on double consciousness, O'Neal remarked that black culture creators suffered from the expectations of 'A white audience ... that refuse[d] to acknowledge the most essential aspect of ... [their] ... consciousness ... [and were] ... further limited by cultural, political and economic institutions that incorporate the premises of racism'.[104]

These institutions shaped the form of the traditional theatre structures which the FST sought to escape. Such was the dominance of

Western white cultural convention that the FST came to prominence outside the South with their production of *Waiting for Godot*. Reflecting on its reception by the white establishment, Dent commented, 'It was cold and nobody black dug it. It was the kind of thing, however, that the *New York Times* would make a big thing.'[105] Yet as a product of the Irish tradition, it was argued that *Godot*'s symbols and meanings were empty to Southern black Americans, existing 'outside of the world view of most Mississippi sharecroppers'.[106] Such accusations were energetically refuted by FST members who condemned the critique as 'a condescending and patronizing argument ... [which] illustrates misplaced western values, presuming education as a prerequisite for intelligence'.[107] The FST's advocates were vindicated in their passionate defence. Their audience was often more astute than cultural stereotypes led white observers to believe. As Fannie Lou Hamer, a cornerstone of the MFDP, commented after seeing *Godot*, 'Every day we see men dressed just like these ... waiting for Godot. But you can't sit around waiting.'[108]

Although Hamer and other saw some truth in its lines, Godot's reception highlighted the FST's profound lack of African-American patronage, despite attempts to obtain additional scripts from luminaries including James Baldwin, Langston Hughes and John Killens. As a result, the Theater primarily performed works culturally alien to its desired audience. The integrationist ethic the FST continued to hold dear inevitably mandated absorption of white cultural values. However, it increasingly appeared that the FST's twin priorities – a relevant black theatre and an integrationist theatre – were contradictory concepts.

In 1965, as militant nationalist-separatist ideology spread through the civil rights movement, and on the eve of Stokely Carmichael's 'Black Power!' declaration, FST began to change. As Carmichael let fly with 'Black Power!' FST unfurled its own slogans: 'the fire next time in Mississippi' and 'goodbye *Godot*'.[109] These were profoundly militant statements, as the Theater sloughed off its dependence on white patrons – be they benefactor, playwright or audience – and clarified its dissatisfaction with the patriarchal benevolence of white America.

Far more than simply soliciting black authors, recruiting black actors or addressing black themes, the newly refined FST required a fundamental redefinition. The theatre needed to be 'as unique as blues, jazz, and gospel', with an equal impact on the African-American mind, and accordingly required the establishment of new forms and approaches designed to express the unique soulfulness of southern black Americans.[110] The FST's talent for documentary theatre, what O'Neal called 'building and improvising from pieces of fact and idea', established a platform for developing a new militant ideology.[111] O'Neal argued that script writing for workshop attendees was a formative process, as 'they'll be dealing with history ... getting their ideas together about what black theatre's all about'.[112] These ideas, once set down, showed a profound connection to the long history of black America. The scripts produced by these workshops emphasised a group unity that resonated with the reality of southern life, stressing that, as one wealthy New Orleans sponsor commented, all black Americans, regardless of their current social status, originated in the 'cotton patch'.[113]

In drawing on historical referents to reintroduce African-Americans into the public consciousness of a region in which they had traditionally been culturally and politically invisible, the FST made a unique cultural and political commitment for its time and one which had the potential to fill the void in the southern civil rights movement created by its lack of 'a sustaining revolutionary cultural dynamic'.[114] In this context, cultural forms were not a weapon used subconsciously, or in an *ad hoc* fashion as with the songs and chants of the traditional civil rights campaigns. Rather the ordinary voices of black Americans, turned into provocative play scripts, became part of a dynamic which constantly informed and was informed by the local context in which it operated.[115]

Moreover, the FST strove to create a medium whereby its message would penetrate the minds of its African-American audience, increasing their political consciousness, and imparting the absolute necessity of change. Much as the Black Panthers attempted to make politics accessible to the illiterate masses through the community-derived art of Emory Douglas, the FST spoke to its audience in terms they could understand.[116] In the process, the group attempted to create a syncretic black language which could use 'the Dozens, the street rap, black liturgical forms ... to make their underlying rhythms and spirit part of the total work' as opposed to merely 'icing on a white cake'. In other words, the FST sought to draw on the broadest range of connected black cultural expressions to reshape its audience's sense of themselves. Even as the BPINS redefined urban African-Americans' political perspectives via vibrant, militant art, the FST reached out to southern black Americans to change them culturally, 'to influence ... their emotions ... their thinking'.[117]

Theatre seldom led to direct changes in the life of its audience, but was an opportunity for critical assessment, of self and society, of hopes and aspirations, a catalyst to wider action and a means of reshaping established modes of thought. The FST, in retrospect, was a unique combination of Southern grassroots militancy and radical northern cultural expression which offered not only a credible reflection of the reality of southern black lives, but encapsulated and expanded the interrelationship between those lives, the cultural heritage of the Black Power movement and militant politics. It existed in a continuity of militant tradition and created characters based on existing archetypes of resistance. These characters evolved in response to their modern and local contexts, becoming transmitters for the concerns and hopes of their audiences, catalysts to militant action, repositories for changing political thought and ultimately, a driving impetus for concrete social change.

The development of an independent African-American cultural world was likewise a central goal for those BAM activists working in the northern cities as the FST battled in the South. From a northern militant perspective, white American culture was nothing but a series of 'tricks and toys that the white man has given to the black man so that he may be docilized and ... exploited'.[118] Especially dangerous were tricks which threatened the development of African-American identity. As S.E. Anderson, eventual author of *The Black Holocaust*, argued, 'Whitey's propaganda mechanism and our self-indoctrination has made us deny our historical, spiritual and political bond with ... Africa.'[119]

Most devastating of all, Anderson claimed, was the trick which strove to convince African-Americans that 'the white man has The Absolute Culture in the world and ... the same holds true for his beauty'.[120] Yet as he pointed out, 'James Brown, the Four Tops, and Abbey Lincoln are boss not because whitey says so, but because you, as a black individual, dig what they are putting down.'[121] From the perspective of urban Cassandras like Anderson acquiescence to white cultural norms was an implicit endorsement of white perspectives and accordingly a lost battle in the struggle for African-American independence, 'The very act of a black person straightening his or her hair' became 'an affirmation of whitey's false claim to have the Absolute Beauty'.[122]

There was a hard core to Anderson's remarks. The political emergence of Black Power in the 1960s placed its advocates at war with the entrenched symbolism of the American nation. The mainstream media was invested in America's 'traditional icons, its metaphors, its heroes, its rituals and narratives'.[123] Dissident voices needed not only to find their own symbols, but a way to chip away at the established frameworks which had calcified around their identity.

In comparison to tricks, toys were defined by some Black Arts militants as specific aspects of white American culture deleterious to African-America's well-being. Unsurprisingly paramount among these, given its omnipresence in American society, was television. Gil Scott-Heron, singing on *Pieces of A Man* was not entirely correct – the revolution in some aspects was televised. Whereas the print media had tended to provide or deny African-Americans a carefully constructed space in the American narrative, while preserving the illusion of a progressive agenda, television, at the outset, appeared more honest.[124] As Anderson explained, for many African-Americans television appeared a panacea, 'With T.V. he is able to escape the daily grind of toiling for "the man"' and yet the same unsuspecting viewer 'receive[d] news ... via the eyes and ears of a pathological liar' and was encouraged by the programmes offered to 'keep on struggling for the entrance into a closed sick society'.[125] Television was almost literally a black and white world characterised by a 'general absence of otherness' and staffed with white newscasters, presenters and reporters.[126] If television held a mirror to society, militants argued that the image it presented of African-America was narrow, distorted and damaging, noting: 'We are either entertainers, sportsmen, tricky James Bond-type spies, or people bleaching away with Artra.'[127]

More problematic still, print and television media worked in combination to control the discourse on African-American identity and mediate the relationship between Black Power and the American people. A twin distortion was effected. Television stations needed the sensationalism, drama and continuing narrative which would attract and keep viewers while print media strove to maintain their declining dominance by setting the framework within which the stories would be told and the agenda which they would serve.[128]

After violence, one of the biggest stories, as always, was sex. The sexual politics which underlay many black/white interactions, saw the plantation stereotypes of the savage, virile and unruly black male articulated in early bodice rippers like *Amber Satyr* resurface in the charged milieu of the late 1960s and early 1970s.[129] As Anderson ruefully surmised, 'This particular toy is quite unique: the more you talk about how bad the racial situation is in this country, the more it wants to go to bed with you.'[130]

Conversation was as dangerous as copulation. For Anderson, both congress and dialogue with white people was pointless, as 'black cats waste their time and energy speaking (or rather spewing) to white liberals'.[131] These white liberals, much like the insincere figures in Hughes's *The Ways of White Folks* were a strange breed, 'a person that lauds another for telling him how diseased his society is, and then does nothing meaningful'.[132] From this perspective, far from being useful allies, white liberals were 'plaything[s] for the black man to help displace his aggression upon the System'.[133]

Yet for all Anderson's vitriol, his castigation of the liberal establishment, the new broadcast media and any interracial couple foolish enough to slip into bed together rang a little hollow. Many black Americans were quite content to have white allies, entertaining programming and enjoyable sex. Far from the rural environs of the South and removed even from the later urban battlegrounds of New Orleans, Atlanta, Watts and Detroit, closeted safely in front of the TV, eating Swanson dinners, smoking Tareyton cigarettes and sipping Tang, enjoying 'all the degenerate benefits of a demented society that accepts them tokenly', were the more prosperous elements of African-America protected from the spreading influence of Black Arts and Black Power culture?[134] Were they indeed immune to the fever? Was deprivation and oppression a necessary component for the revolution of the mind? Stereotypical perceptions of suburban American life certainly suggested so.

How could militancy exist in what Anderson excoriated as a suburban 'concentration camp ... a place ... where every action ... [a black man] ... takes ... attempts to deny his roots?'[135] Were the suburbs still little more than an area where light-skinned black Americans tried fervently to 'pass' as white, as Johnson's *Ex-Coloured Man* had done decades prior? Was it true that suburban African-America was passively ensnared in 'the fascinating game of chromism ... played 24 hours a day everyday of the year' as Anderson claimed?[136] Hardly. The revolution of the mind was also occurring behind the white picket fence and in front of the silver screen, as African-America's cultural landscape was changed forever by the lurid arrival of the controversial, reviled and lauded phenomenon known as Blaxploitation cinema.

Blaxploitation — that heady mix of films suffused in the alleged sex, death and violence of the urban ghetto — swaggered onto the American streets in 1970 in the imposing forms of Sydney Poitier and Raymond St. Jacques. Poitier's lead role in *They Call Me MISTER Tibbs* (1970) accompanied Jacques's riotous performance in *Cotton Comes to Harlem* in the same year. However, both films were merely the first stirring of a new genre which would be defined by a young director named Melvin Van Peebles. Van Peebles, author of *Watermelon Man* (1970) and *Sweet Sweetback's Baadasssss Song* (1971) among others, recalled in an interview the startling rush to adopt the Blaxploitation aesthetic, commenting, 'A nigger couldn't have gotten arrested 16 months ago at Warner Bros.'[137] Yet the success of individuals like Van Peebles was deceptive; making movies in itself did not provide broad-scale empowerment. As he explained, 'Our own racism works against us. Cats will say "Hey man, Melvin did it, so I can do it. He's Black, so I can do it. ["] It's like saying "This cat split an atom, so I can go out and split an atom."'[138]

Nonetheless, the achievements of Van Peebles and similar pioneers were inspiring and in some ways, unprecedented. As Neal put it, 'Young people really want to know how somebody did all of this. It's phenomenal to them. They don't have any models around like that.'[139] The idolising of Van Peebles was significant, as his motivations for entering into the movie industry seemed to reflect the concerns held by the average young African-American in the ghetto. As he recalled, 'I ['d] sit in a movie and say "Shit. I can do better than that." I did not mean lighting, or story sequence, but that I could do better than niggers who are always kissing the white man's ass.'[140] To do better, Van Peebles turned to his community, and its history of struggle. Consequently, his films were defined by a down-to-earth aesthetic which encompassed all aspects of production.[141] As he explained, 'We take the position that the heroes were common Black folks ... we've had plenty of time to see *their* heroes; when are we going to canonise us[?]'[142] This approach resulted in films which, judging by ticket sales, resonated with ordinary black Americans and which carried a deep-rooted ethic of pride, independence and militancy.

Much like Hughes before him, Van Peebles combined the political and humorous in his work. Presenting 'high school students ... [with] ... the political aspect of their seeing apartments with five locks on the door, a beautiful Black woman in a $400 dress etc.' was as important as the realisation that 'we have to recapture the heights of our humor and not be intimidated by it'.[143] Whether in the oppressive climate of urban poverty and economic deprivation, or the repressive suburban atmosphere, with its 'chromic' assumptions and entrenched stereotypes, being able to 'laugh freer' was not an abstract, but a practical and militant goal.[144]

Film critic Diane Williams, commenting in 1996 on the growing influence of African-Americans in Hollywood, argued that the foundations for this success were laid during the Blaxploitation era: 'There is nothing new about this phenomenon ... ticket sales by black consumers ... upheld the black film industry when it was floundering [in the late 1960s].'[145] Blaxploitation was aggressively marketed to African-Americans who comprised only 10 to 15 per cent of the population, but accounted for 30 per cent of total ticket sales during the late 1960s and early 1970s in first-run, major city theatres.[146] Were these dramatic figures merely the result of canny marketing, or did the cultural message contained in such films resonate with audiences?

The 'unstable marriage of Black history and white Hollywood' epitomised by the genre was not without its problems.[147] Many scholars have been scathingly dismissive of Blaxploitation movies. As Donald Bogle accused, 'The films would have us believe the heroes were out to clean up the ghetto of its ills. Actually, the best way to have cleaned up the ghetto might have been to have first rounded up the producers of some of these vehicles.'[148] Critique of the Blaxploitation era contends that as these films were chiefly written, directed and produced by whites, they inevitably played upon the need of African-Americans for culture heroes without addressing these needs substantively.[149]

So it seemed to many civil rights campaigners at the time. Condemnation from both established non-violent groups and militants, including the Panthers, was swift. 'We must insist that our children are not constantly exposed to a steady diet of so-called black movies that glorify black males as pimps, dope pushers, gangsters and super males', warned Junius Griffin, head of the Hollywood NAACP.[150] Many historians have taken Griffin's claims as gospel, arguing that the 'rough-tough-cream-puff militant-stud-buck heroes' of the Blaxploitation era were lacking in authenticity.[151] Such arguments highlight a lack of understanding of Black Power's long history and cultural legacy. That the BPINS railed against 'The movie industry ... using our lives to make money' highlights the fact that these films echoed perceived aspects of *life*, that Blaxploitation heroes such as Sweetback, Shaft or B.G. and Laurie from *Up Tight* were part of a series of connected cultural expressions across time; as strong, wise and crafty as Big Sixteen or Uncle Pleas but incorporating the streetwise sass and militant fervour seen in BAM publications like *Umbra*.[152] Crucially, whether the film was produced by an African-American as with *Sweetback* or by a white American as with *Up Tight*, the militant aesthetic of the Black Arts and Black Power movements remained clearly visible. The absorption of the militant cultural aesthetic was such that even some white producers could not help but express some of its themes in their allegedly inauthentic work.

Jules Dassin's *Up Tight* is the epitome of this cultural mingling. A noted member of the Hollywood 'blacklist' extant between 1947 and 1957, Dassin, along with other entertainment professionals, was viewed with suspicion by the federal government due to his Communist Party ties. Raised in Harlem, Dassin was aware of conditions in the ghetto from his early life, recalling that questioning the status quo was a part of daily existence: 'You grow up in Harlem where there's trouble getting fed and keeping families warm, and live very close to Fifth Avenue, which is elegant ... you fret, you get ideas, seeing a lot of poverty around you, and it's a very natural process.'[153]

This process culminated in Dassin's cinematic output. A remake of the John Ford classic 'The Informer', and scripted by one of its stars, Ruby Dee, *Up Tight* is a fiery and direct presentation of black militancy.[154] Its account of the trials and tribulations of the black radical Johnny and his friend Tank directly and succinctly expresses many of the ideas central to Black Power rhetoric, acknowledging its allure and its dangers in equal measure. As noted critic Roger Ebert commented in his 1969 review, 'It doesn't chicken out. There's no backsliding, toward a conciliatory moderate conclusion. The passions and beliefs of black militants are presented head-on, with little in the way of comfort for white liberals. White racists, I guess, will be horrified beyond measure. Good for them.'[155]

Ebert argued that *Up Tight's* production by a white director had little relevance to its audience, as the messages it contained were analogous to those offered by the BAM, informed by Black Power's long history and thus able to resonate on a profound level. As he explained, 'The black Americans in the audience at the Roosevelt applauded "Up Tight" as a film that said something for them. It had nerve enough to portray the anger of the ghetto. Here was a movie in which the black Americans are really black, and act and think like it.'[156]

Far from evidence of white co-option of the Blaxploitation ethic, *Up Tight* was a signal example of how far African-American militant culture had penetrated into the commercial Hollywood mainstream. Ebert acknowledged that 'It's remarkable that a major studio (Paramount) financed and released this film. Perhaps its success will make it possible for other movies to consider the American reality'.[157] Given its engagement with 'American reality' the success of *Up Tight* amongst an African-American audience is unsurprising. Its language is forthright and direct, its windows onto American life believable and brutal; most notably in its presentation of the police shooting of a militant leader.

The very presence of such scenes in a Paramount film was a profound change in the portrayal of African-America to American cinema audiences. Dassin's cinematic presentations of these 'moments of truth' were signal victories in the struggle for black empowerment and had worth outside of the film's merits.[158] In Ebert's words, 'To see them on the screen is enough'.[159] Unlike in Dassin's source material (Liam O'Flaherty's 1925 novel *The Informer*, set during the aftermath of the Irish Civil War), the revolution in *Up Tight* is very much in the foreground. Throughout the Black Power struggle is central to the plot and its leaders are portrayed as 'direct, brilliant, zealous, and brutal'.[160]

Such representation evidently appealed to an African-American public demanding empowerment in the most direct and rapid fashion possible. Ebert recalled a comment by a white friend who had seen the film and was profoundly disturbed by the audience reaction, 'There was a cheer every time a white guy got hit.'[161] One might suspect Dassin and any number of BAM supporters would have been profoundly unsympathetic, as was Ebert, who summarised the perceived revolutionary nature of the film when he reflected: 'This should have been an educational experience, providing our side with the same sort of feeling that black Americans have had for years when a black guy got hit. Or had to shuffle. Or had to squeeze inside the Stephin Fetchit stereotype. "Up Tight" finishes those days forever.'[162]

This was not merely Hollywood hyperbole. The production of *Up Tight* by a major studio such as Paramount signalled a turning point in white perceptions of African-America and a victory in the attempts by Black Arts militants to introduce a realistic and empowering aesthetic into American mainstream culture. The American people were gradually becoming acquainted with a more complex conception and articulation of Black Power. Two years later, *Sweet Sweetback's Baadasssss Song* produced by Van Peebles was to herald a more resonant triumph.

Independently written, directed, scored, starring and eventually produced by Van Peebles in 1971, *Sweetback* (dedicated to 'All the Brothers and Sisters who had enough of the man') is the lurid neon fable of an African-American fleeing the white authorities after undergoing his own personal 'revolution of the mind' and retaliating to the beating of a Black Panther.[163] The themes and aesthetic of the film are drawn directly from Black Power's long history and its roots in plantation folktales – 'From the slaves' Br'er Rabbit and Slave John to the more recent Great MacDaddy, John Henry, Railroad Bill, Dolemite, Shine and Stackolee [sic]'.[164] In short, Sweetback was a 'bad nigger' a representative of the 'black "bad man" tradition ... characterized by absolute rejection of established authority'.[165] Yet the avatar of the sweetback was a long established trope which also inverted many gender and economic norms; funded by his female lovers, prowling the bars and clubs of the city eternally expected to remain 'master of all situations'.[166] Van Peebles' iteration was the latest in a series of connected cultural expressions of a very particular form of black freedom – fiscal, sexual and personal.

Despite the offer of a three picture deal from Columbia Pictures, Van Peebles rejected what he saw as the 'extreme control' demanded by the movie industry and instead funded the film independently.[167] A great deal of the film's financing came from soundtrack sales, which doubled as cheap advertising.[168] *Jet* reflected in retrospect that 'Melvin Van Peebles both raised eyebrows and good box office with *Sweet Sweetback's Baad Asssss Song*'.[169] This was something of an understatement – the album sold almost one hundred thousand copies in its first year of release and with the addition of a fifty thousand dollar loan from Bill Cosby, allowed

Van Peebles to produce a film which would eventually take over four million dollars in box office sales and nearly ten million gross.[170] Much of this revenue apparently came from a youthful audience, a new militant generation eager for a cinema which appeared to mesh with their changing self-image.[171]

The response by Hollywood was immense. As *Newsweek* noted in October 1972: 'Talented black actors, writer and directors were suddenly plucked out of studio back rooms, modelling agencies and ghetto theatres and turned loose on new black projects.'[172] The economic impetus was clear: 'An astonishing number of black films have been paying off at a rate to put their white counterparts in the shade – [producing] ... the first gold mine in years for a struggling industry.'[173] Historians commonly downplay the significance of such commercial success, attributing the boom to white marketing and co-option, and emphasising the white creators behind many apparently African-American films.[174] The reality, however, is substantially more complex.

The cultural images *Sweetback* offered were more nuanced than commonly assumed in scholarship of the era. All members of law enforcement – black and white – are considered equally villainous, while black preachers are portrayed as duplicitous and disingenuous.[175] Such perspectives were often in line with Black Arts propaganda which frequently sought not merely a rebellion against a white authority, but against all perceived tools of the establishment.[176] Yet these figures, from the perspective of the film's predominantly youthful audience, exemplified the everyday contact points of oppression in the ghetto. As a result, Sweetback's portrayal of life was immediately recognisable and credible to its audience. It spoke to what cinema scholar Mark Reid termed 'a street-oriented film culture'.[177]

A great deal of contemporary critique centred on the allegedly negative perspective of African-American women offered by the film.[178] Van Peebles was dismissive of such concerns, mocking the unrealistic perspectives of white critics and ardent black nationalists alike. Whites and middle-class black Americans, he argued, were culturally conditioned to expect a stereotyped portrayal of the African-American woman, an image, 'romantically nostalgic and ... essentially elitist'.[179] Worse still, overly fervent nationalist Black Power advocates clung to a deluded and fictional idyll with no practical application in everyday life; 'They wanted to see all the women with seven-foot Afros and speaking in

Swahili'.[180] From Van Peebles's perspective, such criticisms were indicative of a failure in the revolution of the mind. As he explained, 'The people who resent these characters haven't really come to terms with Blackness. They really don't like Black people.'[181]

Portrayals of women, particularly working class African-American women had long been a bone of contention for observers of black America's contested relationship with the American psyche. Partially this stemmed from middle class reactions against over-sexualised black stereotypes, coupled with the developing notion throughout the twentieth century that continued migration to the urban north would help unleash black female desire anew. The cities, once again, were the repository for commentators' projected fears, generators of Schuyler's, 'prostitutes, perverts, criminals, drug addicts and bums.'[182] Working class African-Americans, who comprised both subject and audience for *Sweetback*, were considered the most vulnerable. By the late twentieth century, in the wider American sphere changing women's roles threatened the American power structure – as did increasing acknowledgment of their sexuality, but the situation in sections of the African-American community was somewhat different. Alice Dunbar-Nelson had declared in 1927: 'For sixty three years, the Negro woman has been a co-worker with the Negro man.'[183] This opinion had changed only with glacial speed. In many black American households, economic, social and racial pressures meant that black housewives were the novelty, black working women the norm. Accordingly, for a long time African-American middle class women were constructed as 'nonsexual, devoted and demure.'[184] In presenting black women possessed of more complex inner and outer lives, Van Peebles, along with many other black directors, began to diversify perceptions of black identity.

In this vein, the truly empowering nature of *Sweetback* lies in its perceived role in the community and its ability to echo the feelings of its audience. This was recognised by Newton who devoted an entire issue of the BPINS to praising the Van Peebles's opus.[185] The film's opening credits emphasise the theme of community solidarity favoured by the Black Panthers, billing its principal star as 'THE BLACK COMMUNITY' and acknowledging the long history of black empowerment with a credit to 'BRER SOUL [The Black Community]'.[186] As a result, it is unsurprising that Sweetback rapidly became suggested viewing for party members.[187] Billed as a 'hymn from the mouth of reality', the film genuinely seemed rooted in 'the insurgent mood of much of the inner-city black community that propelled the film to megahit status'.[188] Newton dwelt on the theme of solidarity, arguing that it presented 'the need for unity among all the members and institutions among the community of victims'.[189] Yet whether one subscribes to Newton's rhetoric or not, the film is revolutionary on its own merits.

The very fact of Sweetback's survival until the closing credits was a profoundly revolutionary statement for many African-Americans. Van Peebles recalled:

> I go in the theatre and there's all these black folks, but not a sound ... I guess they thought it was some kind of trap or something. I find one seat next to an old black woman. Up on the screen, *Sweetback's* running through the desert and he's wounded and this woman next to me keeps saying, 'Oh, Lord, he's gonna die. He's gonna die. Don't let them kill him.' ... the black always died ... So it was outside anyone's imagination, first, to have a character like Sweetback, and then, to have that character live.[190]

The result of seeing such culturally iconoclastic images on screen was, according to Van Peebles, 'a victorious film ... where niggers could walk out standing tall instead of avoiding each other's eyes'.[191] Importantly, *Sweetback* was not targeted at the revolutionary elite but at the African-American public and unashamedly functioned as a commercial product. The rationale behind this was clear: '[The Man] ain't about to go carrying no messages for you, especially a relevant one, for free.'[192] If a message was to be conveyed to African-Americans in their weekends and nights out, it had to be culturally and aesthetically appealing, a 'work that not only instructs but entertains'.[193] Van Peebles could imagine no more horrifying scenario than to have his work confined to the *cognoscenti* of the militant movement, with *Sweetback* reduced to a 'didactic discourse which would end up playing ... to an empty theater except for ten or twenty aware brothers who would pat me on the back and say "it tells it like it is"'.[194]

His fears proved unfounded. On the first day of the film's release in Detroit it broke all the hosting theatre's sales records. Van Peebles recollected, 'By the second day, people would take their lunch and sit through it three times. I knew that I was finally talking to my audience.'[195] This commercial success was undergirded by another apparent cultural triumph. Van Peebles believed he was making a clear, militant, ideological statement. When *Sweetback* was famously censured by the Motion Picture Association of America (or 'Rated X by an all-white jury' as Van Peebles termed it), he retaliated, claiming that if the white community wanted to 'submit to ... censorship that is its business, but White standards shall no longer be imposed on the Black community'.[196]

Not all contemporary observers were as convinced of Van Peebles's messianic properties as he was. Shortly after the publication of the BPINS article, historian and scholar Lerone Bennett Jr. aired his disgust in an *Ebony* essay, expressively titled 'The Emancipation Orgasm: Sweetback in Wonderland'. In the opening passage, Bennett mused, 'Who would have believed that the Black is Beautiful rhetoric would lead to the Sweetback Doctrine of Black is Misery?'[197] In contrast to both Van Peebles's claims and Newton's belief, Bennett excoriated the film for contradicting his perceived image of the 'black aesthetic' by identifying it with 'empty bellies and big bottomed prostitutes'.[198] The possibility that the ghetto featured a high proportion of both these indicators seems to have escaped Bennett, who, in common with other contemporary academics, appeared to believe that cultural images needed to be founded in revolutionary idealism to be empowering.[199] As a result, Bennett derided the film as 'neither revolutionary nor black' and condemned Sweetback himself as a false culture-hero with no connection to history and no revolutionary ethic.[200] Dwelling on the prevalence of sex in the film, Bennett likewise castigated the plethora of 'emancipation orgasms', wryly remarking 'Nobody ever fucked his way to freedom ... If fucking freed, black people would have celebrated the millennium 400 years ago.'[201]

Bennett's critique is rooted in his differing perception of the black aesthetic, in a pantheon which held as its culture-heroes Malcolm X, Martin Luther King and Angela Davis. What he fails to realise throughout is that differing black aesthetics existed in parallel and each was empowering in its own manner. The often invoked colossi of King and X were perhaps too distant from the experiences of everyday life to convey the revolution of the mind into the cheap seats. *Sweetback*, with his human failings and desires, had more in common with the literary characters of the 1920s or the folk heroes of the plantation, representing as he did an average man asserting himself in the world as best he could.

King and X were dead and martyred, while *Sweetback* seemed vibrantly alive on the silver screen.

As Neal noted, 'Sweetback is a concise metaphor of the *symbolic* condition of the modern day Blood.'[202] Put simply, the film conveyed a militant message, without resorting to complex militant rhetoric. The audience was able to draw its conclusions directly from the viewing itself. As Neal explained, 'There are no long speeches on militancy, but yet it is a militant film. There are no speeches about nationalism and revolution, but yet, somehow, all of this is implied by the *style* of the film.'[203] The accessibility of the piece was primarily due to its simple structure, which shared a great deal of similarity with plantation folktales, a point which was not lost on Neal, who argued, 'Sweetback is a modern day slave; and the film itself is his slave song, or narrative.'[204]

The empowering nature of *Sweetback* lay in the questions it raised among its audience and the verisimilitude of the situations it presented. In many ways it was another catalyst for the revolution of the mind fervently sought by Black Power militants, albeit one presented in the aesthetic of the street. Yet, these queries were fundamental to African-Americans' changing perception of their place within American society. As Neal argued:

> Where does consciousness begin ... ? What is the button that made you a revolutionary? Was it something you read? Or did something happen to you. Were you witness to the death of your brothers and sisters? How? What route to take? By going to the so-called very lowest element in the community, Van Peebles was able to illustrate, in a creative fashion, how various kinds of people, within a certain life-style react to crisis.[205]

Herein lies the essential concept for understanding how Black Arts and Black Power ideals came to inform mainstream American culture and leave a continuing legacy. The multitude of reactions occasioned by *Sweetback* and its successors (from *Shaft* to *Bamboozled*) was a chief goal of BAM; to force a reassessment of how African-America should be represented and what it meant to be black. Neal summarised this best when he reflected:

Some people seem to mean when they say a character in a film is negative, is that the character is *not* like them! That is, he or she doesn't share a particular morality or ideological position the same as we do. But that is the improper way of looking at Black Art. As a filmic character, there is no such thing as a negative. The character is just there, on the screen, he can do positive or negative things ... This is revolutionary film-making.[206]

Regardless of whether an observer favoured or condemned *Sweetback*, the practical effect was the same – African-America was becoming increasingly engaged with its evolving culture, debating its merits and casting it against mainstream societal expectations. *Sweetback* was equally valuable whether he provoked admiration or outrage. As the FST had done in the South, the rise of the Blaxploitation aesthetic in the North energised and engaged the community, presenting stimulating and controversial portrayals of African-American life in a manner accessible to the vast majority of the population. The militant ideals of the BAM, that confrontational, critical and subversive aesthetic drawn from Black Power's long history, had seized the imagination of the American public and penetrated the mainstream media. For good or ill, the cultural legacy of Black Power had cemented itself in the American conceptual landscape. The resulting discussion of what it meant to be black in America, and how that blackness was to be portrayed, was where empowerment truly lay.

One of Bennett's central contentions in his critique of *Sweetback* was the gulf between the hallowed halls of the militant *intelligentsia* and the reality of oppression on the street.[207] From his perspective, 'The Emancipation Orgasm' constituted the beginnings of a dialogue. Bennett apparently failed to realise the brute fact that films like *Sweetback*, through their very existence, obliged those facets of African-American society often divorced from the culture of the street – the mass media, the academics, the critics – to turn their gaze to the art emerging from the ghetto and to acknowledge the blossoming cultural influence of the Black Power and Black Arts Movements. Without *Sweetback*, there would have been no Orgasm.

Bennett might perhaps be heartened to know that in a very real sense, *Sweetback* did inculcate a dialogue between the reality of oppression and the cultural rhetoric of empowerment. The problems highlighted by

Sweetback persist today and cultural forms, informed by connected historical expressions across time, continue to be instrumental in addressing them. In his 2007 address, the President of the Institute of the Black World 21st Century, Dr. Ron Daniels, described modern America as 'a nation where structural-institutional racism and oppression kill the dreams and aspirations of human beings' and railed against 'the cancer decimating marginalized Black communities'.[208]

Dr. Daniels argued that combating these problems required, 'something more than ordinary anti-violence programmes, education and jobs'.[209] In this respect, he appears to have the same fears once held by adherents of Black Power and his predecessors in the IBW, warning that:

> What we are witnessing is the consequence of a loss of 'historical memory' of who we are as people of African descent and the legacy of {our} trials, tribulations and triumphs. Far too many Blacks in this generation, adults and youth, have only a faint recollection of the history and culture of African people, the legacy of struggle and resistance, values, customs and traditions ... While the impact of institutional/structural racism on our people cannot be denied, its most insidious affect {sic} has been robbing our people of a positive/affirmative sense of self and kind. We can readily dismiss and destroy each other because we have internalized the racist premise that to be Black is less than human.

Maulana Karenga, leader of the cultural nationalist US organisation, often contended that 'the key crisis in Black life is the cultural crisis.'[210] Decades later, Karenga's perspective appears to hold weight as scholars like Ramona Edelin, former president of the National Urban Coalition, advocate a 'cultural offensive' to defend African-America.[211] Part of the popularity of this perspective comes from the continuing belief amongst African-American activists that the cultural legacy of Black Power is essential in challenging 'the myth of a "post racial society"'.[212]

The concerns of the cultural Black Power movement and its proposed solutions remain vital. Campaigners speak of a culture 'of the race and for the race', sustained by 'African-centred education' informed by the earliest images from plantation tales and black history, presented as 'the amazing resistance of heroes and sheroes who rebelled against enslavement' and coupled with the more recent account 'of a people who made a way out of no way to create new African communities out of disparate ethnicities in the face of apartheid, violence, lynching and police occupation/terror.'[213]

African-American activists such as Daniels still see themselves as fighting for the revolution of the mind in marginalised and impoverished communities and they promote the same broad engagement at a local level which characterised the cultural thrust of the Black Power movement, arguing that 'churches, fraternities, sororities, business and professional associations, community based organizations, community centers – all segments of Black America must be engaged in this Offensive'.[214] Much as Larry Neal wanted to see the cultural advocates of Black Power opening the way for the 'brother with the heavy and necessary political rap', some modern activists want to see 'Wyclef Jean and Quincy Jones hook-up to ... save the youth'.[215] When Dr Daniels argues that 'The Cultural Offensive must be inclusive, comprehensive and relentless', historians can hear the voice of Larry Neal in the shadows, offering the same perspective infused with the same sense of cultural urgency. In the early twenty-first century, some activists still see the African-American community as existing in 'a moment of accentuated crisis' and turn to the same tropes of empowerment for a way forward, restating 'with urgency prescriptions and remedies which are all too familiar'.[216]

While Black Power activists had great difficulty solving the political problems of African-America, they were much more successful at changing its self-image. While tangible political and economic power was an often impossible goal, convincing people that they deserved that power and had the ability to attain it was a far more successful endeavour.

The acceptance that black was not just beautiful, but strong, intelligent and powerful was a revolution of the mind which endowed the 1960s generation with a pride in blackness never seen before, which in turn gave them the impetus to attempt some truly extraordinary projects. Most importantly, this impetus was transmitted to subsequent generations. As one Oakland native, Larry Dillard, noted in 1986, 'I don't think it's "Black is beautiful" [anymore]. It's "I am beautiful and I'm black". First the black is beautiful thing had to come, so you can know you're beautiful and black ... it's not something that has to be taught or shouted or something people had to unite together to feel. That phase is over and it succeeded. My children feel better about theirselves [sic] and they know that they're black.'[217]

Cultural manifestations of Black Power achieved fundamental changes in the way African-Americans perceived themselves and their place in America. Central to this success was the manner in which Black Power challenged assumptions of what was not just beautiful but aesthetically valuable. The writers, poets and cultural creators of the Harlem Renaissance and Black Arts Movements challenged entrenched myths and stereotypes about not only the presence of African-Americans in art, but the relationship of art to African-America. Publications such as *Fire*, *Ebony and Topaz* and *Umbra* rejected conventional standards of beauty and created that transformation so desired by Larry Neal, a relevant black aesthetic.

In the process, this renewal of art paralleled actual transformations in African-American life. Drawing an absolute distinction between the political and the cultural Black Power movement unjustly ignores the symbiotic nature of a movement which 'made everything political and everything cultural', which Lerone Bennett characterised as an essential historical dialogue, 'a vast and leaping wave ... that started with the first revolt on the first slave ship and will not end until America deals with the revolutionary mandate of its birth.'[218]

Moving forward, historians will need to consider the importance of the revolution of the mind and the legacy it bequeathed — a profound change in self-perception and a reframing of the African-American experience in America. When amateur historian Elena Albert reflected in 1986 on her changed perspective, she reached back to Marcus Garvey in the 1920s and echoed the language of the 1960s Black Power movement, musing:

> We really needed to accept our differentness, to rejoice in it, to enjoy it. You have to realize how it is to be black in America ... when Marcus Garvey said that we were black and beautiful, and when he said, 'Up ye mighty race, you could do what ye will' (*sung exultantly*), that made us look at ourselves. And we are handsome, we are pretty, we are beautiful, we are lovely ... And

we are different, you know (*with immense joy*), and that's all right, isn't it?[219]

Albert's recollections were not drawn solely from history or from memory, but from a series of connected cultural expressions across time; that complex composite of historical fact, renewed myth, plantation heritage and militant rhetoric that categorised the cultural Black Power movement and defined the revolution of the mind. Hers was a personal, private transformation rooted firmly in images and tropes distilled down the decades and shaped by the long history of African-American militancy. In this respect, she epitomises the continuing legacy of the cultural thrust of Black Power.

CONCLUSION

THE LONG HISTORY OF BLACK POWER

A critical reassessment of the Black Power movement presents a picture of an historical phenomenon far different from that in most popular recollections. It is imperative that we begin to reconsider the long history of Black Power and black militancy, viewing it as a series of connected cultural expressions across time, united by common themes and tropes, providing a resilient, malleable reservoir of identity forming concepts. The cultural expressions of resistance which informed the 1960s manifestations of Black Power began long before the political movement and continued long after its demise. The two phenomena existed in parallel for a period and there was a clear reciprocal relationship between the two strands, but the cultural aspects of Black Power which are now so firmly a part of the American consciousness were not merely a product of the political movement. If anything, the converse was true, with fundamental aspects of the political movement's ethos founded upon the long history of Black Power.

As we continue our investigations into the shape of the American past, the evidence suggests that cultural iterations of Black Power operated on a much broader basis and spoke to a wider audience than the political movement. Able to communicate through a variety of media and forms on both an institutional and a personal level, cultural Black Power was accordingly more effective at disseminating, clarifying and distilling the political movement's basic ethos, as well as imparting its own historically enmeshed tropes of empowerment. Thus, cultural

Black Power, fashioned from the long history of black militancy, and sustained via a series of connected cultural expressions through time was not merely an improved tool for communication, but a catalyst for identity reconstruction at a very basic level.

The 'Revolution of the Mind' proposed by militants was not an esoteric concept, but a useful practical term for the changes in perception that were experienced by many black Americans in the late twentieth century as a result of their increased awareness of the long history of Black Power and a greater presence of militant cultural output in their lives as activists, thinkers and creators increasingly mined the black past for new, and newly familiar seams of resistance. The evolution of African-American cultural forms across the centuries served to shape and define the tactics of the political movement and opened avenues for communication with its audience. The use of history and folklore to create a new pantheon of heroes; icons with attributes that could be both aspired to and emulated, identified in political leaders and put into practice in everyday life, was fundamental in cementing militant leaders in the public imagination by placing them firmly within an historical continuity of empowerment. The long history of cultural Black Power not only laid the foundations for the political movement, but helped to set the bounds for its interaction with the American public, and secured its place in the American imagination.

The historical and cultural inheritance of the movement was not a panacea – at its worst, it was as much concerned with image as the political movement, but traded the gun and beret for the dashiki and afro. However, on closer investigation, even the most apparently trivial developments were potent touchstones for black Americans crafting a new identity and reassessing their place in society. It was primarily when the heroes began to believe their own legends and when the myths took the place of new cultural generation that strands of the cultural thrust of Black Power stalled. However, although it was instrumental in the creation and lionising of figureheads through sport, politics, fiction and music, the cultural facets of the movement did not require their existence.

The cultural variants of Black Power which comprised its connected militant expressions across time were essential at the grass roots level; whispered in dive bars, scribbled in the margins of hasty playbills, and shouted on streets and stoops. Yet these same sentiments were also capable of drawing phenomenal attention on the international stage – whether under the halogen glow of the Olympic lights, beamed as cultural catharsis by satellite or shaking the speakers of stages from Berlin to the Bronx.

These memetic, adaptable iterations of resistance were visible artistically, in the iconoclastic publications of the Harlem Renaissance, the community work of the Black Arts Movement, the slick swagger of Blaxploitation and the neon dreams of the Afrofuturists. They were displayed educationally – in the drive of campus groups to help students define their identity and purpose and in the Institute of the Black World, birthed from the dream of a Black University. They also existed in a combination of art, education and practical survival economics, which had been evident from the folktales of the plantation, and was later seen in the work of the Free Southern Theater, the aspirations of returning soldiers and the carefully woven plans of prison groups such as the BCDS. In environments where empowerment was a scarce commodity, the connected cultural expressions of Black Power held a peculiar, powerful resonance.

While these practical concepts may have lost some of the surface gloss and glory of their abstract implementations, they produced enduring, tangible changes in the way their respective audiences perceived the world around them. As a common repository of images, concepts, symbols and tropes that has persisted through the ages, cultural Black Power has existed for as long as it has been possible to draw from these images and use them to convey the desired message. In the plantation, cultural media were used to convey notions of freedom, escape and subtle resistance, in the post-slavery period, cultural forms transmitted notions of retribution and former glory, a casting off of slave heritage writ large. During the Depression era, the same evolving cultural tropes were used to create an aspirational image for the people, incarnated in Joe Louis, or sketched out in the scuffed dust of Negro League baseball stadia. Throughout the Harlem Renaissance, the malleability of cultural Black Power was used to throw off the shackles of cultural expectation from both black and white audiences, creating not only a new corpus of African-American cultural production, but a new manner of perceiving society, which struck out against binaries of skin and sex alike The late 1960s and 1970s finally saw the tropes provided by these connected cultural expressions being appropriated and cast into service of a political objective. However, historians should view this period of synergy between political and cultural Black Power as the culmination of decades of cultural evolution, revolution and empowerment, not merely as the beginning of a comparatively short-lived political movement. In so doing, future scholars will be able to appreciate the long history of Black Power alongside the evolution of other strands of the African-American freedom struggle, providing a more complete history of civil rights and militant protest as a whole and elevating the Black Power movement to a position where it can be compared to other historic civil rights movements, both on a national and an international level.

More importantly, we might be able to get some small sense of what it might have meant for these young men and women seeking new selves in the face of a society which struggled to accept them into its collective imaginations. To borrow from Walter Mosley, Black Power adherents throughout the ages were not simply impassioned demagogues with a flair for violence, nor were they an aberrant symptom of a brutalised era. They 'were far beyond anger ... They were expressing a desire ... for something that didn't exist – had never existed ... they were going to create freedom out of the sow's ear called America.'[1]

For many activists, and for historians like myself, fashioning freedom from the sow's ear seems like an increasingly challenging task. Writing now, we are scant years from the Ferguson protests, punctuated by the arrest of one of today's most prominent African-American academics, Cornel West. We are scant days from the shooting of Philando Castile and countless others. In the town halls of America, presidential hopefuls Hillary Clinton and Bernie Sanders have been pushed into confrontation and engagement with the Black Lives Matter movement, a protest moment which *Time* magazine hailed as a 'new civil rights movement ... turning a protest cry into a political force.'[2] Yet *Time*, and many other commentators, forget that America has a long history of resistance to social change and political protest.

This 'new' movement has its roots in the old; in the fundamental quest for dignity, recognition and respect which colours the relationship between Black Power and the American people. Earlier eras of civil rights and Black Power protest have been softened by the inconsistency of memory, which elides the fact that advocation for the basic rights of black Americans has always met incredible resistance, and nowhere more so than across the long history of Black Power.

America's endemic racism still sings a strong chord in the national symphony, but the men and women who seek to challenge it continue to draw on that most fundamental of images: to be free to be your own person, whatever that might entail and without constraint or condemnation from society. Whether articulated through a clenched fist, a picket line or a science-fiction fable, the connected cultural expressions of Black Power remain a fundamental part of the history of the American people.

NOTES

Preface

1. Noname [Fatimah Nyeema Warner], quoted in 'The Great Fire: A Special Issue', *Vanity Fair*, September 2020, 67.
2. Angela Davis, *Freedom Is a Constant Struggle* (Chicago: Haymarket Books, 2016).
3. Aaron Blake, 'Analysis | What Trump Said before His Supporters Stormed the Capitol, Annotated', *Washington Post*, 11 January 2021, https://www.washingtonpost.com/politics/interactive/2021/annotated-trump-speech-jan-6-capitol/; Mike Ferrara, Shawn Crowley and Magdalene Zier, 'Prosecuting Trump for Role in Jan. 6 Riot Got Easier Thanks to Capitol Officers' Testimony', NBC News, 3 August 2021, https://www.nbcnews.com/think/opinion/prosecuting-trump-role-jan-6-riot-got-easier-thanks-capitol-ncna1275695.
4. Richard Luscombe, 'George Zimmerman Acquitted in Trayvon Martin Case', *The Guardian*, 14 July 2013, https://www.theguardian.com/world/2013/jul/14/zimmerman-acquitted-killing-trayvon-martin.
5. Yashar Ali, Twitter post, 6 June 2020, 9.51 pm, https://twitter.com/yashar/status/1269371427557236736/photo/1. An archived version of the Facebook screencap is available at: https://scalar.usc.edu/works/blacklivesmatter/media/alicia-garzas-facebook-post.
6. Rachel Treisman, 'Nearly 100 Confederate Monuments Removed in 2020, Report Says; More than 700 Remain', NPR.org, 23 February 2021, https://www.npr.org/2021/02/23/970610428/nearly-100-confederate-monuments-removed-in-2020-report-says-more-than-700-remai?t=1622124296938.
7. Aamna Mohdin and Lucy Campbell, 'Black Lives Matter Group Offers Rural People "Insight into Prejudice"', *The Guardian*, 8 August 2020, https://www.theguardian.com/world/2020/aug/08/black-lives-matter-rural-insight-

prejudice-blm-stix. See also George King, 'Rural Activists Stand Together against Racism as Hundreds Line River', *Chelmsford Weekly News*, 11 August 2020, https://www.chelmsfordweeklynews.co.uk/news/colchester/18641112.black-lives-matter-hundreds-join-protest-river-colne/.
8. Ta-Nehisi Coates, 'The Pyromancer's Dream', *Vanity Fair*, September 2020, 20.
9. Patti Waldmeir, 'Black Lives Matter Co-Founder Opal Tometi: "We Have Taken the Baton"', *Financial Times*, 14 August 2020, https://www.ft.com/content/71efd9a2-c1bb-47b6-b4c5-7795b1a66cac.
10. Kate Driscoll Derickson, 'The Racial State and Resistance in Ferguson and Beyond', *Urban Studies* 53, no. 11 (2016): 2223–37, https://www.jstor.org/stable/26151198; Russell Rickford, 'Black Lives Matter: Toward a Modern Practice of Mass Struggle', *New Labor Forum* 25, no. 1 (2016): 34–42, https://www.jstor.org/stable/26419959.
11. Cf. Josh Hafner, 'How Michael Brown's Death, Two Years Ago, Pushed #BlackLivesMatter into a Movement', *USA Today*, 8 August 2016, https://eu.usatoday.com/story/news/nation-now/2016/08/08/how-michael-browns-death-two-years-ago-pushed-blacklivesmatter-into-movement/88424366/; Daniel A. Medina, 'On Mike Brown Anniversary, Activists Remember Birth of a Movement', NBC News, 9 August 2016, https://www.nbcnews.com/news/nbcblk/michael-brown-anniversary-activists-warn-possible-future-unrest-n626546.
12. Alicia Garza, 'We Gon' Be Alright: Black Love, Black Resistance and Black Liberation', *Truthout*, 31 July 2015, https://truthout.org/articles/we-gon-be-alright-black-love-black-resistance-and-black-liberation/
13. For a recent case study of the complexities herein, see Stacy Jenkins-Robinson, 'Black Lives Matter: The Movement's Relevance and Comparison to the 1960s Civil Rights Movement', *OTS Master's Level Projects & Papers*, 1 October 2017, https://digitalcommons.odu.edu/ots_masters_projects/593; Louis M. Maraj, Pritha Prasad and Sherita V. Roundtree, '#BlackLivesMatter: Pasts, Presents, and Futures', *Prose Studies* 40, nos 1–2 (4 May 2018): 1–14, https://doi.org/10.1080/01440357.2019.1668638. For examples of the journalism in question, see Elizabeth Day, '#BlackLivesMatter: The Birth of a New Civil Rights Movement', *The Guardian*, 18 October 2018, https://www.theguardian.com/world/2015/jul/19/blacklivesmatter-birth-civil-rights-movement, through to Adam Serwer, 'The New Reconstruction', *The Atlantic*, October 2020, https://www.theatlantic.com/magazine/archive/2020/10/the-next-reconstruction/615475/. For early essential coverage pushing against this approach, see Jamilah King, 'How Black Lives Matter Has Changed US Politics', *New Internationalist*, 5 March 2018, https://newint.org/features/2018/03/01/black-lives-matter-changed-politics.

14. Dareh Gregorian, '"Dump Trump": Peaceful Protests against the President at First Debate', *NBC News*, 30 September 2020, https://www.nbcnews.com/politics/2020-election/dump-trump-peaceful-protests-against-president-first-debate-n1241449; Kevin Bruyneel, 'Wake Work versus Work of Settler Memory: Modes of Solidarity in #NODAPL, Black Lives Matter, and Anti-Trumpism', in Nick Estes and Dhillon Jaskiran, eds, *Standing with Standing Rock: Voices from the #NoDAPL Movement* (Minneapolis: University of Minnesota Press, 2019), 311–27; Chris Walker, 'Black Lives Matter 5280 Recaps Trip to Standing Rock to Oppose Oil Pipeline', *Westword*, 23 November 2016, https://www.westword.com/news/black-lives-matter-5280-recaps-trip-to-standing-rock-to-oppose-oil-pipeline-8526506.
15. Alicia Garza, 'Foreword: On the Shoulders of Giants', in Institute for Policy Studies, *PAY, PROFESSIONALISM & RESPECT: Black Domestic Workers Continue the Call for Standards in the Care Industry*, 1–5, www.jstor.org/stable/resrep27076.3; Sean Hill, 'Precarity in the Era of #BlackLivesMatter', *Women's Studies Quarterly* 45, no. 3/4 (2017): 94–109, https://www.jstor.org/stable/26421123.
16. Jemima McEvoy, 'Here's How Fox News Spread a False Narrative Black Lives Matter is Standing with Hamas', *Forbes*, 19 May 2021, https://www.forbes.com/sites/jemimamcevoy/2021/05/19/heres-how-fox-news-spread-a-false-narrative-black-lives-matter-is-standing-with-hamas/?sh=3b39c2a55114.
17. Erica Chenoweth and Jeremy Pressman, 'Black Lives Matter Protesters Were Overwhelmingly Peaceful, Our Research Finds', Radcliffe Institute for Advanced Study at Harvard University, 20 October 2020, https://www.radcliffe.harvard.edu/news-and-ideas/black-lives-matter-protesters-were-overwhelmingly-peaceful-our-research-finds?fbclid=IwAR1y--weba6U6C7qhkzZZc9qpRw1Mf6Oj_HE6WTvpBJSyyqyXLTJZFf1xUc.
18. For nuanced analysis on this theme, see Ronald K. Porter, 'A Rainbow in Black: The Gay Politics of the Black Panther Party', *Counterpoints*, no. 367 (2012): 364–75, https://www.jstor.org/stable/42981419; Jakobi Williams, '"Don't No Woman Have to Do Nothing She Don't Want to Do": Gender, Activism, and the Illinois Black Panther Party', *Black Women, Gender Families* 6, no. 2 (2012): 29–54, doi:10.5406/blacwomegendfami.6.2.0029; Antwanisha Alameen-Shavers, 'The Woman Question: Gender Dynamics within the Black Panther Party', *Spectrum: A Journal on Black Men* 5, no. 1 (2016): 33–62, doi:10.2979/spectrum.5.1.03; Amy Abugo Ongiri, 'Prisoner of Love: Affiliation, Sexuality, and the Black Panther Party', *Journal of African American History* 94, no. 1 (2009): 69–86. http://www.jstor.org/stable/25610049.
19. Robyn C. Spencer, *The Revolution Has Come: Black Power, Gender, and the Black Panther Party in Oakland* (Durham, NC: Duke University Press, 2016), 44.

20. Marcia Chatelain and Kaavya Asoka, 'Women and Black Lives Matter: An Interview with Marcia Chatelain', *Dissent Magazine*, 2015, https://www.dissentmagazine.org/article/women-black-lives-matter-interview-marcia-chatelain; For commentary on the importance of intersectional feminism to both BLM and wider feminist movements, see Jessica Watters, 'Pink Hats and Black Fists: The Role of Women in the Black Lives Matter Movement', 24 *William & Mary Journal of Women & Law*, 199 (2017), https://scholarship.law.wm.edu/wmjowl/vol24/iss1/8
21. Sony Salzman, 'From the Start, Black Lives Matter Has Been about LGBTQ Lives', ABC News, 21 June 2020, https://abcnews.go.com/US/start-black-lives-matter-lgbtq-lives/story?id=71320450.
22. Equality Forum, LGBT History Month Bio, 'Alicia Garza – Black Lives Matter Cofounder', https://lgbthistorymonth.com/sites/default/files/icon_multimedia_pdfs/2017/LGBT_HMBio-2017%2014.pdf; Ariel Hall, 'BLM Turns Inward to Ask about LGBTQ Bias', VOA News, 25 June 2020, https://www.voanews.com/student-union/blm-turns-inward-ask-about-lgbtq-bias; Salzman, "From the Start."
23. Darren Sands, "The NAACP and Black Lives Matter Are Talking Past Each Other," BuzzFeed News, 16 July 2015, https://www.buzzfeednews.com/article/darrensands/the-naacp-and-black-lives-matter-are-talking-past-each-other; Michael A. Fletcher, 'NAACP Searches for Relevance in Era Defined by Black Lives Matter and Trump', The Undefeated, 24 July 2017, https://theundefeated.com/features/naacp-searches-for-relevance-in-era-defined-by-black-lives-matter-and-trump; Jamiles Lartey, 'NAACP Considers Role alongside Black Lives Matter at Annual Convention', *The Guardian*, 18 July 2016, https://www.theguardian.com/world/2016/jul/18/naacp-convention-black-lives-matter-cincinnati.
24. #teamebony, 'Elaine Brown Thinks Black Lives Matter Has a "Plantation Mentality"', *Ebony*, 21 October 2016, https://www.ebony.com/news/elaine-brown-black-lives-matter/.
25. To view an original handwritten plan, see the linked image in Andrew Beale et al., 'The Black Panther Party's Ten-Point Program, 50 Years Later', *Oakland North*, 4 November 2016, https://oaklandnorth.net/2016/11/04/the-black-panther-partys-ten-point-program-50-years-later/; 'FRIDAY', M4BL, 1 June 2020, https://m4bl.org/week-of-action/friday/.
26. For a useful introduction to the Panther's wider context, see the excellent Sean L Malloy, *Out of Oakland: Black Panther Party Internationalism during the Cold War* (Ithaca, NY: Cornell University Press, 2017); Elaine Mokhtefi, *Algiers Third World Capital: Freedom Fighters, Revolutionaries, Black Panthers* (Brooklyn, NY: Verso, 2020); or the dated, but useful, Nikil Pal Singh, 'The Black Panthers and the "Undeveloped

Country" of the Left', in Charles E. Jones and Judson L. Jeffries, eds, *The Black Panther Party (Reconsidered)* (Baltimore: Black Classic Press, 1998), 57–105. On the prison and education system, see Lizbet Simmons, 'End of the Line: Tracing Racial Inequality from School to Prison', *Race/Ethnicity: Multidisciplinary Global Contexts* 2, no. 2 (2009): 215–41, https://www.jstor.org/stable/25595013; Nancy A. Heitzen, 'Education or Incarceration: Zero Tolerance Policies and the School to Prison Pipeline', *Forum on Public Policy Online* 2009, no. 2 (2009): 1–21, https://eric.ed.gov/?id=EJ870076; Richard Rothstein, 'For Public Schools, Segregation Then, Segregation Since: Education and the Unfinished March', Economic Policy Institute, 27 August 2013, https://www.epi.org/publication/unfinished-march-public-school-segregation/; 'Criminal Justice Fact Sheet', NAACP, 24 May 2021, https://naacp.org/resources/criminal-justice-fact-sheet.

27. Malkia Devich-Cyril and Ra Malika Imhotep, In Conversation: Black Power Now, Oakland Museum of California, 10 March 2019.
28. See further Ward Leroy Churchill and Jim Vander Wall, *The COINTELPRO Papers: Documents from the FBI's Secret Wars against Dissent in the United States*, 2nd edn (Cambridge, MA: South End Press, 2002); Ward Leroy Churchill and Jim Vander Wall, *Agents of Repression: The FBI's Secret Wars against the Black Panther Party and the American Indian Movement* (London: Turnaround, 2002); Jeffrey Haas, *The Assassination of Fred Hampton: How the FBI and the Chicago Police Murdered a Black Panther* (Chicago: Lawrence Hill, 2019).
29. Lynne Peskoe-Yang, 'How to Dodge the Sonic Weapon Used by Police', Popular Mechanics, 17 June 2020, https://www.popularmechanics.com/military/weapons/a32892398/what-is-lrad-sonic-weapon-protests/.
30. 'Heat Ray "Was Sought" against Protest in Washington's Lafayette Square', BBC News, 17 September 2020, sec. US & Canada, https://www.bbc.co.uk/news/world-us-canada-54187961; Ben Kesslen, '"Plug Your Ears and Run": NYPD's Use of Sound Cannons is Challenged in Federal Court', NBC News, 22 May 2019, https://www.nbcnews.com/news/us-news/plug-your-ears-run-nypds-use-sound-cannons-challenged-n1008916.
31. Janus Rose, 'Audio Engineers Built a Shield to Deflect Police Sound Cannons', *Vice*, 6 September 2020, https://www.vice.com/en/article/dyzpna/audio-engineers-built-a-shield-to-deflect-police-sound-cannons.
32. Sandrine Boudana, Paul Frosh and Akiba A. Cohen, 'Reviving Icons to Death: When Historic Photographs Become Digital Memes', *Media, Culture & Society* 39, no. 8 (3 February 2017): 1210–30, https://doi.org/10.1177/0163443717690818; Raymond Drainville, 'Iconography for the Age of Social Media', *Humanities* 7, no. 1 (26 January 2018): 12, https://doi.org/10.3390/h7010012.
33. Matt Fountain, 'SLO County DA Offers "Slap on the Wrist" Deal for 5 Protesters – but Not Tianna Arata', *San Luis Obispo Tribune*, 3 March 2021, https://www.sanluisobispo.com/news/local/article249611973.html; Katie Fleischer,

'20-Year-Old BLM Activist Faces Five Felonies for Organizing Protest', *Ms. Magazine*, 13 August 2020, https://msmagazine.com/2020/08/13/20-year-old-blm-activist-faces-five-felonies-for-organizing-protest; Andrew Naughtie, 'Black Lives Matter Protesters Facing Life in Jail for Smashing Windows', *The Independent*, 7 August 2020, https://www.independent.co.uk/news/world/americas/black-lives-matter-utah-protesters-life-sentence-a9659791.html; and more generally, Adam Gabbatt, 'Felony Charges against BLM Protesters Are "Suppression Tactic", Experts Say', *The Guardian*, 16 August 2020, https://www.theguardian.com/world/2020/aug/16/felony-charges-blm-protesters-suppression-tactic; Kelly McLaughlin, '2 Black Lives Matter Demonstrators Are Facing Life in Prison. Experts Say the "Deeply Disturbing" Potential Sentences Are an "Unprecedented" Form of Government Overreach', *Insider*, 24 September 2020, https://www.insider.com/black-lives-matter-demonstrators-facing-charges-protests-2020-9.

34. "Introducing the Black Lives Matter Survival Fund," BlackLivesMatter.com, 25 February 2021, https://blacklivesmatter.com/survival-fund; Cheryl Mercedes, 'VERIFY: "Survival Funds" Not Being Provided by Federal Government', KHOU, 18 March 2021, https://www.khou.com/article/news/verify/verify-survival-funds-federal-government/285-1ac00737-60d6-4bb1-a02e-8536a475ab10.

35. Julie Cart, 'California's 2020 Fire Siege: Wildfires by the Numbers', *CalMatters*, 29 July 2021, https://calmatters.org/environment/2021/07/california-fires-2020/; Gwynedd Stuart, 'In Terms of Wildfires, 2021 Is Already Shaping Up to Be a Worse Year than 2020', *Los Angeles Magazine*, 7 July 2021, https://www.lamag.com/citythinkblog/wildfires-california-2021/.

36. Cate Swannell, 'COVID-19, Black Lives Matter and Making a Difference', *Medical Journal of Australia* 213, no. 4 (2 August 2020): C1, https://www.mja.com.au/journal/2020/213/4/covid-19-black-lives-matter-and-making-difference; F. S. Nakhaie and Reza Nakhaie, 'Black Lives Matter Movement Finds New Urgency and Allies because of COVID-19', *The Conversation*, 5 July 2020, https://theconversation.com/black-lives-matter-movement-finds-new-urgency-and-allies-because-of-covid-19-141500.

37. Mindy Fullilove, 'Redlining Trauma', *Race, Poverty & the Environment* 21, no. 2 (2017): 84–6, https://www.jstor.org/stable/44687766; Morgan A. Robinson, 'Thirst for the American Dream: The Lost City of Flint', *Michigan Sociological Review* 32 (2018): 170–86, https://www.jstor.org/stable/26528601; Denise A. Narcisse, 'Beyond Treading Water: Bringing Water Justice to America's Urban Poor', *Race, Gender & Class* 24, nos 1–2 (2017): 27–64, https://www.jstor.org/stable/26529235; Chelsea Grimmer, 'Racial Microbiopolitics: Flint Lead Poisoning, Detroit Water Shut Offs, and the "Matter" of Enfleshment', *The Comparatist* 41 (2017): 19–40, https://www.jstor.org/stable/26254790; Jason Stanley, 'The Emergency Manager:

Strategic Racism, Technocracy, and the Poisoning of Flint's Children', *Good Society* 25, no. 1 (2017): 1–45, https://doi.org/10.5325/goodsociety.25.1.0001.
38. Huey P. Newton, *To Die for the People: The Writings of Huey P. Newton* (New York: Random House, 1972), 104.
39. Cata Gaitán, "Cryptonater Is Watching Me. It's Also Watching You", cata gaitán, 25 August 2020, https://catagaitan.com/2020/08/24/cryptonator-is-watching-me-its-also-watching-you/; NB: I use the long-form 'anti-fascist' here as the modern usage of 'antifa', particularly in the American intonation popularised by Trump, connotes the presence of some potentially sinister, insurgent group, when in fact the vast majority of Black Lives Matter and anti-fascist protestors are simply ordinary people protesting the creeping authoritarianism and burgeoning fascist tendencies in the American state as it staggers from crisis to crisis.
40. For an example, see the 2 May 1967 action against the Mulford Bill at the Sacramento State Capitol.
41. Kelly Mena, 'New Tennessee Law Penalizes Protesters Who Camp on State Property with Felony and Loss of Voting Rights', CNN Politics, 23 August 2020, https://edition.cnn.com/2020/08/22/politics/tennessee-felony-camping-law-right-to-vote/index.html; Sanya Mansoor, 'New Tennessee Law Severely Sharpens Punishments for Some Protesters, Potentially Endangering Their Voting Rights', *Time*, 23 August 2020, https://time.com/5882735/tennesee-law-protest-voting-rights-felony/.
42. Ali Breland, 'Alt-Right Trolls Are Trying to Sabotage Black Lives Matter Chatrooms', *Mother Jones*, 8 June 2020, https://www.motherjones.com/anti-racism-police-protest/2020/06/black-lives-matter-4chan-telegram/; Colin Kalmbacher, 'St. Louis Mayor Lyda Krewson Doxxed Protesters', Law & Crime, 27 June 2020, https://lawandcrime.com/live-trials/live-trials-current/george-floyd-death/calls-for-st-louis-mayors-resignation-intensify-after-she-doxxed-black-lives-matter-protesters-on-facebook-live/; Nellie Bowles, 'How "Doxxing" Became a Mainstream Tool in the Culture Wars', *New York Times*, 30 August 2017, https://www.nytimes.com/2017/08/30/technology/doxxing-protests.html; Scott Morris, 'Doxxed by Berkeley Police', *The Appeal*, 24 August 2018, https://theappeal.org/doxxed-by-berkeley-police/.
43. Martin Pengelly, 'Top US General Warned of "Reichstag Moment" in Trump's Turbulent Last Days', *The Guardian*, 14 July 2021, https://www.theguardian.com/us-news/2021/jul/14/donald-trump-reichstag-moment-general-mark-milley-book; Gavriel D. Rosenfeld, 'An American Führer? Nazi Analogies and the Struggle to Explain Donald Trump', *Central European History* 52, no. 4 (1 December 2019): 554–87, https://doi.org/10.1017/S0008938919000840.
44. Hartwig Fischer, 'A Message from Director Hartwig Fischer', *British Museum Blog*, 5 June 2020, https://blog.britishmuseum.org/a-message-from-director-hartwig-fischer/; Daniel H. Weiss and Max Hollein, 'Standing in Solidarity, Committing to the Work Ahead', The Met, 1 June 2020,

https://www.metmuseum.org/blogs/now-at-the-met/2020/standing-in-solidarity-president-director.
45. Alex Greenberger, 'Minneapolis's Walker Art Center Becomes First Major U.S. Museum to Stop Contracting Police for Events', ARTnews, 3 June 2020, https://www.artnews.com/art-news/news/walker-art-center-police-cut-ties-1202689680/; Julia Jacobs and Zachary Small, 'Whitney Cancels Show That Included Works Bought at Fund-Raisers', *New York Times*, 25 August 2020, https://www.nytimes.com/2020/08/25/arts/design/whitney-museum-exhibition-canceled.html; Nadja Sayej, '"I Felt Taken Advantage Of": The Story of Another Whitney Museum Controversy', *The Guardian*, 29 August 2020, https://www.theguardian.com/artanddesign/2020/aug/29/whitney-museum-black-artists-controversy.
46. Joe Parlock, 'Ubisoft Removes Insensitive Imagery Comparing Black Lives Matter to Terrorists from "Tom Clancy's Elite Squad", but It's Not Enough', *Forbes*, 29 August 2020, https://www.forbes.com/sites/joeparlock/2020/08/29/ubisoft-removes-insensitive-imagery-comparing-black-lives-matter-to-terrorists-from-tom-clancys-elite-squad-but-its-not-enough/.
47. Niall McCarthy, 'Infographic: How Much Do U.S. Cities Spend on Policing?', Statista Infographics, 12 June 2020, https://www.statista.com/chart/10593/how-much-do-us-cities-spend-on-policing/; Polly Mosendz and Jameelah D. Robinson, 'While Crime Fell, the Cost of Cops Soared', *Bloomberg Businessweek*, 4 June 2020, https://www.bloomberg.com/news/articles/2020-06-04/america-s-policing-budget-has-nearly-tripled-to-115-billion; Fola Akinnibi, Sarah Holder and Christopher Cannon, 'Cities Say They Want to Defund the Police. Their Budgets Say Otherwise', *Bloomberg CityLab*, 12 January 2021, https://www.bloomberg.com/graphics/2021-city-budget-police-funding/.
48. John Haltiwanger, 'Democratic Leaders Are Rejecting the Biggest Demand of Black Lives Matter Protesters as They Push Their Police Reform Bill', *Business Insider*, 11 June 2020, https://www.businessinsider.com/democrats-reject-calls-to-defund-the-police-from-blm-protesters-2020-6?r=US&IR=T; Steve Chaggaris, 'Defunding Police: An Idea Most Democrats Don't Want to Talk About', *Al Jazeera*, 15 April 2021, https://www.aljazeera.com/news/2021/4/15/defunding-police-an-idea-most-democrats-dont-want-to-talk-about; Jonathan Bernstein, 'Who Really Wants to Defund the Police?', *Bloomberg Opinion*, 29 June 2021, https://www.bloomberg.com/opinion/articles/2021-06-29/who-really-wants-to-defund-the-police; Maggie McGrath, 'Why Stacey Abrams Is One of the World's Most Powerful Women in 2020', *Forbes*, 8 December 2020, https://www.forbes.com/sites/maggiemcgrath/2020/12/08/in-standing-for-the-power-of-the-vote-stacey-abrams-is-one-of-the-worlds-most-powerful-women/?sh=5c0d85622757; Lauren Dezenski, 'All 4 Members of "the Squad" Reelected to House', CNN, 4 November 2020, https://edition.cnn.com/2020/11/03/politics/alexandria-ocasio-cortez-wins-house-seat/index.html.

49. Claire Bushey, 'Defund the Police: How a Protest Slogan Triggered a Policy Debate', *Financial Times*, 21 April 2021, https://www.ft.com/content/76a8080c-cca9-48cd-be81-891a75676adf.
50. Damon Williams quoted in Noname, 'The Great Fire', 72.
51. Jacob Blake, 'Wisconsin Officer Cleared over Jacob Blake Shooting Returns to Duty', *The Guardian*, April 13, 2021, https://www.theguardian.com/us-news/2021/apr/13/rusten-sheskey-jacob-black-return-to-duty.
52. Black Thought quoted in Noname, 'The Great Fire', 75.
53. Otto Kerner et al., *Report of the National Advisory Commission on Civil Disorders*, 1967, 29.

Introduction

1. Charles H. Fuller, '*What is Black Power, Daddy?* Answer: "?"' (2 November 1979), Box 41, File 34, SCMSS, 1.
2. Ibid., 1–2.
3. Stokely Carmichael quoted in Martin Duberman, *The Uncompleted Past* (1969), 235.
4. Solomon P. Gethers, 'Black Power: Three Years Later', *Negro Digest*, December 1969, 6–7.
5. Jeffrey Ogbonna Green Ogbar, *Black Power: Radical Politics And African American Identity* (Baltimore: Johns Hopkins University Press, 2005), 153.
6. Harold Cruse, *The Crisis of the Negro Intellectual* (New York: Morrow, 1967), 545.
7. Cruse, quoted in Richard J. Meister, *The Black Ghetto: Promised Land or Colony?* (Lexington: D.C. Heath, 1972), 200.
8. Hubert Humphrey quoted in 'Black Power Must Be Defined', *Life*, 22 July 1966, 4.
9. Roy Wilkins, 'Whither "Black Power"?' *The Crisis*, August–September 1966, 354.
10. 'Black Power: Politics of Frustration,' *Newsweek*, 11 July 1966, Box 31, File 14, SCMSS, 26.
11. Ibid., 31.
12. 'The Left: Guns and Butter', *Newsweek*, 5 May 1969, 40.
13. Kwame Ture (Stokely Carmichael) and Charles V. Hamilton, *Black Power* (1967; repr.,1992), 146.
14. Elaine Brown quoted in Jane Rhodes, *Framing the Panthers* (The New Press: New York, 2007), 160.
15. Russell Sackett, 'Plotting A War on "Whitey"', *Life*, 10 June 1966.
16. Ibid.

17. *San Francisco Examiner*, 8 April 1968: *Time*, 19 April 1968.
18. For further analysis see Paul B. Johnson, David D. Sears and John B. McConahay, "Black Invisibility, the Press and the Los Angeles Riot,' *American Journal of Sociology* 76 no 4 (January 1971), 698–721.
19. 'Black Power: Politics of Frustration,' *Newsweek*, 38.
20. *The Times*, 13 March 1968.
21. Mike Phillips and Trevor Phillips, *Windrush* (London: Harper Collins, 1998), 232.
22. *The Times*, 12 December 1969.
23. 'The New Racism.' *Time*, 1 July 1966.
24. Kathleen Cleaver, 'How TV Wrecked the Black Panthers,' *Channels of Communication*, 2 (November–December 1982), 98–9.
25. Emory Douglas in *Eyes On the Prize*, Part 2, 'Fighting Back' (PBS/Blackside, 1988).
26. Fred C. Shapiro, 'The Successor to Floyd McKissick May Not Be So Reasonable,' *New York Times Magazine*, 1 October 1967, 103.
27. Ibid.
28. This was partially an outgrowth of the sensationalism which had followed coverage of the non-violent movement. See Payne, *I've Got The Light of Freedom*, 394.
29. Malcolm X, *The Autobiography of Malcolm X* (1965; repr., 2007), 345.
30. *US News and World Reports*, 29 May 1967.
31. James Forman, *The Making of Black Revolutionaries* (Washington, D.C.: Open Hand Publishing, 1985), 458.
32. Seale, *Seize the Time*, 187.
33. Rhodes, *Framing*, 66–7.
34. Otto Kerner et al., *Report of the National Advisory Commission on Civil Disorders* (1968), 377.
35. Pat Jefferson, 'Stokely's Cool Style', *Today's Speech*, 16, 1968, 19–24.
36. For a useful discussion on the manner in which this media construction took place within a popular culture framework see Stuart Hall, 'The Whites of Their Eyes: Racist Ideologies and the Media' in Gail Dines and Jean M. Humez, eds., *Gender, Race and Class in the Media*, 18–22, alongside Jane Rhodes, *Framing the Panthers*, for an analysis focused more on the political dimensions of black power.
37. Simon Wendt, *The Spirit and the Shotgun: Armed Resistance and the Struggle for Civil Rights* (Gainesville: University Press of Florida, 2007): Jenny Walker, 'A Media Made Movement?: Black Violence and Nonviolence in the Historiography of the Civil Rights Movement,' in Brian Ward, ed., *Media, Culture and the Modern African American Freedom Struggle*, 48.
38. See Carolyn Martindale, *The White Press and Black America* (Westport: Greenwood, 1986) and Rhodes, *Framing the Black Panthers* (2007).
39. Du Bois, 'The Souls of Black Folks', in *Three Negro Classics* (New York: Avon, 1965) 214.

40. Rhodes, *Framing*, 310.
41. Ibid., 308.
42. For examples, see Amy Abugo Ongiri, *Spectacular Blackness: The Cultural Politics of the Black Power Movement and the Search for a Black Aesthetic* (Charlottesville: University of Virginia Press, 2010): William L. Van Deburg, *New Day in Babylon* (London: University of Chicago Press, 1992).
43. Morrison quoted in Paul Gilroy, *The Black Atlantic: Modernity and Double Consciousness* (Cambridge: Harvard University Press, 1993), 221.
44. See Bernice Johnson Reagon, *if You Don't Go, Don't Hinder Me: the African American Sacred Song Tradition* (Lincoln, 2001).
45. Hilliard, Interview.
46. Adam Fairclough, 'State of the Art: Historians and the Civil Rights Movement', Journal *of American Studies*, 24, no. 3 (December 1990), 388.
47. Geertz in Sherry B. Ortner, ed., *The Fate of Culture: Geertz and Beyond* (Los Angeles: University of California Press, 1999), 3. See also Clifford Geertz, *The Interpretation of Cultures: Selected Essays* (New York: Basic Books, 1973), 5.
48. Scholars such as Lila Abu-Lughod have noted that new media, from television to the internet, 'renders more and more problematic a concept of cultures as localized communities of people suspended in shared webs of meaning.' For further discussion of this, see Lila Abu-Lughod, 'The Interpretation of Culture(s) after Television' in Ortner, ed., *The Fate of Culture*, 123.
49. Ibid., 111.
50. Fons Trompenaars and Charles Hampden Turner, *Riding the Waves of Culture: Understanding Diversity in Global Business* (New York: McGraw Hill, 1998).
51. Ibid.
52. Joseph Shaules, *Deep Culture: The Hidden Challenges of Global Living* (Clevedon: Multilingual Matters, 2007), 21.
53. Arjun Appadurai, ed., *Modernity At Large: Cultural Dimensions of Globalization* (London: University of Minnesota Press, 1996), 31–5.
54. See Dayo F. Gore, Jeanne Theoharis and Komozi Woodard eds., *Want to Start a Revolution?: Radical Women in the Black Freedom Struggle* (2009); Vicki Crawford et al., *Women in the Civil Rights Movement: Trailblazers and Torchbearers, 1941–1965* (1990).

Chapter 1 Hotheads and Demagogues: What is Black Power?

1. Stokely Carmichael, 'What We Want,' *The New York Review of Books* 7, no. 4 (22 September 1966), 8.
2. David Hilliard, interview by author, 27 August 2008.
3. Peter Goldman, *The Death and Life of Malcolm X* (1979), 18.
4. Kate Coleman, 'Guess Who's Mything Them Now: The real Black Panthers were a bunch of thugs', *The San Francisco Chronicle*, Sunday, June 15, 2003: Horowitz from Rhodes

5. Van Deburg, *New Day*, 16.
6. Peter Goldman, *Report from Black America* (1969), 100; 'The Black Mood, More Militant, More Hopeful, More Determined', *Time*, 6 April 1970. Louis Harris and Associates, *The Harris Survey Yearbook of Public Opinion, 1970* (1971). Joel D. Aberbach and Jack L. Walker, 'The Meanings of Black Power: A Comparison of White and Black Interpretations of a Political Slogan', *American Political Science Review* 64, no. 2 (June 1970), 383.
7. Gary T. Marx, *Protest and Prejudice* (1969), 217–18.
8. William McCord, John Howard, Bernard Friedberg and Edwin Hardwood, *Life Styles in the Black Ghetto* (1969), 102–3, 275, 283.
9. Russell Sackett, 'Plotting a War on Whitey', *Life*, 10 June 1966, 106.
10. William Brink and Louis Harris, *Black and White: A Study of US Racial Attitudes Today* (1967), 252, 254.
11. Calvin C. Hernton, 'White Liberals and Black Muslims', *Negro Digest*, October 1963, 4.
12. 'Black Mood'.
13. Ibid.; Goldman, *Report*, 156.
14. 'The Stokely Generation', *Newsweek*, 29 May 1967, 24–5: Goldman, *Report*, 205, 263.
15. Marx, *Protest*, 228.
16. Goldman, *Report*, 263.
17. Ibid., 261, 264; Jan E. Dizard, 'Black Identity, Social Class and Black Power', *Psychiatry* 33, no. 2 (May 1970), 199–200; Angus Campbell and Howard Schuman, *Racial Attitudes in Fifteen American Cities* (1968), 18–19. For a thorough discussion of the importance of cultural factors and cultural pluralism in constructing the landscape of late twentieth century America, see Milton Gordon, *Assimilation in American Life* (1964), 77–159.
18. For contemporary commentary on survey research on urban black subjects see Kenneth B. Clark, *Dark Ghetto: Dilemmas of Social Power* (1967), xii–xxv; Robert Blauner and David Wellman, 'Toward the Decolonization of Social Research', in *The Death of White Sociology*, ed., Joyce A. Ladner (1973), 310–30; Ethel Sayer, 'Methodological Problems in Studying So-Called "Deviant Communities"', in Ladner, *Death*, 361–79; Carl O. Word, 'Crosscultural Methods for Survey Research in Black Urban Areas', *Journal of Black Psychology* 3, no. 2 (February 1977), 72–87.
19. Richard D. Tucker and John J. Woodmansee, 'A Scale of Black Separatism', *Psychological Reports* 27, no. 3 (December 1970), 855; Howard Schuman and Shirley Hatchett, *Black Racial Attitudes: Trends and Complexities* (1974), 150. See also, Janet Ward Schofield, *Black and White in School: Trust, Tension, or Tolerance?* (1982), 170. Two studies by the psychologist John Woodmansee illustrate this trend, Brian D. Stenfors and John J. Woodmansee, 'A Scale of Black Power Sentiment', *Psychological Reports* 22, no. 3 (June 1968), 802; Tucker and Woodmansee, 'Black Separatism', 855–8.
20. *Harris Survey*, 1970.

21. Aberbach and Walker, 'Meanings,' 370.
22. Ibid.
23. *San Francisco Examiner*, 24 May 1967: Aberbach and Walker, 'Meanings,' 370.
24. Aberbach and Walker, 'Meanings,' 370.
25. Sackett, 100.
26. Ron Jones and Mike Hancock, Commission of Inquiry into the Black Panthers and Law Enforcement, 'Preliminary Investigation into Relations Between the Black Panther Party and Local Law Enforcement Agencies', 31 January 1970, 18.
27. *New York Times*, 3 and 4 May 1967.
28. For an exemplar of the kind of journalism this engendered see the *New York Times*, 3 May 1967. The broader vision of an armed black populace was encapsulated by Bobby Seale in *Seize The Time*, 162–3.
29. *New York Times*, 13 October 1918.
30. Jane Rhodes, *Framing the Black Panthers*, 42.
31. Jerry Belcher, 'It's All Legal: Oakland's Black Panthers Wear Guns, Talk Revolution.' *San Francisco Sunday Chronicle and Examiner*, 30 April 1967.
32. Ibid.
33. *New York Times*, 7 May 1967.
34. Ibid.
35. Carmichael, 'What We Want', 8.
36. Stokely Carmichael, *Stokely Speaks* (1971), 190.
37. *US News and World Report*, 62 (1967), 12.
38. Kwame Ture (Stokely Carmichael) and Charles V. Hamilton, *Black Power* (1967; repr., 1992), 52.
39. Ibid., 53.
40. James Weldon Johnson, 'The White Witch', in James Weldon Johnson, ed., *The Book of American Negro Poetry* (1922), 111–13; Nathan Hare, 'How White Power Whitewashes Black Power', in *The Black Power Revolt*, ed., Floyd B. Barbour (1968), 182–8.
41. Brown, *Die Nigger!*, 108.
42. Stokely Carmichael, Speech at University of California, Berkeley, 29 October 1966. http://americanradioworks.publicradio.org/features/sayitplain/scarmichael.html.
43. Ture and Hamilton, *Black Power*, 53.
44. Robert L. Scott, 'Justifying Violence: The Rhetoric of Militant Black Power', in *The Rhetoric of Black Power*, ed., Robert L. Scott and Wayne Brockriede (1969), 134–40.
45. John O. Killens et al., 'Black Power: Its Meaning and Measure', *Negro Digest*, November 1966, 34.
46. Wilkins, 'Whither?', 354.
47. Carmichael, 'What We Want', 6, 8; 'In Defense of Self-Defense II: 3 July 1967', in Newton *To Die* (2009), 86–7.
48. Carmichael, 'Black Power Address.'

49. Ibid.
50. C.E. Wilson, 'Black Power and the Myth of Black Racism', *Liberation* 11 (September 1966), 27.
51. Seale, 'Free Huey', 17:00–18:00.
52. Carmichael and Hamilton, *Black Power*, 47, 167; Seale, *Seize*, 281–2; Jackson, *Blood*, 111; Brown, *Die Nigger!*, 17.
53. Robert Scheer, ed., *Eldridge Cleaver: Post-Prison Writings and Speeches* (1969), 142.
54. Hilliard, Interview.
55. Julius Lester quoted in Vincent Harding, 'Black Radicalism: The Road from Montgomery', in *Dissent*, ed., Alfred F. Young (1968), 342.
56. Carmichael, *Stokely Speaks*, 204.
57. Stuart Hall, 'The Whites of Their Eyes: Racist Ideologies and the Media', 20.
58. Kathleen Cleaver 'How TV Wrecked', 98–9.
59. Toni Morrison. *Playing in the Dark: Whiteness and the Literary Imagination* (London: Picador, 1992), 37–9.
60. Ibid., 38.
61. John Fiske, *Media Matters: Race and Gender in U.S. Politics* (Minneapolis: University of Minnesota Press, 1996), xviii.
62. Julius Lester, *Look Out Whitey! Black Power's Gon' Get Your Mama* (1970), 97.
63. Eldridge Cleaver, *Soul on Ice* (New York: Dell, 1968), 164.
64. Fuller, *What is Black Power?*, 1.
65. *Ain't I A Beauty Queen?*, 165.
66. *Ideals of Feminine Beauty*, 153.
67. Maxine Leeds Craig, *Ain't I A Beauty Queen?: Black Women, Beauty, and the Politics of Race* (Oxford: Oxford University Press, 2002), 165.
68. Hare, 'Whitewashes,' 183.
69. The Observer, 'On the Significance of the Black Panther Party to the Nationalists' (n.d., ca. 1968), Box 7, File 9, SCMSS, 2.
70. Aberbach and Walker, 'Meanings', 372.
71. *San Francisco Sun-Reporter*, 17 February 1968.
72. *Oakland Tribune*, 5 July 1966.
73. *San Francisco Sun-Reporter*, 6 April 1968.
74. Ibid., 387.
75. Bayard Rustin quoted in Sackett 'Plotting A War on Whitey', *Life*, 10 June 1966, 100B.
76. Bertram J. Levine, *Resolving Racial Conflict* (2005), 79–80.
77. Franklin Florence, 'The Meaning of Black Power', in Molefi K. Asante, *The Rhetoric of Black Revolution* (1969), 164.
78. 'Fight Leader Speaks on Negroes Plight', *Rochester Institute of Technology Reporter*, 24 February 1967, 1, 4.
79. 'Black Capitalism Re-Analyzed', in Newton, *To Die*, 99.
80. Malcolm X, *By Any Means Necessary* (1970).

81. Marita Sturken, *Tangled Memories: the Vietnam War, the AIDS Epidemic, and the Politics of Remembering* (Berkeley: University of California Press, 1997), 7–9.
82. Forman, *The Making of Black Revolutionaries*, 456–8.
83. Rhodes, *Framing*, 162.
84. Stuart Hall, 'The Whites of Their Eyes: Racist Ideologies and the Media' in Gail Dines and Jean M. Humez, eds., *Gender, Race and Class in the Media*, 18–22.
85. Arthur Hays Sulzberger, '"The Word Negro Is Not To Appear Unless": One Publisher's Attitude on Race', *Nieman Reports*, October 1957, 3.
86. Kerner et al., *Report*, 366.
87. For a useful contemporary example see Jack Lule, 'News Strategies and the Death of Huey Newton', *Journalism and Mass Communication Quarterly*, 70 no. 2 (June 1993), 287–99.
88. See Solomon P. Gethers, 'Black Power: Three Years Later', *Negro Digest*, December 1969, 4–10, 69–81; Alvin F. Poussaint, 'How the "White Problem" Spawned "Black Power"', *Ebony*, August 1967 and 'A Psychiatrist Looks at Black Power', *Ebony*, March 1969.
89. Simeon Booker, 'The New Frontier for Daily Newspapers', *Nieman Reports* (January 1955), 25.
90. Rhodes, *Framing*, 62.
91. 'It's All Legal: Oakland's Black Panthers Wear Guns, Talk Revolution, *San Francisco Examiner*, 30 April 1967.
92. For further analysis of these ideologies, see Gethers's 'Black Power' and 'Black Nationalism and Human Liberation', *Black Scholar* 1 (May 1970), 43–50.
93. Larry Neal, 'Separate State' (n.d.) Box 7, File 15, SCMSS, 2–4.
94. See Aldon D. Morris, *The Origins of the Civil Rights Movement* (1986).
95. See Carmichael and Hamilton, *Black Power*, 44–7; Richard C. Tolbert, 'A New Brand of Black Nationalism', *Negro Digest*, August 1967, 20–3.
96. Van Deburg, *New Day*, 26.
97. Ronald Walters, 'African-American Nationalism: A Unifying Ideology', *Black World*, October 1973, 26.
98. A. Mweusi, 'Steps to Liberation,' (n.d.) Box 42, File 21, SCMSS, 3.
99. Stokely Carmichael, 'Towards Black Liberation', in *Black Fire*, 119.
100. See James Turner, 'The Sociology of Black Nationalism', *Black Scholar* 1 (December 1969), 18–27; Carmichael and Hamilton, *Black Power*, 34–9; Killens, 'Meaning and Measure', 33; Calvin C. Hernton, *Coming Together: Black Power, White Hatred and Sexual Hang-Ups* (New York, 1971), 33–7; Poussaint, 'A Psychiatrist', 142.

Chapter 2 Why Black Power?

1. For successive iterations of this view see, David J. Garrow, *Protest at Selma: Martin Luther King, Jr, and the Voting Rights Act of 1965* (1978); Charles and Barbara Whalen, *The Longest Debate: A Legislative History of the 1964 Civil Rights Act* (1985); John White, *Martin Luther King, Jr., and the Civil Rights*

Movement in America (1991). A more nuanced appraisal of the legislative struggle undergirding the movement can be found in Robert Mann's, *When Freedom Would Triumph: the Civil Rights Struggle in Congress, 1954–1968* (2007).
2. John Alfred Williams, *Flashbacks*, 158.
3. For some anecdotal evidence from the journalist John Alfred Williams, see Williams 45–6, 75–6, 156–7.
4. Neal, *Separate State*, 3.
5. Cleveland Sellers, *The River of No Return* (1973), 166–7.
6. Craig Werner, *A Change Is Gonna Come* (2002), 119.
7. Nathan Hare, 'Black Power: Are Negroes Ready, Willing and Able?' (22 July 1966), Box 31, File 14, SCMSS, 1.
8. Ibid.
9. Larry Neal 'Foreword to Black History' (n.d), Box 21, File 11, SCMSS, 1.
10. Brad Vickers, *Native American Identities: From Stereotype to Archetype in Art and Literature* (Albuquerque: University of New Mexico Press, 1998), xiii.
11. Vickers, *Native American Identities*, 4.
12. Ibid.
13. Ibid., 5.
14. For an excellent discussion on this see Lucy R. Lippard, 'Naming' in William Kelly, ed., *Art and Humanist Ideals: Contemporary Perspectives* (South Yarra: Macmillan, 2003), 81–98.
15. Vickers, *Native American Identities*, 5.
16. Carl Gustav Jung, trans. R.F.C. Hull, *The Archetypes and the Collective Unconscious* (London: Routledge 1991), 5.
17. Ibid., 7.
18. Roland Barthes, trans. Annette Lavers, *Mythologies* (New York: Farrar, Strauss and Giroux, 1972), 150.
19. Jung, *The Archetypes*, 5, 30.
20. Barthes, 142.
21. Ibid., 132.
22. Jung, *The Archetypes*, 38.
23. Stanley Elkins, *Slavery* (1968), 81–139.
24. 'Big Sixteen', in Zora Neale Hurston, *Mules and Men* (1935), 207–8.
25. As told by Caesar Grant, of John's Island, carter and labourer, recorded as 'All God's Chillen Had Wings', in John Bennett, *The Doctor to The Dead* (1946), 139.
26. Ibid., 141.
27. Imamu Amiri Baraka, *Congress of African Peoples – Political Liberation Council: Organizing Manual* (Boston: Black World Foundation, 1971), 8.
28. Larry Neal, *Lenox Avenue Sunday* (1966), Box 14, File 2, SCMSS, 1.
29. Larry Neal, *Black History/Cultural Development* (Fragment, n.d.), Box 6, File 13, SCMSS, 7.
30. Ibid.

31. For further analysis of the robustness of plantation culture, see Ira Berlin, *Many Thousands Gone* (1998).
32. John Mason Brewer, 'Den To De Fiah,' and 'A Laugh That Meant Freedom', in *Tone the Bell Easy*, ed., J. Frank Dobie (1932; repr., 1965), 13–15.
33. Brewer, 'Swapping Dreams', in Dobie, 18, 19.
34. Ibid., 19.
35. Brewer, 'Dey's Auganized', in Dobie, 23–4.
36. Brewer, 'Uncle Pleas's Prayer', in Dobie, 28.
37. 'Slave Song', in Frederick Douglass, *My Bondage and My Freedom* (1855), 252–3.
38. Ibid.
39. 'Promises of Freedom,' in Thomas Washington Talley, *Negro Folk Rhymes* (1922), 25–6.
40. 'An Escaped Convict,' in Edward Clarkson Leverett Adams, *Nigger to Nigger* (1928), 16–17.
41. David Walker, *Appeal in Four Articles* (1830), E147, MHSMSS, 43.
42. Ibid., 13.
43. Ibid.
44. Jonathan Randal, "Collegians Split by 'Black Power,'" *New York Times*, 28 August 1966, 49.
45. Walker, *Appeal*, 15.
46. James Brewer Stewart, 'Modernizing "Difference": The Political Meanings of Color in the Free States, 1776–1840', *Journal of the Early Republic* 19, no. 4 (1999), 702.
47. *A New History of Black America* (New York, ca. 1966), Box 31 File 12, SCMSS, 1.
48. Ibid., 1–3.
49. Christopher James Beshara, 'The Hidden History of Black Militant Abolitionism in Antebellum Boston' (BA Hons. Thesis, University of Sydney, October 2009), 83.
50. A Colored Bostonian, 'Death of Walker', Liberator 1, no. 4 (22 January 1831), 14.
51. Beshara, 'The Hidden History', 37.
52. O. L., 'Causes of Slave Insurrections', *Liberator* 1, no. 38 (17 September 1831), 150.
53. Beshara, 'The Hidden Histpry, 18.
54. Alfred N. Hunt, *Haiti's Influence on Antebellum America: Slumbering Volcano in the Caribbean* (Baton Rouge: LSU Press, 2006), 3.
55. 'Anti-Webster Meeting of the Colored Citizens of Boston and Vicinity', *The Liberator*, 5 April 1850 in *William Cooper Nell, Nineteenth-century African American abolitionist*, ed., Constance Porter Uzelac and Dorothy Porter Wesley (2002), 257.
56. Henry Bibb quoted in Howard H. Bell 'Expressions of Negro Militancy in the North, 1840–1860', *The Journal of Negro History* 45, no. 1 (January 1960), 14.

57. *Minutes of the State Convention of the Colored Citizens of Ohio, Convened at Columbus, January 15th–18th, 1851*, quoted in Bell 'Expressions', 15.
58. 'Letter to the American Slaves', Fugitive Slave Act Convention, Cazenovia, New York, August 1850, http://nationalhumanitiescenter.org/pds/maai/enslavement/text7/freeblacksaddress.pdf (accessed 19 January 2009).
59. Roy Reed, 'The Deacons, Too, Ride by Night', *New York Times Magazine*, 15 August 1965, 20.
60. T. Thomas Fortune, 'It Is Time To Call A Halt', *New York Age*, 25 January 1890.
61. Beshara, 'The Hidden History', 11.
62. John Sweat Rock, 'I Will Sink or Swim With My Race', *Liberator*, 12 March 1858, 7. http://research.udmercy.edu/find/special_collections/digital/baa/item.php?record_id=1238 (accessed 19 January 2009).
63. Samuel E. Cornish, 'Amalgamation', *Colored American* 2, no. 18 (23 June 1838), 73.
64. Lynn Dumenil, *The Modern Temper: American Culture and Society in the 1920s* (New York: Hill and Wang, 1995), 7: George Chauncey, *Gay New York: Gender, Urban Culture, and the Makings of the Gay Male World, 1890–1940* (New York: Basic Books, 1994), 12–13: Kevin J. Mumford, *Interzones: Black/White Sex Districts in Chicago and New York in the Early Twentieth Century* (New York: Columbia University Press, 1997), 79–80, 86–7.
65. Alan Sinfield, *Cultural Politics – Queer Reading* (Hoboken: Taylor and Francis, 2013), 20.
66. David Levering Lewis, *When Harlem Was In Vogue* (New York: Oxford University Press, 1981), 21–2.
67. Alain Locke, 'Harlem', *The Survey Graphic*, Harlem Number (March 1925). http://xroads.virginia.edu/~drbr/locke_2.html (accessed 12 March 2010).
68. Claude McKay, *Harlem: Negro Metropolis*, 16.
69. Locke, *The New Negro*, 11.
70. Ibid., 3.
71. See Roy Flannagan, *Amber Satyr* (1932).
72. Alain Locke, 'Youth Speaks', *Survey Graphic, Harlem: Mecca of the New Negro* (March 1925), online at http://etext.virginia.edu/harlem/LocYoutF.html.
73. Langston Hughes et al., *The Collected Works of Langston Hughes*, Volume 13. Autobiography: The Big Sea (Columbia: University of Missouri Press, 2002), 173.
74. William Edward Burghardt Du Bois, 'Opinion of W.E.B. Du Bois'. *The Crisis*, April 1920, 299.
75. Charles S. Johnson, 'The New Generation', *Opportunity*, Vol. 2, no. 15 (March 1924): 68.
76. Aubrey Bowser, 'The Two-Dollar Woman Out Again', *New York Amsterdam News*, 28 November 1928.
77. Paul Meltsner, Playbill for Wallace Thurman's *Harlem!* (1929), JWJ MSS 12.
78. Ibid.

79. Nathan Irvin Huggins, *Harlem Renaissance* (Oxford: Oxford University Press, 2007), 91: Meltsner, 'Playbill.'
80. Lewis A. Erenber, *Steppin' Out: New York nightlife and the transformation of American culture, 1890–1930* (London: Greenwood, 1981), 95.
81. Edward Margolies, *Native Sons:A Critical Study of Twentieth Century Negro American Authors* (Philadelphia, Lippincott, 1968), 31.
82. 'They Won't Keep Away', *New York Amsterdam News*, 23 October 1929.
83. Wayne Cooper, *Claude McKay*, 242.
84. Paul Guillaume and Thomas Munro, *Primitive Negro Sculpture* (1926), 9.
85. George S. Schuyler, 'Light and Shadows of the Underworld – Studying the Social Outcasts: II. The Folk Farthest Down', *Messenger*, Vol.5, August 1923, 787.
86. Locke, ed., *The New Negro*.
87. Hughes, 'The Negro Artist'.
88. For some examples see Sterling A. Brown, 'The Literary Scene', *Opportunity* Vol. 9 (February 1931): 53–4 and Brown, 'The Negro Writer and His Publisher', *The Quarterly Review of Higher Education Among Negroes* 9 (July 1941): 143.
89. W.E.B. Du Bois, 'Review of Nigger Heaven', *The Crisis*, December 1926, 81.
90. Johnson, *The Book of American Negro Poetry*, vii.
91. Wallace Thurman, 'Tribute' in *The Collected Writings of Wallace Thurman*, Amritjit Singh and Daniel M. Scott III, eds (New Brunswick, Rutgers, 2003), 251.
92. Charles S. Johnson, 'An Opportunity for Negro Writers." Opportunity, 2 no. 21 (September 1924).
93. Alain Locke, 'Spiritual Truancy' in *The Works of Alain* Locke, 226: Cooper, *Claude McKay: Rebel Sojourner*, particularly 171–92.
94. Claude McKay to Harold Jackman, 14 January 1927.
95. Claude McKay to Harold Jackman, 9 May 1928.
96. Huggins, *Voices from the Harlem Renaissance*, 124–5.
97. Claude McKay, *Banjo: A Story Without A Plot* (New York: Harper and Brother, 1929), 252.
98. Ibid., 253.
99. Claude McKay, *Home to Harlem* (Boston: Northeastern University Press, 1987), 108.
100. McKay, *Banjo*, 208.
101. Skip G. Gates, 'Of Negroes Old and New', in Cary D. Wintz, ed., *Analysis and Assessment, 1940–1979*, Vol. 1 (New York: Garland, 1996), 209: Shane Vogel, *The Scene of Harlem Cabaret: Race, Sexuality, Performance* (Chicago, University of Chicago Press, 2009), 14: Hughes quoted in Steven C. Tracy, *Langston Hughes and the Blues* (Urbana: University of Illinois Press, 2001), 44.
102. Langston Hughes, "Café: 3 A.M.', in *The Poems 1951–1967*, 48.

103. Richard Bruce Nugent, 'Lighting Fire' (1982) in *FIRE!!*, ed., Wallace Thurman (1926) [Loose Insert].
104. Ibid.
105. Ibid.
106. Ibid.
107. Ibid.
108. Wallace Thurman quoted in *Remembering the Harlem Renaissance*, ed., Cary D. Wintz (New York: Garland, 1996), 293–4.
109. Thomas H. Wirth, 'Fire!! in Retrospect' (1982) in *FIRE!!* [Loose Insert], 1.
110. Ibid.
111. Langston Hughes, 'Jazzonia' in *The New Negro*, ed., Alain Locke (1925; repr., 1992), 226.
112. Mumford, *Interzones*: Frank Byrd, 'Harlem Rent Parties', U.S. Work Projects Administration, Federal Writers' Project (1939), Library of Congress, MSS55715: BOX A721.
113. Schwartz, *Gay Voices*, 13.
114. Mumford, *Interzones*, 84: Hutchison, *The Harlem Renaissance in Black and White*, 6.
115. Aubrey Bowser, 'An Example for Harlem Writers: The Saturday Evening Quill', *New York Amsterdam News*, 20 June 1928.
116. Ibid., 2.
117. Ibid.
118. Zora Neale Hurston, 'Sweat', in *FIRE!!* 40–5.
119. Langston Hughes, 'Elevator Boy', in *FIRE!!* 20.
120. Wirth, 'Fire!!', 3.
121. Appendix A.
122. Tom Lutz, '"Sweat or Die": The Hedonization of the Work Ethic in the 1920s', *American Literary History* 8, no. 2 (Summer 1996), 283–9.
123. Eleonore Van Notten, *Wallace Thurman's Harlem Renaissance* (Amsterdam: Rodopi, 1994), 138.
124. Wirth, *FIRE!!*, 3.
125. Du Bois, 'Opinion'.
126. Jack B. Moore, *W.E.B. Du Bois* (Boston: Twayne Publishers, 1981), 96.
127. Ibid.
128. Langston Hughes, 'The Negro Artist and the Racial Mountain', *The Nation*, 23 June 1926, http://www.thenation.com/doc/19260623/hughes (accessed 14 June 2008).
129. W.E.B. Du Bois, 'Criteria of Negro Art', *The Crisis*, October 1926, 290–297.
130. Caroline Goeser, 'The Case of *Ebony and Topaz*: Racial and Sexual Hybridity in Harlem Renaissance Illustrations', *American Periodicals* 15, no. 1 (2005), 1.
131. Charles S. Johnson, *Ebony and Topaz: A Collectanea* (1927), 11.
132. Ibid., 12.
133. Ibid.
134. Ibid., 11.

135. For a classic version of the John Henry tale see Hurston, *Mules*, 80–1.
136. W.E.B. Du Bois, 'The Browsing Reader', *The Crisis*, May 1928, 165.
137. Ibid.
138. Countee Cullen, 'Heritage' (1925).
139. Hughes, *Big Sea*.
140. Wallace Thurman, 'Editorial', *Harlem*, Vol. 1, November 1928 in Huggins, *Voices*, 9.
141. Wallace Thurman, 'Review of Infants of the Spring', *Abbott's Monthly Review*, April 1932, 63.
142. Appendix B.
143. Johnson, *Ebony and Topaz*, 13.
144. Charles S. Johnson, 'Jazz Poetry and Blues', *Carolina Magazine* (May 1928), 18.
145. James Weldon Johnson, *Along This Way* (1933; repr., 2000), 152.
146. See Bernard Bell, *The Folk Roots of Contemporary Afro-American Poetry* (1974), 19–31.
147. Booker T. Washington, *The Story of the Negro: The Rise of the Race from Slavery* (1909), 292.
148. Robin Kelley, *Race Rebels: Culture, Politics, and the Black Working Class* (1996), 7.
149. Abraham Chapman, ed., *Black Voices: An Anthology of Afro-American Literature* (1968), 355.
150. Paul Laurence Dunbar, *The Sport of the Gods* (1902; repr., 2005).
151. Charles Waddell Chesnutt, *The Conjure Woman* (1899), 195–229, 103–31, 162–94. http://docsouth.unc.edu/southlit/chesnuttconjure/menu.html (accessed 28 February 2009).
152. Charles Waddell Chesnutt, *The Marrow of Tradition* (1901), http://docsouth.unc.edu/southlit/chesnuttmarrow/menu.html (accessed 1 March 2009); Mike Baker, '1898 Clash Ruled A Coup', *Washington Post*, 1 June 2006, http://www.washingtonpost.com/wp-dyn/content/article/2006/05/31/AR2006053102080.html (accessed 1 March 2009).
153. Joseph R. McElrath, Robert C. Leitz, Jesse S. Crisler, eds., *Charles W. Chesnutt: Essays and Speeches* (1999), xxvi.
154. Larry Neal, 'Eatonville's Zora Neale Hurston: A Profile', *Black Review* 2 ed. Mel Watkins (1979), Box 6, File 27, SCMSS, 15.
155. Charles H. Rowell, 'Sterling A. Brown and the Afro-American Folk Tradition', in *The Harlem Renaissance Re-examined*, ed., Victor Kramer (1987), 317.
156. Sterling A. Brown, quoted in Rowell, 317.
157. Alain Locke, 'Sterling Brown: The New Negro Folk-Poet' (1934), reprinted in Henry Louis Gates Jr. and Gene Andrew Jarrett, eds., *The New Negro: Readings on Race, Representation, and African American Culture, 1892–1938* (Princeton: Princeton University Press, 2007), 120.
158. Sterling Brown, *Southern Road: Poems* (1932), 46–7.
159. Johnson, *American Negro Poetry*, 18.

160. George E. Kent, 'Langston Hughes and Afro-American Folk and Cultural Tradition,' in *Langston Hughes, Black Genius*, ed., Therman B. O'Daniel (1971), 183.
161. Bruce Jackson, ed., *Wake Up Dead Man* (1972), 29–30.
162. 'Southern Road', in *Southern Road*, 46–7; James Weldon Johnson, *God's Trombones: Seven Negro Sermons in Verse* (1927).
163. Jean Wagner, *Black Poets of the United States from Paul Laurence Dunbar to Langston Hughes* (1973), 490.
164. For more detailed analyses see Tony Bolden, *Afro-Blue: Improvisations in African American Poetry and Culture* (Bristol: University of Illinois Press, 2004), 85: Keith D. Leonard, *Fettered Genius: the African American Bardic Poet from Slavery to Civil Rights* (London: University of Virginia Press, 2006), 109–10.
165. First seeing print in *Freedomways* III (Summer 1963), 405–11, 'The Ballad of Joe Meek', Brown notes, was 'written over a score of years ago' placing it ca. 1943. See Robert G. O'Meally, 'An Annotated Bibliography of the Works of Sterling A. Brown', *Callaloo* 14/15 (February – May 1982), 90–105.
166. Sterling A Brown, 'The Ballad of Joe Meek', in *The Collected Poems of Sterling A. Brown*, ed., Michael S. Harper (1996), 159.
167. Ibid., 160.
168. Ibid.
169. Ibid.
170. Bobby Seale quoted in Joseph Harker, 'Loud, Proud and Black', *The New Statesman*, 16 October 2006.
171. Harper, *Collected Poems*, 162.
172. *BPINS*, 23 March 1968.
173. Harper, *Collected Poems*, 162.
174. Joanne V. Gabbin, *Sterling A. Brown: Building the Black Aesthetic Tradition* (1994), 59; Stephen E. Henderson, 'Sterling A. Brown', *Ebony*, October 1976, 129.
175. Jennifer Jordan, 'Sterling A. Brown: A Race Man in the 1960s', *Callaloo* 21, no. 4 (Autumn 1998), 888.
176. Jabari Asim, The *N Word* (2007), 182; Paula J. Massood, *Black City Cinema* (2003), 162–164; mink, *Full Clip*, DVD (2004).
177. James Weldon Johnson, introduction to *Southern Road*, xiv.
178. Sterling A. Brown quoted in Mark A. Sanders, 'The Ballad, the Hero and the Ride', in *The Furious Flowering of African-American Poetry*, ed., Joanne V. Gabbin (1999), 132.
179. David Anderson, 'Sterling Brown's Southern Strategy: Poetry as Cultural Evolution in "Southern Road"', *Callaloo* 21, no. 4 (Autumn 1998), 1023.
180. David Bradley, *The Chaneysville Incident* (1981), 77.
181. Ralph Ellison, *Invisible Man* (1952; repr., 1999), 11.
182. Hortense Spillers, 'Ellison's "Usable Past": Toward a Theory of Myth', in *Black, White, and in Color* (2003), 65–80.
183. Larry Neal, 'Ellison's Zoot Suit' (December 1970) Box 6, File 28, SCMSS, 70.

184. Wesley Brown, 'The Mojo and the Sayso: Myth and Ritual in the Work of Larry Neal' (14 November 1981), Box 1, File 17, SCMSS 8.
185. Larry Neal, 'Politics as Ritual: Ellison's Zoot Suit', *Black World*, December 1970, 40.
186. Brown, 'The Mojo', 9.
187. Charles E. Silberman, *Criminal Violence, Criminal Justice* (1978), 154.
188. Ibid.
189. Ibid., 155.
190. Ibid.
191. Ibid.
192. Brown, 'The Mojo', 1–17.
193. Neal, 'Zoot Suit', 51.
194. Brown, 'The Mojo', 17.
195. Caldwell to [Perce] Pearce, 19 June 1944 in Neal Gabler, *Walt Disney: The Triumph of the American Imagination* (2006), 434.
196. 'Needed: A Negro Legion of Decency', *Ebony*, January 1947, 36–7.
197. Darius James, *That's Blaxploitation!* (1995), 117–23.
198. Karl F. Cohen, *Forbidden Animation* (1997), 61.
199. Richard von Busack, 'Here He Comes to Save the Day: An Interview with Cinequest Maverick Spirit Honoree Ralph Bakshi', *San Jose Metro*, 5 March 2003. http://www.metroactive.com/papers/metro/02.27.03/bakshi-0309.html (accessed 30 March 2009).
200. Ibid.; James, *That's Blaxploitation*, 117–23.
201. 'A Tribute to Langston Hughes: Danny Glover & Randy Weston', Schomburg Center for Research in Black Culture, 23 October 2008; *The Adventures of Brer Rabbit* (2006). http://www.adventuresofbrerrabbitdvd.com (accessed 30 March, 2009).
202. Amazon customer reviews, 25 April 2007 and 25 March 2008. See the other reviews on the product page for similar public disapprobation. http://www.amazon.com/Adventures-Brer-Rabbit-Wanda-Sykes/dp/B000E6V07W/ref=sr_1_2?s = movies-tv&ie = UTF8&qid = 1412563061&sr = 1–2& keywords = brer + rabbit (accessed 10 May 2012).
203. Larry Neal, 'Uncle Rufus Raps on the Squared Circle', *Partisan Review* 39, no. 1 (1972), 45.
204. Ibid., 50.
205. Larry Neal, *Black Power/Liberation* (n.d.), Box 6, File 17, SCMSS 2.
206. Hilliard, interview.
207. Stokely Carmichael with Ekwueme Michael Thelwell, *Ready for Revolution: The Life and Struggles of Stokely Carmichael (Kwame Ture)* (New York: Scribner, 2003), 166.
208. Neal, *Black Power/Liberation*, 3.
209. Ibid., 3.
210. Larry Neal, 'Coming At You Weird', Box 6, File 22, SCMSS, 2.
211. Ibid.

212. Ibid., 3.
213. Ibid.
214. Ibid.
215. Neal, 'Coming At You Weird', Marginalia, 3.
216. Ibid., 4.
217. Larry Neal, 'Larry Neal On Malcolm X (For Rolling Stone)' (n.d.), Box 7, File 1, SCMSS.
218. Lerone Bennett Jr., 'Stokely Carmichael: Architect of Black Power', *Ebony*, September 1966, 26.
219. Ibid.
220. Ibid.
221. Appendix C.
222. Patricia Ann Jefferson, *The Rhetoric of the Magnificent Barbarian, Stokely Carmichael* (1967).
223. Robert Weisbrot, Review of *Ready for Revolution: The Life and Struggles of Stokely Carmichael (Kwame Ture)*, by Stokely Carmichael with Ekwueme Michael Thelwell, *New York Times Book Review*, 23 May 2003, 16: Pat Jefferson, 'Stokely's Cool Style', *Today's Speech* 16 (September 1968): Bernard Weintraub, 'The Brilliancy of Black', *Esquire*, 73 (1967), 132: Len Holt, *The Summer That Didn't End* (1965), 44.
224. Bennett, 'Architect', 26.
225. Ibid.
226. Ibid.
227. Obi Egbuna, *Destroy This Temple: The Voice of Black Power in Britain* (London: Macgibbon & Kee, 1971), 16, 18.
228. Stephen Small, *Racialised Barriers: the Black Experience in the United States and England in the 1980's* (London: Routledge, 1994), 3.
229. Ibid.
230. *Berkeley Barb*, 4 November 1966, in Victoria J. Gallagher, 'Postmodern Constructions in the Rhetoric of Stokely Carmichael', *Quarterly Journal of Speech* 87 (2001), 153.
231. Carmichael, Speech at University of California, Berkeley, 29 October 1966.
232. Ibid.
233. Ibid.
234. Ibid.
235. Ibid.
236. Stokely Carmichael, *Speech Given At Garfield Highschool* (19 April 1967). http://www.aavw.org/special_features/speeches_speech_carmichael01.html (accessed 31 March 2009).
237. For more note on Carmichael's style see Finley C. Campbell, 'Voice of Thunder, Voice of Rage: A Symbolic Analysis of a Selection of Malcolm X's Speech, 'Message to the Grass Roots', *Speech Teacher* 19 (1970), 110.
238. Appendix D.
239. Ibid.

240. Ibid.
241. Bennett, 'Architect', 32.
242. Ibid.
243. Ibid.
244. Carmichael with Thelwell, *Ready for Revolution*, 546.
245. Bennett, 'Architect', 30.
246. Jesse Kornbluth, ed., *Notes From the New Underground: An Anthology* (New York: Viking Press, 1968), xiv.
247. John Downing, *Radical Media: The Political Experience of Alternative Communication* (London: Sage, 2001), 35.
248. Emory Douglas, 'Art for the People's Sake', in *The Black Panther Party Service to the People Programs*, ed. David Hilliard (2008), 122.
249. Ibid.
250. Douglas, quoted in Rhodes, *Framing*, 102.
251. Douglas, 'Art for the People's Sake', 122.
252. Ibid.
253. Ibid., 123.
254. Ibid.
255. Ibid.
256. Rhodes, *Framing*, 113.
257. Seale, *Seize The Time*, 64.
258. Gilbert Stuart Moore, *A Special Rage* (New York: Harper and Row, 1971), 64.
259. John A. Courtright, 'Rhetoric of the Gun: An Analysis of the Rhetorical Modifications of the Black Panther Party', *Journal of Black Studies*, 4, no. 3 (1974), 259–60.
260. Rhodes, *Framing*, 113.
261. David Hilliard and Lewis Cole, *This Side of Glory* (Boston: Little, Brown, 1993), 212.
262. William Lutz and Harry Brent, eds., *On Revolution* (Cambridge: Winthrop Publishers, 1971), 223.
263. Cleaver, 'How TV Wrecked', 99.
264. Douglas, *Art for the People's Sake*, 123.
265. Hilliard, Interview.
266. Caldwell quoted in Elissa Auther and Adam Lerner, eds., *West of Center: Art and the Counterculture Experiment in America, 1965–1977* (Minneapolis: University of Minnesota Press, 2012),
267. Douglas, *Art for the People's Sake*, 123.
268. Ibid., 123–4.

Chapter 3   A Nation of Militants?

1. Hilliard, Interview and David Hilliard, Speech given at George Padmore Institute, London, 4 July 2008.
2. Jama Lazerow, 'Look Out Historians! Black Power's Gon' Get You', *Reviews in American History* 35 (2007), 126–32.

3. William Worthy, 'The Black Power Establishment', *Esquire*, November 1967, Box 31, File 16, SCMSS, 131.
4. Ibid.
5. Ibid.
6. Ibid.
7. Ibid.
8. Ibid.
9. Ibid.
10. Ibid.
11. Ibid.
12. Ibid.
13. Ibid., 132.
14. Ibid.
15. Ibid.
16. Ibid., 133.
17. Ibid., 132.
18. Ibid., 131.
19. Carol Polsgrove, *It Wasn't Pretty, Folks, But Didn't We Have Fun?: Esquire In the Sixties* (Oakland: RDR Books, 2001), 163.
20. William Worthy, 'Aftermath: A Negro Reporter's Dilemma', *Esquire*, 12 October 1967, 60.
21. Sterling Stuckey quoted in *Out of the Revolution: The Development of Africana Studies*, ed., Delores Aldridge and Carlene Young (Lanham: Lexington, 2003), 66.
22. W.E.B. Du Bois, 'The Talented Tenth' in *The Negro Problem*, ed., Booker T. Washington (1903), 33.
23. Ibid., 37.
24. Ibid., 38.
25. Ibid., 40.
26. Ibid., 43–4.
27. Ibid., 45.
28. Ibid.
29. Ibid., 54.
30. William H. Orrick, *Shut It Down! A College In Crisis* (June 1969), 151, 37–41.
31. Ibid., 39.
32. Ibid., 40.
33. Sarah Owen, 'Black Thursday, 40 Years Later', *The Northwestern*, 16 November 2008.
34. Sandra McCreary et al., 'Black Thursday 40 Years Later'. http://www.thenorthwestern.com/00:28–1:24, 2:43–4.00 (accessed 12 April 2009).
35. Milton Mitchell quoted in Owen, 'Black Thursday'.
36. Henry Brown quoted in 'UWO historians unveil "Black Thursday" exhibit', 17 November 2008. http://www.uwosh.edu/news/?p=1472 (accessed 12 April 2009).
37. Sandra McCreary, quoted in Owen, 'Black Thursday'.

38. Ibid.
39. Emily Cohn, 'Tom Jones Reflects on a "Selfless Revolution"', *The Cornell Daily Sun*, 16 April 2009. http://cornellsun.com/section/news/content/2009/04/16/tom-jones-reflects-selfless-revolution (accessed 16 April 2009).
40. Owen, 'Black Thursday'.
41. John Schuh quoted in Owen, 'Black Thursday'.
42. Hammer Housfeld quoted in Owen, 'Black Thursday'.
43. McCreary quoted in Owen, 'Black Thursday'.
44. Ibid.
45. Calvin Trillin, 'U.S. Journal: Oshkosh', *New Yorker*, 4 January 1969, 62–6.
46. McCreary quoted in Owen, 'Black Thursday'.
47. Harry Edwards, *Black Students* (1970), 163, 168–70.
48. Cohn, 'Tom Jones'.
49. George Lowery, 'A Campus Takeover that Symbolized An Era of Change', *Cornell Chronicle Online*, 16 April 2009. http://www.news.cornell.edu/stories/April09/StraightRevisited.gl.html (accessed 16 April 2009).
50. Ibid.
51. 'Universities Under the Gun: Militants at Cornell', *Newsweek*, 5 May 1969.
52. Appendix E.
53. Ibid.
54. Lucy Li, 'Snapshot in History: Remembering the Exit in Photos', *Cornell Daily Sun*, 16 April 2009, http://cornellsun.com/section/news/content/2009/04/16/snapshot-history-remembering-exit-photos (accessed 16 April 2009).
55. *San Francisco Examiner*, 4 May 1967: *Oakland Tribune*, 3 May 1967.
56. Rhodes, *Framing*, 76.
57. Ibid., 153.
58. Ibid.
59. Consider the recent 'All Power to the Imagination! 1968 and its Legacies' program, http://www.1968.org.uk (accessed 4 July 2008). Of the glut of recent works, Rhodes's *Framing the Black Panthers* is an excellent analysis of the presence of Panther iconography in the imagination of the American media.
60. Li, 'Snapshot'.
61. Ibid.
62. Ibid.
63. Ibid.
64. Cohn, 'Tom Jones'.
65. Ibid.
66. Ibid.
67. Cohn, 'Tom Jones'.
68. Hilliard, Padmore.
69. Lerone Bennett Jr., 'Confrontation on the Campus', *Ebony*, May 1968, 30.
70. Ibid., 32.
71. Ibid., 27.

72. Ibid.
73. Ibid., 27–8.
74. Ibid., 28.
75. 'Black Recognition Top Issue in Campus Protests', *Jet*, 29 January 1970, 53.
76. Ibid.
77. Ibid.
78. 'A Proposal to Institute A Black Study and Work Program at San Francisco State College' (1 March 1967) Box 31, File 14, SCMSS, 1.
79. Ernest Dunbar, 'The Black Revolt Hits the White Campus', *Look*, 31 October 1967, Box 31, File 16, SCMSS, 27.
80. Edwards, *Black Students*, 61.
81. 'A Proposal', 1.
82. Ibid.
83. Kofi Lomotey, ed., *Encyclopedia of African American Education* (2010), 301; 'A Proposal', 1.
84. James Turner, 'Black Nationalism', in *Topics in Afro-American Studies*, ed. Henry J. Richards (1971), 70–1.
85. 'A Proposal', 1.
86. Ibid.
87. Ibid.
88. Allan Kornberg and Joel Smith, '"It Ain't Over Yet": Activism in a Southern University,' in *Black Power and Student Rebellion*, ed., James McEvoy and Abraham Miller (1969), 107, 120.
89. Van Deburg, *New Day*, 69.
90. X, *By Any Means Necessary*,: 'A Proposal', 2.
91. S.E. Anderson, 'Toward Racial Relevancy: Militancy and Black Students', *Negro Digest*, September 1967, 13, 16.
92. John Oliver Killens, 'The Artist and the Black University', *Black Scholar* 1, no. 1 (November 1969), 63.
93. Preston Wilcox, 'Black Studies as an Academic Discipline', *Negro Digest*, March 1970, 85.
94. Anderson, 'Towards Racial Relevancy', 17.
95. Ibid.
96. Dunbar, 'The Black Revolt', 27.
97. 'A Proposal', 1.
98. Ibid.
99. Ibid.
100. Dunbar, 'The Black Revolt', 27.
101. Ibid.
102. Ibid.
103. Ibid.
104. 'A Proposal,' 1.
105. Dunbar, 'The Black Revolt', 27.
106. 'A Proposal', 2.

107. Dunbar, 'The Black Revolt', 28.
108. Ibid.
109. Ibid.
110. Ibid.
111. *Ethos Newsletter*, 12 October 1977. http://www.wellesley.edu/Activities/homepage/ethos/site/history.html (accessed 28 May 2009).
112. Ibid.
113. Richard. B.Markham, 'Blacks at Wellesley Discover Indifference Swallows Its Own Children', *The Harvard Crimson*, 19 December 1968.
114. Dunbar, 'The Black Revolt', 28.
115. Ibid.
116. 'A Proposal', 4.
117. Dunbar, 'The Black Revolt', 29.
118. Ibid.
119. Ibid.
120. Ibid.
121. Ibid., 30.
122. Ibid.
123. 'A Proposal', 3.
124. Dunbar, 'The Black Revolt', 30.
125. 'A Proposal', 3.
126. Madeline Johnson, 'Af-Am House to Host Rededication', *Yale Daily News*, 16 November 2007. http://www.yaledailynews.com/news/2007/nov/16/af-am-house-to-host-rededication/ (accessed 28 May 2009).
127. Van Deburg, *New Day*, 72.
128. Bennett, 'Confrontation,' 32.
129. Ibid.
130. Edwards, *Black Students*, 98.
131. Dunbar, 'The Black Revolt', 30.
132. Ibid.
133. Ibid.
134. Ibid.
135. Ibid., 30–1.
136. *Combined Black Youth Workshop, Proposal #2* (ca. 1967), Box 31, File 14, SCMSS.
137. Jimmy Garrett, *The Black Students' Union Philosophy and Goals* (ca. 1967) Box 31, File 14, SCMSS, 1.
138. Ibid.
139. Ibid.
140. Ibid.
141. Ibid.
142. Ibid.
143. Ibid.
144. Ibid.

145. Ibid.
146. Ibid.
147. Ibid.
148. Ibid., 2.
149. Andrew Billingsley, 'The Black Presence in American Higher Education', in *What Black Educators are Saying*, ed., Nathan Wright, Jr (1970), 126–7.
150. Ibid., 146.
151. Mike Thelwell, 'Black Studies: A Political Perspective', *Massachusetts Review* 10 (Autumn 1969). http://www.umass.edu/afroam/dthelwell.html (accessed June 2009).
152. Ibid.
153. Thelwell, 'Black Studies'; Ellison, *Invisible Man*, 103.
154. Turner, 'Black Nationalism', 69–75.
155. John W. Blassingame, 'Black Studies: An Intellectual Crisis,' *American Scholar* 38 (Autumn 1969), 551.
156. Arnold Hano, 'The Black Rebel Who "Whitelists" the Olympics', *New York Times Magazine*, 12 May 1968, 39.
157. Ibid., 39–40.
158. Larry Neal, Diary Excerpt, Box 3, File 14 (May 1968), SCMSS, 2.
159. John H. Johnson, 'Prefatory Notes – The Black University', *Negro Digest* (March 1970), 4.
160. Gerald A. McWorter, 'Struggle, Ideology and the Black University', *Negro Digest*, March 1969, 20; Robert S. Browne, 'Financing the Black University', in Wright, *Black Educators*, 85.
161. Preston Wilcox, 'On the Black University: Movement or Institution?' *Negro Digest*, December 1969, 22.
162. Lowe, 'Black University', 8.
163. Earle H. West, *The Black American and Education* (1972), 228.
164. Ibid.
165. Vincent Harding, 'Toward The Black University', *Ebony*, August 1970, 156.
166. Harding, 'Towards A Black University': Johnson, 'Prefatory Notes'.
167. Coretta Scott King, Announcement of the Martin Luther King Jr., Memorial Center, 15 January 1969.
168. Vincent Harding, 'New Creation or Familiar Death?' *Negro Digest*, March 1969, 14.
169. 'An Approach to Black Studies: Statement of the Planning Staff, Institute of the Black World, Martin Luther King Jr., Memorial Center', Box 31, File 14 (1969), SCMSS, 2.
170. Ibid.
171. Alex Poinsett, 'Think Tank for Black Scholars,' *Ebony*, February 1970, 46–8, 50, 52, 54.
172. Wilcox, 'Black University', 21.
173. 'Approach to Black Studies', 2.

174. Ibid.
175. Ibid.
176. Ibid.
177. Ibid., 3.
178. Ibid.
179. Ibid.
180. Ibid.
181. Ibid., 4.
182. Ibid.
183. Ibid.
184. Ibid.
185. Ibid.
186. Ibid.
187. Max Stanford, 'Black Nationalism and the Afro-american student', *Black Scholar* 2, no. 10 (June 1971) 28–31.
188. Eldridge Cleaver, 'Education and Revolution', *Black Scholar* 1 (November 1969), 50–1.

Chapter 4   'Dramas-of-Aggression': Black Power in Sports

1. David Roediger, *Colored White: Transcending the Racial Past* (Berkeley: University of California Press, 2002), 86.
2. Ibid.
3. Van Deburg, *New Day*, 83.
4. Dick Schaap, 'The Revolt of the Black Athletes', *Look*, 6 August 1968, 74.
5. Ernest Cashmore, *Black Sportsmen* (1982), 46–7.
6. For an overview of the cultural assumptions (both historical and current) surrounding African-American athleticism, see Gary Alan Sailes, 'The African-American Athlete: Social Myths and Stereotypes', in *African Americans in Sport: Contemporary Themes*, ed. Gary Alan Sailes (1998), 188; Patrick B. Miller, 'The Anatomy of Scientific Racism: Racialist Responses to Black Athletic Achievement', in *Sport and the Color Line*, ed. Patrick B. Miller and David K. Wiggins (2004), 327–44 and John Hoberman's *Darwin's Athletes* (1997) for a concise study of Western receptiveness to the idea of a biological basis for black athleticism, in particular 143–68. The media's perpetuation of this stereotype and its historical diversification is elucidated in Laurel R. Davis & Othello Harris, 'Race and Ethnicity in US Sports Media', in *Mediasport*, ed. Lawrence A. Wenner (1998), 154–69.
7. For a summary of the evolution of the quarterback myth and its transition into the contemporary opposition to African-American NFL coaches, see William Rhoden, '1st and Long', *Vibe*, November 1995, 37; Doug Williams with Bruce Hunter, *Quarterblack: Shattering the NFL Myth*

(1990); David K. Wiggins and Patrick B. Miller, eds., *The Unlevel Playing Field* (2003).
8. Montye Fuse and Keith Miller, 'Jazzing the Basepaths: Jackie Robinson and African-American Aesthetics', in *Sports Matters: Race, Recreation and Culture*, ed. John Bloom and Michael Nevin Willard (2002), 119.
9. Grantland Rice, *The Tumult and the Shouting: My Life in Sport* (1956), 248.
10. Fuse and Miller, 'Jazzing', 119–40; Jules Tygiel, *Baseball's Great Experiment* (1983).
11. Fuse and Miller, 'Jazzing', 120.
12. Mark Ribowsky, *The Complete History of the Negro Leagues* (1995), ix; Donn Rogosin, *Invisible Men: Life in Baseball's Negro Leagues* (2007); John Holway, *Voices from the Great Black Baseball Leagues* (1975), xiii.
13. Wilmer Fields, *My Life in the Negro Leagues* (1992), 67.
14. Tom Singer, 'Teddy Ballgame makes difference for Negro Leaguers to enter Hall', http://mlb.mlb.com/mlb/history/mlb_negro_leagues_story.jsp?story=williams_ted# (accessed 19 May 2010).
15. Ibid.
16. Larry Brown in Holway, *Voices*, 212, 213.
17. Cool Papa Bell in Holway, *Voices*, 111.
18. Satchel Paige quoted in Sandy Grady, 'The Return of Satchel Paige', *Baseball Digest*, October 1968, 34.
19. Buck Leonard in Holway, *Voices*, 263.
20. Ibid.
21. Art Rust Jr., *Get That Nigger Off the Field!* (1976), 41.
22. John Holway, *Black Ball Stars*, original typescript (1979), 1. For analysis of Negro League performance across the period 1902–46 see Appendix F.
23. Holway, *Ball Stars*, 1.
24. Forbes quoted in Holway, *Voices*, 4.
25. Ibid.
26. Dean quoted in Rust, *Get That Nigger*, 19.
27. Bruce Chadwick, *When The Game Was Black and White* (1992), 141–2.
28. Holway, *Black Ball*, 4.
29. Ibid., 5.
30. Ibid.
31. Gene Benson, 'Black Star of Philadelphia', in John Holway, *Black Diamonds* (1991), 71.
32. Cool Papa Bell in Holway, *Voices*, 119.
33. Ibid., 124.
34. Young in Ribowsky, *Complete History*, 247–8.
35. Bruce Johnson, 'Clowns of Baseball', *The Clown in Times* 6, no. 3 (2000).
36. Ibid.
37. Stroch quoted in Chadwick, *When The Game*, 46.
38. Renfroe in Holway, *Voices*, 341.
39. Fuse and Miller, 'Jazzing', 130.

40. Carl Rowan and Jackie Robinson, *Wait Till Next Year: The Life Story of Jackie Robinson* (1960), 107–9.
41. Chadwick, 167.
42. Jackie Robinson, *I Never Had It Made* (1972), 73.
43. Jackie Robinson and Wendell Smith, *Jackie Robinson: My Own Story* (1948), 12.
44. Sug Cornelius in Holway, *Voices*, x.
45. Chadwick, 167.
46. Rust, *Get That Nigger*, 38.
47. Red Barber, *When All Hell Broke Loose in Baseball* (1982), 304.
48. Bell quoted in Rust, *Get That Nigger*, 40–1. For other examples of Robinson underperforming in his early shortstop position see Newt Allen, Cool Papa Bell, Hilton Smith, and Othello Renfroe in Holway, *Voices*, 103, 128, 284, 292, 343–5.
49. Tygiel, *Great Experiment*, 190.
50. Roger Kahn, *The Boys of Summer* (1972), xix.
51. Paul Binder, quoted in Chadwick, 168
52. Larry Neal, *Black Boxing* (n.d.), Box 21, File 9, SCMSS, 1.
53. Ibid.
54. Ibid.
55. Ibid.
56. Ibid.
57. Ibid., 2.
58. Ibid., 3.
59. Ibid.
60. Ibid.
61. Al-Tony Gilmore, *Bad Nigger! The National Impact of Jack Johnson* (1975), 12.
62. Neal, *Black Boxing*, 5.
63. Nathan Hare, 'The Psychology of Great Black Boxers', *Ebony*, January 1977, 74.
64. Ibid.,
65. Ibid., 70.
66. Damon Runyan quoted in Jack Johnson, *Jack Johnson: In the Ring and Out* (1927), 14.
67. 'Muhammad Ali You're Still Our Champ', *BPINS*, 17 March 1971, 15.
68. Louie Robinson, 'Joe Louis At Sixty', *Ebony*, October 1973, 65.
69. Neal, *Black Boxing*, 6.
70. Gerald Early quoted in Hoberman, *Darwin's Athletes*, 88.
71. Chester L. Washington, 'Ches' Sez', *Pittsburgh Courier*, 29 February 1936, A5.
72. Thomas Sowell, *Pink and Brown People and Other Controversial Essays* (1981), 6.
73. Hare, 'Psychology', 72.
74. Dizzie Gillespie with Al Fraser, *To Be, Or Not . . . To Bop* (2009), 289.
75. Al Monroe, 'Joe Louis' Arrival In Camp Is Sports Epic', *Chicago Defender*, 15 February 1936, 10.

76. Wright quoted in Lewis A. Erenberg, *The Greatest Fight of Our Generation* (2006), 87.
77. Ibid.
78. William H. Wiggins, 'Joe Louis – American Folk Hero', in Miller and Wiggins, *Sport*, 138.
79. Ibid.
80. Neal, *Black Boxing*, 10.
81. Ibid.
82. Wiggins, *Louis*, 134.
83. Neal, *Black Boxing*, 10.
84. Ibid.
85. Ibid.
86. Ida Peters, 'When Joe Louis' Wife Came to Model', *Washington Afro-American*, 22 August 1978, 6.
87. Robinson, 'Joe Louis', 65.
88. Hare, *Psychology*, 70.
89. Lacy J. Banks, 'The Biggest Fight in History', *Ebony*, March 1971, 135.
90. National Endowment for the Arts, 'Arena Stage Takes a Risk on *The Great White Hope*', 2 February 2007. http://www.nea.gov/about/40th/greatwh.html (accessed 19 June 2009).
91. Howard Sackler, 'The Great White Hope [Revised First Draft]' (1969) Box 45, File 4, SCMSS.
92. Randy Roberts, *Papa Jack Johnson and the Era of White Hopes* (1983), 228.
93. Ken Burns, *Unforgivable Blackness* (2005).
94. Ibid.
95. Drew Brown quoted in Randy Roberts and James S. Olson, *Winning is the Only Thing* (1989), 173.
96. Neal, *Black Boxing*, 12.
97. Ibid.
98. Ibid.
99. Seymour Gray and Larry Neal, *Précis: Boxing as Drama* (n.d.), Box 21, File 18, SCMSS.
100. Ibid.
101. Ibid.
102. Ibid.
103. Banks, 'Biggest', 134.
104. Ibid., 135.
105. Banks, 'Biggest', 135; Kieran Mulvaney, *Ring History: Events That Shaped Madison Square Garden's Ring*, 2 October 2007. http://sports.espn.go.com/espn/print?id=3043786&type=story (accessed 23 June 2009).
106. Joe Frazier, 'Cassius Who?', *Ebony*, May 1972, 68.
107. Ibid., 70.
108. Gray and Neal, *Précis*.
109. Lacy J. Banks, 'Can Anybody Beat This Man?' *Jet*, 18 February 1971, 56.

110. Ibid.
111. Arkush, *Fight*, 193.
112. Frazier, 'Cassius', 68.
113. John Dower, *Thriller in Manila*, DVD (2008).
114. Frazier, 'Cassius', 71.
115. Ibid., 70.
116. Layding Lumumba Kaliba quoted in 'Readers Rap', *Jet*, 11 March 1971, 4.
117. Frazier, 'Cassius', 71.
118. Ibid., 76.
119. Hare, 'Psychology', 69.
120. Dower, *Thriller* (2008).
121. Frazier, 'Cassius', 72.
122. Ibid., 74.
123. Ibid.
124. Edwards quoted in Amy Bass, *Not the Triumph But the Struggle* (2002), 233.
125. Michael E. Lomax, ed., *Sports and the Racial Divide* (2008), 68.
126. Ibid., 69.
127. Mal Whitwell, 'Let's Boycott the Olympics!' *Ebony*, March 1964, 95–100.
128. Bass, *Not the Triumph*, 233.
129. Tommie Smith, *Silent Gesture* (2007), 173.
130. Brian Viner, 'Tommie Smith: "Hate was so entrenched in America, and it took lives"', *The Independent*, 13 October 2008.
131. Tommie Smith quoted in Peter Hossli, 'That Was My Decision', 8 August 2008, http://www.hossli.com/articles/2008/08/08/that-was-my-decision/ (accessed 22 May 2009).
132. Madison Gray, 'John Carlos: Looking Back at a Raised Fist and at a Raised Consciousness', *Time*, 16 October 2012. http://keepingscore.blogs.time.com/2012/10/16/john-carlos-looking-back-at-a-raised-fist-and-at-a-raised-consciousness/ (accessed November 2012).
133. Tommie Smith quoted in Erica McCrae, 'Tommie Smith Recalls His 1968 Olympic Protest', *Black College Wire*, http://www.blackcollegewire.org/index.php?option=com_ywp_blog&task=view&id=5593&Itemid=30 (accessed 7 July 2009).
134. Smith, *Silent*, 173.
135. Brad Herzog, 'Radical Thinker', *Cornell Alumni Magazine*, 11 July 2008, http://cornellalumnimagazine.com/index.php?option=com_content&task=view&id=161 (accessed 7 July 2009).
136. Lipsyte quoted in Herzog, 'Radical Thinker'.
137. Harry Edwards and Dennis Wyss, 'Fighting from the Inside', *Time*, 6 March 1989.
138. Angelou in Introduction, Harry Edwards, *The Struggle That Must Be* (1980), xiii.
139. Edwards, *Struggle*, 133, 146.

140. Ibid., 139.
141. Ibid., 145, 148.
142. Ibid., 148.
143. Harry Edwards, *The Revolt of the Black Athlete* (1969), 47.
144. Bass, *Not the Triumph*, 136; Dave Zirin, *What's my Name, Fool?* (2005), 74.
145. Edwards, *Revolt*, 58–9.
146. Herzog, 'Radical Thinker'.
147. Edwards, *Struggle*, 179; William L. Van Deburg, *Black Camelot* (1997), 119.
148. Herb Boyd and Robert L. Allen, eds., *Brotherman* (1995), 586; Edwards, *Struggle*, 185.
149. Edwards, *Struggle*, 178.
150. Edwards quoted in Douglas Hartmann, *Race, Culture, and the Revolt of the Black Athlete* (2003), 109.
151. Edwards quoted in Herzog, 'Radical Thinker'.
152. Edwards, *Revolt*, xvi.
153. Sports Illustrated Staff, *The Best of Sports Illustrated* (1990), 151.
154. 'Black Complaint', *Time*, 25 October 1968. http://www.time.com/time/magazine/article/0,9171,900397-1,00.html (accessed 8 July 2009).
155. Slava Malamud, 'George Foreman: Hunting Big George', *Sports Illustrated*, 17 August 2006, http://english.sport-express.ru/articles/9_18/ (accessed 22 May 2010).
156. Ibid.
157. Dave Zirin, 'An Interview with George Foreman', *Prince George's Post*, 7–9 November 2003. http://www.counterpunch.org/2003/11/07/an-interview-with-george-foreman/.
158. ABC Olympic host Chris Schenkel quoted in Bass, *Not the Triumph*, 241.
159. Kane quoted in Herzog, 'Radical Thinker.'
160. Jeremy Larner and David Wolf, 'Amidst Gold Medals, Raised Black Fists', *Life*, 1 November 1968, 63.
161. Ibid., 64C.
162. Zirin, *What's My Name?* 76; Brent Musburger quoted in Jeffrey Ogbonna Green Ogbar, *Black Power: Radical Politics and African American Identity* (2004), 119.
163. 'Black Complaint'.
164. Ibid.
165. Robert D. Clark, quoted in Mara Hoogerhuis, 'Why Here, Why Now? The Story of Student Protest on the University of Oregon Campus, April 1970' (PhD thesis, University of Oregon, 2004), 13–14.
166. Ibid., 14.
167. Edwards, *Struggle*, 241.
168. Ibid., 215.
169. Ibid., 248.
170. Edwards in Herzog, 'Radical Thinker'.
171. Tommy Smith quoted in Bass, *Not the Triumph*, 233.

Chapter 5   Behind Bars and Under Fire

1. Wallace Terry II, 'Bringing the War Home', *The Black Scholar* (November 1970), Box 32, File 7, SCMSS, 6.
2. Ibid.
3. Zalin Grant, 'The War and I'. http://www.pythiapress.com/letters/war.htm (accessed 23 May 2010).
4. Terry, 'Bringing the War', 6.
5. Ibid.
6. Edgar Huff quoted in Wallace Terry, *Bloods: An Oral History of the Vietnam War* (1984), 159.
7. Gene Woodley quoted in Terry, *Bloods*, 261.
8. Ibid.
9. Ibid.
10. Goldman, *Report*, 45, 230.
11. Eldridge Cleaver, 'To My Black Brothers In Vietnam', *BPINS*, 2 May 1970, http://www.hippy.com/php/article.php?sid=74 (accessed 5 August 2009).
12. Ibid.
13. Larry Burton in 'Letters', Ebony, December 1970, 24.
14. 'SNCC Position Paper: On Vietnam', quoted in James Forman, *The Making of Black Revolutionaries* (1997), 446.
15. Nathan Hare, 'We Are All Soldiers', *The Black Scholar* (November 1970), Box 32, File 7, SCMSS, 3.
16. 'Ebony Book Shelf', *Ebony*, August 1971, 26.
17. Eldridge Cleaver, 'The Black Man's Stake in Vietnam', in *Soul on Ice*, 119.
18. Appendix G.
19. See Gerard DeGroot, *A Noble Cause?: America and the Vietnam War* (2000).
20. Department of the Army, 'Information Paper: Blacks in the Vietnam Conflict', 3 March 1977 in Martin Binkin et al., *Blacks and the Military* (1982), 76.
21. Ibid.
22. Sol Stern, 'When the Black G.I. Comes Home from Vietnam', in *The Black Soldier*, eds. Elaine Crane and Jay David (1971), 221.
23. Binkin et al., *Blacks and the Military*, 77.
24. 'At the Ready in Vietnam', *U.S News & World Report*, 15 August 1966, 62.
25. Binkin, *Blacks*, 77.
26. For a full statistical break down, by year, of African-American casualties, see Appendix H.
27. Eldridge Cleaver, 'The Black Man's Stake', 120.
28. Robert F. Williams, *Listen, Brother!* (1968). http://www.aavw.org/protest/early_rfw_abstract18.html (accessed 5 August 2009).
29. Hare, 'We Are All Soldiers', 2.
30. Williams, *Listen, Brother!*
31. Ibid.
32. Ibid.
33. Ibid.

34. Ibid.
35. Ibid.
36. Richard Halloran, 'Air Force Racism Charged In Study', *New York Times*, 31 August 1971, 1, Col. 4, 6.
37. Ibid., 23, Col. 6.
38. Ibid.
39. Ibid.
40. Nina Mjagkij, ed., *Portraits of African American Life Since 1865* (2003), 224.
41. James E. Westheider, *The African American Experience in Vietnam* (2008), 51.
42. 'Progress Report 1967', *Ebony*, January 1968, 118.
43. Ibid.
44. Westheider, 48; Andrew J. Huebner, *The Warrior Image* (2008), 186.
45. Steven Morris, 'How Blacks Upset the Marine Corps', *Ebony*, December 1969, 55.
46. Ralph W. Donnelly and Henry I. Shaw, Jr., *Blacks in the Marine Corps* (1975), 69.
47. Morris, 'How Blacks', 58.
48. Ibid.
49. Binkin, *Blacks and the Military*, 34.
50. Mark Rosenman, 'The Negro and the Military', *The Crisis*, May 1967, 197.
51. Lawrence M. Baskir and William A. Strauss, *Chance and Circumstance: The Draft, the War and the Vietnam Generation* (1978), 126–31.
52. Ibid., 57.
53. Ibid.
54. Ibid.
55. Ibid.
56. Morris, 'How Blacks', 58.
57. Ibid., 60.
58. Ibid.
59. Burney and Wilson quoted in Westheider, *African American Experience*, 9–10.
60. Morris, 'How Blacks', 60.
61. Ibid.
62. Ibid.
63. 'Black Army Captain Freed in "Racism" Trial', *Jet*, 2 March 1972, 23.
64. Ibid.
65. Ibid.
66. Ibid.
67. Rhodes, *Framing*, 72.
68. Ibid.
69. Leo Carroll, *Hacks, Blacks and Cons* (1974), xi.
70. Malcolm X, *The Autobiography of Malcolm X*, 244–87.
71. Carroll, *Hacks*, 101–2.
72. Ibid., 105.
73. Ibid., 102.

74. Ibid.
75. Ibid.
76. Ibid.
77. See South Carolina Department of Correction, *The Emerging Rights of the Confined* (1972), Chapter 3.
78. Ibid., 62; Carroll, *Hacks*, 10.
79. Carroll, *Hacks*, 10.
80. Newton, *Revolutionary Suicide*, 282.
81. Huey Newton, 'Lonnie McLucas and the New Haven 9', in *To Die*, 230.
82. Huey Newton, 'I Found Freedom in Jail', *Ebony*, May 1973, 53.
83. Newton, *Revolutionary Suicide*, 1.
84. Jackson, *Soledad Brother*, 85.
85. Ibid., 50.
86. Lester Jackson, 'A Dialogue With My Soledad Son', *Ebony*, November 1971, 72.
87. Ibid.
88. Carroll, *Hacks*, 104.
89. 'What We Want, What We Believe', Newton, *Revolutionary Suicide*, 122–5.
90. Newton, 'Freedom in Jail', 54.
91. Newton, *Revolutionary Suicide*, 2.
92. Newton, 'Freedom in Jail', 58.
93. Bruce Jackson, *Get Your Ass in the Water and Swim Like Me* (London; repr., 2004), 3.
94. Carroll, *Hacks*, 106.
95. Ibid., 10.
96. Min S. Yee, *The Melancholy History of Soledad Prison* (1973), 126.
97. Donald Bogle, 'Black and Proud Behind Bars', *Ebony*, August 1969, 64–5.
98. Ibid., 65.
99. Ibid., 68.
100. Ibid., 65.
101. Ibid., 66.
102. Ibid., 70, 72.
103. Ibid., 68.
104. Ibid., 70.
105. Ibid., 72.
106. Ibid.
107. Carroll, *Hacks*, 91.
108. Ibid.
109. Ulf Hannerz, *Soulside* (1969; repr., 2004), 146.
110. Carroll, *Hacks*, 98.
111. Ibid.
112. Ibid., 99.
113. Ibid.
114. Ibid., 113.
115. Theodore Mead Newcomb, *Social Psychology* (1950), 227.

116. Carroll, *Hacks*, 111–12.
117. For an excellent commentary on the historical and historiographical changes in the perception of African-American prisoners see Helen Taylor Greene and Shaun L. Gabbidon, *African American Criminological Thought* (2000).
118. Ibid., 104.
119. Ibid., 110.
120. Etheridge Knight, *Black Voices from Prison* (1970), 123.
121. Ibid.
122. Ibid.
123. Ibid., 86–7.
124. Etheridge Knight, 'The Day the Young Blacks Came', in *Voices*, 164.
125. Ibid.
126. Ibid.
127. Ibid., 165.
128. Ibid.
129. Ibid.
130. Roberta Ann Johnson, 'The Prison Birth of Black Power', *Journal of Black Studies* 5, no. 4 (June 1975), 396.

Chapter 6   Chariots to the Stars

1. John Akomfrah, *The Last Angel of History*, Smoking Dogs Films, 1995. For further discussion on the origins and evolution of 'black secret technology' see Kodwo Eshun, *More Brilliant Than the Sun: Adventures in Sonic Fiction* (London: Quartet Books, 1998): Alondra Nelson, Thuy Linh N. Tu, Alicia Headlam Hines, eds., *Technicolor: Race, Technology, and Everyday Life* (New York: New York University Press, 2001): Arthur Kroker and Marilouise Kroker, eds. *Critical Digital Studies: a Reader* (Toronto: University of Toronto Press, 2008); Kin-yuen Wong, Gary Westfahl, Amy Kit-sze Chan, eds. *World Weavers: Globalization, Science Fiction, and the Cybernetic Revolution* (Hong Kong: Hong Kong University Press, 2005).
2. Tsutomu Noda quoted in John Wraight, 'Underground Resistance: Designs for a Sonic Revolution', *Straight No Chaser: Interplanetary Sounds: Ancient to Future* (Summer 1999), 28.
3. Alan Greenberg, *Love in Vain: A Vision of Robert Johnson* (New York: Da Capo Press, 1994), vii.
4. Wesley Brown, 'The Mojo and the Sayso: Myth and Ritual in the Work of Larry Neal' (14 November, 1981), Box 1, File 17, SCMSS.
5. Jimmy Klosterman, '6,557 Miles to Nowhere', *Spin* (December 2003), 116.
6. Sherman Alexie, *Reservation Blues* (New York: Warner Books, 1995).
7. For some recent selections, see Peter Meyer, *Can't You Hear the Wind Howl?* (Sweet Homes Pictures, 2011): Paul Sexton, *Hellhounds On His Trail – The Robert Johnson Story* (BBC Radio, 2005/2011): Chris Hunt, *The Search for Robert Johnson* (Sony Music, October 2000): Radio Lab, 'Crossroads', Monday, April 16, 2012. One of the best scholarly analyses available is Patricia R. Schroeder's,

Robert Johnson, Mythmaking, and Contemporary American Culture (Urbana: University of Illinois Press, 2004).
8. Greenberg, *Love in Vain*, vii.
9. Chris Hunt, *The Search For Robert Johnson*.
10. Peter Guralnick, *Searching for Robert Johnson* (London: Pimlico, 1998), 17.
11. Tom Freeland, *Robert Johnson: Some Witnesses to a Short Life in Living Blues*, 150, March/April 2000, 47.
12. Peter Meyer, *Can't You Hear the Wind Howl?*, Winstar, 24th November 1998.
13. Robert Palmer, *Deep Blues* (New York: Viking Press, 1981), 117.
14. Alan Lomax, The *Land Where The Blues Began* (London: Methuen, 1993), 424.
15. Gayle Dean Wardlow, *Chasin' That Devil Music: Searching for the Blues* (San Francisco: Miller Freeman Books, 1998), 197.
16. James H. Cone, *The Spirituals and the Blues: An Interpretation* (Maryknoll, New York: Orbis Books, 1991), 99.
17. Reverend LeDell Johnson quoted in David Evans, *Big Road Blues: Tradition and Creativity in the Folk Blues* (Berkeley: University of California Press, 1982), 115: Tom Graves, *Crossroads: The Life and Afterlife of Blues Legend Robert Johnson* (Demers Books, 2008), xvi.
18. Wardlow, *Chasin' That Devil Music*, 197.
19. Paul Trynka, *Portrait of the Blues* (London: Hamlyn, 1996), 38.
20. Gerhard Kubik, *Africa and the Blues* (Jackson: University Press of Mississippi, 1999), xv.
21. Nelson George, *Hip Hop America* (New York: Penguin, 2005): A Guy Called Gerald, *Black Secret Technology*, Juice Box Records, 1995.
22. *Tennis*, April 1990.
23. Rick Bragg, 'Court Rules Father of the Blues Has a Son', *New York Times*, June 17, 2000.
24. Ibid.
25. Bertram Barnes and Glen Wheeler, 'A Lonely Fork in the Road', *Living Blues*, 94 (November–December, 1990), 26.
26. Marcus Greil, *Mystery Train: Images of America in Rock 'n' Roll Music* (New York: Plume, 2008), 25.
27. Ibid.
28. Henry Louis Gates, Jr., *The Signifying Monkey: A Theory of African-American Literary Criticism* (New York: Oxford University Press, 1988), 5–6.
29. Christopher Douglas, Reciting *America: Culture and Cliché in Contemporary U.S. Fiction* (Urbana, University of Illinois Press, 2001), 55: Isidore Okpewho, Carole Boyce Davies and Ali A. Mazrui, eds., *The African Diaspora: African Origins and New World Identities* (Bloomington: Indiana University Press, 2001), 354.
30. Robert Palmer, *Deep Blues* (New York: Viking Press, 1981), 60.
31. Douglas, *Reciting America*, 55: Anthony B. Pinn, *The African American Religious Experience in America* (Westport, Greenwood Press, 2006), 219–21.
32. Jon Michael Spencer, *Blues and Evil* (Knoxville: University of Tennessee Press, 1993), 11.

33. Heather Russell, *Legba's Crossing: Narratology in the African Atlantic* (Athens: University of Georgia Press, 2009), 30.
34. Okpewho et al., *The African Diaspora*, 354.
35. Julio Finn, *The Bluesman: the Musical Heritage of Black Men and Women in the Americas* (New York: Quartet Books, 1986), 178–9.
36. 180
37. Lanre Bakare, 'Afrofuturism takes flight: from Sun Ra to Janelle Monáe', *Guardian*, 24 July 2014, https://www.theguardian.com/music/2014/jul/24/space-is-the-place-flying-lotus-janelle-monae-afrofuturism, (accessed 3 May 2016).
38. Ibid.
39. William Edward Burghardt Du Bois, *Darkwater: Voices from within the Veil* (New York: Harcourt, Brace & Howe, 1920).
40. Ibid., 253–73.
41. William Edward Burghardt Du Bois, 'The Comet', in *Darkwater: Voices from Beyond the Veil* (New York: Harcourt Brace and Howe, 1920), 254.
42. Ibid., 253.
43. Ibid., 254.
44. Ibid., 258
45. Ibid.
46. Ibid.
47. Ibid., 259.
48. Ibid., 262.
49. Ibid., 263–5.
50. Ibid., 253
51. Ibid., 259.
52. Ibid., 263.
53. Ibid., 260.
54. Ibid., 264.
55. Ibid., 268.
56. Ibid.
57. Ibid., 269.
58. Ibid., 270.
59. Ibid.
60. Ibid., 270–1.
61. Ibid., 272.
62. Ibid., 273.
63. 'W.E.B. Du Bois' "The Comet" and Contributions to Critical Race Theory: An Essay on Black Radical Politics and Anti-Racist Social Ethics', *Ethnic Studies Review: Journal of the National Association for Ethnic Studies* 29, 1 (2006), 26.
64. Du Bois, 'The Souls of Black Folks' in *Three Negro Classics*, 214.
65. Ronald R. Sundstrom, 'The Prophetic and Pragmatic Philosophy of 'Race' in WEB Du Bois's "The Comet"', *APA Newsletter on Philosophy and the Black Experience* 99, no. 1 (Fall 1999), 2.

66. John Clute and Peter Nicholls, *The Encyclopedia of Science Fiction* (London: Orbit, 1993), 947.
67. Sam Moskowitz, *Strange Horizons: The Spectrum of Science Fiction* (New York: Charles Scribner's Sons. 1976), 68–9.
68. For a starting point, see Andrea L. Bell and Yolanda Molina-Gavilan, eds., *Cosmos Latinos: An Anthology of Science Fiction from Latin America and Spain* (Middletown: Wesleyan University Press, 2003): Sheree R. Thomas, ed., *Dark Matter: A Century of Speculative Fiction from the African Diaspora* (New York: Warner Aspect, 2001).
69. Gary G. Wolfe, 'Coming to Terms' in Matthew Candelaria and James Gunn, eds., *Speculations on Speculation. Theories of Science Fiction* (Lanham: Scarecrow Press, 2005), 19.
70. Samuel R. Delany, *Dhalgren* (New York: Bantam Books, 1974).
71. Sun Ra/John Coney, *Space is the Place*, DVD, 1974: Rerelease: Plexi Film, January 2005.
72. Black Audio Film Collective, *The Last Angel of History* (1997). Distributed by LUX London, 2011.
73. Octavia E. Butler, *Kindred* (Garden City, New York: Doubleday, 1979).
74. Mike Banks quoted in Wraight, 'Underground Resistance'.
75. Julianne Burton, *The New Latin American Cinema: an Annotated Bibliography of Sources in English, Spanish, and Portuguese, 1960–1980* (New York: Smyrna Press, 1983): Patricia Aufderheide, 'Latins, Exiles, U.S. Chicanos Attend Havana's Film Fest', *Variety*, December 19, 1979.
76. John Akomfrah, *Handsworth Songs* (Black Audio Film Collective, 1987).
77. Akomfrah quoted in Catlina Ribalta, 'John Akomfrah – Being the Director Who Combines Politics and a Mystical Feeling for Film', *New Internationalist* (April 1998), 33.
78. Lester Friedman, ed., *Fires Were Started: British Cinema and Thatcherism* (London: Wallflower, 2006), 127–31.
79. John Akomfrah, *Sevens Songs for Malcolm X* (Smoking Dogs Films, 1993): John Akomfrah, *Martin Luther King – Days of Hope* (Smoking Dogs Films, 1997).
80. Akomfrah quoted in Ribalta, 'John Akomfrah', 33.
81. William Worthy, 'The Black Power Establishment', *Esquire*, November 1967, Box 31, File 16, SCMSS, 131.
82. Michael Chanan, 'Latin American Cinema: From Underdevelopment to Postmodernism' in in Stephanie Dennison and Song Hwee Lim, eds., *Remapping World Cinema: Identity, Culture and Politics* (London: Wallflower Press, 2006).
83. Akomfrah quoted in Ribalta, 'John Akomfrah', 33.
84. Paul Gilroy, *The Black Atlantic: Modernity and Double Consciousness* (Cambridge: Harvard University Press, 1993).
85. Ibid.
86. John Akomfrah, *The Last Angel of History* (Black Audio Film Collective, 1997).

87. Mark Dery, 'Black to the Future: Interviews with Samuel R. Delany, Greg Tate, and Tricia Rose' in Mark Dery ed., *Flame Wars: The Discourse of Cyber Culture* (Durham: Duke University Press, 1994), 180.
88. Akomfrah, *The Last Angel of History*: Dagmar Buchwald, 'Black Sun Underground: The Music of AlieNation' in Hanjo Berressem, Michael Bucher and Uwe Schwagmeier eds., *Between Science and Fiction: The Hollow Earth as Concept and Conceit* (Berlin: Lit Verlag, 2012), 121–2.
89. Ishmael Reed quoted in 'Space Children: from Dr. Funkenstein to the Archandroid', British Library, 18 June 2011.
90. Black Audio Film Collective, *The Last Angel of History* (1997).
91. Tobias Rapp, 'Underground Resistance', http://www.re-forma.ro/underground-resistance/ (accessed 5 May 2014).
92. Dan Sicko, *Techno Rebels: the Renegades of Electronic Funk* (New York: Billboard Books, 1999), 95–120.
93. Sven von Thülen, "Underground Resistance: Interstellar Fugitives." *De:Bug Magazin*, vol. 109 (February). http://www.de-bug.de/mag/4638.html (accessed 18 February 2009).
94. Rapp, 'Underground Resistance.'
95. Beverly May, 'Techno' in Mellonee V. Burnim and Portia K. Maultsky eds., *African American Music: An Introduction* (New York: Routledge, 2006), 347.
96. Ibid., 331, 333.
97. Sean Albiez, 'Post Soul Futurama: African American cultural politics and early Detroit Techno', *European Journal of American Culture*, Vol 24. No 2 (2005), 146.
98. Sicko, *Techno Rebels*, 60.
99. David Cantwell, '"Detroit City": The anatomy of a record', *The Journal of Country Music*, Vol 23.2 (2003), 43.
100. Jerry Herron, *AfterCulture: Detroit and the Humiliation of History* (Detroit: University of Michigan Press, 1993), 203.
101. For a fuller examination of the process see Susan Welch, Lee Sigelman, Timothy Bledsoe, and Michael Combs, *Race and Place: Race Relations in an American City* (Cambridge: Cambridge University Press, 2001): Mike Rubin, 'Techno: Days of Future Past' in Peter Shapiro, ed., *Modulations: A History of Electronic Music – Throbbing Words on Sound* (New York: Caipirinha Productions, 2000), 112.
102. Kodwo Eshun quoted in Black Audio Film Collective, *The Last Angel of History* (1997).
103. Wraight, 'Underground Resistance', 22.
104. *Requiem for Detroit* (BBC, 2013): Matthew Collin, 'Detroit: the Rebirth of a Techno Utopia', http://www.theguardian.com/music/2014/jun/05/detroit-rebirth-techno-utopia-kevin-saunderson-derrick-may-carl-craig-richie-hawtin (accessed 10 May 2014).
105. Wraight, 'Underground Resistance', 29.

106. Ibid.
107. Ibid.
108. Ibid., 23.
109. Ibid., 22.
110. Ibid.
111. Thomas Meinecke, *Hellblau* (Frankfurt a.M.: Suhrkamp Verlag, 2001) 21 (Trans. Christoph Schaub).
112. Sven von Thülen, 'Mike Banks über Underground Resistance', *De:Bug Magazin*, vol. 109 (February). http://www.de-bug.de/mag/4639.html (accessed 8 May 2014 via web.archive.org).
113. Jon Connell and Chris Gibson, *Sound Tracks: Popular Music, Identity and Place* (London: Routledge, 2003), 160.
114. Albiez, 'Post-soul', 2.
115. Sean Albiez, 'Sounds of Future Past: from Neu! to Numan' in Thomas Phleps and Ralf Von Appen eds., *Pop Sounds: Klangtexturen in der Pop und Rockmusik* (Bielefeld, Germany: Transcript-Verlag, 2003).
116. For some indicative, if problematic discussion of the racial dimension of techno, see Stuart Cosgrove, 'Seventh City Techno', *The Face*, 97 (May 1988), 88: Juan Atkins offers a more contemporary perspective in Mike Shallcross, 'From Detroit to Deep Space', *The Wire*, 161 (July 1997), 21.
117. Suburban Knight, *By Night EP* (UR-036, 12", EP, 1996).
118. Underground Resistance, *Interstellar Fugitives* (UR-045, 1998).
119. Underground Resistance, *World 2 World* (UR20, 1992).
120. Wraight, 'Underground Resistance', 23.
121. Ibid., 24.
122. Ralph Ellison, *Invisible Man* (1952; repr., 1999): David Bradley, *The Chaneysville Incident* (1981): Larry Neal, 'Uncle Rufus Raps on the Squared Circle', *Partisan Review* 39, no. 1 (1972), 45: Adrienne Crew, 'P-Afrofuturism', 16 July 2011, Online at http://hilobrow.com/2011/07/16/p-afrofuturism-1/: Janelle Monae, 'The ArchAndroid', http://www.jmonae.com/album/archandroid
123. Joel Sternfeld, 'Warren Avenue at 23rd Street, Detroit, Michigan' (1993) from *On This Site: Landscape in Memoriam* (San Francisco, Chronicle Books, 1996), 71.
124. Banks quoted in Jimmy Coultas and Alun Johnson, 'Underground Resistance', http://www.plasticsoup.com/article.php?id=17 (accessed 12 May 2014).
125. Wraight, 'Underground Resistance', 22.
126. Stuart Cosgrove, Liner Notes to *Techno! – the new dance sound of Detroit*, 10 Records, DIXCD 75 (1988).
127. X-101, *Whatever Happen To Peace* (UR-013, 1991).
128. Wraight, 'Underground Resistance', 22.
129. Suburban Knight, 'Maroon', *Interstellar Fugitives*, 1:27–2:27.
130. Albiez, 'Post-soul', 12.

131. Banks quoted in Coultas and Johnson, 'Underground Resistance'.
132. Wendy S. Walters, 'Blackness in Present Future Tense: Broadside Press, Motown Records, and Detroit Techno', in Lisa Gail Collins and Margo Natalie Crawford, eds., *New Thoughts on the Black Arts Movement* (New Brunswick, NJ: Rutgers University Press, 2006), 130.
133. Cedric J. Robinson, *Black Marxism. The Making of the Black Radical Tradition* (Chapel Hill: The University of North Carolina Press, 2000), 171.
134. Bank quoted in Thulen, 'Mike Banks Uber Underground Resistance'.
135. Mark Sinker, 'Loving the Alien', *The Wire*, 96 (February 1992). http://www.thewire.co.uk/out/0598_1.html.
136. Mark Antony Neal, *Songs in the Key of Black Life: A Rhythm and Blues Nation* (London: Routledge, 2003), 13.
137. Jana Evans Braziel and Anita Mannur, *Theorizing Diaspora* (Malden, Blackwell Publishing, 2006), 49: Gilroy, *The Black Atlantic*.
138. Steve Goodman, *Sonic Warfare: Sound, Affect, and the Ecology of Fear* (London: MIT Press, 2010), 2.
139. Ibid., 26.
140. Banks quoted in Coultas and Johnson, 'Underground Resistance'.
141. Mark Fisher, 'MikeRe-a2 Banks Interview.' *Wire*, vol. 285 (November 2007). http://www.thewire.co.uk/articles/271/ (accessed 8 May 2014).
142. For recent examples of the impact and influence of Detroit techno on the community, see: *Requiem for Detroit* (BBC, 2013): Collin, 'Detroit: the Rebirth of a Techno Utopia'.
143. Mark Fisher, 'MikeRe-a2 Banks Interview.' *Wire*, vol. 285 (November 2007). http://www.thewire.co.uk/articles/271/ (accessed 8 May 2014).
144. Simon Reynolds, 'Wargasm: Military Imagery in Pop Music', *Frieze*, 28, May 1996. http://www.frieze.com/issue/article/wargasm/ (accessed September 2013).
145. Ibid.
146. Ibid.
147. Immanuel Maurice Wallerstein, *After Liberalism* (New York: New Press, Distributed by W.W. Norton, 1995), 184.
148. United States Congress House Committee on Education and Labor, Extension of Elementary and Secondary Education Programs: Hearings, Ninety-first Congress, first session, on H.R. 514, U.S. Govt. Print. Off., 1969, 2433.
149. Mike Davis, *City of Quartz: Excavating the Future in Los Angeles* (London: Verso, 2006): *The Ecology of Fear: Los Angeles and the Imagination of Disaster* (London: Picador, 2000): *Planet of Slums* (New York: Verso, 2007).
150. Akomfrah, *The Last Angel*.
151. Ibid.
152. Ibid.
153. Eshun, 'Further Considerations of Afrofuturism', 294.
154. Akomfrah, *The Last Angel*.
155. Ibid.

156. Ibid.
157. Ibid.
158. Ibid.
159. Greg Tate quoted in Dery, 'Black to the Future.'
160. Dery, 'Black to the Future', 210–11. Akomfrah, *The Last Angel*.
161. Nona Hendryx at 'Space Children: from Dr. Funkenstein to the Archandroid', British Library, 18 June 2011.
162. Black Audio Film Collective, *The Last Angel of History* (1997).
163. Derrick Bell, *The Space Traders* (1992). Online at http://edweb.tusd.k12.az.us/uhs/APUSH/1st%20Sem/Articles%20Semester%201/Artiles%20Semester%201/Bell.htm.
164. Ibid., 11.
165. John Sayles, *The Brother From Another Planet* (Optimum Releasing, 1984: DVD, MGM 2003).
166. Roger Ebert, 'The Brother from Another Planet', *Chicago Sun Times*, 1 January 1984. Online at http://rogerebert.suntimes.com/apps/pbcs.dll/article?AID=/19840101/REVIEWS/401010318/1023.
167. John F. Kennedy, 'Address Before a Joint Session of Congress, 25 May 1961'. Online at http://www.jfklibrary.org/Asset-Viewer/xzw1gaeeTES6khED14P1Iw.aspx.
168. Akomfrah, *The Last Angel*.
169. Ibid.
170. Ibid.
171. Nicolas quoted in Margaret A. Weitekamp, 'More Than "Just Uhura": Understanding Star Trek's Lt. Uhura, Civil Rights, and Space History' in Nancy R. Reagin, ed., *Star Trek and History* (Hoboken: Wiley, 2013), 31.
172. Ibid.
173. Nicholas in Weitekamp, 'More Than', 30: Nichols quoted in Carrie Rickey, 'Star Recruiter', *The Philadelphia Inquirer*, December 12, 1986. http://articles.philly.com/1986-12-12/news/26068888_1_space-program-nasa-john-yardley (accessed 6 September 2013).
174. Nichols quoted in Akomfrah, *The Last Angel*.
175. Nichols quoted in Weitekamp, 'More Than', 32.
176. Neil DeGrasse Tyson, Startalk Radio Show, 'NASA and Nichelle Nichols', July 18 2011. http://www.startalkradio.net/show/nasa-and-nichelle-nichols/.
177. Hendryx at 'Space Children.'
178. Ibid.
179. Ibid.
180. Clinton at 'Space Children.'
181. Ibid.
182. Ibid.
183. Dave Marsh, *George Clinton and P-Funk: An Oral History* (New York: Avon, 1994), 97.

184. Temporary Services, *Group Work* (New York: Printed Matter, 2007): Adrienne Crew, 'P-Afrofuturism', 16 July 2011, Online at http://hilobrow.com/2011/07/16/p-afrofuturism-1/.
185. Bell quoted in Christopher R. Weingarten, *It Takes A Nation of Millions To Hold Us Back* (New York: Continuum, 2010).
186. Will Hermes, 'Back in the Day', *Spin* (October 2002), 119.
187. Adrienne Crew, 'P-Afrofuturism'.
188. George Clinton at 'Space Children: from Dr. Funkenstein to the Archandroid', British Library, 18 June 2011: Emmett G. Price III, Tammy L. Kernodle and Horace J. Maxile Jr. eds., *Encyclopedia of African-American Music*, Vol.3 (Santa Barbra, ABC-CLIO, 2012), 345.
189. Clinton quoted in Carmen Renee Thompson, 'Brushes with Greatness', *Vibe* (August 2003), 56.
190. George Clinton, *America Eats Its Young* (Westbound Records, 1972).
191. Pedro Bell, Liner Notes of George Clinton, *Greatest Funkin' Hits* (Capitol CDP 724383391127).
192. Ibid.
193. Ibid.
194. Vibe article
195. Larry Neal, *Hoodoo Hollerin' Bebop Ghosts* (Howard University Press Washington D.C., 1968). 13.
196. Rafael Torrubia, 'Slavery, Symbols and Song – The Importance of the African-American Slave Spiritual in the Civil Rights Protest Songs of the 1960s', 24.
197. Mothership Connection (Star Child), *Mothership Connection*, December 15, 1975, Casablanca NBLP 7022.
198. Black Audio Film Collective, *The Last Angel of History* (1997).
199. For some of Bell's influences see Jane Austen, Randy Lancelot and James Porter, 'P-FUNK (Pedro Bell Interview)', *Roctober*, 11, 1994: Abdel Shakur, 'George Clinton's Funky Drawers: Pedro Bell', June 12, 2008. http://misstraknowitall.blogspot.co.uk/2008/06/george-clintons-funky-drawers-pedro.html (accessed 6 September 2013).
200. George Clinton, *Funkadelic* (1970, Westbound W-2000).
201. Adrienne Crew, 'P-Afrofuturism'.
202. Erich von Däniken, *Chariots of the Gods?: Unsolved Mysteries of the Past* (London: Souvenir, 1969).
203. Lightning quoted at 'Space Children.'
204. Hendryx quoted at 'Space Children.'
205. Caterine Milinaire and Carol Troy, *Cheap Chic: Hundreds of Money Saving Hints to Create Your Own Great Look* (New York: Harmony Books, 1976. Reprint, New York: Three Rivers Press, 2015), 301–5.
206. Caterine Milinaire and Carol Troy, *Cheap Chic* (London: Omnibus Press, 1975), 150.
207. Hendryx at 'Space Children.'

208. George Clinton at 'Space Children.'
209. Ibid.
210. Ibid.
211. Ibid.
212. Ibid.
213. Ibid.
214. *Rolling Stone*, 3 July 1975: Patti LaBelle with Laura B. Randolph, *Don't Block the Blessings: Revelations of a Lifetime* (New York: Riverhead Books, 1996), 265: John Clemente, *Girl Groups: Fabulous Females That Rocked the World* (Iola: Krause Publications, 2000), 54–6.
215. Patti Labelle and Nona Hendryx, *Nightbirds* (New Orleans: Epic Records, 1974).
216. Hendryx quoted at 'Space Children.'
217. Ann Powers, 'Labelle was always more than a "Lady"', *Los Angeles Times*, 12 October 2008.
218. Ibid.
219. Ibid.
220. Ibid
221. Ibid.
222. Ibid.
223. Ibid.
224. Ibid.
225. Ibid.
226. Clinton quoted at 'Space Children.'
227. Chris Richards, 'Smithsonian acquires Parliament-Funkadelic Mothership', *Washington Post*, 19 May 2011. Online at http://www.washingtonpost.com/lifestyle/style/smithsonian-acquires-parliament-funkadelic-mothership/2011/05/18/AFHMvj6G_story.html.
228. Ibid.
229. Richards, 'In Maryland.'
230. Ibid.
231. Ibid.
232. Ibid.
233. Richards, 'Smithsonian.'
234. Clinton at 'Space Children.'
235. Ibid.
236. Hendryx at 'Space Children.'
237. Clinton at 'Space Children.'
238. Monae at 'Space Children.'
239. Black Audio Film Collective, *The Last Angel of History* (1997).
240. Lightning quoted at 'Space Children.'
241. Aberjhani and Sandra L. West, eds., *Encyclopedia of the Harlem* Renaissance (New York: Checkmark Books, 2003), 82–3.
242. Leslie Hewitt, 'Cauleen Smith', *Bomb Magazine*, 116, Summer 2011.

243. Nisi Shawl 'Deep End' in Nalo Hopkinson & Uppinder Mehan, eds., *So Long Been Dreaming: Postcolonial Science Fiction & Fantasy* (Vancouver: Arsenal Pulp Press, 2004).
244. Nisi Shawl 'Deep End' in Hopkinson and Mehan, eds., *So Long Been Dreaming*, 13.
245. William Gibson, *Burning Chrome and Other Stories* (London: Harper Collins, 1995), 186.

Chapter 7 Culture from the Midnight Hour

1. Larry Neal, 'Any Day Now: Black Art and Black Liberation' (ca. 1969) Box 6, File 2, SCMSS, 1.
2. Ibid., 1–2.
3. Ibid., 2–3.
4. Ibid.
5. Ibid.
6. Ibid.
7. Ibid., 4.
8. Ibid., 5.
9. W.E.B. Du Bois, *The Souls of Black Folk* (1903) in *Three Negro Classics*, 215.
10. Neal, 'Any Day', 5.
11. Neal, 'Any Day', 9.
12. Ibid., 10.
13. Ibid.
14. Ibid.
15. Ibid., 12.
16. Ibid.
17. Ibid.
18. Ibid.
19. Ibid., 12–13.
20. Ibid., 13.
21. Ibid.
22. Ibid., 14
23. Ibid., 14, 21.
24. LeRoi Jones, 'Black Art', *Black World*, June 1973, 17.
25. James Brown, 'There Was A Time', *Soul on Top*, Decca, 2004; Gylan Kain, 'The Shalimar', *Right On!*, The Last Poets, 1968, 1:02–1:15.
26. Stephen Evangelist Henderson, *Understanding the New Black Poetry* (1973), 348.
27. Jones and Neal eds., *Black Fire* (1968), 337.
28. Ibid.
29. Arthur Pfister quoted in Neal, 'Any Day', 19.
30. Smokey Robinson and the Miracles, *Tears of a Clown*, Tamla-Motown, TMG 745, 1967.

31. Neal, 'Any Day', 19.
32. Keorapetse 'Willie' Kgositsile, 'Toward a Walk in the Sun', in *My Name Is Afrika* (1971), 65.
33. Ibid., 65–6.
34. 'Niggers are Scared of Revolution!' *The Last Poets*, The Last Poets (1970).
35. Neal, 'Any Day', 20.
36. Ibid.
37. Ibid., 23.
38. Baraka quoted in Christopher Funkhouser 'LeRoi Jones, Larry Neal, and "The Cricket": Jazz and Poets' Black Fire', *African American Review* 37, no. 2/3 (Summer – Autumn, 2003), 238.
39. Neal, 'Any Day', 23.
40. Ibid.
41. Ibid.
42. Ibid., 24.
43. Ibid.
44. Ibid.
45. Ibid.
46. Ibid., 25.
47. Ibid.
48. Ibid.
49. Jeff Donaldson, '10 In Search of a Nation', *Black World*, October 1970, 86.
50. Ibid., 85.
51. http://www.blockmuseum.northwestern.edu/wallofrespect/main.htm (accessed 29 June 2010); Larry Neal, 'The Mighty Wall' (n.d.) Box 6, File 36, SCMSS.
52. Don L. Lee, 'The Wall' in Alan W. Barnett, *Community Murals: The People's Art* (1984) 52.
53. Neal, 'Any Day', 25.
54. Ibid.
55. Ibid., 26.
56. Ibid., 28.
57. Williams, *Listen Brother!*.
58. Tom Pendergast and Sara Pendergast, *Contemporary Black Biography* (2006), 71; David Henderson, *Felix of the Silent Forest* (1967).
59. David Henderson, *Keep on Pushing* (1964) Box 42, File 7, SCMSS, 1.
60. Ibid., 2.
61. Ibid., 3.
62. Ibid.
63. Ibid., 5.
64. Ibid., 6.
65. Ibid.
66. Ibid., 7.
67. Ibid.

68. Ibid., 8.
69. Clay Goss, *This Way Before* (1970) Box 42, File 1, SCMSS, 2.
70. Ibid.
71. Ibid.
72. Ibid., 3.
73. Ibid.
74. Ibid.
75. Ibid., 4.
76. Ibid.
77. Ibid.; 'Hot R&B Sides', *Billboard*, 27 July 1959, 46.
78. Goss, *This Way*, 5.
79. Larry Neal, 'Conquest of the South' (ca. 1970), SCMSS, Box 6, File 23, 1–2.
80. Neal, 'Conquest', SCMSS, 3.
81. Rafael Torrubia, 'Slavery, Symbols and Song', M.Litt Thesis, St. Andrews University, 2006.
82. Neal, 'Conquest', 4.
83. Ibid., 5.
84. Ibid., 6.
85. 'Report from the Free Southern Theater' (ca.1964), mz024, University of Southern Mississippi MSS, 1.
86. John O'Neal, 'Motion in the Ocean: Some Political Dimensions of the Free Southern Theatre', *The Drama Review* 12, no. 4 (Summer 1968), 70.
87. Eric Nakamura, 'Farm Working to Organizing', *Giant Robot*, Spring 1998, 73.
88. Carl Heyward, 'El Teatro Campesino: An Interview with Luis Valdez', http://www.communityarts.net/readingroom/archivefiles/2002/09/el_teatro_campe.php (accessed 14 August 2009).
89. Douglas, 'Art for the People's Sake', 122.
90. Neal, 'Conquest', 6.
91. Thomas C. Dent, Richard Schechner and Gilbert Moses, eds., *The Free Southern Theater* (1969), 3–4.
92. Ibid., 4.
93. Ibid.
94. O'Neal, 'Motion', 76.
95. Hughes, 'The Negro Artist'; Johnson, 'Introduction' in *Ebony and Topaz*, 11–12.
96. Morris, *Origins*, v.
97. Dent et al., *FST*, 4–5.
98. Neal, 'Conquest', 9.
99. O'Neal, 'Motion', 76.
100. Dent et al., *FST*, 67–8.
101. Cha Jua quoted in Rachel Breunlin, 'The Legacy of the Free Southern Theater in New Orleans: Interviews with Karen-Kaia Livers and Chakula Cha Jua', http://www.nathanielturner.com/legacyfreesouttheater.htm (accessed 6 November 2009).

102. John O'Neal, 'Free Southern Theatre: Living in the Danger Zone', *Black Scholar* 10 (July–August 1979), 12.
103. Thomas C. Dent, 'The Ghetto of Desire' (ca.1965), Box 41, File 25, SCMSS, 3.
104. O'Neal, 'Motion', 72.
105. Dent, quoted in Neal, 'Conquest', 10.
106. Neal, 'Conquest', 12.
107. O'Neal, 'Motion', 75.
108. Ibid., 76.
109. Dent et al., *FST*, 8, 233.
110. Ibid., 12.
111. O'Neal, 'Performing', 47.
112. Ibid.
113. Ibid.
114. Neal, 'Conquest', 8.
115. Ibid.
116. Hilliard, Interview.
117. O'Neal, 'Danger Zone', 12.
118. S.E. Anderson, 'Tricks and Toys', Box 7, File 23, SCMSS, 1.
119. Ibid., 2.
120. Ibid., 4.
121. Ibid.
122. Ibid.
123. Lauren Berlant, *Anatomy of a National Fantasy* (Chicago: University of Chicago Press, 1991), 20.
124. Wendy Kozol, *America: Family and Nation in Postwar Photojournalism* (Philadelphia: Temple University Press, 1994), 154: 'The Media and the Movement: An Interview with Richard Valeriani', in Juan Williams, ed., *Eyes on the Prize: America's Civil Rights Year, 1954–1965* (New York: Viking, 1987), 270.
125. Anderson, 'Tricks', 5.
126. Rhodes, *Framing*, 162.
127. Anderson, 'Tricks', 5.
128. Edward Jay Epstein, *Between Fact and Fiction: The Problem of Journalism* (New York: Vintage Books, 1975), 182–209.
129. Anderson, 'Tricks', 6.
130. Ibid.; Flannagan, *Amber Satyr*, 4–12.
131. Anderson, 'Tricks', 6.
132. Ibid., 6–7.
133. Ibid., 7.
134. Ibid.
135. Ibid.
136. Ibid.
137. Melvin Van Peebles quoted in Larry Neal, 'Interview with Melvin Van Peebles', Box 26, File 6, SCMSS (n.d.), 1.

138. Ibid.
139. Ibid.
140. Ibid.
141. Ibid., 3.
142. Cheo Tyehimba, *Panthermania*, 2006, online at http://www.iveknownrivers.org/read-2.0.php?id=124 (accessed 17 June 2013).
143. Ibid., 4.
144. Ibid.
145. Diane Williams quoted in 'Who Holds the Power in Hollywood?' *The Crisis*, February/March 1996, 12.
146. Lee Beaupree, 'One-Third Film Public: Negro: Columbia and UA Pitch for Biz', *Variety*, 29 November 1967, 3.
147. Clarence Lusane, 'To Fight For the People: The Black Panther Party and Black Politics in the 1990s', in Charles E. Jones, ed. *The Black Panther Party Reconsidered* (Baltimore: Black Classic Press, 1998), 445.
148. Donald Bogle, *Toms, Coons, Mulattoes, Mammies & Bucks* (2003), 241.
149. Ibid., 241–2.
150. Ibid., 242.
151. Ibid. See also James B. Stewart's, 'Political Commentary in Black Popular Music from Rhythm and Blues to Early Hip Hop', *Journal of African American History* 90, no. 3 (Summer, 2005), 196–225 which argues that Blaxploitation films not only corrupted the community's image, but also its music.
152. *BPINS*, 7 October 1972, 9; David Henderson, ed. *Umbra* (1971), Box 33, File 13, SCMSS.
153. Jules Dassin quoted in Richard Severo, 'Jules Dassin, Filmmaker on Blacklist, Dies at 96', *New York Times*, 1 April 2008, http://www.nytimes.com/2008/04/01/movies/01dassin.html?_r=2&ref=obituaries&oref=slogin (accessed 11 November 2009).
154. Ibid.
155. Ebert, Review 'Up Tight'.
156. Ibid.
157. Ibid.
158. Ibid.
159. Ibid.
160. Ibid.
161. Ibid.
162. Ibid.
163. Melvin Van Peebles, *Sweet Sweetback's BaadAsssss Song*, Bfi Video, 1971.
164. Charles Henry, *Culture and African-American Politics* (1990), 93.
165. Ibid.
166. Wallace Thurman, *The Blacker The Berry* (1929), 147.
167. Jesse Algernon Rhines, *Black Film/White Money* (2000), 43.
168. Mike Gross, 'Black Tracks Cue New Sales Mart', *Billboard*, 24 July 1971, 10.
169. 'Fifty Years of Blacks in Entertainment', *Jet*, 26 November 2001, 51.

170. Nat Freedland, 'Melvin Van Peebles: Multi-media Maverick', *Billboard*, 29 January 1972, Box 36, File 11, SCMSS, 44.
171. Mark A. Reid, *Redefining Black Film* (1993), 79.
172. 'Movies', *Newsweek*, 23 October 1972.
173. Ibid.
174. Bogle, *Toms*, 241–2. For a thorough refutation of this perspective, see Melvin Donalson, *Black Directors in Hollywood* (2003).
175. Ibid.
176. Neal, 'Any Day', 22.
177. Reid, *Redefining*, 79.
178. Lerone Bennett Jr., 'The Emancipation Orgasm: Sweetback in Wonderland', *Ebony*, September 1971, Box 36, File 11, SCMSS; Don L. Lee, 'The Bittersweet of Sweetback/ Or Shake Yo' Money Maker', *Black World*, November 1971.
179. Van Peebles quoted in Neal, 'Interview', 6.
180. Ibid.
181. Ibid.
182. George S. Schuyler, 'Lights and Shadows of the Underworld – Studying the Social Outcasts II. The Folk Farthest Down', *Messenger*, August 193, 787.
183. Alice Dunbar Nelson, 'Woman's Most Serious Problem' (1927).
184. Anne Elizabeth Stavney, 'Harlem in the 1920s: A Geographical and Discursive Site of the Black and White Literary Imagination'. Dissertation, University of Washington, 1994, 128.
185. Huey Newton, 'He Won't Bleed Me: A Revolutionary Analysis of "Sweet Sweetback's Baadasssss Song"', in Newton, *To Die*, 112–48. Originally printed in *BPINS*, 19 January 1971.
186. Van Peebles, *Sweet Sweetback*.
187. John Strausbaugh, *Black Like You* (2008), 256.
188. Van Peebles, *Sweet Sweetback*; Ed Guerrero, *Framing Blackness* (1993), 87.
189. Newton, *To Die*, 130.
190. Van Peebles quoted in Bob Longino, 'The New Black', *Sydney Morning Herald*, 12 June 2004.
191. Van Peebles quoted in Bennett, 'The Emancipation Orgasm', 112.
192. Melvin Van Peebles, *The Making of Sweet Sweetback's BaadAsssss Song* (1972), 15.
193. Van Peebles quoted in Neal, *Soul Babies*, 27.
194. Melvin Van Peebles, *Sweet Sweetback's Baadasssss Song: A Guerrilla Filmmaking Manifesto* (2004), 68.
195. Michael Singer, ed., *Film Directors: A Complete Guide* (1999), 9.
196. Nelson George, *Buppies, B-boys, Baps & Bohos* (1994), 3.
197. Bennett, 'The Emancipation Orgasm', 112.
198. Ibid., 110.
199. Ibid., 114.
200. Ibid., 112.
201. Ibid., 118.

202. Larry Neal (?). *A Note on Sweetback* (ca. 1971), Box 36, File 11, SCMSS, 1.
203. Ibid., 2.
204. Ibid.
205. Ibid., 3.
206. Ibid., 4.
207. Bennett, 'The Emancipation', 106.
208. Ron Daniels, 'Vantage Point', 13 October 2009, http://www.northstarnews.com/columns/dr_ron_daniels/article/1572 (accessed 13 February 2010).
209. Ibid.
210. Maulana Karenga, *Introduction to Black Studies* (1993), 73.
211. 'African-American or Black: What's in a Name? Prominent Blacks and-or African Americans Express Their Views', *Ebony*, July 1989.
212. Daniels, 'Vantage Point'.
213. Ibid.
214. Ibid.
215. Neal, 'Any Day', 12; Daniels, 'Vantage Point'.
216. Daniels, 'Vantage Point'.
217. Larry Dillard quoted in Bob Blauner, *Black Lives, White Lives* (1989), 234.
218. Lerone Bennett Jr., quoted in Mary Schmidt Campbell, *Tradition and Conflict: Images of a Turbulent Decade, 1963–1973* (1985), 10; Lerone Bennett Jr., 'Have We Overcome?', *Ebony*, November 1979, 40.
219. Elena Albert quoted in Blauner, *Black Lives*, 313. Italicised annotations by the interviewer.

Conclusion   The Long History of Black Power

1. Walter Mosley, *Bad Boy Brawly Brown* (Boston: Little, Brown, and Co. 2002), 38.
2. Alex Altman, 'Time Person of the Year Runner Up: Black Lives Matter', *Time*, 21 December 2015. http://time.com/time-person-of-the-year-2015-runner-up-black-lives-matter/ (accessed 14 April 2016).

BIBLIOGRAPHY

Primary Documents

Adams, Edward and Clarkson Leverett. *Nigger to Nigger*. New York: Charles Scribner's Sons, 1928.

Anderson, S.E. 'Tricks and Toys.' n.d. Schomburg Center Manuscripts, Box 7, File 23.

Anonymous. 'Letter to the American Slaves, Fugitive Slave Act Convention, Cazenovia, New York, August 1850.' http://nationalhumanitiescenter.org/pds/maai/enslavement/text7/freeblacksaddress.pdf (accessed 19 January 2009).

Anonymous. *A New History of Black America – Dedicated to Ora Mobley & p.s. 175*. New York, ca. 1966. Schomburg Center Manuscripts, Box 31 File 12.

Anonymous. 'A Proposal to Institute A Black Study and Work Program at San Francisco State College.' 1 March, 1967. Schomburg Center Manuscripts, Box 31, File 14.

Anonymous/Various. *Combined Black Youth Workshop, Proposal #2 – Black Value Commitment and Entertainment*, ca. 1967. Schomburg Center Manuscripts, Box 31, File 14.

Anonymous/Various. 'An Approach to Black Studies: Statement of the Planning Staff, Institute of the Black World, Martin Luther King Jr., Memorial Center.' 1969. Schomburg Center Manuscripts, Box 31, File 14.

Asante, Molefi K. (Arthur L. Smith). *The Rhetoric of Black Revolution*. Boston: Allyn and Bacon, 1969.

Baldwin, James. *No Name in the Street*. New York: Dial Press, 1972.

Baraka, Amiri (LeRoi Jones) and Larry Neal, eds. *Black Fire: An Anthology of Afro-American Writing*. 1968. Reprint, Baltimore: Black Classic Press, 2007.

Bennett, John. *The Doctor to The Dead*. New York: Rinehart & Company, 1946.

Brewer, John Mason. 'Den to De Fiah.' In *Tone the Bell Easy, Publications of the Texas Folk-lore Society*, no. 10, edited by J. Frank Dobie, 13–14. 1932. Reprint, Dallas: Southern Methodist University Press, 1965.

———— 'A Laugh That Mean Freedom.' In *Tone the Bell Easy, Publications of the Texas Folk-lore Society*, no. 10, edited by J. Frank Dobie, 14–15. 1932. Reprint, Dallas: Southern Methodist University Press, 1965.

——— 'Swapping Dreams.' In *Tone the Bell Easy, Publications of the Texas Folk-lore Society*, no. 10, edited by J. Frank Dobie, 18–19. 1932. Reprint, Dallas: Southern Methodist University Press, 1965.

——— 'Dey's Auganized.' In *Tone the Bell Easy, Publications of the Texas Folk-lore Society*, no. 10, edited by J. Frank Dobie, 23–4. 1932. Reprint, Dallas: Southern Methodist University Press, 1965.

——— 'Uncle Pleas's Prayer.' In *Tone the Bell Easy, Publications of the Texas Folk-lore Society*, no. 10, edited by J. Frank Dobie, 26–8. 1932. Reprint, Dallas: Southern Methodist University Press, 1965.

Brink, William and Louis Harris. *Black and White: A Study of US Racial Attitudes Today*. New York: Simon & Schuster, 1967.

Brown, Sterling. *Southern Road: Poems*. New York: Harcourt, Brace and Co., 1932.

——— 'The Ballad of Joe Meek.' In *The Collected Poems of Sterling A. Brown*, edited by Michael S. Harper, 158–62. Evanston: TriQuarterly Books, 1996.

Brown, Wesley. 'The Mojo and the Sayso: Myth and Ritual in the Work of Larry Neal.' 14 November 1981. Schomburg Center Manuscripts Box 1, File 17.

Campbell, Angus and Howard Schuman. *Racial Attitudes in Fifteen American Cities*. Survey Research Center Institute for Social Research: The University of Michigan, Ann Arbor, June 1968.

Carmichael, Stokely. 'Towards Black Liberation.' In *Black Fire: An Anthology of Afro-American Writing*, edited by Amiri Baraka and Larry Neal, 119–32. 1968. Reprint, Baltimore: Black Classic Press, 2007.

Chapman, Abraham, ed. *Black Voices: An Anthology of Afro-American Literature*. New York, New American Library, 1968.

Clark, Kenneth B. *Dark Ghetto: Dilemmas of Social Power*, foreword by Gunnar Myrdal. New York: Harper & Row, 1967.

Cleaver, Eldridge. *Soul On Ice*. 1968. Reprint, London: Panther Modern Society, 1970.

Dent, Thomas C. 'The Ghetto of Desire', ca.1965. Schomburg Center Manuscripts, Box 41, File 25.

Dent, Thomas C., Richard Schechner and Gilbert Moses, eds. *The Free Southern Theater, by the Free Southern Theater: A Documentary of the South's Radical Black Theater, with Journals, Letters, Poetry, Essays, and a Play Written By Those Who Built It*. Indianapolis Bobbs-Merrill Co., 1969.

Dobie, J. Frank, ed. *Tone the Bell Easy, Publications of the Texas Folk-lore Society*, no. 10. 1932. Reprint, Dallas: Southern Methodist University Press, 1965.

Douglas, Emory. 'Art for the People's Sake.' In *The Black Panther Party: Service to the People Programs*, edited by David Hilliard, 121–4. Albuquerque: University of New Mexico Press, 2008.

Douglass, Frederick. *My Bondage and My Freedom*. New York: Miller, Orton & Co., 1855.

Duberman, Martin. *The Uncompleted Past*. New York: Random House, 1969.

Du Bois, W.E.B. 'The Talented Tenth.' In *The Negro Problem*, edited by Booker T. Washington, 31–75. New York: James Pott & Co., 1903.

——— 'Criteria of Negro Art.' *The Crisis*, October 1926.

——— 'The Browsing Reader.' *The Crisis*, May 1928.

——— 'The Souls of Black Folks.' In *Three Negro Classics*, New York: Avon, 1965.

Du Bois, W.E.B., James Weldon Johnson and Booker T. Washington. *Three Negro Classics*, introduction by John Hope Franklin. New York: Harper Collins, 1999.

Dunbar, Ernest. 'The Black Revolt Hits the White Campus.' 31 October 1967. Schomburg Center Manuscripts, Box 31, File 16.

Dunbar, Paul Laurence. *The Sport of the Gods: And Other Essential Writings*, edited and introduced by Shelley Fisher Fishkin and David Bradley. 1902. Reprint, New York: Modern Library, 2005.

Edwards, Harry. *The Revolt of the Black Athlete with a foreword by Samuel J. Skinner Jr.* New York: Free Press, 1969.

——— *Black Students*. New York: Free Press, 1970.

Ellison, Ralph. *Invisible Man*. 1952. Reprint, London: Penguin, 1999.

Erikson, Erik with Huey P. Newton. *In Search of Common Ground: Conversations with Erik H. Erikson and Huey P. Newton*, introduced by Kai T. Erikson. New York: Norton, 1973.

Flannagan, Roy. *Amber Satyr*. New York: Doubleday, Doran & Co., 1932.

Florence, Franklin. 'The Meaning of Black Power.' In *The Rhetoric of Black Revolution*, Molefi K. Asante, 161–5. Boston: Allyn and Bacon, 1969.

Free Southern Theater. 'Report from the Free Southern Theater.' ca.1964. mz024, University of Southern Mississippi MSS, Box 1, Folder 4.

Fuller, Charles H. 'What is Black Power, Daddy? Answer: "?".' 2 November 1979. Schomburg Center Manuscripts, Box 41, File 34.

Garrett, Jimmy. *The Black Students' Union Philosophy and Goals*. ca. 1967. Schomburg Center Manuscripts, Box 31, File 14.

Gilmore, Al-Tony. *Bad Nigger! The National Impact of Jack Johnson*. Port Washington: Kennikat Press, 1975.

Grant, Caesar. 'All God's Chillen Had Wings.' In *The Doctor to The Dead*, John Bennett, 139–42. New York: Rinehart & Company, 1946.

Goldman, Peter. *Report from Black America*. New York: Simon and Schuster, 1969.

Gordon, Milton. *Assimilation in American Life*. New York: Oxford University Press, 1964.

Goss, Clay. *This Way Before*. Schomburg Center Manuscripts, Box 42, File 1.

Gray, Seymour and Larry Neal. *Précis: Boxing as Drama*. n.d. Schomburg Center Manuscripts Box 21, File 18.

Guillaume, Paul and Thomas Munro. *Primitive Negro Sculpture*. New York: Harcourt, Brace & Co., 1926.

Hannerz, Ulf. *Soulside: Inquiries into Ghetto Culture and Community*. 1969. Reprint, Chicago: Columbia University Press, 2004.

Harding, Vincent. 'Black Radicalism: The Road from Montgomery.' in *Dissent: Explorations in the History of American Radicalism*, edited by Alfred F. Young, 321–354. DeKalb: Northern Illinois University Press, 1968.

Hare, Nathan. '"Black Power: Are Negroes Ready, Willing and Able?", statement to the Commission on Religion and Race, National Council of Churches, Bethel A.M.E. Church, New York, Friday, 22 July 1966.' Schomburg Center Manuscripts, Box 31, File 14.

——— 'How White Power Whitewashes Black Power.' In *The Black Power Revolt*, edited by Floyd B. Barbour, 182–8. Boston: Porter Sargent, 1968.

Harris, Louis. *The Harris Survey Yearbook of Public Opinion, 1970*. New York: Louis Harris and Associates, 1971.

Henderson, David. *Keep on Pushing*. 1964. Schomburg Center Manuscripts. Box 42, File 7.

——— *Felix of the Silent Forest*. New York: Poets Press, 1967.

―――― *Umbra*. 1971. Schomburg Center Manuscripts. Box 33, File 13.
Henderson, Stephen Evangelist. *Understanding the New Black Poetry: Black Speech and Black Music as Poetic References*. New York: Morrow, 1973.
Holt, Len. *The Summer That Didn't End: The Story of the Mississippi Civil Rights Project of 1964*. New York: Morrow, 1965.
Holway, John. *Voices from the Great Black Baseball Leagues*. 1975. Reprint, New York: Da Capo Press, 1992.
―――― *Black Ball Stars*, typescript. Manassas, 1979.
―――― *Black Diamonds: Life in the Negro Leagues from the Men Who Lived It*. New York: Stadium Books, 1991.
―――― *The Complete Book of Baseball's Negro Leagues: The Other Half of Baseball History*. Edited by Lloyd Johnson & Rachel Borst. Fern Park: Hastings House Publishers, 2001.
Hughes, Langston. 'Jazzonia.' In *The New Negro*, edited by Alain Locke, 226. 1925. Reprint, New York: Atheneum, 1992.
―――― 'Elevator Boy.' In *FIRE!!* edited by Wallace Thurman, 20. New York: Opportunity, 1926.
Hurston, Zora Neale. 'Sweat.' In *FIRE!!* edited by Wallace Thurman, 40–5. New York: Opportunity, 1926.
―――― *Mules and Men with an introduction by Franz Boas, Ph.D., LL.D., 10 Illustrations by Miguel* Covarrubias. Philadelphia: J.B. Lippincott Company, 1935.
Jackson, George L. *Soledad Brother: The Prison Letters of George Jackson*. 1970. Reprint, London: Jonathan Cape/Penguin, 1971.
―――― *Blood in My Eye*. 1972. Reprint, Baltimore: Black Classic Press, 1990.
Jefferson, Patricia Ann. 'The Rhetoric of the Magnificent Barbarian, Stokely Carmichael.' PhD Diss, Indiana University, Department of Speech and Theatre, 1967.
Johnson, Charles S. *Ebony and Topaz: A Collectanea*. New York: Opportunity, 1927.
Johnson, Jack. *Jack Johnson: In the Ring and Out*. Chicago: National Sports Publishing Company, 1927.
Johnson, James Weldon James Weldon Johnson, 'The White Witch.' In *The Book of American Negro Poetry: Chosen and Edited with an Essay on the Negro's Creative Genius by J.W. Johnson*, edited by James Weldon Johnson, 111–13. New York: Harcourt, Brace & Co., 1922.
Johnson, James Weldon, ed. *The Book of American Negro Poetry: Chosen and Edited with an Essay on the Negro's Creative Genius by J.W. Johnson*. New York: Harcourt, Brace & Co., 1922.
―――― 'The Creation.' In *The New Negro*, edited by Alain Locke, 138–41. 1925. Reprint, New York: Atheneum, 1992.
―――― 'Harlem: the Culture Capital.' In *The New Negro*, edited by Alain Locke, 301–11. 1925. Reprint, New York: Atheneum, 1992.
―――― *God's Trombones: Seven Negro Sermons in Verse, Drawings by Aaron Douglas, Lettering by C.B. Falls*. New York: Viking Press, 1927.
―――― *The Autobiography of an Ex-Colored Man*. New York: A.A. Knopf, 1927.
―――― *Along This Way: The Autobiography of James Weldon Johnson*; with a new introduction by Sondra Kathryn Wilson. New York: Da Capo Press, 2000.

Kent, George E. 'Langston Hughes and Afro-American Folk and Cultural Tradition.' In *Langston Hughes, Black Genius: A Critical Evaluation*, edited by Therman B.O. Daniel, 183–210. New York: William Morrow & Co., Inc., 1971.

Kerner, Otto, John V. Lindsay, Fred. R. Harris, Edward W. Brooke, James C. Corman, William M. McCulloch, I.W. Abel, Charles B. Thornton, Roy Wilkins, Katherine G.Paden and Herbert Jenkins. [United States National Advisory Commission on Civil Disorders.] *Report of the National Advisory Commission on Civil Disorders*. Washington: US Government Printing Office, 1968.

Kahn, Roger. *The Boys of Summer*. New York: Harper & Row, 1972.

Kgositsile, Keorapetse 'Willie'. *My Name is Afrika*, Introduction by Gwendolyn Brooks. Garden City, New York: Doubleday & Company, Inc., 1971.

Kornberg, Allan and Joel Smith. '"It Ain't Over Yet": Activism in a Southern University.' In *Black Power and Student Rebellion*, edited by James McEvoy and Abraham Miller, 100–21. Belmont: Wadsworth, 1969.

Knight, Etheridge (and other inmates of Indiana State Prison). *Black Voices from Prison*, with an introduction by Roberto Giammanco. New York: Pathfinder, 1970.

Last Poets, The. *Niggers are Scared of Revolution!* The Last Poets, AMG, 1970.

Lester, Julius. *Look Out Whitey! Black Power's Gon' Get Your Mama*. London: Allison & Busby, 1970.

Locke, Alain, ed. *The New Negro*. 1925. Reprint, New York: Atheneum, 1992.

Marx, Gary T. *Protest and Prejudice: A Study of Belief in the Black Community*. New York: Harper and Row, 1969.

McCord, William, John Howard, Bernard Friedberg and Edwin Hardwood. *Life Styles in the Black Ghetto*. New York: W.W. Norton, 1969.

McEvoy, James and Abraham Miller eds. *Black Power and Student Rebellion*. Belmont, California: Wadsworth, 1969.

Meyer, Frank S. 'The Negro Revolution – A New Phase.' *National Review*, 4 October 1966. In *The Conservative Mainstream*, Frank S. Meyer, 209–12. New York: Arlington House, 1969.

Mweusi, A. 'Steps to Liberation.' n.d. Schomburg Center Manuscripts, Box 42, File 21.

Neal, Larry. *Black History/Cultural Development* [Fragment]. n.d. Schomburg Center Manuscripts, Box 6, File 13.

——— *Black Power/Liberation*, n.d. Schomburg Center Manuscripts Box 6, File 17.

——— 'Coming At You Weird.' n.d. Schomburg Center Manuscripts, Box 6, File 22.

——— 'The Mighty Wall.' n.d. Schomburg Center Manuscripts, Box 6, File 36.

——— 'Larry Neal On Malcolm X (For Rolling Stone).' n.d. Schomburg Center Manuscripts, Box 7, File 1.

——— *Separate State*. n.d. Schomburg Center Manuscripts, Box 7, File 15.

——— *Black Boxing*. n.d. Schomburg Center Manuscripts, Box 21, File 9.

——— 'Foreword to Black History.' n.d. Schomburg Center Manuscripts, Box 21, File 11.

——— 'Interview with Melvin Van Peebles.' n.d. Schomburg Center Manuscripts, Box 26, File 6.

——— *Lenox Avenue Sunday*. 1966. Schomburg Center Manuscripts, Box 14, File 2.

——— Diary Excerpt. May 1968. Schomburg Center Manuscripts, Box 3, File 14.

——— 'Any Day Now: Black Art and Black Liberation.' ca. 1969. Schomburg Center Manuscripts, Box 6, File 2.
——— 'Conquest of the South.' ca. 1970. Schomburg Center Manuscripts.
——— 'Ellison's Zoot Suit.' December 1970. Schomburg Center Manuscripts, Box 6, File 28.
——— *A Note on Sweetback*. ca. 1971. Schomburg Center Manuscripts, Box 36, File 11.
Nell, William C. 'Anti-Webster Meeting of the Colored Citizens of Boston and Vicinity.' In *William Cooper Nell, nineteenth-century African American abolitionist, historian, integrationist: selected writings from 1832–1874*, edited by Constance Porter Uzelac and Dorothy Porter Wesley, 256–9. Baltimore: Black Classic Press, 2002.
Newcomb, Theodore Mead. *Social Psychology*. New York, The Dryden Press, 1950.
Newton Huey P. 'In Defense of Self-Defense II: 3 July 1967.' In *To Die for the People*, Huey P. Newton, edited by Toni Morrison, 85–90. 1972. Reprint, San Francisco: City Lights, 2009.
——— *Revolutionary Suicide*. 1972. Reprint, New York: Penguin, 2009.
——— 'Lonnie McLucas and the New Haven 9.' In *To Die for the People*, Huey P. Newton, 227–31. 1972. Reprint, San Francisco: City Lights, 2009.
——— 'Black Capitalism Re-Analyzed.' In *To Die for the People*, Huey P. Newton, edited by Toni Morrison, 85–90. 1972. Reprint, San Francisco: City Lights, 2009.
——— 'He Won't Bleed Me: A Revolutionary Analysis of "Sweet Sweetback's Baadasssss Song".' In *To Die For The People: The Writings of Huey P. Newton*, Huey P. Newton, 112–48. 1972. Reprint, San Francisco: City Lights, 2009.
——— *To Die For The People: The Writings of Huey P. Newton*. 1972. Reprint, San Francisco: City Lights, 2009.
——— 'War Against The Panthers: A Study Of Repression In America.' PhD diss., University of California Santa Cruz, 1 June 1980.
Nugent, Richard Bruce. 'Lighting Fire.' 1982. In *FIRE!!* edited by Wallace Thurman [Loose Insert]. New York: Opportunity, 1926.
Orrick, William H. *Shut It Down! A College In Crisis – San Francisco State College October, 1968–April*, 1969. Washington: U.S. Government Print Office, June 1969.
Porter, James Amos. *Modern Negro Art {With Eighty-Five Half-Tone Plates}*. New York: Dryden Press, 1943.
Robinson, Jackie and Wendell Smith. *Jackie Robinson: My Own Story*. New York: Greenberg, 1948.
Robinson, Jackie and Carl Rowan. *Wait Till Next Year: The Life Story of Jackie Robinson*. New York: Random House, 1960.
Robinson, Jackie. *I Never Had It Made: As Told to Alfred Duckett*. New York: Putnam, 1972.
Rice, Grantland. *The Tumult and the Shouting: My Life in Sport*. London: Cassell, 1956.
Rust, Art Jr. *Get That Nigger Off the Field! A Sparkling, Informal History of the Black Man in Baseball*. New York: Delacorte Press, 1976.
Sackler, Howard. 'The Great White Hope [Revised First Draft].' 1969. Schomburg Center Manuscripts, Box 45, File 4.

Stanford, Max. 'Black Nationalism and the Afro-american student.' *Black Scholar* 2, no. 10 (June 1971): 27–31.

Scheer, Robert, ed. *Eldridge Cleaver: Post-Prison Writings and Speeches.* New York: Jonathan Cape Ltd., 1969.

Schuyler, George S. 'The Negro-Art Hokum.' *Nation* 122 (16 June 1926): 662–3.

Scott, Robert L. 'Justifying Violence: The Rhetoric of Militant Black Power.' In *The Rhetoric of Black Power*, edited by Robert L. Scott and Wayne Brockriede, 132–46. New York: Harper & Row, 1969.

Seale, Bobby. *Seize the Time: The Story of the Black Panther Party and Huey P. Newton.* 1968. Reprint, London: Arrow Books, 1970.

——— *A Lonely Rage: the Autobiography of Bobby Seale*, foreword by James Baldwin. New York: Times Books, 1978.

Shakur, Assata. *Assata: An Autobiography.* Westport: Lawrence Hill, 1987.

South Carolina Department of Correction. *The Emerging Rights of the Confined.* Columbia: The Correctional Development Foundation, 1972.

Talley, Thomas Washington. *Negro Folk Rhymes: Wise and Otherwise, With an Introduction by Walter Clyde Curry and With a Study by T.W. Talley.* New York: The Macmillan Company, [Press of J.J. Little & Ives Company, New York], 1922.

The Observer. 'On the Significance of the Black Panther Party to the Nationalists.' [1968?] Schomburg Center Manuscripts, Box 7, File 9.

Thurman, Wallace, ed. *FIRE!!* New York: Opportunity, 1926.

Ture, Kwame and Charles V. Hamilton. *Black Power: The Politics of Liberation.* 1967. Reprint, New York: Vintage Books, 1992.

Van Peebles, Melvin. *The Making of Sweet Sweetback's Baadasssss Song.* New York: Lancer Books, 1972.

Walker, David. *Appeal in Four Articles, together with a Preamble, to the Colored Citizens of the World, but in particular, and very expressly to those of the United States of America.* Boston: Printed for the Author, 1830. Massachusetts Historical Society, Shelfmark E187.

Washington, Booker T. *The Story of the Negro: The Rise of the Race from Slavery*, Vol.2. London: T. Fisher Unwin, 1909.

Washington, Chester L. 'Ches' Sez.' *Pittsburgh Courier*, 29 February 1936.

Whitwell, Mal. 'Let's Boycott the Olympics!' *Ebony*, March 1964.

Wilkins, Roy. 'Whither "Black Power"?' *The Crisis*, August-September 1966.

Williams, John Alfred. *This Is My Country Too.* New York: New American Library, 1966.

——— *Flashbacks: A Twenty-Year Diary of Article Writing.* Garden City, New York: Anchor/Doubleday, 1973.

Wirth, Thomas H. *Fire!! in Retrospect*, 1982. In *FIRE!!* edited by Wallace Thurman [Loose Insert]. New York: Opportunity, 1926.

Worthy, William. 'The Black Power Establishment.' *Esquire*, November 1967. Schomburg Center Manuscripts, Box 31, File 16.

Wright, Nathan Jr., ed. *What Black Educators are Saying.* New York: Hawthorn, 1970.

X, Malcolm. *The Autobiography of Malcolm X.* 1965. Reprint, London: Penguin, 2007.

——— *By Any Means Necessary.* New York: Pathfinder, 1970.

BIBLIOGRAPHY 333

Books

Aldridge, Delores and Carlene Young, eds. *Out of the Revolution: The Development of Africana Studies*. Lanham: Lexington, 2003.

Asim, Jabari. *The N Word: Who Can Say It, Who Shouldn't, and Why*. Boston: Houghton Mifflin, 2007.

Barber, Red. *When All Hell Broke Loose in Baseball*. Garden City: New York, 1982.

Barbour, Floyd B., ed. *The Black Power Revolt*. Boston: Porter Sargent, 1968.

────── *The Black Seventies*. Boston: Sargent, 1970.

Barnett, Alan W. *Community Murals: The People's Art*. Philadelphia: The Art Alliance Press, 1984.

Baskir, Lawrence M. and William A. Strauss. *Chance and Circumstance: The Draft, the War and the Vietnam Generation*. New York: Knopf, 1978.

Bass, Amy. *Not the Triumph but the Struggle: The 1968 Olympics and the Making of the Black Athlete*. Minneapolis: University of Minnesota Press, 2002.

Bell, Bernard. *The Folk Roots of Contemporary Afro-American Poetry*. Detroit: Broadside Press, 1974.

Benson, Gene. 'Black Star of Philadelphia.' In *Black Diamonds: Life in the Negro Leagues from the Men Who Lived It* compiled by John Holway, 70–88. New York: Stadium Books, 1991.

Berlin, Ira. *Many Thousands Gone*. Cambridge: Belknap, 1998.

Billingsley, Andrew. 'The Black Presence in American Higher Education.' In *What Black Educators are Saying*, edited by Nathan Wright, Jr., 126–49. New York: Hawthorn Books, 1970.

Binkin, Martin. Mark J. Eitelberg, Alvin J. Schexnider and Marvin M. Smith. *Blacks and the Military*. Washington, D.C.: The Brookings Institution, 1982.

Blauner, Bob. *Black Lives, White Lives: Three Decades of Race Relations in America*. Berkeley: University of California Press, 1989.

Blauner, Robert and David Wellman.'Toward the Decolonization of Social Research.' In *The Death of White Sociology*, edited by Joyce A Ladner, 310–30. New York: Random House, 1973.

Bloom, John and Michael Nevin Willard, eds. *Sports Matters: Race, Recreation and Culture*. New York: New York University Press, 2002.

Bogle, Donald. *Toms, Coons, Mulattoes, Mammies & Bucks: An Interpretive History of Blacks in American Films*. New York: Continuum, 2003.

Boyd, Herb and Robert L. Allen, eds. *Brotherman: The Odyssey of Black Men in America*. New York: Ballantine, 1995.

Bradley, David. *The Chaneysville Incident*. New York: Harper & Row, 1981.

Brown, Elaine. *A Taste of Power: a Black Woman's Story*. New York: Pantheon Books, 1992.

Brown, H. Rap. *Die Nigger Die!* 1969. London: Allison & Busby Limited, 1970.

Browne, Robert S. 'Financing the Black University.' In Wright, *Black Educators*, edited by Nathan Wright, Jr., 88–93. New York: Hawthorn Books, 1970.

Bush, Rod. *We Are Not What We Seem: Black Nationalism and Class Struggle in the American Century*. New York: New York University Press, 1999.

Campbell, Mary Schmidt. *Tradition and Conflict: Images of a Turbulent Decade, 1963–1973*. New York: Studio Museum in Harlem, 1985.

Carmichael, Stokely. *Stokely Speaks: Black Power Back to PanAfricanism*. New York: Random House, 1971.

Carroll, Leo. *Hacks, Blacks and Cons.* D.C. Heath and Company, Lexington, 1974.
Cashmore, Ernest. *Black Sportsmen.* London: Routledge & Kegan Paul, 1982.
Cayton, Horace R. and St. Clair Drake. *Black Metropolis: A Study of Negro Life in a Northern City, with an introduction by Richard Wright and a new foreword by William Julius Wilson,* Revised and Enlarged Edition. Chicago: University of Chicago Press, 1993.
Chadwick, Bruce. *When the Game was Black and White: The Illustrated History of the Negro Leagues.* New York: Abbeville, 1992.
Cleaver, Eldridge. 'The Black Man's Stake in Vietnam.' In *The Black Panthers Speak*, edited by Philip S. Foner, 100–4. New York: Da Capo Press, 1995.
Cleaver, Kathleen and George Katsiaficas, eds. *Liberation, Imagination and the Black Panther Party.* New York: Routledge, 2001.
Cohen, Karl F. *Forbidden Animation: Censored Cartoons and Blacklisted Animators in America.* Jefferson: McFarland & Company, Inc., 1997.
Cunard, Nancy, ed. *Negro: An Anthology*, collected and edited by Nancy Cunard; edited and abridged with an introduction by Hugh Ford. New York: Continuum, 2002.
Crawford, Vicki, Jacqueline Anne Rouse and Barbara Woods. *Women in the Civil Rights Movement: Trailblazers and Torchbearers, 1941–1965.* Brooklyn: Carlson, 1990.
Davis, Laurel R. and Othello Harris. 'Race and Ethnicity in US Sports Media.' In *Mediasport*, edited by Lawrence A. Wanner, 154–69. London: Routledge, 1998.
Davis, Sharon. *Stevie Wonder: Rhythms of Wonder.* London: Robson, 2006.
DeGroot, Gerard. *A Noble Cause?: America and the Vietnam War* (Harlow: Longman, 2000).
Donalson, Melvin. *Black Directors in Hollywood.* Austin: University of Texas Press, 2003.
Donnelly, Ralph W. and Henry I. Shaw, Jr. *Blacks in the Marine Corps.* Washington D.C.: History and Museums Divisions Headquarters, U.S. Marine Corps, 1975.
Edwards, Harry. *The Struggle That Must Be.* New York: Macmillan, 1980.
Elkins, Stanley M. *Slavery: A Problem in American Institutional and Intellectual Life.* London: University of Chicago Press, 1968.
Erenberg, Lewis A. *The Greatest Fight of Our Generation: Louis vs. Schmeling.* New York: Oxford University Press, 2006.
Fields, Wilmer. *My Life in the Negro Leagues: An Autobiography By Wilmer Fields with a Foreword by John B. Holway.* Westport: Meckler, 1992.
Forman, James. *The Making of Black Revolutionaries.* London: University of Washington Press, 1997.
Fuse, Montye and Keith Miller. 'Jazzing the Basepaths: Jackie Robinson and African-American Aesthetics.' In *Sports Matters: Race, Recreation and Culture*, edited by John Bloom and Michael Nevin Willard, 119–140. New York: New York University Press, 2002.
Gabbin, Joanne V. *Sterling A. Brown: Building the Black Aesthetic Tradition.* Charlottesville: University Press of Virginia, 1994.
——— *The Furious Flowering of African-American Poetry.* Charlottesville: University Press of Virginia, 1999.
Gabler, Neal. *Walt Disney: The Triumph of the American Imagination.* New York: Alfred A. Knopf, 2006.

Garrow, David J. *Protest at Selma: Martin Luther King, Jr, and the Voting Rights Act of 1965*. New Haven: Yale University Press, 1978.
George, Nelson. *Buppies, B-boys, Baps & Bohos: Notes On Post-Soul Black Culture*. New York: HarperPerennial, 1994.
Gillespie, Dizzie with Al Fraser. *To Be, Or Not ... To Bop*. Minneapolis: University of Minnesota Press, 2009.
Goldman, Peter. *The Death and Life of Malcolm X*. Urbana: University of Illinois Press, 1979.
Gore, Dayo F., Jeanne Theoharis and Komozi Woodard eds. *Want to Start a Revolution?: Radical Women in the Black Freedom Struggle*. New York: New York University Press, 2009.
Gottsegen, Michael G. *The Political Thought of Hannah Arendt*. Albany: State University of New York Press, 1994.
Greene, Helen Taylor and Shaun L. Gabbidon. *African American Criminological Thought*, with a foreword by Julius Debro. Albany: State University of New York Press, 2000.
Guerrero, Ed. *Framing Blackness: The African-American Image in Film*. Philadelphia: Temple University Press, 1993.
Harper, Michael S., ed. *The Collected Poems of Sterling A. Brown* (1996), 159.
Hartmann, Douglas. *Race, Culture, and the Revolt of the Black Athlete: The 1968 Olympic Protests and their Aftermath*. Chicago: University of Chicago Press, 2003.
Henry, Charles P. *Culture and African-American Politics*. Bloomington: Indiana University Press, 1990.
Hernton, Calvin C. *Coming Together: Black Power, White Hatred and Sexual Hang-Ups*. New York: Random House, 1971.
Herron, Jerry. *After Culture: Detroit and the Humiliation of History* (Detroit: University of Michigan Press, 1993).
Hilliard, David and Lewis Cole. *This Side of Glory: the Autobiography of David Hilliard and the Story of the Black Panther Party*. 1993. Reprint, Chicago: Lawrence Hill Books, 2001.
Hilliard, David, ed. *The Black Panther Party: Service to the People Programs*. Albuquerque: University of New Mexico Press, 2008.
Hoberman, John Milton. *Darwin's Athletes*. Boston: Houghton Mifflin Co., 1997.
Hoogerhuis, Mara. 'Why Here, Why Now? The Story of Student Protest on the University of Oregon Campus, April 1970.' PhD diss., University of Oregon, 2004.
Huebner, Andrew J. *The Warrior Image: Soldiers in American Culture from the Second World War to the Vietnam Era*. Chapel Hill: University of North Carolina Press, 2008.
Hurston, Zora Neale. *Hurston: Novels and Stories*. New York: Library of America, 1995.
Hutchinson, George. *The Harlem Renaissance in Black and White* (1995). Cambridge: Belknap Press of Harvard University Press, 1995.
Jackson, Bruce, ed. *Wake Up Dead Man*. Cambridge: Harvard University Press, 1972.
——— *Get Your Ass in the Water and Swim Like Me: Narrative Poetry from Black Oral Tradition*. 1974. Reprint, New York: Routledge, 2004.
James, Darius. *That's Blaxploitation! Roots of the Baadasssss 'Tude (Rated X by an All-Whyte Jury)*. New York: St. Martin's Griffin, 1995.
Jones, Charles E., ed. *The Black Panther Party {Reconsidered}*. Baltimore: Black Classic Press, 1998.

Joseph, Peniel E. *Waiting 'Til The Midnight Hour: A Narrative History of Black Power in America*. New York: Henry Holt & Co., 2006.

Karenga, Maulana. *Introduction to Black Studies*. Los Angeles: University of Sankore Press, 1993.

Kelley, Robin. *Race Rebels: Culture, Politics, and the Black Working Class*. New York: Free Press, 1996.

King, Richard H. *Civil Rights and the Idea of Freedom*. Athens: University of Georgia Press, 1996.

Kramer, Victor, ed. *The Harlem Renaissance Re-examined*. New York: AMS Press, 1987.

Ladner, Joyce. 'What "Black Power" Means to Negroes in Mississippi.' In *Old Memories, New Moods: Americans from Africa*, Vol. 2, edited by Peter I. Rose, 249–265. New York: Atherton, 1970.

——— *The Death of White Sociology*. New York: Random House, 1973.

Lazerow, Jama and Yohuru Williams, eds. *In Search of the Black Panther Party: New Perspectives on a Revolutionary Movement*. Durham: Duke University Press, 2006.

Lazerow, Jama and Yohuru Williams. eds. *Liberated Territory: Untold Local Perspectives on the Black Panther Party*. Durham: Duke University Press, 2008.

Lee, Don L. 'The Wall'. In *Community Murals: The People's Art*, Alan W. Barnett, Philadelphia: The Art Alliance Press, 1984.

Levine, Bertram J. *Resolving Racial Conflict*. London: University of Missouri Press, 2005.

Lomax, Michael E., ed. *Sports and the Racial Divide*. Jackson: University Press of Mississippi, 2008.

Lomotey, Kofi, ed. *Encyclopedia of African American Education*. London: Sage, 2010.

Marable, Manning. *Blackwater: Historical Studies in Race, Class Consciousness, and Revolution*. Dayton: Black Praxis Press, 1981.

——— *Black American Politics: from the Washington Marches to Jesse Jackson* London: Verso, 1985.

——— *African and Caribbean Politics: from Kwame Nkrumah to Maurice Bishop*. London: Verso, 1987.

Mann, Robert. *When Freedom Would Triumph: the Civil Rights Struggle in Congress, 1954–1968*. Baton Rouge: Louisiana State University Press, 2007.

Marqusee, Mike. *Redemption Song: Muhammad Ali and the Spirit of the Sixties*. London: Verso, 2005.

Martindale, Carolyn. *The White Press and Black America*. Westport: Greenwood, 1986.

Massood, Paula J. *Black City Cinema: African American Urban Experiences In Film*. Philadelphia: Temple University Press, 2003.

McElrath, Joseph R., Robert C. Leitz and Jesse S. Crisler, eds. *Charles W. Chesnutt: Essays and Speeches*. Stanford: Stanford University Press, 1999.

Miller, Patrick B. 'The Anatomy of Scientific Racism: Racialist Responses to Black Athletic Achievement.' In *Sport and the Color Line*, edited by Patrick B. Miller and David K. Wiggins, 327–44. New York: Routledge, 2004.

Miller, Patrick B. and David K. Wiggins, eds. *The Unlevel Playing Field: A Documentary History of the African American Experience in Sport*. Urbana: University of Illinois Press, 2003.

——— *Twentieth-Century America*. New York: Routledge, 2004.

Mjagkij, Nina, ed. *Portraits of African American Life Since 1865.* Wilmington: SR Books, 2003.
Morris, Aldon D. *The Origins of the Civil Rights Movement: Black Communities Organising for Change.* New York: Free Press, 1986.
Nakamura, Eric. 'Farm Working to Organizing.' *Giant Robot*, Spring 1998.
Neal, Mark Anthony. *Soul Babies: Black Popular Culture and the Post-Soul Aesthetic.* London: Routledge, 2002.
O'Daniel, Therman B., ed. *Langston Hughes, Black Genius: A Critical Evaluation.* New York: William Morrow & Co., Inc., 1971.
Ogbar, Jeffrey Ogbonna Green. *Black Power: Radical Politics and African American Identity.* London: John Hopkins University Press, 2004.
Pendergast, Sara and Tom Pendergast. *Contemporary Black Biography: Profiles from the International Black Community.* Detroit: Gale Group, 2006.
Popeau, Jean Baptiste. *Dialogues of Negritude: An Analysis of the Cultural Context of Black Writing.* Durham: Carolina Academic Press, 2003.
Quarles, Benjamin, ed. *Blacks on John Brown.* Urbana: University of Illinois Press, 1972.
Reagon, Bernice Johnson. *If You Don't Go, Don't Hinder Me: the African American Sacred Song Tradition.* London: University of Nebraska Press, 2001.
Reed, Adolph. *Race, Politics, and Culture: Critical Essays on the Radicalism of the 1960s.* Westport: Greenwood, 1986.
Reid, Mark A. *Redefining Black Film.* Berkeley: University of California Press, 1993.
Rhines, Jesse Algernon. *Black Film/White Money.* New Brunswick: Rutgers University Press, 2000.
Rhodes, Jane. *Framing the Black Panthers.* New York: The New Press, 2007.
Ribowsky, Mark. *The Complete History of the Negro Leagues.* New York: Citadel Press, 2002.
Richards, Henry J. *Topics in Afro-American Studies.* Buffalo: Black Academy Press, 1971.
Roberts, Randy. *Papa Jack Johnson and the Era of White Hopes.* New York: Free Press, 1983.
Roberts, Randy and James S. Olson. *Winning is the Only Thing: Sports in America Since 1945.* London: Johns Hopkins University Press, 1989.
Rogosin, Donn. *Invisible Men: Life in Baseball's Negro Leagues.* London: University of Nebraska Press, 2007.
Rose, Peter I., ed. *Old Memories, New Moods: Americans from Africa*, Vol. 2. New York: Atherton, 1970.
Rowell, Charles H. 'Sterling A. Brown and the Afro-American Folk Tradition.' In *The Harlem Renaissance Re-examined* edited by Victor Kramer, 316–37. New York: AMS Press, 1987.
Sailes, Gary Alan. 'The African-American Athlete: Social Myths and Stereotypes.' In *African Americans in Sport: Contemporary Themes*, edited by Gary Alan Sailes, 183–97. New Brunswick: Transaction Publishers, 1998.
——— *African Americans in Sport: Contemporary Themes.* New Brunswick: Transaction Publishers, 1998.
Sanders, Mark A. 'The Ballad, the Hero and the Ride: A Reading of Sterling A. Brown's *The Last Ride of Wild Bill.*' in *The Furious Flowering of African-American Poetry*, edited by Joanne V. Gabbin, 118–34. Charlottesville: University Press of Virginia, 1999.

Sayer, Ethel. 'Methodological Problems in Studying So-Called "Deviant Communities".' In *The Death of White Sociology*, edited by Joyce A Ladner, 361–379. New York: Random House, 1973.
Schofield, Janet Ward. *Black and White in School: Trust, Tension, or Tolerance?* New York: Praeger, 1982.
Schuman, Howard and Shirley Hatchett. *Black Racial Attitudes: Trends and Complexities*. Ann Arbor, Survey Research Center, Institute for Social Research: University of Michigan, 1974.
Scott, Robert L. and Wayne Brockriede, eds. *The Rhetoric of Black Power*. New York: Harper & Row, 1969.
Sellers, Cleveland. *The River of No Return: The Autobiography of a Black Militant and the Life and Death of SNCC*. New York: William Morrow, 1973.
Silberman, Charles E. *Criminal Violence, Criminal Justice*. New York: Random House, 1978.
Singer, Michael, ed. *Film Directors: A Complete Guide*. Los Angeles: Lone Eagle, 1999.
Smethurst, Edward James. *The Black Arts Movement: Literary Nationalism in the 1960s and 1970s*. Chapel Hill: University of North Carolina Press, 2005.
Smith, Tommie with David Steele. *Silent Gesture: The Autobiography of Tommie Smith*. Philadelphia: Temple University Press, 2007.
Sowell, Thomas. *Pink and Brown People and Other Controversial Essays*. Stanford: Hoover Institution Press, 1981.
Spillers, Hortense J. *Black, White, and in Color: Essays on American Literature and Culture*. Chicago: University of Chicago Press, 2003.
———— 'Ellison's "Usable Past": Toward a Theory of Myth.' In *Black, White, and in Color: Essays on American Literature and Culture*, 65–80. Chicago: University of Chicago Press, 2003.
Sports Illustrated Staff. *The Best of Sports Illustrated*. New York: Oxmoor House, 1990.
Stern, Sol. 'When the Black G.I. Comes Home from Vietnam.' In *The Black Soldier: from the American Revolution to Vietnam*, edited by Elaine Crane and Jay David, 215–27. New York: Morrow, 1971.
Strausbaugh, John. *Black Like You: Blackface, Whiteface, Insult & Imitation in American Popular Culture*. New York: Penguin, 2008.
Terry, Wallace. *Bloods: An Oral History of the Vietnam War*. New York: Random House, 1984.
Theoharis, Jeanne and Woodard, Komozi, eds. *Freedom North: Black Freedom Struggles Outside the South, 1940–1980*. New York: Palgrave Macmillan, 2003.
Torrubia, Rafael. 'Slavery, Symbols and Song.' M.Litt diss., St. Andrews University, 2006.
Turner, James. 'Black Nationalism.' In *Topics in Afro-American Studies*, edited by Henry J. Richards, 59–76. Buffalo: Black Academy Press, 1971.
Tygiel, Jules. *Baseball's Great Experiment: Jackie Robinson and His Legacy*. New York: Oxford University Press, 1983.
Tyson, Timothy B. *Radio Free Dixie: Robert F. Williams & the Roots of Black Power*. Chapel Hill: University of North Carolina Press, 1999.
Uzelac, Constance Porter and Dorothy Porter Wesley, eds. *William Cooper Nell, nineteenth-century African American abolitionist, historian, integrationist: selected writings from 1832–1874*. Baltimore: Black Classic Press, 2002.

Van Deburg, William L. *New Day in Babylon: The Black Power Movement and American Culture, 1965–1975*. London: University of Chicago Press, 1992.
——— *Black Camelot: African-American Culture Heroes in Their Times, 1960–1980*. Chicago: University of Chicago Press, 1997.
Van Peebles, Melvin. *Sweet Sweetback's Baadasssss Song: A Guerrilla Filmmaking Manifesto*. New York: Thunder's Mouth Press, 2004.
Vargus, Ione D. *Revival of Ideology: The Afro-American Society Movement*. San Francisco: R & E Research Associates, 1977.
Wagner, Jean. *Black Poets of the United States from Paul Laurence Dunbar to Langston Hughes* translated [from the French] by Kenneth Douglas. London: University of Illinois Press, 1973.
Wallace, Michele. *Black Macho and the Myth of the Superwoman*. New York: Dial Press, 1978.
Wanner, Lawrence A., ed. *Mediasport*. London: Routledge, 1998.
Wendt, Simon. *The Spirit and the Shotgun: Armed Resistance and the Struggle for Civil Rights*. Gainesville: University Press of Florida, 2007.
Werner, Craig. *A Change Is Gonna Come: Music, Race and the Soul of America*. Edinburgh: Canongate, 2002.
West, Earle H. *The Black American and Education*. Columbus: Charles E. Merrill, 1972.
Westheider, James E. *The African American Experience in Vietnam: Brothers in Arms*. Lanham: Rowman & Littlefield, 2008.
Whalen, Barbara and Charles. *The Longest Debate: A Legislative History of the 1964 Civil Rights Act*. Washington, D.C.: Seven Locks Press, 1985.
White, John. *Martin Luther King, Jr., and the Civil Rights Movement in America*. London: British Association for American Studies, 1991.
Wiggins, William H. 'Joe Louis – American Folk Hero.' In *Sport and the Color Line: Black Athletes and Race Relations in Twentieth-Century America*, edited by Patrick B. Miller and David K. Wiggins, 127–46. New York: Routledge, 2004.
Williams, Doug with Bruce Hunter. *Quarterblack: Shattering the NFL Myth*. Chicago: Bonus Books, 1990.
Williams, Yohuru R. *Black Politics/White Power: Civil Rights, Black Power and Black Panthers*. New York: Brandywine Press, 2000.
Wintz, Cary D. *Black Culture and the Harlem Renaissance*. Houston: Rice University Press, 1988.
Word, Carl O. 'Crosscultural Methods for Survey Research in Black Urban Areas.' *Journal of Black Psychology* 3, no. 2 (February 1977): 72–87.
Wright, Richard. *Native Son*. London: Vintage, 2000.
Yee, Min S. *The Melancholy History of Soledad Prison: In Which a Utopian Scheme Turns Bedlam*. New York: Harper's Magazine Press, 1973.
Zirin, Dave. *What's my Name, Fool? Sports and Resistance in the United States*. Chicago: Haymarket Books, 2005.

Scholarly Journals

Aberbach, Joel D. 'The Meanings of Black Power: A Comparison of Walker, Jack L. White and Black Interpretations of a Political Slogan.' *The American Political Science Review* 64, no. 2 (June 1970): 367–88.

Anderson, David. 'Sterling Brown's Southern Strategy: Poetry as Cultural Evolution in "Southern Road"'. *Callaloo* 21, no. 4 (Autumn 1998): 1023–37.

Bell, Howard H. 'Expressions of Negro Militancy in the North, 1840–1860.' *The Journal of Negro History* 45, no. 1 (January 1960): 11–20.

Blassingame, John W. 'Black Studies: An Intellectual Crisis.' *American Scholar* 38 (Autumn 1969): 548–61.

Cleaver, Eldridge. 'Education and Revolution.' *Black Scholar* 1 (November 1969): 49–51.

Dizard, Jan E. 'Black Identity, Social Class and Black Power.' *Psychiatry* 33, no. 2 (May 1970): 195–207.

Fabre, Genevieve. 'The Free Southern Theatre 1963–1979.' *Black American Literature Forum* 17, no. 2, Black Theatre Issue (Summer 1983): 55–9.

Fairclough, Adam. 'State of the Art: Historians and the Civil Rights Movement', *Journal of American Studies*, 24, no. 3 (December 1990): 387–98.

Flacks, Richard. 'The Liberated Generation: An Exploration of the Roots of Student Protest.' *Journal of Social Issues* 23 (July 1967): 52–75.

Funkhouser, Christopher. 'LeRoi Jones, Larry Neal, and "The Cricket": Jazz and Poets' Black Fire.' *African American Review* 37, no. 2/3 (Summer–Autumn 2003): 237–44.

Gallagher, Brian. 'Explorations of Black Identity from The New Negro to Invisible Man.' *Perspectives on Contemporary Literature* 8 (1982): 1–9.

Gethers, Solomon P. 'Black Nationalism and Human Liberation.' *Black Scholar* 1 (May 1970): 43–50.

Goeser, Caroline. 'The Case of *Ebony and Topaz*: Racial and Sexual Hybridity in Harlem Renaissance Illustrations.' *American Periodicals* 15, no. 1 (2005): 86–111.

Gruber, Murray. 'Four Types of Black Protest: A Study.' *Social Work* 18 (January 1973): 42–51.

Hare, Nathan. 'We Are All Soldiers.' *The Black Scholar* (November 1970). Schomburg Center Manuscripts, Box 32, File 7.

Johnson, Roberta Ann. 'The Prison Birth of Black Power.' *Journal of Black Studies* 5, no. 4 (June 1975): 395–414.

Jordan, Jennifer. 'Sterling A. Brown: A Race Man in the 1960s.' *Callaloo* 21, no. 4 (Autumn 1998): 888–94.

Killens, John O. 'The Artist and the Black University.' *Black Scholar* 1 (November 1969): 61–5.

Lazerow, Jama. 'Look Out, Historians! Black Power's Gon' Get You.' *Reviews in American History* 35, no. 1 (March 2007): 126–32.

Lutz, Tom. '"Sweat or Die": The Hedonization of the Work Ethic in the 1920s.' *American Literary History* 8, no. 2 (Summer 1996): 259–83.

Mason, Julian. 'James Weldon Johnson: A Southern Writer Resists the South.' *College Language Association Journal* 31, no. 2 (December 1987).

McWorter, Gerald A. 'Struggle, Ideology and the Black University.' *Negro Digest*, March 1969.

Neal, Larry. 'Uncle Rufus Raps on the Squared Circle.' *Partisan Review* 39, no. 1 (1972).

——— 'Eatonville's Zora Neale Hurston: A Profile.' *Black Review* 2, edited by Mel Watkins. New York. William Morrow & Co., Inc., 1979. Schomburg Center Manuscripts, Box 6, File 27.

O'Meally, Robert G. 'An Annotated Bibliography of the Works of Sterling A. Brown.' *Callaloo* 14/15 (February–May 1982): 90–105.
O'Neal, John. 'Motion in the Ocean: Some Political Dimensions of the Free Southern Theatre.' *The Drama Review* 12, no. 4 (Summer 1968).
——— 'Free Southern Theatre: Living in the Danger Zone.' *Black Scholar* 10 (July–August 1979).
Pitts, James P. 'The Politicalization of Black Students: Northwestern University.' *Journal of Black Studies* 5, no. 3 (March 1975): 277–319.
Porter, James A. 'Four Problems in the History of Negro Art.' *The Journal of Negro History* 27, no. 1 (January 1942): 9–36.
Stenfors, Brian D. and John J. Woodmansee. 'A Scale of Black Power Sentiment.' *Psychological Reports* 22, no. 3 (June 1968): 802.
Stewart, James B. 'Political Commentary in Black Popular Music from Rhythm and Blues to Early Hip Hop.' *Journal of African American History* 90, no. 3, The History of Hip Hop (Summer, 2005): 196–225.
Terry II, Wallace. 'Bringing the War Home.' *The Black Scholar* (November 1970). Schomburg Center Manuscripts, Box 32, File 7.
Tucker, Richard D. and John J. Woodmansee. 'A Scale of Black Separatism.' *Psychological Reports* 27, no. 3 (December 1970): 855–8.
Turner, James. 'The Sociology of Black Nationalism.' *Black Scholar* 1 (December 1969): 18–27.
Walters, Ronald. 'African-American Nationalism: A Unifying Ideology.' *Black World*, October 1973.

Newspapers and Magazines

Anderson, S.E. 'Toward Racial Relevancy: Militancy and Black Students.' *Negro Digest*, September 1967.
Anonymous. 'Fight Leader Speaks on Negroes Plight.' *Rochester Institute of Technology Reporter*, 24 February 1967.
Banks, Lacy J. 'Can Anybody Beat This Man?' *Jet*, 18 February 1971.
——— 'The Biggest Fight in History.' *Ebony*, March 1971.
Beaupree, Lee. 'One-Third Film Public: Negro: Columbia and UA Pitch for Biz.' *Variety*, 29 November 1967.
Bennett, Lerone Jr. 'Stokely Carmichael: Architect of Black Power.' *Ebony*, September 1966. Schomburg Center Manuscripts, Box 31, File 14.
——— 'Confrontation on the Campus.' *Ebony*, May 1968.
——— 'The Emancipation Orgasm: Sweetback in Wonderland.' *Ebony*, September 1971.
——— 'Have We Overcome?' *Ebony*, November 1979.
Billboard. 'Hot R&B Sides.' *Billboard*, 27 July 1959.
Black Panther Intercommunal News Service. *Black Panther Intercommunal News Service*, 23 March 1968.
Bogle, Donald. 'Black and Proud Behind Bars.' *Ebony*, August 1969.
Browne, Robert S. 'The Case for Two Americas – One Black, One White.' *New York Times Magazine*, 11 August 1968.
Burton, Larry. 'Letters.' *Ebony*, December 1970.
Carmichael, Stokely. 'What We Want.' *The New York Review of Books*, 22 September 1966.

Davis, J. Don. 'The Black University: In Peril Before Birth.' *Negro Digest*, March 1970. [N.B: This article was originally attributed to 'Ronald Davis' and corrected in the May 1970 issue.]
Donaldson, Jeff. '10 In Search of a Nation.' *Black World*, October 1970.
Ebony Magazine. 'Needed: A Negro Legion of Decency.' *Ebony*, January 1947.
—— 'Progress Report 1967.' *Ebony*, January 1968.
—— 'Ebony Book Shelf.' *Ebony*, August 1971.
—— 'African-American or Black: What's in a Name? Prominent Blacks and-or African Americans Express Their Views.' *Ebony*, July 1989.
Edwards, Harry and Dennis Wyss. 'Fighting from the Inside.' *Time*, 6 March 1989.
Frazier, Joe. 'Cassius Who?' *Ebony*, May 1972, 68.
Freedland, Nat. 'Melvin Van Peebles: Multi-media Maverick.' *Billboard*, 29 January 1972. Schomburg Center Manuscripts, Box 36, File 11.
Gethers, Solomon P. 'Black Power: Three Years Later.' *Negro Digest*, December 1969.
Grady, Sandy. 'The Return of Satchel Paige.' *Baseball Digest*, October 1968.
Gross, Mike. 'Black Tracks Cue New Sales Mart.' *Billboard*, 24 July 1971.
Halloran, Richard. 'Air Force Racism Charged In Study.' *New York Times*, 31 August 1971.
Hano, Arnold. 'The Black Rebel Who "Whitelists" the Olympics.' *New York Times Magazine*, 12 May 1968.
Harding, Vincent. 'New Creation or Familiar Death?' *Negro Digest*, March 1969.
Hare, Nathan. 'The Psychology of Great Black Boxers.' *Ebony*, January 1977.
Harker, Joseph. 'Loud, Proud and Black.' *The New Statesman*, 16 October 2006.
Henderson, Stephen Evangelist. 'Sterling A. Brown.' *Ebony*, October 1976.
Hernton, Calvin C. 'White Liberals and Black Muslims.' *Negro Digest*, October 1963.
Herzog, Brad. 'Radical Thinker.' *Cornell Alumni Magazine*, 11 July 2008.
Jackson, Lester. 'A Dialogue With My Soledad Son.' *Ebony*, November 1971.
Jet Magazine. 'Black Recognition Top Issue in Campus Protests.' *Jet*, 29 January 1970.
—— 'Black Army Captain Freed in "Racism" Trial.' *Jet*, 2 March 1972.
—— 'Fifty Years of Blacks in Entertainment.' *Jet*, 26 November 2001.
Jones, LeRoi. 'Black Art.' *Black World*, June 1973.
Kaliba, Layding Lumumba. 'Readers Rap.' *Jet*, 11 March 1971.
Killens John O. Julian Bond, Anita R. Cornwell, Roland Fair, Eloise Greenfield, Nathan Hare, Brooks Johnson, Dudley Randall, Conrad Kent Rivers, Sterling Stuckey, Eugene Walton and Francis Ward. 'Black Power: Its Meaning and Measure.' *Negro Digest*, November 1966.
Larner, Jeremy and David Wolf. 'Amidst Gold Medals, Raised Black Fists.' *Life*, 1 November 1968.
Lawson, James R. Benjamin E. Mays, Benjamin E. Payton and Samuel D. Proctor. 'The Black University Concept: Educators Respond.' *Negro Digest*, March 1969.
Lee, Don L. 'The Bittersweet of Sweetback/Or Shake Yo' Money Maker.' *Black World*, November 1971.
Life Magazine. 'Black Power Must Be Defined.' *Life*, 22 July 1966.
Longino, Bob. 'The New Black.' *Sydney Morning Herald*, 12 June 2004.
Monroe, Al. 'Joe Louis' Arrival In Camp Is Sports Epic.' *Chicago Defender*, 15 February 1936.
Morris, Steven. 'How Blacks Upset the Marine Corps.' *Ebony*, December 1969.
Neal, Larry. 'Politics as Ritual: Ellison's Zoot Suit.' *Black World*, December 1970.

Newsweek. 'Black Power: Politics of Frustration.' *Newsweek*, July 1966. Schomburg Center Manuscripts, Box 31, File 14.
——— 'Universities Under the Gun: Militants at Cornell.' *Newsweek*, 5 May 1969.
——— 'Black (Studies) Vatican.' *Newsweek*, 11 August 1969.
——— 'Movies.' *Newsweek*, 23 October 1972.
Newton, Huey P. 'I Found Freedom in Jail.' *Ebony*, May 1973.
Owen, Sarah. 'Black Thursday, 40 Years Later.' *The Northwestern*, 16 November 2008.
Poinsett, Alex. 'Think Tank for Black Scholars.' *Ebony*, February 1970.
Poussaint, Alvin F. 'How the "White Problem" Spawned "Black Power".' *Ebony*, August 1967.
——— 'A Psychiatrist Looks at Black Power.' *Ebony*, March 1969.
Reed, Roy. 'The Deacons, Too, Ride by Night.' *New York Times Magazine*, 15 August 1965.
Rhoden, William. '1st and Long.' *Vibe*, November 1995.
Robinson, Louie. 'Joe Louis At Sixty.' *Ebony*, October 1973.
Rosenman, Mark. 'The Negro and the Military.' *The Crisis*, May 1967.
Sackett, Russell. 'Plotting a War on Whitey.' *Life*, 10 June 1966.
Schaap, Dick. 'The Revolt of the Black Athletes.' *Look*, 6 August 1968.
Shapiro, Fred C. 'The Successor to Floyd McKissick May Not Be So Reasonable.' *New York Times Magazine*, 1 October 1967.
Time Magazine. 'The New Racism.' *Time*, 1 July 1966.
——— 'Black Complaint.' *Time*, 25 October 1968.
——— 'The Black Mood, More Militant, More Hopeful, More Determined.' *Time*, 6 April 1970.
Tolbert, Richard C. 'A New Brand of Black Nationalism.' *Negro Digest*, August 1967.
Trillin, Calvin, 'U.S. Journal: Oshkosh.' *New Yorker*, 4 January 1969.
Turner, James. 'Black Students: A Changing Perspective.' *Ebony*, August 1969.
U.S. News and Report. 'At the Ready in Vietnam.' *U.S News & World Report*, World 15 August 1962.
Viner, Brian. 'Tommie Smith: "Hate was so entrenched in America, and it took lives"'. *The Independent*, 13 October 2008.
Wilcox, Preston. 'On the Black University: Movement or Institution?' *Negro Digest*, December 1969.
——— 'Black Studies as an Academic Discipline.' *Negro Digest*, March 1970.
Williams, Diane. 'Who Holds the Power in Hollywood?' *The Crisis*, February/March 1996.
Wilson, C.E. 'Black Power and the Myth of Black Racism.' *Liberation* 11 (September 1966): 27–9.

Other Media

Anonymous. http://www.blockmuseum.northwestern.edu/wallof respect/main.htm (accessed 29 June 2010).
Baker, Mike. '1898 Clash Ruled A Coup.' *Washington Post*, 1 June 2006. http://www.washingtonpost.com/wp-dyn/content/article/2006/05/31/AR2006053102080.html (accessed 1 March 2009).

Breunlin, Rachel. 'The Legacy of the Free Southern Theater in New Orleans: Interviews with Karen-Kaia Livers and Chakula Cha Jua.' http://www.nathanielturner.com/legacyfreesouttheater.htm (accessed 6 November 2009).

Brown, James. 'There Was A Time.' *Soul on Top*, Decca, 2004.

Burns, Ken. *Unforgivable Blackness: The Rise and Fall of Jack Johnson*. Crystal City: PBS, 2005.

Carmichael, Stokely. 'Speech Given At Garfield Highschool, Seattle, Washington, 19 April 1967.' http://www.aavw.org/special_features/speeches_speech_carmichael01.html (accessed 31 March 2009).

Chesnutt, Charles Waddell. *The Conjure Woman*. Boston: Houghton, Mifflin and Company, 1899. http://docsouth.unc.edu/southlit/chesnuttconjure/menu.html (accessed 28 February 2009).

——— *The House Behind the Cedars*. Boston: Houghton, Mifflin and Company, 1900. http://docsouth.unc.edu/southlit/chesnutthouse/menu.html (accessed 28 February 2009).

——— *The Marrow of Tradition*. Boston: Houghton, Mifflin and Company, 1901. http://docsouth.unc.edu/southlit/chesnuttmarrow/menu.html (accessed 1 March 2009).

——— *The Colonel's Dream*. New York: Doubleday, Page & Company, 1905. http://docsouth.unc.edu/southlit/chesnuttcolonel/menu.html (accessed 28 February 2009).

Cleaver, Eldridge. 'To My Black Brothers In Vietnam.' *The Black Panther Intercommunal News Service*, 2 May 1970. http://www.hippy.com/php/article.php?sid=74 (accessed 5 August 2009).

Cohn, Emily. 'Tom Jones Reflects on a "Selfless Revolution"'. *The Cornell Daily Sun*, 16 April 2009. http://cornellsun.com/section/news/content/2009/04/16/tom-jones-reflects-selfless-revolution (accessed 16 April 2009).

Daniels, Ron. 'Vantage Point', 13 October 2009. http://www.northstarnews.com/columns/dr_ron_daniels/article/1572 (accessed 13 February 2010).

Douglass, Frederick. *The Heroic Slave: Autographs for Freedom*. Cleveland: John P. Jewett and Company, 1853. http://etext.virginia.edu/etcbin/toccer-new2?id=DouHero.sgm&images=images/modeng&data=/texts/english/modeng/parsed&tag=public&part=all (accessed 27 March 2009).

Dower, John. *Thriller in Manila*, DVD, Darlow Smithson, 2008.

Ebert, Roger. 'Review *Up Tight*.' 19 February 1969. http://rogerebert.suntimes.com/apps/pbcs.dll/article?AID=/19690219/REVIEWS/902190301/1023 (accessed 17 November 2009).

Ethos. *Ethos Newsletter*, 12 October 1977. http://www.wellesley.edu/Activities/homepage/ethos/site/history.html (accessed 28 May 2009).

Garnet, Henry Highland. *An Address to the Slaves of the United States of America*. http://www.pbs.org/wgbh/aia/part4/4h2937t.html (accessed 27 March 2009).

Glover, Danny and Randy Weston. 'A Tribute to Langston Hughes: Danny Glover & Randy Weston.' Schomburg Center for Research in Black Culture, 23 October 2008.

Grant, Zalin. 'The War and I.' http://www.pythiapress.com/letters/war.htm (accessed 23 May 2010).

Heyward, Carl. 'El Teatro Campesino: An Interview with Luis Valdez.' http://www.communityarts.net/readingroom/archivefiles/2002/09/el_teatro_campe.php (accessed 14 August 2009).

Hilliard, David. Speech at George Padmore Institute, 4 July 2008.
——— Interview conducted by the author, Oakland, California, 27 August 2008.
Hossli, Peter. 'That Was My Decision.' 8 August 2008. http://www.hossli.com/articles/2008/08/08/that-was-my-decision/ (accessed 22 May 2009).
Hughes, Langston. 'The Negro Artist and the Racial Mountain.' *The Nation*, 23 June 1926. http://www.thenation.com/doc/19260623/hughes (accessed 14 June 2008).
Johnson, Bruce. 'Clowns of Baseball.' *The Clown in Times* 6, no. 3 (2000). http://www.charliethejugglingclown.com/baseball.htm (accessed 19 May 2009).
Johnson, Madeline. 'Af-Am House to Host Rededication.' *Yale Daily News*, 16 November 2007. http://www.yaledailynews.com/news/2007/nov/16/af-am-house-to-host-rededication/ (accessed 28 May 2009).
Kain, Gylan. 'The Shalimar'. *Right On!*, The Last Poets, Juggernaut, 1968.
Li, Lucy. 'Snapshot in History: Remembering the Exit in Photos; Through different lenses, the Associated Press and The Sun capture iconic moment at Cornell.' *Cornell Daily Sun*, 16 April 2009. http://cornellsun.com/section/news/content/2009/04/16/snapshot-history-remembering-exit-photos (accessed 16 April 2009).
Lowery, George. 'A Campus Takeover That Symbolized An Era of Change.' *Cornell Chronicle Online*, 16 April 2009. http://asrc.cornell.edu/turner.html (accessed 15 May 2009).
Malamud, Slava. 'George Foreman: Hunting Big George.' *Sports Illustrated*, 17 August 2006. http://english.sport-express.ru/articles/9_18/ (accessed 22 May 2010).
McCrae, Erica. 'Tommie Smith Recalls His 1968 Olympic Protest.' *Black College Wire*. http://www.blackcollegewire.org/index.php?option=com_ywp_blog&task=view&id=5593&Itemid=30 (accessed 7 July 2009).
McCreary, Sandra, Herb Gaede and Henry Brown. 'Black Thursday 40 Years Later.' http://www.thenorthwestern.com/ (accessed 12 April 2009).
Mink. *Full Clip*, DVD. Lions Gate, 2004.
Mulvaney, Kieran. 'Ring History: Events That Shaped Madison Square Garden's Ring.' 2 October 2007. http://sports.espn.go.com/espn/print?id=3043786&type=story (accessed 23 June 2009).
National Endowment for the Arts. 'Arena Stage Takes a Risk on *The Great White Hope*.' 2 February 2007. http://www.nea.gov/about/40th/greatwh.html (accessed 19 June 2009).
News Bureau, University of Wisconsin-Oshkosh. UWO historians unveil "Black Thursday" exhibit.' 17 November 2008. http://www.uwosh.edu/news/?p=1472 (accessed 12 April 2009).
Robinson, Smokey. *Tears of a Clown*, Smokey Robinson and the Miracles, Tamla-Motown, TMG 745, 1967.
Rock, John Sweat. 'I Will Sink or Swim With My Race.' *Liberator*, 12 March 1858. http://research.udmercy.edu/find/special_collections/digital/baa/item.php?record_id=1238 (accessed 19 January 2009).
Seale, Bobby. 'Free Huey.' Pacifica Radio Archive BB 5471. http://sunsite.berkeley.edu/VideoTest/pantherstape1.ram (accessed 4 June 2010).
Severo, Richard. 'Jules Dassin, Filmmaker on Blacklist, Dies at 96.' *New York Times*, 1 April 2008. http://www.nytimes.com/2008/04/01/movies/01dassin.html?_r=2&ref=obituaries&oref=slogin (accessed 11 November 2009).

Singer, Tom. 'Teddy Ballgame makes difference for Negro Leaguers to enter Hall.' http://mlb.mlb.com/mlb/history/mlb_negro_leagues_story.jsp?story=williams_ted# (accessed 19 May 2010).

Stackleberg, Verena and Gareth Evans. 'All Power to the Imagination! 1968 and its legacies.' http://www.1968.org.uk (accessed 4 July 2008).

Thelwell, Mike. 'Black Studies: A Political Perspective.' *Massachusetts Review* 10 (Autumn 1969). http://www.umass.edu/afroam/dthelwell.html (accessed June 2009).

Van Peebles, Melvin. *Sweet Sweetback's BaadAsssss Song*. Bfi Video, 1971.

Various. *The Adventures of Brer Rabbit*. 2006. http://www.adventuresofbrerrabbitdvd.com (accessed 30 March 2009).

Von Busack, Richard. 'Here He Comes to Save the Day: An Interview with Cinequest Maverick Spirit honoree Ralph Bakshi.' *San Jose Metro*, 5 March 2003. http://www.metroactive.com/papers/metro/02.27.03/bakshi-0309.html (accessed 30 March 2009).

Williams, Robert F. *Listen, Brother!* New York: World View Publishers 1968. http://www.aavw.org/protest/early_rfw_abstract18.html (accessed 5 August 2009).

INDEX

A Guy Called Gerald, 187
African Commune of Bad Relevant Artists (AFRICOBRA), 233
Afro-American Society (Cornell), 104–6
Afrofuturism, 21, 25, 189, 194–5, 197, 199, 208–9, 214–15, 217–18, 221–5, 267
Afrogroups, 116–17, 121–2, 126, 129, 178
Akil, Salim, 224
Akomfrah, John, 197–9, 209
Albert, Elena, 263
Albert II, 212
Alexie, Sherman, 185
Ali, Muhammad, 77, 82–3, 89, 95, 143–4, 146–52, 156, 160, 164, 167, 222
Amber Satyr, 249
American football (NFL), 134
Anderson, S.E., 114, 247–9
Andrews, Lee, 237
Angelou, Maya, 155
Anti-Slavery Standard, 56
Aptheker, Herbert, 99
Armstrong, Louis, 79, 223
assimilation, definition of, 42

Association of American and Afro-American Students (AAAS), 116, 119–21
Atkins, Juan, 200, 209
Attucks, Crispus, 167
Austin, Junius Caesar, 144

Bakshi, Ralph, 82
Baldwin, James, 168, 206, 245
Banks, Lacy, 150
Banks, Mike, 197, 200, 204–7
Baraka, Amiri, 77, 99, 124, 127, 230–2, 234
Barber, Red, 141
Barkley, Gnarls, 221
Barthes, Roland, 49
baseball
  Major League, 134, 135, 137–8, 141, 160
  Negro Leagues, 135–9, 141–2, 267
basketball, 134
Bassett, Lloyd, 139
Beatles, The, 91, 229
Belafonte, Harry, 87
Bell, Cool Papa, 135–6, 138, 140–2
Bell, Derrick, 211
Bell, Pedro, 214–17

Benjamin, Alexander, 163
Bennett, Lerone, 86–7, 90, 110–11, 182, 258, 260, 263
Benson, Eugene, 138, 140, 142
Berkeley Barb, 88
Bibb, Henry, 55
Big Sixteen, 50, 75–7, 86, 144, 181, 217, 252
Black Arts Movement (BAM), 22, 26, 72, 86, 143, 146, 149, 198, 226–7, 231–2, 234, 236–7, 241, 247–9, 252–5, 259–60, 263, 267
Black Audio Films, 197
Black Communications Project, 124
Black Cultural Development Society (BCDS), Colorado State, 177–9, 267
Black Holocaust, The, 247
'Black Is Beautiful', 30, 55, 87, 110, 147, 169, 171
Black Lives Matter, 268
Black Muslims, *see* Nation of Islam
Black Panther Intercommunal News Services (BPINS), 76, 91–2, 246, 252, 256, 258

Black Panther Party, 3–6, 8, 10, 28, 30–2, 35, 83, 88, 91, 93, 107, 162–4, 176, 211, 251, 256
Black Power, political definition of, 11
Black Power, cultural definition of, 11
Black Rage, 174
Black Scholar, journal, 162
black studies movement, 109–17, 123–4, 126–7, 129–31
Black University, 127–8
Black World magazine, 233
Blaxploitation, 20, 26, 218, 223, 250–2, 267
Bogle, Donald, 251
Boston Globe, 100
Bowser, Aubrey, 59, 64
boxing, 82–3, 142–53, 160
Bradley, David, 78, 204
Br'er Rabbit, 81–2, 254
Brooklyn Royal Giants, 139
Brooklyn Dodgers, 135
Brooks, Darryl, 222
Brother From Another Planet, The, 212, 217
Brown, Carolyn, 230
Brown, Drew, 148
Brown, Elaine, 5
Brown, H. Rap, 7, 33, 99, 164, 173, 233
Brown, Henry, 103
Brown, James, 90, 222, 230, 237, 247
Brown, John, 99
Brown, Larry, 136
Brown, Ralph, 139
Brown, Sterling, 61, 74–8, 92, 95
Brundage, Avery, 156
Buckley, Jeff, 185
Bunche, Ralph, 130
Burney, Willie E. Jr., 171
Burton, Larry, 164
Butler, Barbara, 121

Butler, Jerry, 231
Butler, Octavia E., 194, 196, 208

Caldwell, Earl, 94
Caldwell, Vern, 81
Camp Lejeune, 169, 171
Carlos, John, 154, 157–60
Carmichael, Stokely, 3, 6–8, 22, 29–30, 32–5, 46, 54, 72, 76, 83, 86–91, 94–5, 99, 103, 148, 164–5, 222, 226, 245
Carroll, Lee, 173–5, 177–80
Cavett, Dick, 35
Cha Jua, Chakula, 244
Chantels, The, 236
Charleston, Oscar, 138
Chepulis, Ionas, 157
Chesnutt, Charles, 59, 72–4, 95
Chicago American, 158
Chicago Defender, 138, 145–6
Civil Rights Act 1964, 45
Clark, Dee, 236
Clark, Hilton, 115–17
Clark, Kenneth Dr., 115, 119
Clark, Robert D., 158
Clay, Cassius, *see* Ali, Muhammad
Cleaver, Eldridge, 8, 35, 93, 164, 173–4
Cleaver, Kathleen, 6
Clinton, George, 204, 209, 210, 213–19, 222–3
Clinton, Hillary, 268
Cobb, Ty, 137
Cohen, Jim, 139
Cohen, Octavus Roy, 74
Cole, Terry Joseph, 235
Coleman, Kate, 29
Colt, Len, 87
Coltrane, John, 86
Comet, The, 190–3, 217, 224
Cone, James, 186
Congress of Racial Equality (CORE), 6, 43, 82, 84, 87, 242

Connell, John, 203
Cooper, Wayne, 60
Corbett, John, 209, 216
Cornelius, Sug, 141
Cornell Sun, 107
Cornell University, protests (1969), 105–10, 112, 114, 159, 161
Cornish, Samuel E., 57
Cortez, Dave, 236
Cosby, Bill, 254
Cosgrove, Stewart, 205
Cotton Comes To Harlem, 250
Crisis, The, 64
Cruse, Harold, 4, 6
Cullen, Countee, 70–1, 224
cultural nationalism, 11–12

Daniels, Ron, 261–2
Dark Tower Project, the, 224
Dassin, Jules, 252–3
Davenport, Willie, 157
Davis, Angela, 221, 258
Davis, Mike, 208
Davis, Ossie, 77
De Priest, Oscar, 146
Deacons for Defence, 56
Dean, Jay, 137
Dee, Ruby, 252
Delany, Samuel R., 194–6, 208, 223
Dellums, Ron, 122
Dent, Thomas C., 241, 243–5
Dery, Mark, 189, 199, 214, 225
Dhalgren, 195–6
Diamond, King, 185
Dillard, Larry, 262
DJ culture, 202, 209–10
Donaldson, Jeff, 233–4
Douglas, Aaron, 63, 65, 70
Douglas, Emory, 6, 91–5, 215, 240, 246
Douglass, Frederick, 53, 63
Dower, John, 151
Downing, John, 91
Drifters, The, 237

INDEX 349

Du Bois, William Edward Burghardt, 10, 46, 59–60, 64, 66–9, 71, 88, 99, 101–2, 109, 114, 125, 130, 190–4, 217, 224, 228, 233, 242, 244
Dunbar, Ernest, 112, 115–16, 122
Dunbar, Paul Laurence, 59, 65, 72–4, 95, 99
Dylan, Bob, 127, 229

Early, Gerald, 144
East Wind Poetry Workshop, 232
Eastern Correctional Institution (ECI), 173–4, 176, 178–80
  Afro-American Society, 178–9
  Uptight Program, 179
Ebert, Roger, 212, 252–3
Ebony magazine, 26, 81, 86–7, 89, 111, 144, 147, 152, 168, 170, 175, 258
Ebony and Topaz, 68–71, 86, 263
Edelin, Ramona, 261
Edwards, Harry, 24, 122, 127, 153–60
Edwards, Honeyboy, 187
Egbuna, Obi, 88
Elbert, Donny, 237
Electric Light Orchestra, 218
Elkins, Stanley, 50, 108, 173
Ellison, Ralph, 79, 126, 135, 204
Epps, Archie III, 120
Eshun, Kodwo, 200, 209–11
Esquire magazine, 98, 198
Ethos (Wellesley College), 118, 119
Evans, Eric, 106
Evans, Lee, 158
Evers, Medgar, 99

Fairclough, Adam, 14
Fanon, Frantz, 193

Fauset, Jessie Redmond, 59
Federal Bureau of Investigation, 160
Feller, Bob, 137
Ferguson protests, 1, 268
FIRE!! magazine, 63–7, 71, 86, 217, 263
Fiske, John, 36
'Five Percenters', 29
Flobots, The, 231
Flood, Curt, 160
Florence, Franklin, Reverend, 38, 39
folklore, significance, 50–3
Forbes, Frank, 137
Forman, James, 7, 8, 40
Fortune, T. Thomas, 56
Foxx, Jimmy, 137
Frazier, Joe, 82–3, 149–52
Free Southern Theater, (FST), 22, 26, 237–47, 260, 267
Freedom Independence God Honor Today (FIGHT), 38
Fugitive Slave Bill, 1850, 55–6
Fuller, Charles H., 1, 3, 37, 217, 226
Fuse, Montye, 135

Gabbin, Joanne, 77
Gagarin, Yuri, 212
Gamble, Kenneth, 221
Garnet, Henry Highland, 54, 56–7
Garrett, Jimmy (James P.), 122–6
Garvey, Marcus, 99
Gates, Skip, 62
Geertz, Clifford, 15
Gehrig, Lou, 138
George, Nelson, 187
Gethers, Solomon P., 3
Gibson, Chris, 203
Gibson, Josh, 136
Gibson, William, 194, 225
Gillespie, Dizzy, 145
Gilmore, Al-Tony, 143

Gilroy, Paul, 21, 199, 207
Giovanni, Nikki, 221
Glenn, Stanley, 137
Glover, Danny, 82
Goeser, Caroline, 68
Goldie, 210
Goss, Clay, 236–7
Gray, Seymour, 149–50
Greenberg, Alan, 185
Griffin, Junius, 251
Guevara, Che, 175
Guiles, Roger, 102–3
Guillaume, Paul, 60

Hall, Robert, 119
Hall, Stuart, 36
Hamer, Fannie Lou, 245
Hands Up, Don't Shoot, 2
Handsworth Songs, 197
Handy, William Christopher, 187
Hannerz, Ulf, 179
Hard Rock, 181
Harding, Vincent, 128–9, 232
Hare, Nathan, 46, 144, 152
Harlem Globetrotters, 139
Harlem magazine, 70
Harlem Rebellion/Riot, 84
Harlem Renaissance, 22, 26, 57–61, 63–4, 66, 70–2, 74, 86, 125, 230, 242, 263, 267
Harlem Youth Federation, the, 232
Harris, Bernard, 213
Harris, Joel Chandler, 73, 81–2
Hegg, Owen, 163
Henderson, David, 235–6
Hendryx, Nona, 211, 213–14, 218–21, 223
Henry, John, 69, 75, 77, 86, 144, 254
Hernton, Calvin C., 30
Herron, Jerry, 202
Hilliard, David, 8, 28, 82, 93–4, 110
Hitler, Adolf, 145

Hodges, Harold, 127
Holiday, Billie, 232
Holt, Len, 238
Hoover, John Edgar, 156
Hopkins, Donald R., 122–3
Hopkins, Raymond, 171–2
Horne, Lena, 223
Horowitz, David, 29
House, Son, 186
Howard, Jeff, 121
Huff, Edgar, 163
Hughes, Langston, 60–3, 65, 67, 70, 74, 95, 98–9, 135, 235, 242, 245, 249, 251
Humphrey, Hubert, 4
Hurd, L.C., 178
Hurston, Zora Neale, 61, 63, 65, 70, 74, 95, 135, 242, 250

Indianapolis ABCs, 138
Indianapolis Clowns, 139–40, 142
Institute of the Black World (IBW), 23, 128–31, 261, 267
twenty-first century, 261
International Olympic Committee (IOC), 156, 158, 160

Jackson, Bruce, 75, 177
Jackson, George, 173–4, 177, 180
Jackson, Jesse, 164
Jackson, Lester, 175
Jean, Wyclef, 262
Jet magazine, 112, 151, 254
Johnson, Charles Spurgeon, 64, 68–70, 130
Johnson, Jack, 77, 140, 143–8
Johnson, James Weldon, 59, 61, 72, 75, 77, 242, 250
Johnson, John Henry, 134
Johnson, Lyndon Baines, 34
Johnson, Robert, 25, 184–9
Johnson, Tommy, 186
Johnson, Walter, 137

Jones, James Earl, 147
Jones, LeRoi, *see* Baraka, Amiri
Jones, Quincy, 262
Jones, Tom, 104, 106, 109
Joplin, Janis, 232
Jung, Carl, 48, 49

Kahn, Roger, 141
Kain, Gylan, 230–1
Kaliba, Layding Lumumba, 151
Kane, Bob, 158
Kansas City Monarchs, 141
Karenga, Maulana, 233, 261
Kennedy, John F., 212
Kent State shootings (1970), 108
Kerner Report (National Commission on Civil Disorders Report, 1968), 8, 41
Kgositsile, Keorapetse, 231
Killens, John Oliver, 34, 114, 245
Kindred, 196–7
King, Coretta Scott, 128, 164
King, Martin Luther, Jr., 29, 83, 85–6, 99, 104, 151, 164, 198, 211, 213, 230, 258–9
Klosterman, Chuck, 185
Knight, Etheridge, 181–2
Kravitz, Lenny, 221
Krowter, George, 9
Ku Klux Klan, 4, 34, 35, 151, 156, 163
Kubik, Gerhard, 187
Kuti, Fela, 199

L'Ouverture, Toussaint, 99
Labelle, 25, 210, 219–21
LaBelle, Patti, 25, 219–21
Lang, Fritz, 194, 224
Last Angel of History, The, 199
Last Poets, The, 231
Lee, Don L., 233
Lee, Spike, 82
LeGaspi, Larry, 218, 220
Legba, 188

Lenin, Vladimir Ilyich Ulyanov, 175
Leonard, Buck, 136
Lester, Julius, 35, 61, 192
Li, Lucy, 107
Liberator, The, 55
Life magazine, 5, 93, 168
Lightning, Chuck, 218, 224
Lincoln Giants, 137
Lippmann, Walter, 80
Lipsyte, Robert, 155
Little, Malcolm, *see* X, Malcolm
Locke, Alain, 57–8, 60, 70–1, 74, 130
Los Angeles Times, 158
Louis, Joe, 143–7, 149, 206, 267
Loyd, Overton, 215
Luciano, Felipe, 231
Lynyrd Skynyrd, 185

Mack, Connie, 136
'Magnificent Barbarian, The', 87, 148, 150
Manson, Marilyn, 165
Marcus, Greil, 188
Martindale, Caroline, 41
Martin Luther King – Days of Hope, 198
Marx, Karl, 175
Maxwell, Hurdle L., 170
May, Derrick, 200, 210
Mayfield, Curtis, 235
McCreary, Sandra, 103, 105
McEnroe, John, 187
McGraw, John, 138
McKay, Claude, 58, 61–2
McKissick, Floyd, 6, 7, 8
Meek, Joe, 75–6, 86, 181
Meinecke, Thomas, 203
Meredith, James, 46
Meredith March, 3, 46, 84, 87
Michaux, Lewis, 87
Middle Passage, 216
Miller, Booker, 186
Miller, Keith, 135
Mills, Jeff, 200
Minh, Ho Chi, 175

INDEX 351

Mississippi Freedom Democratic Party (MFDP), 240, 245
Mitchell, Milton, 103
Mix Master Mike, 210
Mojo and Sayso, 81
Monae, Janelle, 204, 223–4
Monro, John, 122
Monroe, Al, 145
Moore, Gilbert, 93
Morehouse College, 224
Morris, Steven, 170
Morrison, Toni, 13, 36
Moses, Gilbert, 238, 241
Moskowitz, Samuel, 194
Mosley, Walter, 268
Motown, 201
Mumford, Kevin, 64
Munro, Thomas, 60
myth, importance of, 78

Nation, The, 67
Nation of Islam, 30, 149, 174, 217
National Advisory Commission on Selective Service, 165
National Afro-American League, 56
National Association for the Advancement of Colored People (NAACP), 4, 43, 74, 84, 164, 251
National Black Theater, 232
National Coalition of Negro Churchmen (NCNC), 4
National Urban Coalition, 261
National Urban League, 84, 168
nationalism, definition, 42
Neal, Gaston, 232
Neal, Larry, 45, 51, 79, 81, 84–6, 127, 142–4, 146, 149–50, 185, 204, 216, 226–34, 238–9, 241, 243, 246, 258, 262–3

Negro Digest, 3, 114, 132
Nelson, David, 231
New Lafayette Theatre, 232
New School for Afro-American Thought, 232
'New Wave' authors, 195–6
New York Amsterdam News, 59
New York Times, 31, 32, 94, 187, 245
Newark rebellion/riot, 84, 112
Newsweek magazine, 4, 106, 255
Newton, Huey, 8, 39, 55, 72, 86, 94, 100, 175, 180, 206, 233, 256–8
Nichols, Nichelle, 213
'Niggerati, the', 63–4, 66, 70
Nkrumah, Kwame, 175
Noda, Tsutomu, 184, 202
Norman, Peter, 154
Nugent, Richard Bruce, 62–3, 66–7, 70–1
Nyro, Laura, 220–1

Oakland Tribune, 38
Obama, Barack, 109
Olympic Games
  Berlin 1936, 153
  Melbourne 1956, 153
  Mexico 1968, 24, 88, 153–60
  Moscow 1980, 159
  Montreal 1976, 159
  Munich 1972, 159
  Tokyo 1964, 153
Olympic Project for Human Rights (OPHR), 155–7
O'Neal, John, 238, 240, 244, 246
Opportunity magazine, 65, 68

Paige, Jimmy, 185
Paige, Satchel, 135–6, 138
Parker, Charlie, 86
Parks, Rosa, 206

Parliament Funkadelic, 25, 214–19
  the Mothership, 216, 219, 221–2
Pearce, Perce, 81
Perry, Lee, 200, 209, 214
Pfister, Arthur, 231
Philadelphia Athletics, 136
Philadelphia Stars, 137
Plain Truth, The, 243
pluralism, definition, 42
Poitier, Sidney, 87, 250
Pollock, Syd, 139
Presley, Elvis, 185
prison life, 173–83
Project One Hundred Thousand, 169
Pryor, Richard, 82

Quarry, Jerry, 148

Rabaka, Reiland, 193
Randolph, Asa Philip, 64
Reagan, Ronald, 153
Reece, Dwandalyn R., 221–2
Reed, Clarence, 232
Reed, Ishmael, 200, 208, 210
Reid, Mark, 255
Renfroe, Othello, 140
Reynold, Simon, 208
Rhodes, Jane, 10, 41, 107
Rice, Grantland, 135
Richards, Chris, 222
Rickey, Branch, 135, 140–2
Roberts, Randy, 148
Robeson, Paul, 145, 156, 206
Robinson, Cedric, 206
Robinson, Jackie, 30, 135, 140–2, 160
Robinson, Smokey, 231
Robinson, Sugar Ray, 144–5
Rock, John Sweat, 56
Rolling Stone magazine, 84–5, 86
Roosevelt, Franklin D., 145
Roots, The, 231
Rowan, Carl, 140
Ruggles, David, 56
Rusan, Francille, 118

Rustin, Bayard, 5, 38
Ruth, Babe, 137
Ryan, Michael P., 169

Sackett, Russell, 31
Sackler, Howard, 147
Sacramento State Capital, protest, 8, 33
San Francisco State Black Students' Union (BSU), 102, 116, 119, 122–6
San Francisco Chronicle, 29
San Francisco Examiner, 41
San Francisco State College protests (1968), 102
San Francisco Sunday Chronicle, 32
Sanchez, Sonia, 77
Sanders, Bernie, 268
Sanders, Mark, 77
Santigold, 221
Saturday Evening Post, 156
Saunderson, Kevin, 200
Savio, Mario, 100
Sayles, Jon, 212, 217
Schechner, Richard, 241
Schmeling, Max, 145–6
Schuh, John, 104
Schuyler, George, 60, 256
Scorsese, Martin, 185
Scott, Ridley, 194
Scott-Heron, Gil, 199, 221, 248
Seale, Bobby, 8, 35, 76, 93, 100
Selassie, Haile, 146
Selma March, 84
Semple, Jesse, 62
Seven Songs for Malcolm X, 198
Sharpton, Reverend Al, 82
Shawl, Nisi, 224
Silberman, Charles, 80–1, 177
Simeon, Booker, 41
Simone, Nina, 221
'Simple' stories, *see* Semple, Jesse
Sinfield, Alan, 57

Small, Stephen, 88
Smith, Cauleen, 224
Smith, Hilton, 138
Smith, Tommie, 154–5, 157–61
Southern Christian Leadership Conference (SCLC), 46, 164
Sowell, Thomas, 145
Space Is The Place, 196, 217
Space Traders, The, 211
Spellman, Alfred Bailey, 232
Sports Illustrated magazine, 157
Spriggs, Ed, 230
Sputnik flight, 212
St. Jacques, Raymond, 250
Stagolee, 77, 230, 254
Stanley, Thomas, 222
Starr, Marilynne, 108
Starr, Steve, 106, 108
Stevens, Cat, 220
Stewart, James, 54
Stewart, Maria, 56, 57
Stroch, Nelson, 139
Stuckey, Sterling, 100
Student Non-Violent Coordinating Committee (SNCC), 32, 84, 164, 238–9, 242
Students' Afro-American Society (SAS), 116, 119
Students for a Democratic Society (SDS), 105–6, 110, 122, 162
Sturken, Marita, 40
Sulzberger, Arthur Hayes, 41
Sun Ra, 196, 200, 201, 209, 214, 217
Sundstrom, Ronald R., 194
Sweet Sweetback's Baadasssss Song, 250, 252, 254–60

Taber, George, 106
Talented Tenth, The, 70, 101, 125, 131
Tate, Greg, 196, 208–10, 214
Teatro Campesino (TC), 240

Teer, Barbara Ann, 232
Terry, Wallace II, 162
They Call Me MISTER Tibbs, 250
Thomas, Queen Elizabeth, 186
Thurman, Wallace, 59, 61, 63, 65, 70
Time magazine, 158, 162
Times, The, 5, 6
Toomer, Jean, 61, 74
Trompenaars, Fons, 15
Trotter, Marva, 146
Truman, David B., 117
Truth, Sojourner, 99
Tubman, Harriet, 99
Turner, Nat, 50, 99, 156
Tse-Tung, Mao, 100, 175
Tygiel, Jules, 135

Umbra, 30, 252, 263
Uncle Remus, 73, 82, 149
Uncle Rufus, 81, 83–4, 149, 152, 204
Underground Resistance (UR), 200–7, 214
United Colored People's Association (UCPA), 88
United Neighbors for Progress, 3
Unknown Writer, 204, 206
Up Tight, 252–3
US News and World Report, 7, 33
US organization, 261

Valdez, Luis, 240
Van Deburg, William L., 43, 113
Van Peebles, Melvin, 62, 77, 223, 250, 254–8
Van Vechten, Carl, 59, 64
Vesey, Denmark, 50, 99
Vickers, Brad, 47
Vietnam Solidarity Campaign, 165
Vietnam War, 162–73
 casualty statistics, 165–6

INDEX

Vincent, Rickey, 219
von Däniken, Erich, 217
Voting Rights Act 1965, 45

Walker, A'Leila, 64, 224
Walker, David, 53–7, 99, 209
Walker, Jenny, 9
Wall of Respect, 233–4
Wallerstein, Immanuel, 208
Wardlow, Gayle, 187
Washington, Booker T., 72
Washington, John, 78
Washington Post, 222
Watermelon Man, 150
Watts rebellion/riot, 84, 112, 155, 238, 249
Wells, Herbert George, 216
Wendt, Simon, 9
West, Cornell, 268
Westmoreland, William, 168
Wheatley, Phyllis, 59

Wheatstraw, Peetie, 186
Whitfield, Mal, 153
Wickham, Vicky, 220
Wiggins, William, 152
Wilkins, Roy, 4, 34
Willard Straight Hall occupation, *see* Cornell University, protests
Williams, Diane, 251
Williams, Robert, 99, 152, 167, 223, 235
Williams, Saul, 231
Williams, Stick, 178
Williams, Ted, 136
Williamson, Tom Jr., 119–20
Wilson, Wesley C., 171
Wirth, Thomas, 64–5
Wisconsin State University-Oshkosh, protests (1968), 102–5, 110, 161

Wondaland Arts Society, 218, 224
Woodley, Gene, 163
Worthy, William, 98–100, 198
Wraight, John, 202
Wright, Richard, 145
Wright, John, 77

X, Malcolm, 7, 28, 84–7, 95, 99, 104, 114, 155–6, 173, 198, 230–1, 258–9

Yette, Samuel, 165
Young, A.Z., 56
Young, Coleman, 206
Young, Frank A., 138

Zinermon, Ike, 186
Zulu Cannibal Giants Baseball Tribe, 139